SPORT TOURISM

Joy Standeven, D.Phil

Joy Standeven Leisure and Tourism
Consultancy and Research

Paul De Knop, PhD

Vrije Universiteit Brussel
Brussels, Belgium
and the University of Brabant
Tilburg, Netherlands

Human Kinetics

Library of Congress Cataloging-in-Publication Data

Standeven, Joy, 1933-
    Sport tourism / Joy Standeven, Paul De Knop.
      p.   cm.
    Includes bibliographical references and index.
    ISBN 0-87322-853-7
    1. Sports and tourist trade.   I. Knop, Paul De.   II. Title.
    G155.A1S662   1998
    338.4'791--dc21

ISBN: 0-87322-853-7

Copyright © 1999 by Joy Standeven and Paul De Knop

All rights reserved. Except for use in a review, the reproduction or utilization of this work in any form or by any electronic, mechanical, or other means, now known or hereafter invented, including xerography, photocopying, and recording, and in any information storage and retrieval system, is forbidden without the written permission of the publisher.

Developmental Editor: Christine Drews; **Assistant Editors:** John Wentworth and Sandra Merz Bott; **Copyeditor:** Tony Callihan; **Proofreader:** Jane Hilken; **Graphic Artist:** Kathleen Boudreau-Fuoss; **Text Designer:** Nancy Rasmus; **Photo Manager:** Boyd LaFoon; **Cover Designer:** Jack Davis; **Photographer (cover): Photo Network/Bachmann; Illustrator:** Tom Roberts; **Printer:** Edwards Bros.

Printed in the United States of America   10 9 8 7 6 5 4 3

Human Kinetics
Web site: www.HumanKinetics.com

United States: Human Kinetics
P.O. Box 5076
Champaign, IL 61825-5076
800-747-4457
e-mail: humank@hkusa.com

Canada: Human Kinetics
475 Devonshire Road, Unit 100
Windsor, ON N8Y 2L5
800-465-7301 (in Canada only)
e-mail: orders@hkcanada.com

Europe: Human Kinetics
107 Bradford Road
Stanningley
Leeds LS28 6AT, United Kingdom
+44 (0)113 255 5665
e-mail: hk@hkeurope.com

Australia: Human Kinetics
57A Price Avenue
Lower Mitcham, South Australia 5062
08 8277 1555
e-mail: liaw@hkaustralia.com

New Zealand: Human Kinetics
Division of Sports Distributors NZ Ltd.
P.O. Box 300 226 Albany
North Shore City, Auckland
0064 9 448 1207
e-mail: blairc@hknewz.com

Contents

Preface vii

Part I   Rethinking Sport Tourism as an Experience
of Physical Activity, Travel, and Place 1

Chapter 1   **Sport and Tourism: An International Overview 3**
Overview of Sport and Tourism 4
Working Definitions of Key Concepts 7
Historical Development of Connections
Between Sport and Tourism 14
Democratization of Sport and Tourism
in the Twentieth Century 28
Summary 38
References 39

Chapter 2   **Sport and Tourism: Investigating the Relationship 47**
The Nature of Sport, Tourism, and Sport Tourism 49
Our Classification Scheme for Sport Tourism 62
The Infrastructure of Sport, Tourism, and Sport Tourism 66
The Characteristics of Participants 70
Summary 75
References 75

Chapter 3   **Sport in the Development of Tourism 81**
Sport as a Growing Segment of the Tourism Industry 82
The Influence of Increased Sport Participation 83
The Influence of Increased Sport Tourism 83
Active Sports on Holidays 88
Passive Sports on Holidays 111
Active Sports During Nonholiday Time 118
Passive Sports During Nonholiday Time 122
Summary 124
References 125

Chapter 4   **Tourism in the Development of Sport 129**
Sports Development 130
Development of Sport Activity Based
on Available Tourism Resources 134
Sports Development as a Result
of Visiting Tourist Resources 136

Tourism-Generated Sports Development
Through Programs and Instruction 146
Major Events Used to Stimulate Sports Development 150
The Influence of Elite Performers and Coaches
on Sports Development 156
Sports Development as a Spin-Off "At Home" 158
Constraints That Inhibit Sports Development
Being Initiated by Tourism 159
Summary 162
References 162

Part II   The Impact of Sport Tourism 167

Chapter 5   The Economic Impact of Sport Tourism 169
Michael F. Collins and Guy A.M. Jackson
Sport and Tourism as Economic Activities 170
Sport Activity Holidays 176
Major Sport Facilities and Events as an Attraction
for Visitors 179
Sport and Tourism as Part of Regeneration Strategies
for Cities and Regions 189
Summary 195
References 197

Chapter 6   The Sociocultural Impact of Sport Tourism 203
Conceptual Background to Sociocultural Impacts 205
Positive Impacts 210
Negative Impacts 216
Violence in and Surrounding Sport and Tourism 221
Sport Tourism for All: The Issue of Social Equity 223
Cultural Homogeneity 226
Summary 229
References 230

Chapter 7   The Environmental Impact of Sport Tourism 235
A Growing Concern for the Natural Environment 237
Increasing Participation in Outdoor Sports 240
Damage to the Natural Environment
Caused by Tourism 242
The Impact of Holiday Resorts
on the Natural Environment 246
The Impact of Sport Tourism Activities
on the Natural Environment 247
Minimizing the Influence of Outdoor Sports
on the Environment 252
The Impact of Sport Tourism on Urban Environments 262

Summary 266
References 266

Chapter 8   The Health Impact of Sport Tourism **271**
Health Implications of Sport Tourism Activities 273
Special Interest Health and Fitness Holidays 278
Sport Tourism for People With Disabilities 281
Sport Tourism to Raise Sponsorship to Fight Disease 284
Summary 286
References 286

Part III   Present Status and Future Prospects **291**

Chapter 9   Administrative and Policy Issues **293**
Overview of Administration and Policy 295
Sport Tourism Administrative Infrastructures
in Various Countries 297
Implications of Administrative Infrastructures
for Sport Tourism Policy 306
Sport Tourism Policy Issues 308
Summary 315
References 316

**Chapter 10   Conclusions and Implications: Sport Tourism
in the Twenty-First Century** **321**
Sport Tourism Today: A Summary 324
Future Trends 332
Summary 347
References 348

Index 353

About the Authors 367

Preface

Since the 1960s *sport* has become an international affair of huge proportions, attracting a considerable amount of media attention, money, participants, and political interest. Meanwhile, *tourism*—with well over a billion participants and billions of dollars generated in revenue annually—remains the world's largest industry as well as its fastest growing. It is hardly surprising then that a symbiotic relationship exists between sport and tourism. As the two nourish and complement one another, they each become more lucrative and culturally influential. Mass sports events are held in many parts of the world, often deliberately staged to attract tourists and generate income. As an example, of the 28,000 participants in the 1997 New York Marathon, more than 12,000 were from outside the United States. Of course this kind of tourism translates into big revenue for the host location and its surrounding areas. Indeed, it is probably its financial clout that has finally given sport tourism its credibility in academic settings.

The purpose of this text is two-fold. First, we hope to provide a solid introduction to this relatively new area of study. The available texts focusing exclusively on sport tourism are few and far between, and none of them is as comprehensive as we've designed this one to be. Second, we hope the book promotes inquiring thought among students. As enthusiastic sport tourists ourselves, we have written the book in the hopes of inspiring enthusiasm in others.

An increasing number of undergraduate and postgraduate courses are now being offered in several academic fields associated with tourism and sport. This is true not only in North America and Europe but also in Australia and other parts of the world. With this in mind, our goal has been to take an international perspective of the discipline. Since the experience, the business, and the study of sport tourism are global in scope, it only makes sense that its text should be as well.

The text is organized into three parts. The four chapters of part I offer a theoretical overview of the relationship between sport and tourism. In chapter 1 we define our terms, laying the groundwork for the in-depth discussions of later chapters, and look at the historical development of sport tourism. In chapter 2 we form a theoretical foundation and provide a conceptual framework for the rest of the book. An original model is introduced to help you recognize the basic relations between sport and tourism and understand how the two intertwine.

In chapter 3, titled "Sport in the Development of Tourism," and chapter 4, titled "Tourism in the Development of Sport," we look separately at how sport and tourism contribute to each other. Chapter 3 describes the ways that tourism has used sport to develop and further its own interests. Chapter 4 then reverses in focus to illustrate the less well-attested contribution made by tourism to sport.

These first four chapters provide you with an excellent base from which to move into a more critical level of investigation in part II, which is concerned with the implications and consequences of sport tourism interactions. Chapters 5 through 8 contain discussions on how sport tourism influences the economy, the sociocultural environment, the natural environment, and physical health. For many students, these chapters will constitute the core of the book, as it is here that the theories and constructs described in the early chapters are shown to apply to each of our lives.

The third and final part of the text examines the organization of sport tourism today and challenges you to conceptualize future directions. Chapter 9 explores national models to illustrate that only in rare instances are the administrative bodies responsible for functions of sport and tourism co-located in central government. The implications of this co-location are discussed, as are the reasons why common quarters for the two administrative systems have been slow to emerge.

The book closes in chapter 10 with a projection for the future of sport tourism. Here we speculate on how the future demand for sport tourism will be influenced by globalization, technology, population changes, politics, economics, leisure, and consumer tastes. We explain in some detail our view of how these variables may give rise to significant opportunities, and perhaps problems, for future generations.

Finally, to supplement and illustrate the points we make in the text, interesting and detailed case studies give you examples of sport tourism drawn from around the world. Several of these studies have been contributed by other authors, and we feel they offer a broad international perspective.

While it is predominantly the work of its two authors, ably assisted in chapter 5 by Michael Collins and Guy Jackson, this text would not have been possible without extensive reference to past work in the area and to the practical help offered by a number of colleagues worldwide. We are also very grateful to Peter Clarijs, Paul McNaught Davis, Laurents Wetts, and Paul Wylleman for their contributions to chapter 8 and to Lisa Delpy, Cynthia Stacey, and David Rowe for writing case studies in chapters 3, 4, and 9, respectively. We owe a special thanks, as well, to Phil Dolby of Exodus for providing many of the photos for the book on very short notice. We feel indebted to Heather Gibson for contributing useful information on sport tourism in the United States. Many thanks go to Cherry Clementson and Ruth Cooper for editorial assistance with the manuscript. Last, we would like to thank our developmental editor at Human Kinetics, Christine Drews, for her encouragement, support, and expertise throughout the project.

Part I

Rethinking Sport Tourism as an Experience of Physical Activity, Travel, and Place

Chapter 1
Sport and Tourism: An International Overview   3

Chapter 2
Sport and Tourism: Investigating the Relationship 47

Chapter 3
Sport in the Development of Tourism   81

Chapter 4
Tourism in the Development of Sport   129

Chapter 1
Sport and Tourism: An International Overview

Exodus

Alpine walking beneath the snows of Mt. Everest in Nepal.

The following topics are covered in this introductory chapter:

1. An overview of the varied activities described as sport tourism.
2. Definitions of the concepts of sport, tourism, and sport tourism.
3. Development of connections between sport and tourism from the ancient world to the twentieth century.
4. Democratization of sport and tourism in the twentieth century.

Sport tourism is a prevalent and growing phenomenon; however, it did not just magically appear in the twentieth century. Connections between sport and tourism can be traced to ancient times. In this chapter, we will provide a brief overview of sport and tourism and will define the three key terms necessary to understanding this field: sport, tourism, and of course, sport tourism. Finally, we will look at the development of connections between sport and tourism from the Olympic Games of ancient Greece to the increased access to, or democratization of, sport tourism in the twentieth century.

Overview of Sport and Tourism

Today vast numbers of people participate in or watch sports and almost everyone aspires to a holiday. Though the connections between sport and tourism have long been established, the relationship is now gaining global significance. Media attention has increased and people are becoming more aware of the health and recreational benefits that sport and tourism provide. Elliott (1995) has shown that the televised production of England's cricket tour to the West Indies increased ongoing package tourism to those islands by as much as 60 percent, an outcome also noted by Ritchie and Lyons (1990) in their postevent study of the 1988 Calgary Winter Olympics, where holiday visits to Calgary increased dramatically after the Games.

The growing number of travel companies that now produce brochures to advertise their sports and adventure holidays—for example, white-water rafting through the Arctic, scuba diving in Kenya, or trekking in Nepal—testify to the increasing interest in sport tourism. In travel-and-tourist magazines, resort advertising continues to emphasize the availability of sport facilities and opportunities. Spectator vacations are also increasingly popular with huge numbers of visitors attracted to sports events. Le Tour, France's prestigious three-week cycle race, claims to be the world's largest annual sports spectating event, attracting several million spectators along its 2,500-mile route, while in Britain it is claimed that around 2.5 million people watch outdoor sport and another 1 million watch indoor sport while on holiday there (NOP Market Research Ltd., 1989).

Congresses, seminars, and workshops on sport and tourism have been documented as taking place since 1971 when the International Council for Sport Science and Physical Education (ICSSPE) held a congress in Helsinki, Finland, on the topic "Activity Holiday-Making" (De Knop, Wylleman, De Martelaer, Van Puymbroeck, and Wittock, 1994). ICSSPE and the International Council for Health, Physical Education and Recreation (ICHPER) jointly sponsored the first congress that specifically addressed sport tourism which was held in Israel in 1986. The first journal dedicated to sport tourism, *The Journal of Sports Tourism,* began publication in October 1993. As the official publication of the Sports Tourism International Council, this journal is now produced quarterly in the E-zine format with access through the Internet.

The relationship between sport and tourism in the modern world is symbiotic. It is not simply that sport furthers tourism by offering an ever-increasing range of valued visitor experiences; tourism also aids sport. This is illustrated in figure 1.1 as an interdependent relationship. The figure

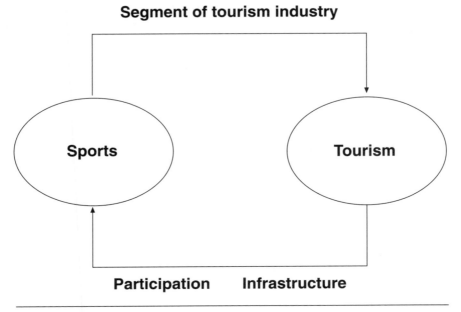

Figure 1.1   Basic model of sport tourism.

identifies sport as a special segment of the tourism industry. Our model illustrates the relationship between sport and tourism as interactive with tourism, which in turn influences sports participation and the sports infrastructure. Sport and tourism are now inextricably linked, and as globalization advances, new and exciting possibilities are opening up to enrich touristic experiences through sport and enhance sport development through tourism.

Changes in the international travel market are leading to an increasing variety of tourist types, needs, and patterns (Martin and Mason, 1987). Adventure and activity holidays are a recognized and growing segment of the tourist industry (Cooper, 1988; Leisure Consultants, 1992; Terry, 1996; Weiler and Hall, 1992; World Tourism Organization, 1985), and sports training (e.g., the regular practice of sport) is acknowledged as an important and potentially health-enhancing activity for which tourism can be the catalyst (Glyptis, 1991).

Health care and training of the body have become an important part of the tourism industry. From the start tourism was promoted for its health-improving functions. People used to go to seaside resorts because of the "presumed health-giving properties of sea bathing" (Urry, 1990, p. 37). Sea bathing led to sunbathing, but the risk of skin cancer has shifted emphasis toward a fit body, a body that is trained through exercise and sport. Sport as therapy is another growing segment of the tourism industry, with an estimated 15 million annual visits to spas in Europe alone, a figure that is similar to the markets in the United States and Asia (Benton, 1995).

Sport as part of business hospitality is big, profitable, and growing, with most of the clients spectating at events miles away from their place of work. Active sport associated with business tours is also increasingly widespread. However, due to space limitations and a stronger commitment to sporting holidays, we must treat this type of sport tourism cursorily in this book.

Travel agents are always on the lookout for new markets as a way of broadening their business. Jolley and Curphey (1994) report that the six thousand agents who were at the American Society of Travel Agents' World Travel Congress in Portugal in 1994 identified the sports sector as a major growth market of niche travel: "Whatever the special interest a company somewhere will organise a holiday around it" (p. 35).

It has become almost impossible for professional sportsmen and sportswomen to pursue their careers without engaging in travel. Team tours are also popular with amateur clubs who engage agents to find matches and make accommodation and transport arrangements (Jackson and Glyptis, 1992).

These examples provide an introduction to the sport tourism phenomenon, which we will now define.

Working Definitions of Key Concepts

It is important to clarify the humanistic perspective from which this book is written before we establish detailed definitions. Neither sport nor tourism are adequately described as *industries;* they are *activities* in which *people* engage. Sport is about an *experience of physical activity,* tourism about an *experience of travel and place.* The *sport product* is not the activity itself; nor is the *tourism product* equal to its vehicle or destination. Rather, "their value is a function of the quality and quantity of *experience* they promise" (MacCannell, 1976, p. 23).

Sports activity does not mean the same thing to all people; nor does its experience mean the same thing even for the same person at different stages of life. Likewise, travelers do not all experience place in the same way. Yet the special significance of both sport and tourism is the meaning that each can have for different people, or for the same person at different times in life.

Such variation makes definitions difficult. However, working definitions of the key concepts of *sport, tourism,* and *sport tourism* are needed in order to identify more adequately the phenomena we are discussing.

Definition of Sport

There is no universally accepted definition of sport; in fact, according to Slusher (1967) the concept defies definition. Widely differing views are held as to which activities come under the heading of sport, although sport is often thought of as being highly competitive and organized. For example, North American definitions often characterize sport as a pursuit that

- requires complexity of physical skill and vigorous physical exertion;
- involves some form of rule-governed competition; and
- has organized and structured relations but keeps a sense of freedom and spontaneity (Coakley, 1990).

The sense of institutionalized competition and formalized rules integral to this definition of sport differentiates Olympic and other elite events from the exertions of the weekend walker or skier. Activities that do not follow formalized rules and that are noncompetitive are usually described in North America as *recreation* (Coakley, 1990).

European definitions of sport are generally looser, accepting that the "traditional value patterns of the sports system has lost its formerly rather homogeneous purpose structure" (Digel, 1994, p. 75). As a result of a process of value differentiation a wide range of models of sports have developed. For example, the Council of Europe (1992) formally defined *sport* as

> all forms of physical activity, which through casual or
> organized participation, aim at improving physical fitness

and mental well being, forming social relationships, or obtaining results in competition at all levels. (p. 1)

This definition does not separate competitive from noncompetitive activity or distinguish between professional and nonprofessional participation—all of these categories are referred to as *sport*. Some American authors acknowledge this broader concept as a legitimate interpretation (Bennett, Howell, and Simri, 1983; Coakley, 1990; Spears and Swanson, 1983), and support for this way of thinking can be found in Africa (Anyanwu, 1988; Macdonald, 1988), Asia (Jones, 1993; Sagawa, 1996), the Indian subcontinent (Fleming, 1991), and elsewhere (Best, Blackhurst, and Makosky, 1992). Indeed the differentiation of recreation from sport on the basis of standardized conditions and formalized rules can seem somewhat arbitrary given that the activities themselves remain the same, as do the facilities and equipment normally required. According to Wilcox (1994), "America has redefined the meaning of sport in the post-industrial world" (p. 73). That author suggests that there is a cultural uniqueness to American sport linked to capitalism, commercialism, and competition with "little genuine interest in and support for the egalitarian provision of 'Sport for All'" (p. 81). This may explain, in part, the identification by North Americans of a separate category of recreation.

 In this text, however, we use the term *sport* in its widest possible sense to include the whole range of competitive and noncompetitive active pursuits that involve skill, strategy, and/or chance in which human beings engage, at their own level, simply for enjoyment and training or to raise their performance to levels of publicly acclaimed excellence.

 The advantage of this definition is that it embraces *sports equity*, the first principle of the European Sports Charter, which charges governments "to enable every individual to participate in sport" (Council of Europe, 1992, p. 1). This was also considered to be important by the United Nations Educational, Scientific, and Cultural Organization (UNESCO). Almost 20 years ago (in 1978), that organization adopted its International Charter of Physical Education and Sport, which is based on the premise that "every human being has a fundamental right of access to physical education and sport, which are essential for the full development of his/her personality" (p. 5). Although both charters are only recommendations to governments (neither holds any status in law), they have initiated a "Sport for All" policy in many countries, though not in America (Standeven, Hardman, and Fisher, 1991; Wilcox, 1994). Nonetheless, *recreation* in America embraces much of the wider concept of sport.

We believe that the opening up of all manner of sports to popular participation at all levels has increased the significance of the links between sport and tourism, and for this reason the broader definition of sport is preferred.

Forms of Sport Involvement

Going beyond the definition of sport itself, involvement in sport can take different forms. A distinction is often made between *active* and *passive* sport involvement. Active sport involvement requires the participant to be physically active. This is perhaps the most commonly recognized form of sports participation, though not necessarily the most prevalent. Passive sport involvement comprises watching others engage in sport. This can include watching both live and televised performances and might even embrace reading about sport. However, in this book we focus on watching live performances, since only that type of passive sport involvement includes travel, and thus tourism.

Definition of Tourism

Holloway (1994) begins his book by attempting to define tourism. Following a review of a number of definitions he concludes, "Conceptually, then, to define tourism precisely is an all but impossible task" (p. 3). Urry (1990) writes in this respect, "There is no single tourist gaze as such. It varies by society, by social group and by historical period" (p. 1).

No universal definition has yet been adopted. *Tourism* is derived from the English word *tour* (i.e., journey), derived itself from the French *tour* (i.e., a movement of going away and returning to its starting point). The first characteristic of tourism, then, is that travel is involved. However, travel itself is not a sufficient condition of tourism. Tourism and travel are not synonymous. Tourism is a relatively modern concept, whereas travel has taken place for almost as long as the earth has been inhabited.

Tourism first appeared in the Oxford English Dictionary in 1811. In 1937 the League of Nations recommended what may have been the first official definition of tourism (cited by Mill, 1990, p. 17): "any person visiting a country, other than that in which he usually resides, for a period of at least 24 hours." This was subsequently ratified in 1963 by the United Nations, and in 1968 the United Nations Statistical Commission identified the overnight stay as a necessary condition to distinguish a tourist. The definitions of a *tourist* as someone who stays overnight and an *excursionist* as a visitor who does not stay overnight have been widely adopted even though they fail to identify the nature of tourist activity. Accordingly, the International Association of Scientific Experts in Tourism (AIEST) redefined tourism in 1981 as follows:

> Tourism may be defined in terms of particular activities, selected by choice and undertaken outside the home environment. Tourism may or may not involve overnight stays away from home (De Groote, 1995, p. 28).

In other words, leisure and tourism are both part of a continuum, travel being the discriminating factor.

The second characteristic of tourism is that the stay away from home must be temporary. Essentially, tourism is a circular journey. MacCannell (1996) argues that returning home is the first condition of being a tourist, that is, "one goes only to return" (p. 5), and is a point clearly supported by Urry (1990): "There is a clear intention to return home within a relatively short period of time" (p. 3).

The third element most scientists have adopted to describe tourism is the purpose of the trip. In his writings, MacCannell (1996) focuses on the nature of the experience, proposing that a condition necessary to be a tourist is the expectation of having "some kind of experience of 'otherness'" (p. 5). Urry (1990) describes "otherness" as experiences "which are different from those typically encountered in everyday life" (p. 1).

MacCannell's emphasis on the cultural experience involved in tourism appeals to us since sport tourism is bound up with the nature of the activities engaged in rather than with the site of accommodation. For the purposes of this text, our working definition of tourism is as follows:

> The temporary movement of people beyond their own home and work locality involving experiences unlike those of everyday life. The experiences might take place as part of a holiday or as an ancillary to business travel.

Iberotel

Tourism involves travel, a stay in a place other than one's home, and experiences unlike those of everyday life.

Forms of Tourism

Most countries accept that an *international tourist* is a temporary visitor who spends at least one night but not more than one year in a country other than his or her own for the purposes of leisure or business (Boniface and Cooper, 1994; Mill, 1990). An *international day_excursionist* is a visitor who does not stay overnight but who visits a country other than his or her own for the purposes of leisure or business (Mill, 1990).

A *domestic tourist* is defined by the World Tourism Organization (1981) as

> any person residing within a country, irrespective of na-
> tionality, travelling to a place within this country other
> than his usual residence for a period of not less than 24
> hours or one night.

A *domestic excursionist* is someone who meets the above definition but who does not stay overnight (World Tourism Organization, 1981).

In other literature on the subject, tourists are divided into three categories, according to the main purpose of their visit:

1. Holiday tourists
2. Business tourists
3. Other tourists (Holloway, 1994)

Holiday tourists are those who travel to engage in a touristic experience in their leisure time including visits to friends and relatives. *Business tourists* include those who travel as part of their work obligation (Boniface and Cooper, 1994). Boniface and Cooper resolve the complication of considering business visitors as tourists by analyzing the "degree of freedom" each purpose-of-visit category implies. The holiday visitor is relatively free to choose both time of departure and destination; the common interest visitor less so; and the business traveler is usually highly constrained in terms of where and when to travel. The category *other tourists* comprises those who travel for miscellaneous reasons, such as study or religious pilgrimages.

The inclusion of a *nonholiday* (business) category as a legitimate form of tourism has a distinct advantage so far as this text is concerned since it permits the inclusion of professional sports players, their coaches, team officials, and media personnel who engage in business tourism for a wholly sport-oriented purpose. *Other* tourism is not generally concerned with sport (except students on educational sporting exchanges) and is therefore excluded. Therefore a two-part division of tourism is used here that distinguishes between *holiday* and *nonholiday* tourism.

Definition of Sport Tourism

As a concept, sport tourism is often seen as of more recent origin than either sport or tourism. Yet what may be the earliest published work specifically linking sport and tourism can be traced to 1887. Victor Balck, the father of modern Swedish sport, included in a book dealing with different sports a chapter describing "Tourism and Sport" (Olson, 1993). The terms *sport tourism* or *sport tourist* are found increasingly in recent literature (Barnard, 1988; De Knop, 1987; Deveen, 1987; Glyptis, 1982; Redmond, 1990; Standeven and Tomlinson, 1994) though few definitions are available. Hall (1992) states that

> Sport tourism falls into two categories, travel to participate in sport and travel to observe sport. Therefore, sport tourism may be defined as travel for non-commercial reasons, to participate or observe sporting activities away from the home range. (p. 147)

Although we accept this definition, we also include the category of business and commercial tourism. That is, sport tourism can occur while a person is traveling for business or commercial reasons.

Sport

The whole range of competitive and noncompetitive active pursuits that involve skill, strategy, and/or chance in which human beings engage, at their own level, simply for enjoyment and training or to raise their performance to levels of publicly acclaimed excellence.

Tourism

The temporary movement of people beyond their own home and work locality involving experiences unlike those of everyday life. The experiences might take place as part of a holiday or as an ancillary to business travel.

Sport Tourism

All forms of active and passive involvement in sporting activity, participated in casually or in an organized way for noncommercial or business/commercial reasons, that necessitate travel away from home and work locality.

Forms of Sport Tourism

Figure 1.2 sets out our typology of the sport tourist. It categorizes the various types of participation and distinguishes one type of sport tourist from another. As you can see, sport tourists may be *active* or *passive*. Active sport tourists may engage in *sport activity holidays,* in which sport is a main intention of the trip, or in *holiday sport activities,* where sport is incidental. There are two types of sport activity holidays: (1) the single sport activity holiday, where a specific sport is the overriding objective of the holiday, and (2) the multiple sport activity holiday, where participation in several sports forms an important part of the holiday experience (for example, a holiday taken at a sports club or camp).

Two types of holiday sport activities are identified: (1) incidental participation in organized sport, provided during holidays (usually in groups such as competitive beach games), and (2) private or independent sports activity on holiday (for example, taking a walk or playing a round of golf).

Passive sport tourists can also be grouped according to how important sport is to the purpose of their trip. *Connoisseur observers* are those who have extensive passive involvement and are discriminating in the sports activity they watch as spectators or officiators—the "connoisseur consumer" was

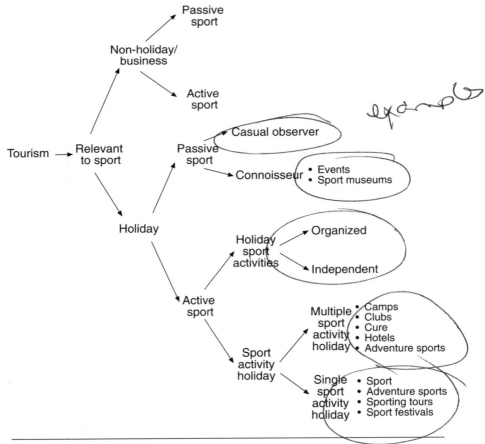

Figure 1.2   Types of sport tourism.

introduced as a lifestyle concept by The Henley Centre (Tomlinson, 1990). *Casual observers* are those who simply enjoy watching an event and who usually happen across it rather than plan their visit.

In chapter 2 we shall examine some theoretical approaches to sport and tourism in order to increase our understanding of how the two are related. However, since sport and tourism have been linked for a long time, one must first appreciate the historical development of sport tourism in order to understand it in its contemporary form. It is to the historical connections that we now turn.

Historical Development of Connections Between Sport and Tourism

Links between travel and sport were evident in ancient Greece. Though the evolution of sport tourism to its modern-day concept has been neither steady nor smooth, we document selected connections to show how both sport and tourism have benefited from their relationship and how the modern-day links are established on an old foundation. Historical periods can rarely be precisely defined. It takes time for influences to be felt and legacies spill over, resulting in overlapping periods. Most dates, therefore, are simply approximations.

Connections in the Ancient World

The ancient Olympic Games, the most celebrated of the Greek multisport festivals, took place every four years and lasted for over a thousand years. They were first conducted in 776 B.C. (Finley and Pleket, 1976). Held over five days, they are amongst the earliest examples of a connection between sport and tourism.

> Athletes, peasants, noblemen, politicians, and splendid state embassies from all parts of Greece made their way to the games. A city of tents mushroomed on the fields near Olympia. (Van Dalen and Bennett, 1971, p. 51)

People came in tens of thousands:

> There was probably no other occasion in the ancient world when so many people were on the road (or the sea) for the same destination at the same time (Finley and Pleket, 1976, p. 55).

A modern estimate suggests that as many as 40,000 people crowded into the stadium (Finley and Pleket, 1976), but the main problem at the event was the lack of housing, particularly for the athletes, who slept in the open air until the first hostel was provided in the fourth century B.C. (Baker, 1982;

Finley and Pleket, 1976). Clearly, then, spectators in ancient Greece traveled with a sport intention, as did elite athletes who toured professionally, some as far as Rome and as early as 186 B.C. (Baker, 1982).

With the disintegration of Greek civilization and the subsequent development of the Roman world empire (circa 200 B.C.-480 A.D.), athletic activity became more health and socially oriented: the Greek games were "paradoxically too openly competitive, yet too tame for the Romans" (Baker, 1982, p. 28). As spectators Romans preferred gladiatorial combats, as participants the baths or *thermae*. Towns became famous because of their natural mineral springs, and where no natural waters existed, the Romans constructed artificial bathing facilities. In Rome alone there were almost nine hundred baths. Caracalla, the largest, could accommodate 3,200 bathers at once. The ease of travel and the spread of the Empire led to the patronage of foreign towns such as Spa in Belgium, Bath (Aquae Sulis) in England, Baden-Baden (Aquae Aureliae) in Germany, and Tiberias in Israel, all of which became fashionable resorts for traveling Roman officials because they had bathing facilities.

The popularizing of bathing and the survival of ball games (two currently popular forms of sport tourism) are probably both due to the Romans' disposition to travel. Had their ideology of games as a means to fitness not been disseminated throughout Europe, ball play would most likely have disappeared due to its association with pagan customs.

An artist's depiction of an ancient stadium for the Olympic Games.

Connections in the Middle Ages and the Renaissance

During the Middle Ages (approximately 500-1400 A.D.), the Catholic Church dominated most aspects of European life, adapting various "pagan" rites for Christian worship (Baker, 1982). The Church also provided both the "holy days" and, in the cloisters, the physical places for people to play their ball games. Gradually, however, the Church's association with ball games diminished as religious reforms led to a period of puritan prohibition in the late sixteenth and early seventeenth centuries. Had not Spanish, French, and English monarchs taken to jousting, horse racing, hunting, court tennis, and yachting, sporting activities may not have survived the puritan purge (Baker, 1982).

Jousting tournaments in medieval times were dominated by professional knights who chose "touring the tournaments" as a way to make their living (Spears and Swanson, 1983, p. 28). Medieval Strasbourg's crossbow contest attracted bowmen from all over Germany and Switzerland. Royal patronage of the tournaments and a tolerant attitude toward the generally rough popular pastimes such as football that ordinary people enjoyed on festivals and holidays ensured the survival of sport. Travel also attracted royal attention in 1388 when Richard II required pilgrims to carry travel permits, the precursor of today's passport (Mill, 1990).

The period of the Renaissance (circa 1400-1600) was characterized by an emphasis on intellectual activity that sharply differentiated scholars and aristocrats from the common folk. Sports suitable for promoting the health of young "gentlemen" were promoted (Baker, 1982). Dancing, wrestling, tennis, and archery were popular, but fencing was regarded as of sufficient importance to require the tutelage of imported Italian masters (Baker, 1982; Van Dalen and Bennett, 1971), the sixteenth century's professional sport tourist coaches.

Extensive trade between The Netherlands and Scotland in the sixteenth century led the Dutch to merge their style of golf (*kolven*) with the way the Scots played the game (Baker, 1982). Adventurers traveled farther than traders and in 1520-1521 the Spaniard Hernando Cortes, following his conquests in Mexico, is reputed to have returned to Europe with a team of Aztec ball players to demonstrate and introduce their games there (Baker, 1982).

Another game that spread beyond national boundaries was real tennis which was popular among sixteenth century aristocrats. Records of international games include one at Windsor in 1505 between Philip I of Castile (Spain) and the Marquis of Dorset (England). The need for a rudimentary set of rules, which were first published in Italy in 1555 and translated into most European languages before the end of the century, attests to the game's widespread appeal and its connections with tourism.

Connections in the Premodern World: 1600-1800

The quest for learning combined with the development of the sprung coach in the fifteenth and sixteenth centuries, which made travel more comfortable, led to a form of tourism in Europe known as the Grand Tour (Holloway, 1994). This was initially a sixteenth century idea designed to train ambassadors and statesmen for the courts of Europe. According to Baker (1982), "young gentlemen strove to be more active than contemplative and physically adroit as well as learned" (p. 61). Thus the Grand Tour established travel, combined with physical activity, as fashionable and desirable for anyone aspiring to knowledge and position. The tour commenced in France, where wealthy young men from England (as many as 20,000 a year), Scandinavia, Russia, and Germany studied French, as well as dancing, fencing, riding, and drawing (Mill, 1990). The men then traveled to Italy to study the arts and returned by way of Germany, the Alpine towns of Switzerland, Holland, Belgium, and Luxembourg. In its original concept the Grand Tour was brought to an end by the French Revolution (1789 to 1792) and the Napoleonic wars.

Another formative influence on the development of tourist destinations in this period were the *spas*. From 1660 onwards, when the medical profession recommended the medicinal properties of mineral waters, spa towns became established as fashionable centers in which to stay and find commercial recreation (Walton, 1983). Since comparatively few people could afford the travel involved, spa visiting was initially exclusive, and the older spa towns became important high-class social centers as well as health resorts (Walton, 1983). "Common folk" meanwhile swam in rivers, and swimming races were an annual feature on the Thames in London (Baker, 1982).

By the middle of the eighteenth century the inland spa centers experienced a challenge. Medical recommendation and aristocratic patronage led to the popularizing of sea bathing and sea water drinking as an alternative to spa visiting (Holloway, 1994; Walton, 1983). Early visitors to the seaside soon discovered that these resorts offered more spacious areas for recreation and the benefit of "fresh" sea air—thus the fashion for seaside holidays began to be established.

During this period, America was colonized, but the sportslike activities adopted differed from colony to colony in part due to their isolation from one another. Settlers came from different social and religious backgrounds, and some, like the New England Puritans, were strongly opposed to sport (Van Dalen and Bennett, 1971). Further, harsh conditions in the new land were hardly conducive to leisure activities. Nevertheless, there is a record of football being played in Massachusetts in 1686 (Baker, 1982). Horse racing was established and the Schuylkill Fishing Club was founded in 1732

(Spears and Swanson, 1983). European explorers also found indigenous North American Indians participating in forms of wrestling, archery, competitive running, swimming, and canoe racing (Baker, 1982) and around 1840 adopted from them the game which became lacrosse (Compton's Interactive Encyclopedia, 1992). The game was first introduced to England by a touring party of 18 Indians in 1867 (Hutchinson, 1996). In contrast to the white settlers, most Africans (by 1790 almost 700,000 had been brought to North America) were slaves and exercised in boxing only to provide betting opportunities for their white masters (Spears and Swanson, 1983). The context of sport in North America during this period of colonization was both a matter of class and geography. The movement of people was not tourism in today's terms; however, the result of travel created conditions in which sport could take root and thrive. In a sense, then, North America provides an early example of sport development arising from travel.

China is attributed with the origins of *wushu*, the collective name given to the martial arts that were introduced to other Asian cultures, where they developed into distinctive styles such as *jiujitsu* in Japan and *tae kwon do* in Korea. Jean Joseph Amiot (1718-1793), a French Jesuit priest, was among the first foreign visitors to China to see wushu, which he referred to as *cong-fou*, during his stay at the Chinese imperial court (Crompton, 1975; Hsu, 1986). Of its two aspects, military combat and health improvement, Amiot emphasized wushu's therapeutic benefits. A French scientist, Dally, who wrote 60 years after Amiot's death, believed that the system deserved wider publicity than it had received in Europe following Amiot's return—thus he detailed its characteristics in his own work. As happened with other sport and exercise systems, when wushu's devotees immigrated to other parts of the world, they sought to preserve wushu as part of their own cultural tradition, and by so doing spread the practice of martial arts through travel beyond Asia (Gast, 1984; Hallander, 1986).

Connections in the Nineteenth and Early Twentieth Centuries

The nineteenth century was a hugely significant period in the development of both sport and tourism due to the industrial revolution. During this century major developments increased the geographical diffusion of sport and tourism from the older countries (primarily of Europe) to the newer nations (i.e., European colonies in Africa, Australia and New Zealand, Canada, the expanding United States after its War of Independence). But "old" values remained and social differentiation persisted, resulting in the experiences of sport and tourism expressing the social inequalities present in society.

The industrial revolution was precipitated by the application of steam power to machinery, first in 1771 in the cotton industry in Britain. From there mechanization developed rapidly. Manufacturing was drawn into factories that were set up in the main centers of population. This led to the urbanization of society, as more and more people eager for work crowded into the towns. Urban life created a new milieu that revolutionized sport, as work-weary laborers sought relaxation and entertainment and became conscious of the values of their former rural surroundings.

Urbanization, stipulated working hours, automatization, the monotony of the workplace, and slowly rising standards of living were all factors that contributed to the development of both sport and tourism in the nineteenth century.

Colonialism was another outcome of industrialization that played a major role in the cultural diffusion of sport. The exploitation of foreign territories, as European imperialistic powers expanded, provided the wealth as well as the markets that stimulated commerce and in turn encouraged industry (Giddens, 1993). But economic motives were not the only reason for acquiring colonies. Colonies also increased the power of parent countries and provided sites for military bases. In return colonial powers engaged with missionary zeal to educate and civilize "primitive" peoples (Giddens, 1993). Travel that arose from imperialism—the power to subjugate other peoples—and the cultural diffusion that happened as a result should not be confused with today's concept of tourism. Tourism is a voluntary activity undertaken for the experiences it promises the individual. Imperialism is a nationalistic activity designed to extend political and economic power and influence. What they share in common is the possibility for cultural diffusion.

Undoubtedly colonialism was a very important influence on the development of both sport and tourism. As populations moved around the globe, so sport spread from its "homelands" and was often used in the "transmission of imperial and national ideas" (Holt, 1989, p. 203).

The industrial revolution fanned the flames of nationalism. Immigrants and exiles from Europe, attracted to the cities of North America, took with them their patriotic pride and culture, which found expression in various forms of gymnastics and sports. Thus the Turnerverein societies, formed by German immigrants to provide classes on the German system of gymnastics, became established in North America where, by 1867, there were 148 societies with 10,200 members (Metzner, 1974). Similarly, immigrant Scotsmen formed Caledonian Clubs in the United States to preserve their native Highland Games. These games were the catalyst for the growth of track and field (athletics) in America (Spears and Swanson, 1983).

The industrial revolution had an enormous impact on the development of transport. The distance people can travel is directly related to the modes and costs of transportation available. Technological improvements in the late eighteenth and nineteenth centuries made travel safer, more reliable, more comfortable, quicker, and cheaper. In Europe in the eighteenth century, new roads were created and main road surfaces improved, making it possible for people, goods, and services to be more mobile (Holloway, 1994). During this period, the stagecoach was replaced by the horse-drawn tram, which later was supplanted by the steam train.

In the nineteenth century the steam train, probably more than any other invention, revolutionized travel, making it possible for sports participants and spectators to move beyond their own locality. The first public railway to carry goods and passengers opened in 1825 in northeast England. By 1840 1,400 miles of track had been laid in Britain and a decade later that figure had risen to 6,000 (Peacock, 1982). In the United States 2,800 miles of track had been completed by 1840, by 1860 all the major eastern U.S. cities were linked by rail, and by 1869 the first trans-American railroad link was completed. The year 1886 saw the completion of the Canadian Pacific Railway, and by 1901 the Trans-Siberian Railway in Russia had opened for single-track traffic.

In the United States at least, the railroad did not maintain the popularity it had in Europe, since the distances between cities were often great and other forms of transport soon challenged it. Nevertheless, the rise and success of professional major league baseball in the 1870s and 1880s depended on rail transportation (Spears and Swanson, 1983).

Schrodt (1988) describes how advances in transportation in the late nineteenth and early twentieth centuries also had a significant impact on the development of sport in Canada, particularly with respect to competitions between neighboring communities.

Although travel by water had been possible for centuries, steam power made it possible for Sir Samuel Cunard to inaugurate the first regular steamship service between Britain and the United States in 1840 (Mill, 1990). In those days the transatlantic crossing took 15 days.

Since Britain was both a prestigious world power and the originator of many modern sports, it is hardly surprising that sport followed its politics, trade, and travel to the four corners of the earth (Baker, 1982; Holt, 1989; Redmond, 1977). But Britain, of course, was not alone either in the practice of colonizing distant places or inventing sports. So although this section of the chapter has focused on the diffusion of British culture and its sports, other nations, too, played a formative role in the transmigration of sports around the globe, as we shall see.

We shall now look at some examples of the prolific connections between sport and tourism that occurred during the nineteenth century. Space limits the specific sports we can discuss, making only a small selection possible. Many sports have been omitted altogether, most notably water sports— from swimming to yachting—not because they were unconnected to tourism, but rather because our purpose here is simply to demonstrate that sport tourism is not a recent development.

Skiing

Perhaps more than any other popular sport, skiing is associated with tourism. The small (in population) country of Norway played an important part in the development of skiing. Using the kind of skis that they had used for centuries for transportation, Norwegians held the first of their annual jumping and racing competitions in Christiania (now known as Oslo) in 1866 (Schwartz, 1989). Norwegian travelers and immigrants took their sport with them; thus its development in America and Australia can be attributed to travel and tourism (Hutchinson, 1996; Schwartz, 1989).

John "Snowshoe" Thompson left his small Norwegian village north of Oslo in 1851 and moved to California to join the gold rush (Schwartz, 1989). In the winter of 1856 and for 13 winters after that, he delivered mail to the miners on homemade skis (Porter, 1996). Early in the 1860s the miners held skiing contests, and by 1867 racing had become so popular that La Porte skiers formed the Alturas Snowshoe Club, which became the center of skiing development in North America and one of the first ski associations in the world. The first is claimed to be at Kiandra, the highest of Australia's "gold rush" towns (Porter, 1996).

The catalyst for the spread of the sport throughout Europe can be attributed in large measure to early British skiers who imported Norwegian skis and then traveled to the Swiss Alpine resorts of Davos, Grindlewald, and Adelboden, introducing holiday skiing to these resorts in the 1880s (Schwarz, 1989). The resorts themselves had been popularized as part of the eighteenth-century Grand Tour (Lavery, 1989). The first group ski holidays from Britain took place in the same decade when Sir Henry Lunn (the world's first ski tour operator) organized holidays to Chamonix in Switzerland for some of his friends (Holloway, 1994; Porter, 1996). He was responsible for organizing the first senior challenge cup for downhill ski racing in 1911, and his son, Arnold, pioneered the timed slalom ski run through gates at the Alpine town of Murren, made famous as a ski resort by the family travel agency (Hutchinson, 1996).

Climbing

Climbing is another sport dependent on terrain that developed as a result of travel. The Alpine districts of Switzerland, popularized by the Grand Tour, saw a utilitarian activity transformed into a sport.

To the Swiss, climbing was serious, an activity undertaken to move animals to higher pastures or to conduct scientific research. But by 1827 the Britons Frederick Slade and Yeats Brown's unsuccessful attempt to climb the Jungfrau was described as "for the fun of the thing" (Cleare, 1975). Thus it was foreign tourists who introduced the idea of climbing for pleasure.

Mountaineering as a sport owes much to young British visitors, mainly university students, who between 1854 and 1872 made 31 of the 39 first ascents of the highest European Alpine peaks (Whymper, 1871). The deaths of four leading climbers on the Matterhorn in 1865 gave the new sport a tragic prominence. According to Holt (1989), "What had begun as little more than energetic and adventurous tourism came to be a competitive activity surrounded by an aura of quiet heroism and patriotic endeavour" (p. 88). Thus mountaineering as a sport was first associated with the privileged classes of British society and their families, who could afford both the time to travel and the equipment and guiding services needed to attempt such ascents.

In New Zealand, prior to the 1880s, most travel in the mountains was undertaken in search of natural resources or in aid of exploration or surveying. It took three visitors (two Swiss and one Irish) to open up the South Island's Alps to the sport of mountaineering (Johnston, 1992).

Football (Soccer)

Association Football (soccer) can reasonably claim to be the world's most international game; it is played and watched on a regular basis more than any other single sport. Just over a hundred years ago the game was in its infancy but growing at a phenomenal rate in England and spreading out from there equally as rapidly. Mason (1986) comments,

> From Calais to the Urals, Helsinki to Genoa, football was being played to an increasingly sophisticated standard. And the feet of the English were everywhere, playing the game. (p. 67)

Three forces were mainly responsible for the transmission of football to other countries: commerce, education, and the armed forces. However, Mason (1986) tells us that touring teams were responsible for nurturing the game to a consolidated state and stimulating spectator interest: "For club members, touring became a regular attraction in which football, seeing the sights, and socializing with your side and theirs were of equal importance" (p. 67). He goes on, "The touring team showed what could be achieved and the coach came to help local players to achieve it" (p. 71).

One well-known club, the Corinthians, composed of upper-class young men, toured widely and frequently—in South Africa in 1897, 1903, and 1907; Canada and the United States in 1906, 1911, and 1924; and Brazil in 1910, 1913, and 1914. Visits to Europe were even more common after their first trips to Hungary and Scandinavia in 1904 (Mason, 1986).

Football in North America was, in its original form, adopted from Britain, though it did not survive long unchanged (Baker, 1982). According to Salisbury (1997), the first recorded soccer club formed in the United States was the Oneida Football Club which played on Boston Commons from 1862-1865. But following an 1878 meeting of the Intercollegiate Football Association, new rules began to emerge, and by the early years of the twentieth century, the game was unmistakably different, described by Baker as "a mild form of trench warfare" (p. 130). American football has only recently gained an audience in Europe, where it has been popularized by exhibition games and television.

Tennis

Lawn tennis was an adaptation of the much older game of real or royal tennis, which originated in France. The "real" tennis court evolved from monastery courtyards where the game, played with the palm of the hand much like *pelota* is today in the Basque provinces of northern Spain, was called *jeu de paume*. Transforming tennis into a popular sport can be attributed to an entrepreneurial Englishman, Maj. Walter Wingfield, who patented a complete kit of equipment in 1874 following publication of the first book of rules in 1873. In its newly commercialized form, the game gained instant popularity and spread rapidly in Europe through the agency of British holidaymakers (Hutchinson, 1996). Baker (1982) tells us,

> In 1893, two years after the founding of the French championships, a similar tournament was held in a German Baltic seacoast town, Bad Homburg, where English Victorians vacationed. The pattern repeated itself all over Europe in the 1890s. On Dutch asphalt courts at the Hague, at St. Moritz in the Swiss Alps, at Marienbad in the Hapsburg Empire, and in St. Petersburg, wherever Englishmen visited or worked, they carried their tennis equipment and met with an enthusiastic response from upper-class Europeans. (p. 183)

The spread and popularizing of tennis owed much to the enthusiasm, status, and affluence of its devotees. Lawns on which to play, sufficient disposable income to purchase the equipment, and the "right" social connections were all important. In the early days, even more than today, private incomes were essential to any who aspired to cross the Atlantic to play or spectate. Lawn tennis was introduced to the United States by Mary Ewing Outerbridge following a visit to Bermuda from New York in 1874 (Hutchinson, 1996; Spears and Swanson, 1983). Seeing the game played by British garrison officers during her visit, she took a set of Wingfield's equipment back to America with her, and her brother established the game at the Staten Island Cricket and Base Ball Club. Elsewhere in the country James Dwight, following a visit to Europe in 1874, influenced the development of the game and in 1876 played the first recorded tennis tournament in the United States at Nahant, Massachusetts. The first lawn tennis club in the United States was founded in New Orleans in 1876, which suggests there could well have been French influences at work also (Spears and Swanson, 1983).

Golf

Both the Scots and the Dutch claim to have invented golf. That the game is old there can be no doubt—the first clubs were formed in the area of Edinburgh and the first rules of the game were established in that city in

1744. Although the game did not immediately appeal to the English, Scots took their game abroad where in 1829 a club was formed in Calcutta, followed by one in Bombay in 1842, and in Pau, France, in 1856 (Baker, 1982).

In the 1870s clubs were established in Australia, New Zealand, and Canada; wherever the Scots emigrated, golf went with them. In England in particular, high fees led to social exclusivity of the clubs and attracted memberships from the newly affluent. As this group took their holidays at the developing seaside resorts, courses were constructed there to cater to their needs (Walton, 1983). The more wealthy increasingly took their holidays abroad; thus it was the same upper middle classes who first took golf to Germany, Belgium, and Spain (Ford, 1977).

The first permanent golf club in the United States was founded in 1888 in New York, having been introduced there by a Scottish immigrant who laid out a three-hole course in a cow pasture in Yonkers (Baker, 1982). In the early 1900s, the English club professional Harry Vardon was invited to the United States, where he was sponsored by A.G. Spalding and Company to promote the game. This piece of sponsored tourism, coupled with Haskell's invention of a rubber-cored ball, contributed significantly to America's rapid dominance of the game (Baker, 1982).

Cycling

The bicycle was an independent means of transport that offered new opportunities to get out of the towns and into the countryside. Founded in 1878, the Cyclists' Touring Club in Britain promoted cycling holidays and by the turn of the century had attracted 60,449 members (Alderson, 1972). Around 1890 the machine underwent a metamorphosis, with improvements to the tires that made riding more comfortable (Baker, 1982). Since bicycles were initially available to the rich, the upper classes established the habit of bicycle riding and formed the early clubs. In the 1890s cycling boomed across Europe, with the first competitive race being held from Bordeaux to Paris in 1891. During the same year, a race from Paris to Brest and back again attracted cyclists from all over Europe (Baker, 1982).

Bicycling, described as "the most phenomenal craze of all" (Redmond, 1977, p. 490) in the United States, began when Colonel Pope saw a display of English machines at the Centennial Exposition in Philadelphia in 1876. Subsequently he visited England, studied their manufacture, imported machines into the United States, and then developed his own product (Redmond, 1977). As early as 1893, a million bicycles had been sold in America. To assist bicycle touring, the League of American Wheelmen developed a system of approval and certification of suitable lodgings and established a directory (Tobin, 1974). The league also published a range of tour guides, which they issued to wheelmen. Yet in the United States the bicycle never attained the popularity it achieved in Europe, where by the 1920s cycling trips were commonplace and where, due to mechanized production of the bicycle, it was available to those of more modest means (Baker, 1982). An estimated 10 million cyclists were on the roads of Britain alone by the 1930s, and organized holidays to Europe were available.

Hiking

Hiking is usually distinguished from walking by its use of the countryside while walking is done anywhere. Hiking involves distances of at least two miles.

Together with swimming, hiking (often termed walking or trekking) is the most popular form of sport tourism (Kamphorst and Roberts, 1989). Like so many other sporting activities, hiking was popularized toward the end of the nineteenth century once walking's major function as a utilitarian activity had been superseded by the emergence of mechanized forms of transport. Hiking depended on people's financial capability to travel to rural areas and often on suitable accommodation.

Born in 1864 and educated in Germany in the 1880s, T.A. Leonard returned to Britain and took up a post as a church minister. Eager to provide social as well as religious teaching, he organized a holiday in the English Lake District in 1891 for 30 men of his congregation to scale the "fells" (hills). This led to the establishment of the Co-operative Holidays Association (CHA), which by 1893 was placing advertisements in *Christian World* for rambling holidays in the Lake District (Tomlinson and Walker, 1990). In establishing the CHA, Leonard was motivated by social concerns and a desire "to bring holidays within the reach of poorer folks" (Tomlinson and Walker, 1990, p. 230). One of the earliest clubs was the Manchester YMCA Rambling Club formed in 1880; rambling is a peculiarly British term for hiking (Tomlinson and Walker, 1990).

The German youth movement emerged in the last decade of the nineteenth century and in 1896 a group of Berlin boys under the leadership of Karl Fischer took up hiking. In 1904 the *Wandervogel* (literally, wandering birds) organization was formed. In 1911 the Prussian parliament voted a large sum of money and placed 17 buildings at the disposal of the wanderers. Two years later there were 83 hostels providing shelter for 20,000 overnight hikers (Van Dalen and Bennett, 1971). There are now around 4,500 youth hostels worldwide.

Founded in 1892, just 20 years after the establishment of the first national park at Yellowstone in Wyoming, Montana, and Idaho, the *Sierra Club* in the United States was formed with similar motives—to conserve the nation's resources and realize their value for scenic as well as aesthetic and scientific purposes (Kraus, 1984). Not restricted to conservation, the club claims to be the nation's largest hiking and skiing club. The Appalachian Mountain Club, founded in 1876 to explore the mountains of New England, has contributed to the exploration and mapping of one of the longest national scenic trails designated by the U.S. Congress. Stretching more than 2,000 miles from Maine to Georgia, the Appalachian trail crosses 13 states and is the subject of Bill Bryson's recent travel book, *A Walk in the Woods* (1997). Each year around 200 people now hike the full length and millions more complete sections of the trail.

Tom Stephenson, a rambler and journalist, was impressed by the long-distance wilderness hiking trails in America, and visualized the application of the idea in England (Hopkins, 1989). An article appeared in the *Daily Herald* in 1935 proposing a path along the backbone of the English Pennine hills. The Rambler's Association together with the Youth Hostels Association undertook preparatory field work in the late 1930s. The interruption caused by World War II and the need to open up linking paths, delayed the official opening of the first national trail path in England—the 256-mile Pennine Way from Edale south of Manchester to Kirk Yetholm over the Scottish border—until 1965 (Hopkins, 1989).

Cricket and Baseball

The origins of cricket are ancient and unrecorded. Early references document the game being played in England about 1550, but its popularity grew in the eighteenth century with the establishment of a club in Hampshire and the founding of a cricket ground (Lord's) in London.

Originally a village game, cricket broadened its scope when the railways made more distant travel possible. English immigrants also took the game with them to various parts of the world including Canada, where a match in 1835 involved a team from Sherbrooke (east of Montreal) who trekked to Hamilton and Toronto on foot and horseback (Booth and Batts, 1977). Possibly the first touring team of any sport, the Surrey (England) Cricket Club was on its way to Paris in 1789. It never reached its destination due to the French Revolution (Hutchinson, 1996).

Overseas tours by an English cricket team commenced with visits to North America in 1859 and to Australia in 1861-62 (Green, 1982) via the newly established passenger steamship services. According to Baker (1982), cricket was described as "the leading game played out of doors" (p. 139) in the United States in 1858. The international match played in Hoboken a year later supports this claim since it drew 25,000 spectators and required "extra ferries to carry people over from Manhattan" (Baker, 1982, p. 139). Beginning in 1861 English cricketers regularly visited Australia, and by the end of the century, teams were touring all parts of Queen Victoria's far-flung empire (Holt, 1989).

It was America, not Britain, that developed and codified baseball early in the nineteenth century, though it, too, was a "colonial implantation" (Hutchinson, 1996). Like cricketers, America's first baseballers "prided themselves on being exclusively 'gentlemen'" (Baker, 1982, p. 139). The Civil War (1861-65) was the watershed that caused Americans to "recognize baseball as their 'national game' in contrast to cricket" (Baker, 1982, p. 143).

The heritage of sport tourism—England's cricket team heading to America in 1859.

Anglo-American relations deteriorated during the Civil War as England declared itself neutral but in subtle ways backed the Confederacy against the Union. This led to strong anti-British feelings and a wave of patriotism that led to the popularizing of an American game rather than one more obviously British. Further, by the end of the war, the "New York rules" were widely adopted, providing uniform government of the game that had previously been played following a variety of rules. The Cincinnati Red Stockings' tour from Maine to California in 1869 is described as a "first" since it used the Union Pacific Railroad, local lines, and steamships to cross the continent (Spears and Swanson, 1983). And as early as 1874 the Philadelphia Athletics and the Bostons toured England (Hutchinson, 1996). By the turn of the century baseball had been introduced to America's colony in the Philippines (Beran, 1989), and Finland had derived its own variant—*pesapallo*—following Tahko Pihkala's visit to the United States in 1907 (Silvennoinen, 1989).

The Modern Olympic Games

After a hiatus of 1,500 years, the first modern Olympic Games took place in Athens in 1896 and were seen by an American visitor at the time as a spectacular attraction (Holmes, 1984). Holmes's conception of the 1896 Games and his record of them is bound up with a guided tour of Greece. He viewed the sporting activity as a tourist and wrote about it in the same touristic fashion as he wrote about the architecture, the food, the Greeks, and their money. His destination was Greece, not the Games, yet his account is indicative of the way in which sports activities were often linked to touristic experiences and were considered part "of the same whole" (McFee, 1990).

The 311 athletes who attended the first modern Games came from 13 countries, although 230 were from Greece itself (Szymiczek, 1976). Most of the visiting athletes traveled to Athens at their own expense, many on their own initiative, and between them won 17 out of the 22 first prizes, receiving a diploma, a silver medal, and a crown of olive branches (Szymiczek, 1976).

The expenses of the first modern Olympics were projected at approximately 200 drachmas; however, the Games ended up costing more than a million (Gruneau, 1984). In order to meet such costs, early Games were linked to other tourist attractions. For example, the 1900 Olympic Games were held in conjunction with the Universal Exhibition in Paris; the 1904 celebration was timed to coincide with the St. Louis World's Fair. Given the inaccessibility of St. Louis (New York, as a transatlantic port, would have been a better choice) only the desire to link the Games to the World's Fair can explain the selection of St. Louis. The distance, cost, and difficulty of travel to St. Louis more than halved the number of competitors in 1904. Four years earlier, Paris had registered 1,330 contestants. St. Louis managed a mere 617 who represented 12 nations, but 525 of them were Americans and another 41 were Canadians, leaving just 51 overseas competitors (Meyer, 1976).

Numbers of participants and countries represented in the Olympics climbed steadily as long as the Games were held in Europe, clearly indicative of the greater ease of travel. In London in 1908, where the events were linked with an Anglo-French exhibition, there were 2,056 competitors representing 22 countries, and by 1912 in Stockholm this number had grown by a further 25 percent representing 28 nations (Tomlinson and Whannel, 1984).

In summary, sport's geographical diffusion around the world from its various "homelands" was closely tied to travel. Since sport is part of cultural experience, as people traveled they took their sport with them and established it in new milieus. Thus much of the early development of sport can be attributed to the spread of travel and tourism.

Democratization of Sport and Tourism in the Twentieth Century

The twentieth century has seen the unparalleled growth of sport and tourism. The period has been characterized by social diffusion and the development of mass tourism and mass sport, rather than their geographical diffusion characteristic of the nineteenth century. Democratization—the process by which increasingly more members of a community gain access to opportunities previously restricted to the upper classes—has taken place. This is not to suggest that people at all levels of society have equal access to sport and tourism. This is clearly false (for a general sociological analysis see Giddens, 1993; for sport see Clarke and Critcher, 1985; Coakley, 1990; Gruneau, 1984; and Hargreaves, 1986; for tourism see Lea, 1988; MacCannell, 1976; Tomlinson and Walker, 1990; Urry, 1990; and Walton, 1983). However, a much wider cross section of people are now sport tourists.

Conditions That Have Favored the Democratization of Sport and Tourism

A number of conditions have influenced the democratization of both sport and tourism. We have singled out four factors as major twentieth-century developments that have encouraged mass sport and mass tourism: economic forces, technological innovations, political movements, and attitudinal and value changes.

Economic Forces

In order to take part in either sport or tourism, people must have adequate time and money. Major changes this century in how and what kind of work people are doing (among them, a decrease in manual occupations and an increase in nonmanual ones) have led to a lessening of material inequalities and increasing affluence. Giddens (1993) tells us:

> Blue-collar workers in Western societies now earn three or four times as much as their counterparts at the turn of the century. Gains for white-collar, managerial and professional workers have been slightly higher. In terms of earnings per head of the population and the range of goods and services which can be purchased, the majority of the population today are vastly more affluent than any other people have been before in human history. (p. 223)

Although the quantity of leisure time has not increased at such a dramatic pace as some might believe, more people are experiencing more leisure than their predecessors. Mill (1990) notes that by the turn of the century, the workday had been reduced from 12 to 10 hours and vacations were beginning to be recognized. He says, "While travel had been for the few, now it began to come within the reach of more and more people" (p. 11). In broad terms, hours of employment have decreased quite significantly over the past century, particularly as holiday entitlements have increased and technological improvements have led to more disposable time for many people. Parker (1983) observes that "Shorter working weeks, longer holidays, [and] a longer period of retirement because we tend to give up employment earlier and live longer . . . are giving us more leisure" (p. xi), and Capernerhurst (1994) notes that "In the richer countries tourism has grown in importance as household real incomes and leisure time have increased" (p. 146). So, for most people in the Western-style democracies of Europe, North America, Japan, and Australia, economic changes this century have created the time and money that have encouraged them to participate more in both sport and tourism.

Technological Innovations

Equally important in enabling sport and tourism to spread to a wider cross section of the population are the technological innovations of this century. New methods of transportation have encouraged the expansion of tourism and in turn this has had an impact on sport.

The last quarter of the nineteenth century saw the appearance of the first motor cars. Within two decades the car was being mass-produced, first in America and later in England. Henry Ford's comparatively inexpensive Model T, introduced in 1908, brought the motor car within reach of the masses and offered an independent form of leisure transport capable of greater distances than the bicycle. Private car ownership has expanded since 1950, and today more than 90 percent of all pleasure trips in the United States are taken by car (Mill, 1990). In Great Britain the car is used as the main method of transport by 78 percent of those who take holidays of four nights or more. (Ward, Higson, and Campbell, 1994).

The invention of air transport had the most significant impact on international travel. The first regular scheduled service was begun in 1919 by the German airline Lufthansa. The introduction of jet aircraft in 1958 drastically reduced the time it took to travel almost anywhere in the world, encouraging people to travel longer distances. The 1970 development of the jumbo jet, capable of carrying nearly five hundred passengers at speeds of over one thousand kilometers per hour, increased the attractiveness of long-haul leisure travel (Davidson, 1993). Today the Concorde crosses the Atlantic in just over three hours (Mill, 1990). Compare this with the 15 days taken by the early transatlantic liners when the journey itself was a holiday but available only to the well-off.

Although charter flights were organized as early as the 1920s (the trip run by Thomas Cook in 1927 to take fans from New York to Chicago to see the Dempsey-Tunney title fight was one of the first), they were not widely available until the 1960s (Holloway, 1994).

The introduction of charter air travel led to the development of package holidays. By filling every seat on the aircraft and making block bookings in accommodation, holiday packages could be offered to some international destinations almost as cheaply as an independent domestic holiday. The attraction of the sunny coasts of the Mediterranean increased the popularity of moderately priced package holidays, particularly for northern Europeans.

Larger aircraft made it possible to keep fares down, making it possible for more people to travel farther. Up to 1980 only about 20 percent of the world's international tourists traveled interregionally, while 80 percent of international tourism was *intraregional*. Long-haul travel has virtually doubled and by 1987 accounted for nearly 40 per cent of world tourism (Burton, 1995).

As each successive form of transport has been popularized, lower fares have been introduced. Longer distances have thus become less expensive and more accessible. Technological advances in transport thus have enabled a more broadly based market to engage in sport tourism.

People who travel beyond their homes require lodgings. The introduction of the stagecoach led to the development of inns, which were used for sleeping, stabling, eating, and drinking. By the eighteenth century the advent of the railways led to the development of the modern grand hotels, of which Tremont House, opened in Boston in 1829, is often regarded as the first (Mill, 1990). At that time it was the largest hotel in the world, with 170 rooms (Mill, 1990). It also offered cold baths, water closets, gas lights, a different key for each room, and free soap (regarded as an extravagance).

The origins of the holiday camp as a more modest tourist accommodation can be traced to the Co-operative Holidays Association in England in the 1890s. The first such camp was opened by Billy Butlin at Skegness in 1936. Operated on the principle of visitor volume (the first camp took three thousand guests) and a small profit margin, the self-contained, all-weather facilities provided for sport and fitness as well as dancing and other forms of entertainment. The all-inclusive cost and a child-minding service popularized the holiday camp concept and kept middle to lower income families happy.

Prewar Germany also took to the concept of camps for health and recreation, though of a more militaristic type, and in France the "villages de vacance" was similarly designed (Holloway, 1994). In the United States in the 1930s, hotels with leisure complexes had become a popular development (Holloway, 1994). The range of "club" type holidays now available—including, for example, Center Parcs and Club Med—appeals to a broad segment of the holiday market.

As more families traveled independently by car, hotels failed to cater to their needs. Kemmons Wilson, in America, is attributed with opening the first motel as a new form of accommodation in 1952 (Mill, 1990). Motels were situated on highways, rather than in town centers where hotels were principally located; they offered free parking, family occupancy, and a telephone in every room; and generally they welcomed animals. Offering more flexibility to the tourist, their occupancy increased while in hotels it decreased. In response, the accommodation sector has diversified and segmented its market by opening new properties of all kinds designed to meet the needs of the budget conscious, the middle market, and the most elite luxury travelers.

While transport and accommodation have played crucial roles in opening up tourism, important technological innovations in the media have helped develop sport. Spectator sport in particular was first popularized by the press, followed by radio and then by television (Holt, 1989). Baker (1982) believes television has been the "most decisive" technological influence on modern sport. He says, "For sports, television is the great popularizer, benefactor and dictator" (p. 262).

Technological advances in the production of sports equipment have also contributed to the development and the popularizing of sport. Vulcanized rubber revolutionized balls as well as transport in the nineteenth century. The sewing machine and various wood-crafting tools contributed to the mass production of uniforms and equipment, making them more moderately priced. Electric light was another innovation that made sport more accessible to the masses, illuminating courts and playing fields after work.

More recently, information technology has brought massive changes to tourism. Travel agents can now call up hotel availability from thousands of miles away and transact bookings instantly. Computerization has revolutionized virtually every aspect of travel—from the issue of tickets to the navigation of aircraft—and is contributing to lower pricing.

A whole raft of technological innovations have thus helped to open up travel and widen the appeal of sport. Increased access, expanded availability, and ease of participation have contributed to the democratization of sport tourism.

Political Movements

In antiquity traveling was dangerous and undertaken mainly for trade. The Romans created conditions—including excellent roads, staging inns suitably located for travelers, a single currency, and a system of law that provided protection—that made it safer, but as their empire collapsed at the end of the fourth century, established political structures were destroyed and the countryside became unsafe for travelers.

Agricultural innovations and an increase in productivity improved the welfare of the people and caused the cities in the Middle Ages to flourish. This led to the setting up of guilds, whose purpose was to protect political and economic interests. From 1500 onward traveling became safer again and "tourism" gathered momentum. This clearly shows that in times of peace and prosperity tourism flourishes. In countries with unstable political situations or where there is a threat of war, tourism suffers.

As foreign travel grew, currency exchange assumed increased importance. The need to carry large sums in cash acted as a deterrent as it increased the risk of robbery and encouraged cheating by money exchangers (Holloway, 1994). The increased political stability since the Second World War, ease of exchange through international monetary arrangements, and, more recently, cashless innovations like the credit card have eased uncertainties and encouraged travel.

In the decades since World War II, the civil rights movement has contributed to the reduction of gender and racial barriers in sport, opening up sports participation to more participants and spectators. Baker (1982) notes that "a wave of vast social change . . . has opened the door of opportunity for blacks and females" (pp. 283-284). In 1945 black sports heroes were almost unknown in America—where they were largely segregated—and elsewhere. As many black nations won independence in the 1950s, black athletes began to show in international competitions that they were as skillful at sport as whites. In the 1960s the black athletes of America protested and by their sporting expertise demonstrated their right to be on national and professional teams (Baker, 1982; Spears and Swanson, 1983). During the 1970s athletic teams even in southern states became fully integrated (Baker, 1982). In both professional and amateur sports the doors were being pried open to allow more people to participate.

The women's movement also benefited from skilled athletes and militant feminists who "won for women an enlarged, more equal participation not only in business and professional fields, but also in sports" (Baker, 1982, p. 262). In this respect America became the model for elsewhere. Gradually old attitudes and practices of discrimination have been modified and sport is becoming democratized.

Attitudinal and Value Changes

Bart Crum (1991, 1994), writing primarily about West European societies, describes a shift to postmaterialist values in sport as "the sportification of the society" (p. 6). In this context, by postmaterialist values he is referring to the shift from work ethic values to values emphasizing leisure, hedonism, and self-realization. The sportification of society denotes that sport and sports values in general have a greater societal influence than before. An obvious example is how sports clothing has become fashionable in nonsport contexts. Along with this change we see the rapid growth of commercial fitness clinics that appeal to consumers whose values are more hedonistic, individualistic, and cosmetic than most organized sports club members'. The more sport is "used for objectives outside sport itself," Crum (1994) maintains, "the more its traditional social values and characteristics will be blurred" (p. 7). This dilution of the once homogeneous traditions of sport (Digel, 1994) has resulted in two opposing trends: the "sportification of sport" and the "de-sportification of sport." Intrinsic to the sportification of sport are excesses such as doping and injurious training in order to win and the massive financial support for an elite system. The de-sportification of sport refers to changes embraced by the "sport for all" movement with its focus on participation more than performance, on fun experiences rather than on competitive challenges.

The de-sportification of sport is seen as a reaction to the sportification of sport, a countermove involving a rejection of traditional sporting values and a move toward greater pluralism. Increasing differentiation in levels of performance, and a growing lack of interest on the part of many participants in conventional sporting roles and traditional sports institutions, is affecting sports clubs, according to Crum (1994) and Digel (1994). Although achievement and competition remain meaningful to some, others see these characteristics as less desirable and simply want to practice an activity for its own sake. This tendency has lowered the barrier to sports participation as people who would previously have considered sport as not being for them now seek to participate independently at their own level. Kamphorst and Roberts (1989) point out that instead of joining formal organizations such as sports clubs, recreational participants now more often choose family or friends as their playing companions. It is no longer necessary to boast a single-figure handicap in order to be seen on a prestigious golf course. As the client base of sport (and tourism) has widened, and as sport tourists have broadened their horizons, so the conventions and expectations have relaxed.

In summary, sport and tourism have historically been closely tied to social stratification. Because of the resources needed to participate in these activities, they tended to be reserved for privileged groups in society. However, as economic, technological, political, and attitudinal factors have changed this century, resources have become more widely available. These conditions have favored the democratization of both sport and tourism and contributed to the establishment of sport tourism.

Increased Participation Due to Democratization

Increased access to sport and tourism has caused more and more people to participate in sport tourism. In looking at adventure travel, Kearsley (1990) reports a trend toward participatory activity rather than passive viewing, and McKie (1994) states that the 1980s and 1990s have seen a rapid growth in activity holidays in the United Kingdom, a view supported by Clark, Darrell, Grove-White, Macnaghten, and Urry (1994). Johnston (1992), writing about New Zealand, similarly describes the 1980s as "a key decade for the growth and promotion of the commercial provision of adventure tourism opportunities for not only international visitors, but also domestic participants" (p. 159). This trend continued according to a report published in 1995 by Deloitte Touche Tohmatsu (1995). Other researchers agree on the growth trend for Britain (Churchill, 1990; Ogilvie and Dickinson, 1992), Europe (Smith and Jenner, 1990), America (Mudge, 1991), and worldwide (Weiler and Hall, 1992).

The Commonwealth of Independent States (i.e., Russia and the former Soviet Republics) has experienced some growth in domestic tourism since the end of 1991 when the USSR ceased to exist, and activity holidays are noted to be growing in popularity there, especially canoeing and camping (Boniface and Cooper, 1994). The advanced industrial economies of the Czech and Slovak Republics also report a growing demand for a wide range of outdoor recreation activities (Boniface and Cooper, 1994). In Australia large numbers head for the ski slopes between June and September, and the Great Barrier Reef provides opportunities for scuba diving and snorkeling unequaled anywhere else in the world. The Japanese search for good golfing holidays has resulted in the development of championship golf courses in the Philippines and the Middle East (Boniface and Cooper, 1994).

In Great Britain, according to the English Tourist Board (1992), holidays mainly for the purpose of activity accounted for around 12 percent of all holiday trips in 1991, a figure with which Leisure Consultants (1992) agrees, though the United Kingdom Tourism Survey (British Tourist Authority/ English Tourist Board, 1992) puts the percentage higher with 26 percent of their respondents claiming "sport" as a main purpose of their trip. Support for this higher percentage was found by Mintel International Group (1995) who reports that the activity holiday sector accounted for 22 percent of total domestic holidays. Similar figures are reported from southwest England, where it was estimated that almost a quarter of the market were activity holidaymakers (West Country Tourist Board/The Sports Council [South West], 1992).

Similar percentages emerge from the United States. According to Gibson and Yiannakis (1995), a survey commissioned by Marriott International (1994) found that 22 percent of all respondents considered opportunities to participate in sports important when planning a vacation. The demand for participation in recreational activities such as sailing, backpacking, and skiing is also reported to have markedly increased (Boniface and Cooper, 1994; Ewert, 1983).

This marked interest in active holidays is clearly matched by data from Germany (Studienkreis für Tourismus, 1990), where 18 percent of the holidaymakers mentioned sport as their most important motive for going on holiday and 7 percent of all tourists could be classed as "real" sport tourists (Studienkreis für Tourismus, 1990). Belgium's figures for participation in sports during domestic holiday trips are rather higher but still of the same order: 27.1 percent participate in sports during domestic holiday trips, and this increases to 30.4 percent for holidays spent abroad (Westvlaams Economisch Studiebureau, 1991). That around one in four to one in five holidaymakers of more advanced economies are involved in (sport) activity tourism is supported elsewhere, namely, in New Zealand (Kliskey and Kearsley, 1993) and in France (Burton, 1995). Further support comes from the Sports Tourism International Council Research Unit, which conducted a content analysis of 22 tourism schedules—10 from different countries and 12 from urban centers in North America (STIC Research Unit, 1997). Over one-third (34 percent) of the 865 listed tourism activities were devoted to sport tourism and tourism sport activities were offered on 42 percent (mean percentage) of days. The highest percentages of tourism sport days were found in the Caribbean and Europe, which had 56 percent and 54 percent, respectively. The Orient and South America were found to be in the low 30 percent range.

By identifying favorite sport activities of various countries, we can determine possible trends in sport tourism activities. In view of differences in definition, the activities reported here must be seen only as an indication of relative popularity. Kamphorst and Roberts (1989) compared the main trends in sport in 15 countries from all parts of the world, namely, Bulgaria, Canada, Czechoslovakia, Finland, France, Great Britain, India, Italy, Japan, The Netherlands, New Zealand, Nigeria, Poland, Portugal, and the United States. From the 15 contributions they concluded that the leading activities worldwide are walking, running, and swimming. Research in Australia confirms the popularity of walking and swimming and includes exercise and keep-fit activities, including aerobics and jogging/running (Darcy and Veal, 1996). The same sporting activities are identified as the favorites in Canada (Zuzanek, 1996) and Germany (Tokarski and Michels, 1996); while in Hong Kong, badminton, basketball, table tennis, and soccer have emerged as the most commonly practiced (Sivan and Robertson, 1996); and in Brazil, soccer, walking (Bramante, 1998), and beach volleyball have been identified (Channel 4, 27 December 1997). The popularity of different sports can vary from year to year, which is influenced by fashion, national heritage, and even the success of sports stars. The most notable feature is the fragmentation of participation across dozens of different activities.

So, as far as sport tourism is concerned, data sources are scarce and are not directly comparable from one country to another. The Sports Tourism International Council's research (STIC Research Unit, 1997) of 22 tourism schedules found that, of the top sports tourism activities noted, there were major games traditional to the host and geographic region. Other top 20 sport tourism activities were equestrian events, motor sports and boat racing, ballooning, kite flying, and wind surfing. A recent study in the United Kingdom (Mintel International Group, 1995) identified the most popular type of holiday activity as walking, with swimming as second. Dutch holidaymakers chose a subtropical swimming pool as their favorite facility on a domestic package holiday, cycling opportunities were their second choice, and walking was third (Zom and van Hal, 1997). In France cycling is the most popular recorded sport tourism activity, beach sport activities are second, hiking is third, followed by water sports and alpine skiing (Pigeassou, 1997). Research in Germany established swimming as the most practiced sport on holiday, walking was second, ball games third, followed by cycling, jogging, and gymnastics (Studienkreis für Tourismus, 1989).

Specific research into short break holidays in Britain found that "sports and interest" trips accounted for around 10 percent of the market (Withyman, 1994). Surveys of British domestic tourists between 1986 and 1988 showed that over a quarter of all holidaymakers went walking, hiking, or rambling, though only 6 percent (1.5 million) were "serious" walkers. A further half million took part in each of the following: cycling, fishing, horse riding, and rock climbing. Adventure activities such as caving or parachuting attracted fewer people (Smith and Jenner, 1990).

Taking these figures into consideration, it seems reasonable to suggest that between 10 and 20 percent of the holidaymaking population of affluent nations are interested in, and take, sports activity holidays each year.

If, instead of holidays in which sport is the main purpose, we consider holidays in which sport is an incidental aspect, participation rates rise significantly to somewhere between 25 and 80 percent. In Scotland McKie (1994) found that up to 25 percent of holidaymakers claimed to have taken part in some form of activity during their holiday, whereas in Germany research by Studienkreis für Tourismus (1990) suggested that 80 percent of all tourists were in some way active in sport during their holidays. This figure is supported by research in Corfu where 96 percent of German and 87 percent of British holidaymakers reportedly swam on holiday (Tokarski,

Toerisme Vlaanderen

In Europe, water sports are the fourth most popular sport tourism activity following cycling, beach sports, and hiking.

1993). Walking was participated in by around half of these visitors; "other sports" attracted 24 percent (of German women) and 41 percent (of British men) (Tokarski, 1993).

In England, the Tourist Board (English Tourist Board, 1987) more than doubled its estimate for participation where sport is incidental rather than the "main purpose" of a holiday, suggesting that 29 million trips involved tourists as either sport players or spectators. Of these, two-thirds were domestic trips and one-third was foreign.

Despite the lack of reliable data for many countries, several points need to be made regarding levels of participation. First, other than identifying walking and swimming as the two most common holiday activities (and when these are included participation soars), it is impossible to determine the relative popularity of sports such as skiing, golf, and a wide range of other outdoor pursuits because the data that does exist is rarely differentiated at the sport-specific level. It is self-evident that when the destination is a beach, swimming is likely to be the most popular activity—but in the mountains the season will largely dictate the activities. Thus topography, climate, and markets combine to influence the relative popularity of specific activities in different regions.

Second, the following question needs to be asked of all the data: what counts as sport tourism or as, say, swimming? The narrow definition used by Leisure Consultants (1992) in the United Kingdom, by omitting holidays in which instruction was not taken and many club tours, underrepresented what most people would genuinely regard as a sport activity holiday. Yet accepting the most casual participation in swimming and walking as activity holidays artificially inflates the number of holidayers and undervalues the significance of authentic experiences. Datzer (1993) goes so far as to say that sport as the whole intention of the holiday is vastly overestimated: "The holidaymakers who are playing tennis from morning to evening or those standing until sundown on their surfboard, belong to a minority" (p. 62). However, the number of people who are looking for a more recreational, not so "sporty," activity is high and still growing. The trend is to practice several activities, looking for variety.

In summary, data problems indicate the need for cautious interpretation. However, there is ample evidence to support the claim that participation in sports activities has increased significantly as a feature of holiday taking and as a focus of holidays. Sport is thus considered to be an important element of the enlarging spectrum of the touristic product.

Summary

Neither sport nor tourism are adequately described as *industries*; they are *activities* in which *people* engage. Sport is about an *experience of physical activity*, tourism about an *experience of travel and place*.

We have chosen to use relatively wide definitions of both sport and tourism. The term sport is taken to mean the whole range of competitive and noncompetitive active pursuits that involve skill, strategy, and/or chance in which human beings engage, at their own level, simply for enjoyment and training or to raise their performance to levels of publicly acclaimed excellence.

We use a similarly broad definition of tourism, defining it as the temporary movement of people beyond their own home and work locality involving experiences unlike those of everyday life. The experiences might take place as part of a holiday or as an ancillary to business travel.

Our definition of sport tourism is that it comprises all forms of active and passive involvement in sporting activity, participated in casually or in an organized way for noncommercial or business/commercial reasons, that necessitate travel away from home and work locality.

By identifying connections between sport and tourism that originated in the ancient world and have continued into the modern world, though not in any directly linear progression, this chapter has demonstrated that the extensive connections we see today are rooted in old foundations established between the two active experiences of sport and tourism. Appreciating the links between them in the past is necessary to understanding their contemporary relation.

The nineteenth century was a hugely significant period in the development of both sport and tourism due to the industrial revolution. During that century major developments encouraged the spread of sport and tourism from the older countries (primarily of Europe) to the newer nations. Both sport and tourism as leisure pursuits were first the preserve of the wealthy, but given that "mass follows class," contemporary sport tourists are somewhat different (that is, the majority of society eventually takes up the activities enjoyed by their social superiors).

Unparalleled growth of sport and tourism has taken place this century and the period is characterized by social diffusion and the development of mass tourism and mass sport. Contextualized by the democratization that has taken place in society, sport tourism has become a prevalent and growing phenomenon.

References

Alderson, F. (1972). *Bicycling: A history.* Newton Abbot, Great Britain: David Charles.

Anyanwu, S.U. (1988). Sport: Its perceptions as an instrument for nationalism in Nigeria. In K. Hardman (Ed.), *Physical education and sport in Africa. ISCPES Monograph No.1* (pp. 12-17). Manchester, Great Britain: University of Manchester.

Baker, W.J. (1982). *Sports in the western world.* Totowa, NJ: Rowman and Littlefield.

Barnard, C.L.P. (1988). *Sport tourism . . . for you? A guide to develop a sport tourism strategy.* Victoria, Australia: Ministry of Tourism, Recreation and Culture (Recreation and Sport Branch).

Bennett, B.L., Howell, M.L., and Simri, U. (1983). *Comparative physical education and sport.* Philadelphia: Lea & Febiger.

Benton, N. (1995). Taking the waters. *The Leisure Manager, 13*(4), 40.

Beran, J. (1989). Americans in the Philippines: Imperialism or progress through sport? *The International Journal of the History of Sport, 6*(1), 62-87.

Best, J.C., Blackhurst, M., and Makosky, L. (1992). *Minister's task force on federal sport policy: The way ahead.* Ottawa, ON: Ministry of State, Fitness and Amateur Sport.

Bollettieri, N. (1996, September). Young talent. *High Life,* pp. 64-71.

Boniface, B., and Cooper, C. (1994). *The geography of travel and tourism.* Oxford, Great Britain: Butterworth-Heinemann.

Booth, B.F., and Batts, J.S. (1977). Cricket and the British sporting ethic in Victorian Canada, 1829-1867. In G. Curl (Ed.), *Proceedings of the VIth International Congress— International Association for the History of Physical Education and Sport (HISPA),* Supplement (pp. 26-37). Dartford, Great Britain: HISPA.

Bramante, A.C. (1998). Leisure lifestyles in a developing country: Reasons for non-participation. In M.F. Collins and I.S. Cooper (Eds.), *Leisure management issues and applications.* (pp. 49-64). Wallingford, Great Britain: CAB International.

British Tourist Authority/English Tourist Board. (1992). *The UK tourist: Statistics 1991.* London: Author.

Bryson, B. (1997). *A walk in the woods.* New York: Doubleday.

Burton, R. (1995). *Travel geography.* London: Pitman.

Capernerhurst, J. (1994). Community tourism. In L. Haywood (Ed.), *Community leisure and recreation.* (pp. 144-171). Oxford, Great Britain: Butterworth-Heinemann.

Channel 4. (1997, December 27). *Transworld sport.* London: Channel 4.

Churchill, D. (1990, September 22/23). A sense of adventure. *Financial Times Weekend,* p. vii.

Churchill, D. (1995, July 20). Boom in golf breaks. *The Times,* p. 36.

Clark, G., Darrall, J., Grove-White, R., Macnaghten, P., and Urry, J. (1994). The diversity and specialization of leisure and tourism. Background Paper No. 13. *Leisure landscapes. Leisure, culture, and the English countryside: Challenges and conflicts.* Lancaster University, Great Britain: Centre for the Study of Environmental Change.

Clarke, J., and Critcher, C. (1985). *The devil makes work.* London: Macmillan Educational.

Cleare, J. (1975). *Mountains.* London: Macmillan.

Coakley, J. (1990). *Sport in society: Issues and controversies.* 4th ed. St. Louis: Times Mirror/Mosby College Publishing.

Compton's Interactive Encyclopedia. (1992). [CD-ROM].

Cooper, C. (1988). Global tourism. *Leisure Management, 8*(3), 36-38.

Council of Europe. (1992). *European Sports Charter.* Strasbourg, France: Author.

Crompton, P. (1975). Kung-fu. In B. Williams (Ed.), *Martial arts of the Orient* (pp. 150-157). London: Hamlyn.

Crum, B. (1991). *Over versporting van de samenleving* [On the sportification of the society]. Rijswijk, The Netherlands: Ministerie van Welzijn, Volksgezondheid en Cultuur.

Crum, B. (1994, June). *Changes in movement culture: A challenge for sport pedagogy.* Paper presented at the L'Association internationale des écoles d'éducation physique supérieures World Congress, Berlin, Germany.

Darcy, S., and Veal, A.J. (1996). Australia. In G. Cushman, A.J. Veal, and J. Zuzanek (Eds.), *World leisure participation: Free time in the global village* (pp. 17-34). Wallingford, Great Britain: CAB International.

Datzer, R. (1993). Zukünftige marktentwicklungen im urlaubssport [Market trends in the future regarding leisure sport]. In H.J. Neuerburg, T. Wilken, K. Fehres, and N. Sperle (Eds.), *Sport im urlaub* [Sport in holiday] (pp. 59-70). Aachen, Germany: Meyer & Meyer.

Davidson, R. (1993). *Tourism.* London: Pitman.

De Groote, P. (1995). *Panorama op toerisme* [Panorama on tourism]. Leuven, Belgium: Garant.

De Knop, P. (1987). Some thoughts on the influence of sport on tourism. In M. Garmise (Ed.), *International Seminar and Workshop on outdoor education, recreation and sport tourism. Proceedings* (pp. 38-45). Netanya, Israel: Wingate Institute.

De Knop, P. (1989). The reciprocal development of sport and tourism. In M. Blagajac and O. Urednik (Eds.), *Programmes of sport recreation in the process of work and tourism* (pp. 185-204). Rovinj, Yugoslavia: International Council for Sports Science and Physical Education.

De Knop, P., Wylleman, P., De Martelaer, K., Van Puymbroeck, L., and Wittock, H. (1994). New professions in sport and tourism. In J. Mester (Ed.), *Sport sciences in Europe 1993: Current and future perspectives* (pp. 33-54). Aachen, Germany: Meyer & Meyer.

Deloitte Touche Tohmatsu. (1995). *Small business survey 1994: New Zealand tourism industry.* Auckland, New Zealand: Author.

Deveen, M. (1987). Sport et tourisme. In M. Garmise (Ed.), *International Seminar and Workshop on outdoor education, recreation and sport tourism. Proceedings* (pp. 46-52). Netanya, Israel: Wingate Institute.

Digel, H. (1994). *Sports in a changing society.* International Council for Sports Science and Physical Education (ICSSPE). Manuscript Sports Science Series. Schorndorf, Germany: Karl Hofmann.

Elliott, H. (1995, August 3). Test series gives big boost to West Indies tourism. *The Times*, p. 19.

English Tourist Board. (1987). *Tourism strategy: A vision for England.* London: Author.

English Tourist Board. (1992). *Activity holidays 1993.* London: Author.

Ewert, A. (1983). Perceived importance of outdoor adventure activities. *Recreation Research Review, 10*(2), 28-34.

Finley, M.I., and Pleket, H.W. (1976). *The Olympic Games.* Edinburgh, Great Britain: R. and R. Clark.

Fleming, S. (1991). The role of sport in South Asian cultures in Britain and the Indian subcontinent. In J. Standeven, K. Hardman, and D. Fisher, *Sport for all: Into the 90s. Comparative physical education and sport. Vol. 7* (pp. 230-242). Aachen, Germany: Meyer & Meyer.

Ford, J. (1977). *This sporting land.* London: New English Library.

Gast, P. (1984). Should a white man learn kung-fu? The Chinese in white America. *Inside Kung-Fu, 11*(9), 86-89.

Gibson, H., and Yiannakis, A. (1995, November). *Some characteristics of sport tourism: A life span perspective.* Paper presented at the Annual Conference of the North American Society for the Sociology of Sport, Savannah, GA.

Giddens, A. (1993). *Sociology.* Oxford, Great Britain: Polity Press.

Glyptis, S.A. (1982). *Sport and tourism in western Europe.* London: British Travel Educational Trust.

Glyptis, S.A. (1991). Sport and tourism. In C. Cooper (Ed.), *Progress in tourism, recreation and hospitality management. Vol. 3* (pp. 165-183). London: Belhaven Press.

Green, S. (1982). *Cricketing bygones.* Princes Risborough, Great Britain: Shire Publications.

Gruneau, R. (1984). Commercialism and the modern Olympics. In A. Tomlinson and G. Whannel (Eds.), *Five ring circus* (pp. 1-15). London: Pluto Press.

Hall, C.M. (1992). Adventure, sport and health. In C.M. Hall and B. Weiler (Eds.), *Special interest tourism* (pp. 141-158). London: Belhaven Press.

Hallander, J. (1986). San Francisco. Gateway to the Orient. *Inside Kung-Fu, 13*(5), 57-58.

Hargreaves, J. (1986). *Sport, power and culture.* Oxford, Great Britain: Polity Press.

Hawkins, D.E. (1994). Ecotourism: Opportunities for developing countries. In W. Theobald (Ed.), *Global tourism* (pp. 261-273). Oxford, Great Britain: Butterworth-Heinemann.

Holloway, J.C. (1994). *The business of tourism.* London: Pitman.

Holmes, B. (1984). *The Olympian Games in Athens, 1896: The first modern Olympics.* London: Grove Press.

Holt, R. (1989). *Sport and the British.* Oxford, Great Britain: Oxford University Press.

Hopkins, T. (1989). *Pennine Way North. National Trail Guide 6.* London: Aurum Press.

Hsu, A. (1986). Chinese martial arts. Bridging the cultural gap between East and West. In S. Kleinman (Ed.), *Mind and body. East meets West* (pp. 89-95). Champaign, IL: Human Kinetics.

Hutchinson, R. (1996). *Empire games.* Edinburgh, Great Britain: Mainstream Publishing.

Jackson, G.A.M., and Glyptis, S.A. (1992). *Sport and tourism: A review of the literature.* Unpublished report to the Sports Council, London.

Johnston, M. (1992). Facing the challenges: Adventure in the mountains of New Zealand. In B. Weiler and C.M. Hall (Eds.), *Special interest tourism* (pp. 159-169). London: Belhaven Press.

Jolley, R., and Curphey, M. (1994, November 10). Agents race for niche markets. *The Times,* p. 35.

Jones, R. (1993). Sport in China: A current view. In A. DeLacey (Ed.), *International sports' systems: Past, present and future.* (pp. 25-34). Liverpool, England: Liverpool Institute of Higher Education.

Kamphorst, T., and Roberts, K. (Eds.). (1989). *Trends in sports. A multinational perspective.* Voorthuizen, The Netherlands: Giordano Bruno Culemborg.

Kearsley, G.W. (1990, November 2). Tourism development and users' perceptions of wilderness in Southern New Zealand. *The Australian Geographer,* pp. 127-140.

Kliskey, A., and Kearsley, G.W. (1993). Mapping multiple perceptions of wilderness so as to minimise the impact of tourism on natural environments: A case-study of the North West South Island of New Zealand. In A.J. Veal, P. Jonson, and G. Cushman (Eds.), *Leisure and tourism: Social and economic change* (pp. 104-119). Sydney, Australia: University of Technology.

Kraus, R. (1984). *Recreation and leisure in modern society,* 3rd ed. Glenview, IL: Scott, Foresman.

Lavery, P. (1989). *Travel and tourism.* Suffolk, Great Britain: St. Edmundsbury Press.

Lea, J. (1988). *Tourism and development in the third world.* London: Routledge.

Leisure Consultants. (1992). *Activity holidays: The growth market in tourism.* Suffolk, Great Britain: Author.

MacCannell, D. (1976). *The tourist.* London: The Macmillan Press.

MacCannell, D. (1996). *Tourist or traveller?* London: BBC Educational Developments.

Macdonald, A.I. (1988). Physical education and sport in Botswana: A view from the outside. In K. Hardman (Ed), *Physical education and sport in Africa. International Society for Comparative Physical Education and Sport Monograph No.1* (pp. 87-92). Manchester, Great Britain: University of Manchester.

Martin, B. and Mason, S. (1987). Social trends and tourism futures. *Tourism Management, June,* 112-114.

Mason, T. (1986). Some Englishmen and Scotsmen abroad: The spread of world football. In A. Tomlinson and G. Whannel (Eds.), *Off the ball* (pp. 67-82). London: Pluto Press.

McFee, G. (1990). The Olympic Games as tourist event: An American in Athens, 1896. In A. Tomlinson (Ed.), *Sport in society: Policy, politics and culture. Conference papers No. 43* (pp. 146-157). Eastbourne, Great Britain: Leisure Studies Association.

McKie, L. (1994). Signs of activity. *Leisure Management, 14*(9), 32-34.

Metzner, H. (1974). *History of the American Turners.* Rochester, NY: National Council of the American Turners.

Meyer, G. (1976). St. Louis 1904. In Lord Killanin and J. Rodda (Eds.), *The Olympic Games* (pp. 32-36). London: Book Club Associates.

Mill, R.C. (1990). *Tourism: The international business.* Englewood Cliffs, NJ: Prentice Hall.

Mintel International Group. (1995). *Activity holidays in the UK.* London: Author.

Mudge, S. (1991). *Notes on ecotourism.* Washington, DC: Ernst & Young.

Nogawa, H. (1992). A study of sport tourism. *Annals of Fitness and Sports Sciences, 7,* 43-55.

NOP Market Research Ltd. (1989). *Activities by the British on holiday in Britain.* London: British Tourist Authority/English Tourist Board/National Opinion Poll.

Ogilvie, J., and Dickinson, C. (1992). The UK adventure holiday market. *EIU Travel and Tourism Analyst, 3,* 37-50.

Olson, H.E. (1993). Leisure policy in Sweden. In P. Bramham, I. Henry, H. Mommaas, and H. vander Poel, (Eds.), *Leisure policies in Europe* (pp. 71-100). Wallingford, Great Britain: CAB International.

Parker, S. (1983). *Leisure and work.* London: George Allen & Unwin Ltd.

Peacock, H.L. (1982). *A history of modern Britain.* London: Heinemann Educational Books.

Pigeasseau, C. (1997). Sport and tourism: The emergence of sport into the offer of tourism. An overview of the French situation and perspective. *Journal of Sports Tourism,* 4(1), Available from http://www.mcb.co.uk/journals/jst/archive/vol4no1/htm: World Wide Web.

Porter, I. (1996). The evolution of a downhill skier. *The Skier and Snowboarder, December,* 52-54.

Prentice, R. (1992). Market segmentation and the prediction of tourist destinations. In P. Johnson and B. Thomas (Eds.), *Choice and demand in tourism* (pp. 73-92). London: Mansell.

Redmond, G. (1977). Aspects of British influence on sport in the United States during the nineteenth century. In G. Curl (Ed.), *Proceedings of the VIth International Congress—International Association for the History of Physical Education and Sport (HISPA)* (pp. 481-492). Dartford, Great Britain: HISPA.

Redmond, G. (1990). Points of increasing contact: Sport and tourism in the modern world. In A. Tomlinson (Ed.), *Sport in society: Policy, politics and culture. Conference papers No. 43* (pp. 158-169). Eastbourne, Great Britain: Leisure Studies Association.

Redmond, G. (1991). Changing styles of sports tourism: Industry, consumer interactions in Canada, the USA and Europe. In M.T. Sinclair and M.J. Stabler (Eds.), *The tourism industry: an international analysis* (pp. 107-120). Wallingford, Great Britain: CAB International

Ritchie, J., and Lyons, M. (1990). Olympulse VI: A post-event assessment of resident reaction to the XV Olympic Winter Games. *Journal of Travel Research, 28*(3), 14-23.

Sagawa, T. (1996, August). *The changes of sports in Thailand: From traditional sports to modern sports.* Paper presented at the International Society of Comparative Physical Education and Sport Conference, Tokyo.

Salisbury, M. (1997). American attitudes toward soccer. Available at http://almond.srv.cs.cmu.edu/afs/cs/usr/mdwheel/www/soccer/history/histl.html: World Wide Web.

Schrodt, B. (1988). Taking the tram: Travelling to sport and recreation activities on Greater Vancouver's interurban railway—1890s to 1920s. *Canadian Journal of the History of Sport, XIX*(1), 52-62.

Schwartz, G. (1989). *The art of skiing.* Tiburon, CA: Wood River.

Silvennoinen, M. (1989). Finnish baseball: From folk game to sport machine—A short sociohistorical analysis. In F. Fu, M. Ng, and M. Speak (Eds.), *Compar-*

ative physical education and sport. Vol. 6 (pp. 165-172). Hong Kong: The Chinese University.

Sivan, A., and Robertson, B. (1996). Hong Kong. In G. Cushman, A.J. Veal, and J. Zuzanek (Eds.), *World leisure participation: Free time in the global village* (pp. 131-140). Wallingford, Great Britain: CAB International.

Slusher, H.S. (1967). *Men, sport and existence: A critical analysis.* Philadelphia: Lea & Febiger.

Smith, C., and Jenner, P. (1990). Activity holidays in Europe. *EIU Travel and Tourism Analyst, 5,* 58-78.

Spears, B., and Swanson, R.A. (1983). *History of sport and physical activity in the United States.* Dubuque, Iowa: Wm. C. Brown.

Sport Tourism International Council Research Unit. (1997). Content analysis of tourism schedules. *Journal of Sport Tourism, 4*(1). Available at http://www.mcb.co.uk/journals/jst/archive/vol4no1/htm: World Wide Web.

Standeven, J., Hardman, K., and Fisher, R. (1991). *Sport for all: Into the 90s.* Aachen, Germany: Meyer & Meyer.

Standeven, J., and Tomlinson, A. (1994). *Sport and tourism in South East England.* London: South East Council for Sport and Recreation.

Studienkreis für Tourismus. (1990). *Reiseanalyse* [Analysis of the holidays]. Starnberg, Germany: Studienkreis für Tourismus.

Szymiczek, O. (1976). Athens 1896. In Lord Killanin and J. Rodda (Eds.), *The Olympic Games* (pp. 56-59). London: Book Club Associates.

Terry, L. (1996). Holidayers seek thrills. *Leisure Management, 16*(6), 14.

Tobin, G.A. (1974). The bicycle boom of the 1890s: The development of private transportation and the birth of the modern tourist. *Journal of Popular Culture, 7,* 838-849.

Tokarski, W. (1993). Leisure, sports and tourism: The role of sports in and outside holiday clubs. In A.J. Veal, P. Jonson, and G. Cushman (Eds.), *Leisure and tourism: Social and economic change* (pp. 684-686). Sydney, Australia: University of Technology.

Tokarski, W., and Michels, H. (1996). Germany. In G. Cushman, A.J. Veal, and J. Zuzanek (Eds.), *World leisure participation: Free time in the global village* (pp. 107-112). Wallingford, Great Britain: CAB International.

Tomlinson, A. (1990). *Consumption, identity and style.* London: Routledge.

Tomlinson, A., and Walker, H. (1990). Holidays for all: Popular movements, collective leisure and the pleasure industry. In A. Tomlinson (Ed.), *Consumption, identity and style: Marketing, meanings and the packaging of pleasure* (pp. 221-241) London: Routledge.

Tomlinson, A., and Whannel, G. (1984). Introduction. In A. Tomlinson and G. Whannel (Eds.), *Five ring circus* (pp. v-x). London: Pluto Press.

United Nations Educational, Scientific, and Cultural Organization. (n.d.). *Chartre internationale de l'éducation physique et du sport.* New York: Author.

Urry, J. (1990). *The tourist gaze: Travel, leisure and society.* London: Sage Publications Ltd.

Van Dalen, D.B., and Bennett, B. (1971). *A world history of physical education.* Englewood Cliffs, NJ: Prentice Hall.

Walton, J.K. (1983). *The English seaside resort.* Leicester, Great Britain: Leicester University Press.

Ward, J., Higson, P., and Campbell, W. (1994). *Advanced leisure and tourism.* Cheltenham, Great Britain: Stanley Thornes.

Weiler, B., and Hall, C.M. (Eds.). (1992). *Special interest tourism.* London: Belhaven Press.

Westvlaams Economisch Studiebureau. (1991). *Reisgedrag en -opinies van de Belgen* [Traveling behavior and opinions of Belgians]. Brugge, Belgium: Author.

West Country Tourist Board and the Sports Council (South West). (1992). *Tourism and sport: A joint policy statement.* Exeter/Crewkerne/Devon, Great Britain: West Country Tourist Board and the Sports Council (South West).

Whymper, E. (1871). *Scrambles amongst the alps in the years 1860-69.* London: Murray.

Wilcox, R. (1994). The cultural uniqueness of American sport. In R. Wilcox, (Ed.), *Sport in the global village* (pp.73-102). Morgantown, WV: Fitness Information Technology Inc.

Withyman, M. (1994, September). Out for the day. *Insights,* pp. B19-34. 1.

World Tourism Organization. (1981) *Guidelines for the collection and presentation of domestic and international tourism statistics.* Madrid, Spain: Author.

World Tourism Organization. (1985). The role of recreation management in the development of active holidays and special interest tourism and consequent enrichment of the holiday experience. Madrid, Spain: Author.

Zom, J., and van Hal, W. (1997). Holiday decision-making in The Netherlands; selection processes with regard to domestic and foreign holiday destinations. *Revue De Tourisme, 3,* pp. 19-26.

Zuzanek, J. (1996). Canada. In G. Cushman, A.J. Veal, and J. Zuzanek (Eds.), *World leisure participation: Free time in the global village* (pp. 35-74). Wallingford, Great Britain: CAB International.

Chapter 2
Sport and Tourism: Investigating the Relationship

Mountain biking in the Austrian Alps, near Kitzbuhel.

World Pictures

The following topics are covered in this chapter:

1. The nature of sport, tourism, and sport tourism in terms of physical activity and place experiences.
2. Theoretical frameworks relevant to investigating the sport-tourism relationship.
3. Our classification scheme for sport tourism.
4. The infrastructure that supports sport, tourism, and sport tourism.
5. Characteristics of sportists, tourists, and sport tourists.

In chapter 1 we saw that there are different definitions of sport and tourism. For example, in some schemes competition is a necessary condition for an activity to be described as sport and an overnight stay is essential for it to be described as tourism. Our scheme, on the other hand, is not bound by these conditions; we emphasize other aspects of the sport and touristic experience (see chapter 1 for this discussion).

How any of us sees the world is dependent on our diverse cultural experience and heritage, and the different conceptual schemes we have are all, in principle, equally valid. Thus there is no simple, single, or universally correct understanding. What is accepted as sport or tourism, and therefore the relationship between them, relies entirely on the way these concepts are understood and used.

This chapter, then, has two important purposes: first, to examine more analytically the nature of the experiences we are discussing and, second, to build a model of their reciprocal relationship. To deepen this investigation of the relationship between sport and tourism, theories proposed by other authors will be discussed. We shall retain our fundamental structure (see figure 1.1 on page 5) throughout this chapter as we look at sport, tourism, their infrastructure, and their participants.

At the outset of this discussion, a comment on the concept of cultural experience is important. In recent years leading social theorists have shown increasing interest in the phenomenon of cultural experience (Bourdieu, 1978; Eliot, 1962; Goffman, 1974; Laing, 1967; Swingewood, 1977; Williams, 1965, 1977, 1981). Bourdieu (1978) in particular has addressed sport as a component of culture. The articulation between sport and culture has been noticeably expanded since the 1980s in the writings of Jennifer and John Hargreaves (1982, 1986) and in articles in a number of sports journals (see *International Review of Sports Sociology* and *Journal of Sport and Social Issues*). The Hargreaves' studies focus on sport as a phenomenon intimately related to other features of social life, a "central component of popular culture"

(Hargreaves, 1982, p. 16). John Hargreaves writes, "One cannot begin to understand the structure and meaning of sport without also appreciating that it is intimately tied up with conceptions and evaluations of the social order" (Hargreaves, 1982, p. 33). About culture he says, "Culture . . . is not just a mental product: it is a lived practice formed by conscious human beings from their lived experience, and constituting for them a whole way of life" (p. 47). In our view, then, sport itself is a cultural form and, as such, also an integral component of popular culture.

The same theoretical interests in the concept of cultural experience that has influenced writers on sport has influenced writers on other aspects of social experience, such as the media and tourism (Becker, 1974; Hoffman, 1967; McLuhan, 1964). MacCannell's (1976) work parallels that of the sport theorists. In the first full-scale sociological examination of modern tourism, he constructs sight-seeing as a cultural form, integrally part of culture.

Thus both sport and tourism (along with the arts, media, and so on) are, in themselves, a culture. They offer cultural experiences as well as being important constituents of popular culture. In our examination of the nature of sport, tourism, and sport tourism we adopt this stance.

To begin our analysis, sport will be considered as a cultural experience of physical activity and tourism as a cultural experience of place. This leads to our proposal that sport tourism is a cultural experience of physical activity tied to a cultural experience of place.

In the second section of the chapter we outline a theoretical framework to support the concept of sport tourism as cultural experience on two dimensions: sport and tourism. Independent of each other, sport and tourism are significant aspects of the leisure industry. Although their interdependence is not yet fully recognized in theory or practice, the new genre in leisure of sport tourism is becoming increasingly important.

The third section of the chapter deals with the material ingredients that make up sport, tourism, and sport tourism. By studying the major factors that are a necessary part of the infrastructure of sport and tourist "products," the potential for sport tourism is identified.

A more profound understanding of sport tourism must include an analysis of the participants. We have already distinguished between holidaymakers and business travelers, and between active and passive sport tourists (see chapter 1). In the final part of this chapter we develop a profile of the types of people who engage in these experiences.

The Nature of Sport, Tourism, and Sport Tourism

In chapter 1 we provided our definitions of the words sport, tourism, and sport tourism. In spite of the difficulties encountered in defining the terms, our intention was to bring out their salient features. In this chapter the intention is somewhat different. To examine the *nature* of sport, tourism, and sport tourism is to engage in a conceptual inquiry wherein we examine our terms more closely and attempt to trace out some of their "logical interdependencies" (Best, 1978).

The Nature of Sport

In order to explore the diverse phenomenon of sport, it is helpful to examine some of the roots of conceptual analysis of games and sport. First, we shall look at some seminal ideas regarding the concepts of sport, work, and play since the sport experience from professional to casual types of involvement crosses the spectrum from work to play. Second, we shall outline a model of sport (Haywood, 1994) that focuses on it as an experience of physical activity.

Seminal Conceptions of Sport

Huizinga (1949) argued that play was the foundation of human culture. Although sport was not the same as play, he saw the play element as a valuable ingredient of sport. According to Huizinga, sport without play becomes separated from culture and then holds little worth for mankind. His definition of play involves three characteristics: (1) freedom and spontaneity: the player cannot be forced to play, (2) separateness: play has boundaries of time and place, and (3) regulation: during play the only "rules" are those inherent to play itself. Although Huizinga referred to "sports and athletics," he made no attempt to classify them, but his analysis of play is relevant given our view that sport is necessarily a playlike activity.

Critical assessments of sport's role in modern society began to emerge in Europe and America in the 1970s (Brohm, 1978; Guttman, 1978). Luschen (1972) defined sport as institutionalized, competitive physical activity located on a continuum between work and play. His view illustrated the relevance of Huizinga's formative play thesis but suggested that sport contained elements of both play and work. Rigauer (1981) went further than this—he started his critique from the point that sport and work were structurally analogous and claimed that top-level sport had lost its playful, spontaneous character. Sport in the modern world, in its obsession with measurement, technique, standards, and competition, had become work. Elite athletes who failed to achieve would, like workers, be eliminated. Sport's potential to improve health and reduce time lost through illness was its main justification. Thus Rigauer's critique embraced all levels of sport, from the elite professional to the recreational.

Though Rigauer's views are thought-provoking, he puts too much emphasis on professional sport on the one hand, and on the other, leads us to think that "it is largely workers who take part in sport" (Mason, 1988, p. 76). Guttman (1978) countered this assumption from an American perspective, noting that movement up sport's achievement ladder to the top levels was disproportionately weighted in favor of the socially advantaged, and Mason (1988) concurred that this was also the case in Britain. Further, Rigauer's critique tends to disregard the huge volume of participants who, voluntarily and independently, seek little more than enjoyment from their participation.

The resolution of this difficulty seems to be to make a separate category called *recreation* for nonprofessional levels of sports participation. Yet, because recreationists engage in the same physical activities and use, very largely, the same facilities as professional sports people, and because the dividing line between amateur and professional athletes is now meaningless (e.g., Olympic Games participation is now open to all—true amateurs and sports persons still claiming amateur status while receiving large financial rewards), our conceptualization of sport sees it as crossing the whole spectrum from work to play, embracing sportists who are serious and competitive as well as those who are merely casual and playful.

Given our broad conceptualization and definition of sport, we looked for a similarly comprehensive analysis of its nature, one that could be applied to sport at all levels, and one that actually examined its structural properties. We have located this in a classification offered by Haywood and Kew (Haywood, 1994).

The Haywood and Kew Model of Sport

Haywood and Kew (Haywood, 1994) examined three broad dimensions of the nature of sport forms as the basis for their analysis:

- the characteristics of the basic *challenge* present in any given sport,
- the *conditions* imposed upon that challenge, and
- the *response* resulting from the interaction of the challenge and conditions.

Their model is robust and provides a very satisfactory form of analysis through which a wide range of activities can be categorized as sport without ambiguity (a problem of some other analyses). It also helps us to understand the nature of the appeal of selected sporting activities and sensitizes us to extant and potential links with tourism. Thus it can help us identify those connections more effectively. Our examination of their model, to which we now turn, is heavily dependent upon Haywood (1994); and Haywood, Kew, Bramham, Spink, Capernerhurst, and Henry (1995) who should be consulted for further detail.

Challenge in Sport

The first dimension of Haywood and Kew's model, that is, the challenge, takes one of two forms—it can be either *environmental* or *interpersonal*. Environmental challenges have to do with the physical laws of gravity and friction and are a result of pitting the body against those natural forces.

Environmental challenges can be subdivided into those posed by natural phenomena such as water or snow and those that are mainly artificially contrived by apparatus such as trampolines or bungees. A further subdivision of both types of environmental challenges distinguishes *purposive* activities from *aesthetic* activities (Haywood, 1994). See figure 2.1.

Purposive challenges are those in which the *outcome* of the activity is of prime importance, whereas in aesthetic challenges *style* of performance is paramount (Best, 1978).

Environmental challenges appear obvious in an activity such as climbing, but to the casual observer the movements involved in walking appear relatively simple. However, kinesiologic analysis shows that even these movements are exceedingly complex. The initial challenge is to overcome the inertia of the body. Variations in terrain, and the need to cope with up and down gradients involving the economic and effective use of friction, comprise the specific challenge in walking. In other recreational activities, such as cycling or ice skating, the challenge more obviously involves a balancing of forces to obtain movement. And, in swimming, the challenge concerns bouyancy, not gravity, and overcoming the resistance of the medium of water.

There are numerous examples of environmental challenge sports being converted into interpersonal competitions. For example, gymnastics, athletics (track and field), ski jumping, slalom canoe races, and others are usually thought of as competitive activities. Nonetheless, the primary challenge in all of these activities is the environmental one, and until that is mastered competition cannot take place. In that sense, competition is secondary and not the raison d'être of the activity itself (Haywood, 1994).

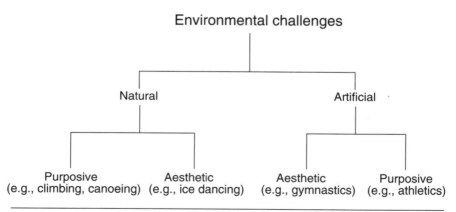

Figure 2.1   Nature of environmental challenges in sports (Haywood, 1994, p. 118).

Copyright 1994 Butterworth-Heinemann. Reprinted by permission.

Conversely, interpersonal challenge sports are inherently competitive—competition is not simply necessary; it is the sufficient condition to define the nature of the activity. Winning (or losing or drawing) is unavoidable; it is the ultimate goal, the whole purpose of engaging in the activity. Of course it is possible to play these sports simply for fun, disregarding the outcome, but, ultimately, unless players attempt to outwit and outplay each other, individually or in teams, the whole point of the game is lost.

Interpersonal challenge sports are of two main types: combat and contest (see figure 2.2). In combat sports, opponents essentially "fight" one another, with or without implements, with the intention of overcoming, literally or figuratively, the other combatant (for example, judo and fencing). Contest sports depend on the manipulation of an object toward a target in order to better an opponent. Targets take many forms, from the more traditional goals of football to the boundaries of tennis, the baskets of basketball, the stumps in cricket, and so on. Contest sports may be further subdivided according to the spatial relationship between the contestants and the target. Five distinct forms of contest emerge:

1. Aiming games (i.e., shared territory, common targets) such as golf and archery.
2. Net games (i.e., own territory to defend, opponents' territory as target) such as volleyball and tennis.

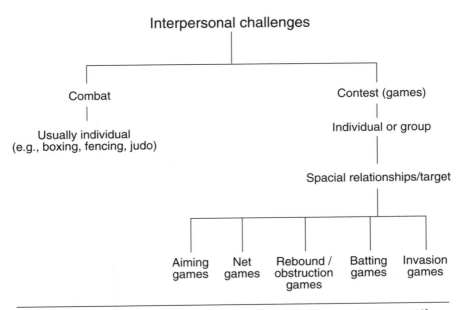

Figure 2.2 Nature of interpersonal challenges in sports (Haywood, 1994, p. 119).

Copyright 1994 Butterworth-Heinemann. Reprinted by permission.

3. Rebound/obstruction games (i.e., shared and disputed territory, common targets) such as squash, snooker, and bowls.

4. Batting games (i.e., alternative uses of common territory and targets requiring different attacking and defensive skills) such as cricket and baseball.

5. Invasion games (i.e., shared and disputed territory, separate targets) such as football and basketball. (Haywood, 1994)

Conditions Imposed on Sport

We now turn to the second dimension of Haywood and Kew's (Haywood, 1994) model, the conditions that are imposed upon the environmental and interpersonal challenges. Conditions take the form of equipment, rules, and conventions. Conditions in the form of equipment include the handling of the bat in batting games and the use of a racket instead of the hand in net games. Equipment used for protection, though in some sports an accepted aspect of the rules, is not itself part of the fundamental challenge. Rules both protect players and further refine the challenge of the game, such as the rule in soccer that a player may not tackle from behind. Conventions include such things as ideas of fair play and respect for referees.

Response to the Challenges and Conditions

This brings us to the third component of Haywood and Kew's model, that is, the response by the participants to the challenge and its conditions (Haywood, 1994). Haywood writes: "The nature of *the response* to the conditioned challenges offered by sports to individual players varies enormously from sport to sport in terms of both the psychomotor skills and the strategies employed" (Haywood, 1994, p. 121). In some sports the response involves performing a series of set bodily movements (some apparently simple, others more complex) at the appropriate time. The dinghy sailor, for example, must adjust his or her balance at just the right moment to accommodate the environmental conditions, the walker (less obviously) must do the same. Where the challenge is interpersonal and the sport is inherently competitive, the participants have to continually adapt their movements to counter those of other participants (for example, basketball and football). These two situations make different demands on the body.

Summary of the Nature of Sport

In summary, the model of the nature of sport that we shall work with in this book is broad, like our definition. However, it has distinct boundaries and analytical rigor, distinguishing sport from other activities yet not limiting that distinction to competition. Our focus is on the nature of the sport experience as a cultural experience of physical activity.

Sport must have the essential ingredients of play—spontaneity and uncertainty occurring within fixed limits of time and space. These ingredients separate sport from ordinary life, yet it can be a form of work for skilled opponents.

Sport will comprise either an environmental or an interpersonal challenge; where it appears to have both kinds of challenge, one is essential to the activity and the other is imposed upon it, as in the case of competition climbing, for example.

Sports are differentiated from each other also by the rules (and equipment) adopted, that is, by the sport's conditions. All sports make some, yet different, kinds of physical demands on the body.

We have shown that sport is an experience of many different kinds of physical activity. We shall now turn to an examination of the nature of tourism.

The Nature of Tourism

Our definition of tourism concentrates on the nature of the visitor's experience rather than upon the trip's duration or site of accommodation (see chapter 1). We see tourism as a cultural experience of place. For an analysis of tourism as a cultural experience, the work of MacCannell (1976) is particularly pertinent.

Tourism as an Experience of Culture

The term *tourist* can be derisory. Tourists are sometimes criticized not for their wish to see the sights but rather "for being satisfied with superficial experiences of other peoples and other places" (MacCannell, 1976, p. 10). "Sightseers are motivated," according to MacCannell, "by a desire to see life as it is really lived" (p. 94). He says, "All tourists desire (this) deeper involvement with society and culture to some degree" (p. 10). However, constraints of time and place too often lead to staged events that, by their nature, can be described as inauthentic.

Thus MacCannell's (1976) analysis of the touristic experience hinges on the notion of authenticity, and on whether the tourist's experience of place is staged or real. An example of an inauthentic event from sport tourism would be Thai boxing staged at the Rose Garden in Bangkok as part of a touristic display of cultural events. In its natural, unstaged environment this sport activity is authentic, real combat. But witnessed as a packaged, some would say trivialized, performance for tourists, it is a "staged" and not a genuine combat. Thus the value of tourists' cultural experiences depend on their depth of involvement and the degree of authenticity achieved in their interaction with the place they visit.

There are, then, different levels and qualities of the touristic experience of place, just as there are different levels and qualities of the sport experience of physical activity. We shall now examine tourist destinations as cultural experiences of place.

Tourism as an Experience of Place

An early classification of tourist places was proposed in America by the Outdoor Recreation Resources Review Commission (ORRRC, 1962). Their system categorized areas based on physical resource characteristics, level of development, management, and intensity of use (Boniface and Cooper, 1994). Six categories were derived: high-density recreation areas; general outdoor recreation areas; natural environment areas; unique natural areas; primitive areas; and historic and cultural sites (Boniface and Cooper, 1994). However, Clawson (1966) proposed a simpler scheme that is still regarded as "one of the most useful" (Boniface and Cooper, 1994, p. 20). He suggested three basic categories:

- User-oriented. These destinations are close to population centers and are based on whatever resources are available, frequently man-made.
- Intermediate. These areas are within an accessible distance and make use of the best resources available, sometimes man-made but usually natural.
- Resource-based. These places are often distant from the users because natural resources determine their use. (Boniface and Cooper, 1994)

When arranged on a continuum this simple classification embraces natural resources such as wilderness places on through artificial resources such as museums. It is therefore comprehensive because virtually any type of place experience can be included.

However, more recently, Burton (1995) has identified five geographical features that form the resource base for tourism:

- Climatic resources
- Coastal resources
- Landscape and wildlife resources
- Historic resources
- Cultural, entertainment, and man-made resources

This refinement of Clawson's three categories is particularly relevant for sport tourism, including, as it does, climatic conditions. For as Burton (1995) points out,

> tourists must be physically comfortable in the climatic conditions at the holiday destination. They must be comfortable irrespective of their activity, be it passive (sunbathing) or at the other extreme, very active (e.g., surfboarding, horse riding, snow skiing and so on). (p. 6)

Historically, the most popular type of tourist destination was the seaside resort. The appeal of sea and sand remains the most popular combination

Thomson Holidays

A typical seaside resort in Cyprus provides many opportunities for holiday activities.

of resources in one place after consideration of climatic features (Burton, 1995). Countryside tourism may be the most varied natural category because it includes landforms from lowlands to mountains, which give a very different experience of place from sand and sea. Historic resources include archeological, architectural, and landscape features of the place visited, as well as artifacts and day-to-day objects that have survived from the past (Burton, 1995). Cultural tourism comprises an enormous range of activities. It includes "exposure to and appreciation of another group's culture, and also the enjoyment of aspects of one's own culture" (p. 51). Traditions, customs, events, festivals, and performances as well as "the whole living expression of existing cultures" (p. 51) are included. The strength of this classification is its appropriateness for sport touristic cultural experience. Its weakness, if it has one, is its apparent failure to specifically identify urban areas as touristic experience places, but of course it can be argued that Burton's last two categories embrace all that is involved in urban tourism.

   Thus the nature of tourism is rooted in authentic cultural experience of places away from home that have different characteristics. Those characteristics are unique to each place, and the tourist views, feels, hears, smells, and touches them. Their differences (and their similarities) become a part of his or her conscious experience.

Summary of the Nature of Tourism

In summary, we have chosen a broad definition that focuses on tourism as a cultural experience of place (see chapter 1). The quality of such experience is directly related to the depth of tourists' involvement in their host society and destination culture. MacCannell (1976) and Ryan (1991) have both argued that tourists achieve greater satisfaction from deeper experiences. However, constraints, such as time availability, often lead to superficial experiences of place. To accommodate tourists, host societies offer packaged, staged events, rather than truly authentic experiences, but, according to MacCannell, the irony is that tourists themselves desire authenticity in their cultural experiences (1976).

These experiences—staged or real—result from tourists' interactions with *place*. The various classification schemes of tourist places basically identify two kinds: *natural,* or those dependent on the world's physical resources, and *man-made,* or those that use resources related to man's social behavior.

Burton's (1994) five-part scheme, in its identification of climatic, coastal, landscape and wildlife, historic, and cultural entertainment and man-made resources, is selected as the most comprehensive and relevant classification of tourists' experience of the place visited.

We have defined sport in a broad sense and explained that by its nature, sport has a challenge, conditions imposed upon the challenge, and a response resulting from the interaction of the challenge and conditions. We have focused on tourism as a cultural experience of place. We now examine the nature of sport tourism.

The Nature of Sport Tourism

According to the definition we have adopted in chapter 1, sport tourism falls into two categories: travel to participate in sport and travel to observe sport. Therefore, we have defined sport tourism as the temporary movement of people beyond their own home and work locality involving experiences unlike those of everyday life. The experiences might take place as part of a holiday or as an ancillary to business travel.

However, an examination of the nature of sport tourism must go beyond a definition. In analyzing the natures of sport and tourism, we have taken a specifically humanistic viewpoint. We have essentially treated sport and tourism as cultural experiences—sport as a cultural experience of physical activity; tourism as a cultural experience of place. It will come as no surprise, therefore, that the nature of sport tourism, as we analyze it, is about an experience of physical activity tied to an experience of place.

The Significance of Place in Sport Tourism

Place is a milieu away from the home range, but in sport tourism it has more significance than that. Herva Lyytinen (1993) (cited in Bale, 1994) found that top-level athletes in orienteering and cross-country skiing cited "nature" as the primary motive for taking part in these sports. Dunleavy (1981) focused on the importance of the environmental experience for the skier and Bannister (1957) eloquently described running on the beach. Climbers' views of mountains and nonclimbers' views of mountains differ according to Tomlinson (1996):

> Extreme athletes look at the landscape differently than "normal" people. Climbers travelling through mountainous regions look at the series of potential routes on each face as they pass by. "Normal" folk simply see nice mountains. (p. 49)

Bale (1994), another author whose work is particularly relevant to sport tourism, describes his own running experience:

> One of my routes takes me along undulating country lanes and, coming to the crest of a gentle hill in the clear air following heavy rain showers . . . the early evening summer sunlight seems to accentuate and enhance the colours of the light and dark greens of the fields and woods, the red bricks and grey tiles of the farm buildings . . . and the different blues and greys of the sky . . . They seem to stand out in sharp contrast to the dreariness of much modern life . . . Running in such a landscape can become more than running; it is almost a spiritual, sensual, poetic experience which, in large part because of the landscape, undeniably enhances in a small but important way the quality of my life. (p. 2)

However, in spite of this emphasis on place experience, in his book *Landscapes of Modern Sport,* Bale discusses the ways in which sportscapes—places that are man-made for sport—can be manifestations of placelessness (Relph, 1976). Because many of them are uniform, internationally standardized, and "other-directed," they may be seen to replace "geography by geometry" and tend toward placelessness (Bale, 1994, p. 189). But for all that Bale concludes that "place has not been totally replaced by space nor has the affection which people have for sports landscapes been eroded" (p. 189).

For a more detailed, academic study of place, Bale's (1994) entire thesis is highly relevant to our theme of sport tourism. Much of his work concentrates on sportscapes. He acknowledges that sports like orienteering and sailing take place in natural landscapes and that "They remain landscapes and never become sportscapes" (p. 10). In analyzing sport tourism, we would strongly support Bale's claim that "for the sports participant—performer or spectator—the experience of place, therefore, could be argued to contribute to the overall sporting experience or, indeed, the sports performance" (p. 13). We adopt the view that the experience of place is a key component of the sport tourism experience.

Categorizing that experience is difficult. Here we look at two possible schemes to categorize sport tourism and then propose a new classification scheme that we feel best represents the field of sport tourism.

Pybus's Classification Scheme

The publication *Adventure Holidays* (Pybus, 1995) organizes holidays into 12 categories: multiactivity holidays; young people's holidays; air sports; cycling; hiking and rambling; mountain pursuits; overland; riding and trekking; specialist activities and courses; special tours and expeditions; water sports; and wildlife. One of the problems with this analysis by sport activity is the ever-lengthening number of categories and its lack of differentiation of one type of sport tourism from another. Its categorization remains one-dimensional, based only on the sport activity, and offers little to anyone seeking to understand the nature of the relationship between sport and tourism.

Hall's Classification Scheme

Hall's (1992) recent academic work is more useful. It examines three significant segments of special interest travel: adventure, sport, and health tourism. These interest areas are differentiated according to the nature of the activity they involve. Adventure tourism is defined as the deliberate seeking of risk and danger. Sport tourism's defining characteristic, according to Hall, is competition; here Hall reveals a North American interpretation of sport. Health tourism includes travel for medical treatment and the more general motive of improving overall health and fitness. Hall noted "significant commonalities" among the three sectors where distinct overlaps exist. His examples of adventure activities include backpacking, bicycle touring, fishing, and a range of other activities that we regard as sports. Not all fishermen nor all cyclists "deliberately seek risk and danger"—indeed several of the activities listed as adventure tourism are not necessarily characterized by risk at all. Similarly, Hall concedes that many sports activities can be undertaken as "recreational" activities rather than as a form of competition. The differentiation, then, between adventure and sport tourism is indistinct. The same may be said of health tourism, except for activities deliberately undertaken for the purpose of medical treatment. As a way of classifying special interest tourism this three-part segmentation of the market has some ambiguities.

Hall's classification scheme is shown in figure 2.3. By using two criteria— (1) the degree of active involvement, from more active to less active, and (2) competition, from competitive to noncompetitive—he develops a framework with nine segments.

This typology is limited, in our opinion, because of its definition of a sport activity as being necessarily competitive, of adventure travel as entailing

Activity

Less active ————————————————— More active

	Less active		More active
Noncompetitive	**Health tourism** (e.g., spa tourism health travel)	**Health tourism** (e.g., fitness retreats)	**Adventure travel** (e.g., whitewater rafting, SCUBA diving, hiking)
	Adventure travel (e.g., yacht chartering)	**Tourism activities** which contain elements of health, sport, & adventure (e.g., cycling, sea-kayaking)	**Adventure travel** (e.g., climbing)
Competitive	**Sport tourism** (e.g., spectating)	**Sport tourism** (e.g., lawn bowls)	**Sport tourism** (e.g., ocean racing)

Figure 2.3 A conceptual framework of the motivation and activities of participants in adventure, health, and sports tourism (Hall, 1992, p. 142). Copyright 1992 Hall. Reprinted by permission.

risk, and of health tourism as being limited to less active forms of participation. Recreational participation in activities such as walking, beach games, and fishing is difficult to position on the grid. White-water rafting can be competitive, ocean racing can be as adventurous as yacht chartering, and strenuous activity can have positive health benefits. Thus there are ambiguities that render this unidimensional framework less useful than one would hope.

A New Model Is Needed

We have identified the nature of sport tourism as a cultural experience of physical activity tied to a cultural experience of place. The two schemes of analysis we have reviewed (Hall, 1992; Pybus, 1995) are one-dimensional—that is, they are based only on the characteristics of the physical activity. Such frameworks present problems of classification and contribute only a little to our understanding of the relationship between sport and tourism

Saltmarsh Partnership

Rafting the mighty Shotover river in Queenstown, New Zealand.

and the different kinds of experience their interaction gives rise to. For this reason we propose a new scheme to depict the nature of sport tourism.

Our Classification Scheme for Sport Tourism

We can trace no fully developed classification of sport tourism that satisfies us. This is hardly surprising since no other book has set out to deal exclusively with sport tourism. Its manifestations are enormously diverse, and the topic is comparatively new and underresearched.

Since we are dealing with two types of cultural experience, namely sport and tourism, we propose a two-dimensional classification to embrace the experiences of physical activity and place. The experience of sport is not the same as the experience of tourism—much of the activity in sport takes place entirely independent of tourism and vice versa. It is in the areas of intersection between the two that sport tourism takes place. The nature of sport tourism is seen as a cultural experience of physical activity tied to a cultural experience of place. This kind of special characteristic of active sport holidays was recognized by the World Tourism Organization (1985). They believed that such holidays had the potential to enrich the tourist experience by allowing greater integration with the place visited and fuller involvement in the social and cultural life of the destination.

Two models underpin our classification. First, we use a modified version of Haywood's classification of sport for one dimension of our scheme (Haywood, 1994); for the other dimension we use a modified version of Burton's (1995) tourism resources, because it is consistent with our interpretation of sport tourism. By incorporating two dimensions, our model seeks to treat both sport and tourism evenhandedly. Sport tourism offers a *two-dimensional* experience of physical activity tied to a particular setting.

Our classification scheme can be seen in figure 2.4. In it, we illustrate the functional relationship between the sport and the touristic activity using two criteria:

- The nature of the sport experience (environmental or interpersonal)
- The nature of the touristic experience (natural or man-made)

From these criteria a grid of eight segments is derived. Each of the segments of the grid illustrates particular sport tourism experiences located in their particular touristic resource setting.

The framework illustrated in figure 2.4 establishes a classification system of sport tourism that takes account of the nature of the activity at the intersection of the two core experiences. The grid allows us to plot the position of different sporting activities in different touristic settings according to the nature of the activities and the geographical resources in which they take place.

At any time the participant may give primacy to one or the other core experiences. For example, an individual or group may be engaged in the same activity, such as hiking, but whereas for one it will be the sole intention of the touristic trip, for another it will be no more than incidental. However, this is a matter of emphasis and does not alter the basic nature of the two experiences, only their relative importance to the individual.

We allow for this in our typology of sport tourists (see chapter 1 and figure 1.2 on page 13) where we differentiate active sport holiday takers into two groups: (1) sport activity holiday takers for whom sport is the overriding objective of the trip and (2) holiday sport activity vacationers for whom sport is incidental. In sport activity holidays, the sport experience is dominant, but to be categorized as sport tourism its setting and experience must be in the touristic dimension. In holiday sport activities, on the other hand, the touristic dimension is dominant, and the sport experience is integral but subsidiary. Passive sport holidays are similarly divided between those where the sport experience dominates (connoisseur sport tourism) and those where tourism is dominant (casual observer). In the nonholiday/business sector the pattern is replicated.

The eight sport tourism segments shown in figure 2.4 offer a means to classify different cultural experiences in terms of the nature of the physical activity in interaction with its setting. Imposed on the nature of the sport tourism experience is the relative importance attached by the sport tourists

Touristic Experience

Sport Experience		Natural		Manmade	
		COASTAL	LANDSCAPE	HISTORIC	CULTURAL/ENTERTAINMENT
Environmental	*Natural*	Surfing Boardsailing Fishing Scuba diving Sailing Swimming Yachting Snorkeling Land yachting	Walking / hiking Climbing Cycling Canoeing Skiing Angling Rowing Jogging Triathlon Orienteering Sky diving Abseiling Ballooning Hang gliding Caving Horse riding Hunting Canyoning Kite flying Hot springs Rafting	Trips to historic sites (e.g., Olympia)	Ice skating Roller skating Skateboarding Yoga
	Artificial	Water skiing Jet skiing Paragliding	Equestrian — 3-day event Ski jumping Luge Bobsleigh Tobogganing	Sports museums Halls of fame Historic sports buildings	Athletics Trampolining Gymnastics Health farms Fitness retreats Bungee jumping Artificial climbing Weight lifting
Interpersonal	*Combat*			Jousting	Fencing Boxing Judo Wrestling Kendo Stick fighting Karate (Indonesia)
	Contest	Beach volleyball Boules	Traditional games Road bowls (Ireland) Tira del bola (Spain) Street football (England) Palla (Italy) Street hockey	Tennis	Football Hockey Tennis Golf Baseball Bowls Cricket Handball Basketball Volleyball Badminton Archery Croquet Curling Ice hockey Lacrosse Raquetball Tenpin Squash Softball Table tennis Tug of war Pool/billiards/snooker

Figure 2.4 A conceptual classification of sport tourism.

to the two components: sport and tourism. The bold black line defines the dominant experience, the divided line the subsidiary experience. Thus, where the sport experience is most important (on the vertical dimension) the touristic experience (on the horizontal dimension) is, by definition, subsidiary, and vice versa. For example, by its position on the grid, shown below, the sport experience (hiking) is dominant, the challenge is provided by the natural environment and the touristic experience takes place in the natural landscape. This case illustrates a single sport holiday. Had the horizontal line been bold (and the touristic experience dominant), this would have been classed as a holiday sport activity. However, in historic sports buildings, the touristic experience is dominant, it takes place in the historic man-made environment, and its challenge in sport terms is artificial. This case illustrates the passive sport experience of a casual observer. Had the vertical line been bold (and the sport experience dominant) the observer would be classed as a connoisseur.

	Hiking		

		Historic sports buildings	

Spectating sport tourism is a vicarious form of participation, wholly dependent on the participation of other people. Spectators may well influence the activity they watch, but they do not materially alter its nature. We therefore identify sport tourism spectating as one form of participation within our typology of sport tourists (see chapters 1 and 3).

The Infrastructure of Sport, Tourism, and Sport Tourism

As we saw in chapter 1, and, in particular, figure 1.1 (on p. 5), sport is a special segment of the tourism industry. We also say that sport tourism takes place in the infrastructure of sport and tourism. We have just discussed the way in which the nature of sport tourism is a two dimensional experience involving a synergy of sport and tourism experiences. Therefore, we will now examine the infrastructure of sport, tourism, and sport tourism in more detail. By infrastructure, we mean the underlying foundations needed to carry out these activities (for example, the facilities, organizations, and transportation).

The Infrastructure of Sport

Sport could not take place without an infrastructure to support it. Today, this infrastructure is becoming more complex and diverse, but we can identify three main components—private individuals and groups (often characterized as the voluntary or not-for-profit sector), commercial providers and operators, and public authorities. Recent changes, however, in attitudes toward public funding, have blurred the distinctions between the three sectors. At least some of the provisions made by the voluntary sector could not occur without public support, and many publicly provided community sports facilities now operate on at least a semicommercial basis. Partnerships and other forms of collaboration have become both practically desirable and politically important.

In table 2.1, we have identified the factors needed to sustain sport and divided them into seven categories: natural features, constructed facilities, services, entertainment, transport, heritage, and organizations. This table helps to identify the complex and costly underpinning needed for sport.

A range of facilities is needed—both indoor and outdoor, in the countryside, and in the urban environment—to satisfy the demands made by individuals, families, clubs, and a host of other groups. These facilities are of two types: natural landscapes and man-made constructions.

Yet facilities alone cannot meet the demands for sport. A whole range of services are required, from coaching, leadership, and administration to the merchandising of equipment and clothing. Most facilities, even natural

Table 2.1   Factors Necessary to Support Sport

Natural features	Services	Entertainment	Transport	Goods
Parks (national, country, community) Mountains Rocks Spas Beaches & sea Lakes Rivers Open-amenity spaces Wilderness	Coaching/leadership Hire facilities Shopping Administration Commercial providers Marketing Operators/agents	Events Performances Matches	Road Rail Air Sea River	Equipment Clothing

Constructed facilities	Heritage	Organizations
Marinas Golf courses Ice rinks Arenas Stadia Leisure centers Artificial ski slopes Climbing walls Tennis & other racquet courts Swimming pools Race courses Bowling greens/rinks Athletic tracks	Museums Historic sports buildings	Volunteer groups Associations Governing bodies Public sector/community authorities Clubs

national parks, need to be managed in such a way that they attract people to use but not overuse them. The majority of participants need forms of transport to enable them to engage in sports.

Much of the demand for sport is for spectating rather than participating; thus, part of the infrastructure consists of the arrangement of entertainment—that is, matches, events, and performances. Heritage is a small though important factor embracing, for example, the wide range of sports museums. Finally, organizations of many types are essential to support the practice of sport, ranging from volunteer and community groups to governing bodies, clubs, and public authorities.

The sporting infrastructure clearly must share with tourism the need for administration and policy if full use is to be made of existing resources and the potential for development effectively realized. Marketing is a further important component of the delivery system, if the "right" experiences are to be developed at the "right" price in the "right" place, and prospective participants made aware of them. Operators and agents are responsible for the provision and delivery of the sport experiences and linking the participants with them.

The Infrastructure of Tourism

Mill (1990) identified four dimensions of tourism, all of which refer to the infrastructure needed to support it.

- Attractions
- Facilities
- Transportation
- Hospitality

Attractions, according to Mill, are the features that draw visitors to a destination and may be based on natural resources, culture, ethnicity, or entertainment. Facilities service the visitors once they have arrived at their destination and include lodging, food and beverage, and support services such as souvenir shops, laundries, and recreational amenities. Transportation is obviously essential to tourism. Improvements in the conditions of travel have encouraged tourism, and conversely, the expansion of tourism has increased the need for better transportation. Hospitality refers to the quality of the interaction between visitors and the people they come into contact with at the destination.

Recently, Davidson (1993) provided a categorization of six types of tourist attractions that shows clearly how sport is a component of tourism (see table 2.2).

Note that a comparison of table 2.1 and table 2.2 shows a degree of overlap indicating the potential for relationships between sport and tourism. The categories of facilities (or attractions, as Davidson describes them) are, again, indicative rather than exhaustive but are useful in helping us to place the range of facilities and events that attract visitors to a particular place. In this scheme natural features and sports facilities are the most obvious categories of sport tourism attractions, stadiums for spectator sport fit the entertainment category, special interests such as go-carting circuits or pony trekking can be included, sports museums have a place, and specialty

Table 2.2   Categories of Tourist Attractions

Natural features	Rides & transport	Entertainment
Beaches & sea	Steam railways	Cinemas
Volcanoes	Canals	Fairgrounds
Parks & gardens	Gondolas	Nightclubs
Spas	Hot air balloons	Zoos
Lakes	Camel rides	Racecourses
Mountains	Coaches	Theme parks
Rivers		

Sports facilities	Shopping	Artistic & cultural heritage
Leisure centers	Leisure shopping complexes	Historic buildings
Golf courses		Archeological sites
Ski slopes	Oriental bazaars	Arts/music festivals
Tennis courts	Specialty shopping	Tribal customs & crafts
Swimming pools	Hypermarkets	Museums
Ice rinks	Duty-free shopping	

See Davidson, 1993, p. 91. Reprinted by permission of Addison Wesley Longman Ltd.

shopping (e.g., for ski or diving gear) is covered. Davidson's (1993) categorization clearly identifies the importance of sport within tourism. Matley's (1983) earlier work similarly comprehended sports activities as attractions within tourist destinations and Graburn (1983), writing about Japan, likewise included "sportive tourist sites" as one of the variety of tourist site types in domestic tourism there.

Other factors required to support tourism include organizational structures, administration, and agreements within and between countries. Regional, national, international, and transnational organizations have been developed to implement tourism policies in our increasingly globalized world. Frequently conflicts of interests arise not only between the different levels but also within any one level. Such conflicts occur in sport also. At the transnational level, a current hot issue concerns the European Community's sports policy to ban tobacco advertising at sporting events and the Spanish government's refusal to comply for the Formula One event when it takes place on the Spanish motor racing circuit at Barcelona. For example, regional (and even local) organizations concerned with promoting tourism for its economic contribution to a community can be aligned with, or opposed by, other organizations concerned with its sociocultural or environmental impact on the community.

Like sport, tourism has special characteristics that differentiate it from other industries such as manufacturing. By definition, the tourist experience is consumed away from home. Tourism is not a single service, but a combination of services that have to be coordinated to deliver the touristic experience. Marketing and distribution of the opportunities are the specialist processes that have to be implemented to bring about tourism.

The Infrastructure of Sport Tourism

Sport tourism, by definition, must depend upon some combination of factors already outlined as necessary to support sport and tourism separately. The considerable overlap that has already become apparent indicates their shared needs and interests, and identifies the potential closeness of the relationship between the two types of experience (see table 2.3).

Here it is important to stress that this relationship generates myriad connections that together amount to more than the sum of the two separate experiences. The relationship depends upon interaction—a process to be stimulated and managed, since it creates a new genre of leisure. The facilities and the interests common to sport and tourism suggest the advantages of an integrated administrative and marketing approach.

The overlapping of sport and tourism may have positive or negative consequences. Duplication of resources, overuse or underuse of resources, and conflicts of interest in administration are the potential downside of the relationship. On the other hand, coordinated policy, administration, and marketing, and the efficient and effective use of joint resources can be the outcome. The administration of the sport-tourism relationship is the theme of chapter 9.

The Characteristics of Participants

Having examined the infrastructure of sport tourism, we now turn our attention to the important aspect of the characteristics of those who participate, thus completing our analysis of the relationships in our basic model of sport tourism (please refer to figure 1.1 on p. 5).

The Characteristics of Sportists

We are familiar with the label *tourists*. *Sportists* are those who engage, actively or passively, in sport. Active sportists are in the minority—more people watch sports than participate actively (Kamphorst and Roberts, 1989).

Nonprofessional participation tends to be concentrated in specific groups and is influenced by age, gender, social class, geographical setting, race,

Table 2.3   The Infrastructure of Sport Tourism

Natural features	Services	Entertainment
Parks (national, country, community) Mountains Rocks Spas Beaches & sea Lakes Rivers Open-amenity spaces Wilderness	Travel agents Tour operators (domestic, inbound, outbound) Animateurs/leaders/coaches/teachers Equipment & clothing merchandising outlets Tour escorts/representatives/guides Tourist information bureaus Facility & event managers Marketing Currency exchange Insurance Catering Management information systems Equipment hire Maps and guide books Sports injury clinics	Events Matches Performances Festivals

Transport	Constructed facilities	Accommodations
Rail networks National bus networks Cars Airlines Shipping lines Ferries	Marinas Golf courses Ice rinks Arenas Stadia Swimming pools Sports pitches Leisure centers Artificial ski slopes Artificial climbing walls Sports courts Bowling greens/rinks Race courses Athletics tracks Mountain lifts	Hotels Motels Villas Holiday camps Clubs Camp sites Hostels Cruise ships Guest houses Mountain huts

(continued)

Table 2.3   *(continued)*

Heritage	Built amenities	Organizations
Museums Archeological sites Historic stadia/arenas	Car parks Toilets Signposts Shelters	National Government Agencies Legislative/Regulative bodies Regional & local public agencies Governing bodies of sport Airline associations Travel trade marketing associations Professional associations Voluntary organizations

ethnicity, and religion. Sports participation, generally, is increasing through-out most of the developed world due to a growing awareness of health issues and of the implications of lack of exercise.

Characteristically, sport participation is highest among young people. Most young children at schools in Western democracies take part in physical education as part of their curriculum. But this participation is often compulsory, and once it becomes voluntary it tends to decline with age. However, in many countries, comparisons over the last 10 to 15 years show that sports participation is increasing across all age groups, particularly among people in their 40s to 50s (Ban, 1990; Clearing House, 1988a, 1988b; Harada, 1993; Maiztegui-Onate, 1996; Sports Council, 1994; De Knop, Laporte, Van Meerbeek, and Vanreusel, 1991).

Men are more likely than women to participate in sport in general and in outdoor sport in particular (Coakley, 1990; Laidler and Cushman, 1993; Maiztegui-Onate, 1996; Sports Council, 1994; Thurley, 1993). But participation among women—especially in indoor sport—has increased significantly, stimulated by the fitness and health boom (Coakley, 1990; Norwegian Confederation of Sports Women's Committee, 1990; Sports Council, 1994). Coakley (1990) identified the increase in participation among girls and women as "the single most dramatic change in sport" since the 1970s (p. 177). He goes on to say, "This has occurred in many countries around the world, especially industrial countries" (p. 177). Women now participate in a wider range of sports than ever before. Even so, there are more sporting competitions and events for men than women.

Patterns of participation in sport "are closely tied to social stratification in any society," according to Coakley (1990, p. 233). Socioeconomic status has been found to be an important influence in many countries, with participation higher among nonmanual workers, and highest among professional groups (Coakley, 1990; Maiztegui-Onate, 1996; Sports Council, 1994). Furthermore, regarding the pattern in North America, Coakley states that "overall participation rates in middle- and upper-middle-income white communities is much higher than in the vast majority of predominantly black communities" (p. 208).

The Characteristics of Tourists

In terms of the percentage of people who engage in a leisure activity, tourism is more popular than sport. The reader is referred to chapter 6 (see table 6.3 on p. 223) which shows that in at least 12 countries, and the European Community (EC) countries on average, the majority of people normally take a holiday away from home. However, developing a profile of holiday takers is complex given the tremendous range of experiences on offer including short and long breaks, domestic and international locations, package and independent tours and so on.

Two prerequisites for the consumption of tourism are time and money, and these are not universally available, nor evenly spread where they are available. People less likely to be tourists are those groups who are short of money, those who experience time constraints, and those who are subject to both of these disadvantages or ill health. Those most likely to be tourists are those who have time and money at their disposal. Beyond this generalized picture it is difficult to profile the "tourist," since tourism has wide appeal to both sexes, all ages, singles, families, and other groups including the disabled.

The Characteristics of Sport Tourists

Sport tourists as a type of tourist have been identified for the past 20 years (see Finger, Gayler, Hahn and Hartmann, 1975, in Germany; Goodrich, 1980, in the United States; Perreault, Darden and Darden, 1977, in Belgium; American Express, 1989, in Japan, Germany, the United States, and the United Kingdom; and the World Tourism Organization, 1985, worldwide).

Research in Great Britain (Mintel International Group, 1995) profiled activity holiday takers as predominantly those in the 15-to-34-year-old age group and nonmanual occupations, that is, people in the upper socioeconomic groups. An earlier study by Leisure Consultants (1992) found much the same profile, though they noted that more males than females participated in active holidays, an observation also made by Nogawa, Yamaguchi, and Hagi (1996) in relation to Japanese sport tourists. French sport tourists share a similar profile, with men or women in higher management positions always overrepresented (Pigeasseau, 1997).

Yiannakis (1992) reported research undertaken in America from which he identified four tourist roles: the action seeker, the explorer/adventurer, the sport lover, and the organized mass tourist. He found a similar profile to Mintel International Group's British participants. Yiannakis's sport lovers tended to be mostly male college graduates from 18 to 41 years of age with comparatively high incomes. His profile of the explorer/adventurer tourist identifies someone from 18 to 34 or 42 to 49 years old, successful in his or her career, financially comfortable, and moderately to highly educated. Confirmation of this profile can be found elsewhere (Dearden and Harron, 1992; Hall, 1992; Hall and McArthur, 1991; Johnston, 1992; Olsen and Granzin, 1989; Tabata, 1992; Wooder, 1992).

However, Hall (1992) and Johnston (1992) noted that the profile of adventure tourists differed from activity to activity and from location to location. In particular, Johnston (1992) noted different activity preferences among male and female mountain recreationists. Males dominated the hunting and climbing groups, and although females were present in most groups, they favored walking, hiking, and skiing. Operators in this sector of special interest tourism confirm these general characteristics but report that an increasingly broader spectrum of people are choosing activity holidays. Elliott (1994), commenting on British involvement, found that the fastest growth area in adventure holidays has recently been among the older, wealthier, and more sophisticated travelers.

Hall's (1992) typology distinguished three groups of active tourists based on their level of activity: first, nonparticipating (passive) spectators; second, moderately active tourists (for example, lawn bowlers); and third, "more active" tourists (for example, those who enjoy "ocean racing"). Positioning specific activities on a three-point scale as a means of differentiating active tourists is problematic given that many activities can be pursued at different levels even when "competition" is accepted as the baseline for inclusion.

There is no recognized scale against which to identify the degree of intensity involved in activity. The definition of an activity in terms of its physical demands involves a high degree of subjectivity. Research in western Canada (Tourism Research Group, 1988) has pointed out that

> while river rafting may be a "softer" activity in terms of physical exertion than whitewater kayaking, participants on a river rafting trip, who have never been outside an urban environment before, may find the experience extremely risky, exhausting and therefore "hard." (p. 8)

Young and able-bodied people will rate as only "moderately active" sports that the older, or a disabled, participant would find "more active." The activity and risk demands of a sport can be as much a function of the age and health of a participant as they are of the activity itself.

Visitors to sports events, Mazitelli (1987) noted, were more likely to travel long-haul, stay more days, stay in costlier accommodation, and spend more per day. However, international events do not always attract big-spending visitors. Collins (1991) refers to youth events, such as the World Student

Games, and events for veterans or masters where hosts are expected to cover costs such as accommodation for the visitors whose budgets, even for sightseeing, are limited.

Summary

In this chapter we identified the nature of active sport as a cultural experience of physical activity and analyzed it following Haywood and Kew's classification (Haywood, 1994). Their scheme differentiates sports for which the raison d'être is environmental challenge from those for which it is interpersonal challenge.

We characterized the nature of tourism as a cultural experience of place. We prefer Burton's (1994) analysis of its nature, because her identification of tourist resources in terms of coastal, landscape, historic, and cultural and entertainment resources embraces all touristic places and, in addition, recognizes the overall importance of climate.

From the above points, it follows that the nature of sport tourism is a cultural experience of physical activity tied to a cultural experience of place. The key point is the two-dimensional nature of the experience they induce.

Not fully satisfied with any extant classification of the nature of sport tourism, we propose our own. Our scheme illustrates the functional relationships in the two-dimensional experience of sport tourism. The grid derived from these relationships enables us to identify the nature of the different experiences at the intersection between sport and tourism. Thus our classification focuses on the inherent nature of sport tourism experiences, not on the participants or the forms of participation.

There are seven categories of factors that make up the infrastructure to support sport: natural and constructed environments, services, entertainment, transportation, heritage, and organizations. The same support structures are necessary for tourism with the addition of attractions and hospitality. The potential for a close relationship between sport and tourism is identified by their utilization of a very similar infrastructure.

Participants will engage in these experiences in different ways at different times. For some the sport experience will be dominant, while for others the touristic experience will be more important. This difference in participation is at the root of our typology of sport tourist experiences described in detail in chapter 3.

References

American Express. (1989). Unique four nation travel study reveals traveller types. London: American Express. News release.

Bale, J. (1994). *Landscapes of modern sport*. Leicester, Great Britain: Leicester University Press.

Ban, D. (1990, May). *Participation of youth in sports organization*. Paper presented at the meeting of the IVth Congress of Yugoslav Pedagogics of Physical Culture, Bled, Yugoslavia.

Bannister, R. (1957). *First four minutes*. London: Corgi Books.

Becker, H. (1974). Art as collective action. *American Sociological Review, 39*(6), 767-776.

Best, D. (1978). *Philosophy and human movement*. London: Allen & Unwin.

Boniface, B., and Cooper, C. (1994). *The geography of travel and tourism*. Oxford, Great Britain: Butterworth-Heinemann.

Bourdieu, P. (1978). Sport and social class. *Social Science Information, XVIII*(6), 820-833.

Brohm, J. (1978). *Sport—Prison of measured time*. London: Ink Links.

Burton, R. (1995). *Travel geography*. London: Pitman Publishing.

Clawson, M., and Knetsch, J. (1966). *The economics of outdoor recreation*. Baltimore, MD: John Hopkins University Press.

Clearing House. (1988a). Sportparticipatie in de Bondsrepubliek Duitsland [Sports participation in the Federal Republic of Germany]. In Clearing House (Ed.), *Sports Information Bulletin. Vol. 13* (pp. 697-703). Brussels, Belgium: Author.

Clearing House. (1988b). Sportparticipatie in Noorwegen [Sports participation in Norway]. In Clearing House (Ed.), *Sports Information Bulletin. Vol. 13* (pp. 719-721). Brussels, Belgium: Author.

Coakley, J. (1990). *Sport and society: Issues and controversies*. 4th ed. St. Louis: Times Mirror/Mosby College Publishing.

Collins, M.F. (1991). The economics of sport and sport in the economy: Some international comparisons. In C.P. Cooper (Ed.), *Progress in tourism, recreation, and hospitality management* (pp. 184-214). London: Belhaven Press.

Davidson, R. (1993). *Tourism*. London: Pitman.

Dearden, P. and Harron, S. (1992). Tourism and the hill-tribes of Thailand. In B. Weiler and C.M. Hall (Eds.), *Special interest tourism* (pp. 95-104). London: Belhaven Press.

De Knop, P., Laporte, W., Van Meerbeek, R. Vanreusel, B. (1991). *Fysieke fitheid en sportbeoefening van de Vlaamse jeugd* [Physical fitness and sports participation of Flemish youth]. Brussels, Belgium: Interuniversitair Onderzoekscentrum voor Sportbeleid.

Dunleavey, J. (1981). Skiing: The worship of Ullr in America, *Journal of Popular Culture, 4*, 74-85.

Eliot, T.S. (1962). *Notes toward the definition of culture*. London: Faber & Faber.

Elliott, H. (1994, November 10). You're never too old for an adventure. *The Times*, p. 35.

Finger, K., Gayler, B., Hahn, H., and Hartmann, K.D. (1975). *Animation in Urlaub* [Animation in holiday]. Stranberg, Germany: Studienkreis für Tourismus.

Goffman, E. (1974). *Frame analysis: An essay on the organization of experience*. New York: Harper Row.

Goodrich, J.N. (1980). Benefit segmentation of US international travellers: An empirical study. In D.E. Hawkins, E.L. Shafer, and J.M. Rovestad (Eds.), *Tourism marketing and management issues* (pp. 133-147). Washington, DC: George Washington University.

Graburn, N.H. (1983). *To pray, pay and play: The cultural structure of Japanese domestic tourism* (Series B), 26. Aix-en-Provence, France: Centre de Hautes Etudes Touristiques: Cahiers du Tourisme.

Guttman, A. (1978). *From ritual to record—The nature of modern sports*. New York: Columbia University Press.

Hall, C.M. (1992). Adventure, sport and health. In C.M. Hall and B. Weiler (Eds.), *Special interest tourism* (pp. 141-158). London: Belhaven Press.

Hall, C.M., and McArthur, S. (1991). Commercial whitewater rafting in Australia: History and development. *Leisure Options: Australian Journal of Leisure and Recreation, 1*(2), 25-30.

Harada, M. (1993). Longitudinal perspectives on sport participation among the active 'aged' population in Japan. In A.J. Veal, P. Jonson, and G. Cushman (Eds.), *Leisure and tourism: Social and economic change* (pp. 310-317). Sydney, Australia: University of Technology.

Hargreaves, Jennifer. (1982). Theorising sport: An introduction. In Jennifer Hargreaves (Ed.), *Sport, culture and ideology* (pp. 1-29). London: Routledge & Kegan Paul.

Hargreaves, John. (1982). Sport, culture and ideology. In Jennifer Hargreaves (Ed.), *Sport, culture and ideology* (pp. 30-61). London: Routledge & Kegan Paul.

Hargreaves, John. (1986). *Sport, power and culture*. Cambridge, Great Britain: Polity Press.

Haywood, L. (1994). Community sports and physical recreation. In L. Haywood (Ed.), *Community leisure and recreation* (pp. 111-143). Oxford, Great Britain: Butterworth-Heinemann.

Haywood, L., and Kew, F.C., Bramham, P., Spink, J., Capernerhurst, J., and Henry, I. (1995). *Understanding leisure*. Cheltenham, Great Britain: Stanley Thornes.

Hoffman, P. (1967, June 5). Hippies hangout draws tourists. *The New York Times*, p. 43.

Huizinga, J. (1949). *Homo ludens*. London: Routledge & Kegan Paul.

Johnston, M. (1992). Facing the challenges: Adventure in the mountains of New Zealand. In B. Weiler and C.M. Hall (Eds.), *Special interest tourism* (pp. 159-169). London: Belhaven Press.

Kamphorst, T., and Roberts, K. (Eds.). (1989). *Trends in sports. A multinational perspective*. Voorthuizen, the Netherlands: Giordano Bruno Culemborg.

Laidler, A., and Cushman, G. (1993). Life and leisure in New Zealand. In A.J. Veal, P. Jonson, and G. Cushman (Eds.), *Leisure and tourism: Social and economic change* (pp. 342-349). Sydney, Australia: University of Technology.

Laing, R.D. (1967). *The politics of experience*. New York: Ballantine.

Leisure Consultants. (1992). *Activity holidays: The growth market in tourism*. Sudbury, Great Britain: Author.

Luschen, G. (1972). On sociology of sport: General orientation and its trend in the literature. In O. Grupe, D. Kurz, and J. Teipel (Eds.), *The scientific view of sport.* Heidelberg, Germany: Springer.

MacCannell, D. (1976). *The tourist.* London: Macmillan.

Maiztegui-Onate, C. (1996). Spain. In G. Cushman, A.J. Veal, and J. Zuzanek (Eds.), *World leisure participation: Free time in the global village* (pp. 199-214). Wallingford, Great Britain: CAB International.

Mason, A. (1988). *Sport in Britain.* London: Faber & Faber.

Matley, I.M. (1983). Physical and cultural factors influencing the location of tourism. In N.S. Starr (Ed.), *Tourism for the travel agent.* Wellesley, MA: Institute of Certified Travel Agents.

Mazitelli, D. (1987). *The benefits of hosting major sporting events.* Paper presented at the 60th National Conference of the Royal Australian Institute of Parks and Recreation, Canberra, Australia.

McLuhan, M. (1964). *Understanding media: The extensions of man.* New York: McGraw-Hill.

Mill, R.C. (1990). *Tourism: The international business.* Englewood Cliffs, NJ: Prentice Hall.

Mintel International Group. (1995). *Activity holidays in the UK.* London: Author.

Nogawa, H., Yamaguchi, Y., Hagi, Y. (1996). An empirical research study on Japanese sport tourism in sports-for-all events: Case studies of a single-night event and multiple-night event. *Journal of Travel Research, 35*(2), 46-54.

Norwegian Confederation of Sports Women's Committee. (1990). *Women in Sport. Program 1985-1990.* Norway: Author.

Olsen, J.A. and Granzin, K.L. (1989). Life style segmentation in a service industry: The case of fitness spas. *Visions in Leisure and Business: An International Journal of Personal Services. Programming and Administration, 8*(3), 4-20.

Outdoor Recreation Resources Review Commission (ORRRC). (1962). *Outdoor recreation for America* (pp. 96-120). Washington, DC: U.S. Government Printing Office.

Perrault, W.D., Darden, D.K., and Darden, W.R. (1977). A psychographic classification of vacation styles. *Journal of Leisure Research, 9,* 208-224.

Pigeasseau, C. (1997). Sport and tourism: The emergence of sport into the offer of tourism: An overview of the French situation and perspective. Available at http://www.mcb.co.uk/journals/jst/archive/vol4no1/htm.

Pybus, V. (1995). *Adventure holidays.* Oxford, Great Britain: Vacation Work.

Relph, E (1976). *Place and placelessness.* London: Pion.

Rigauer, B. (1981). *Sport and work.* New York: Columbia Press

Ryan, C. (1991). *Recreational tourism.* London: Routledge.

Sports Council. (1994). *Trends in sports participation, fact sheet.* London: Author.

Swingewood, A. (1977). *The myth of mass culture.* London: Macmillan.

Tabata, R. (1992). Scuba diving holidays. In B. Weiler and C.M. Hall (Eds.), *Special interest tourism* (pp. 171-184). London: Belhaven.

Thurley, A. (1993). National recreation participation surveys. In A. J. Veal, P. Jonson, and G. Cushman (Eds.), *Leisure and tourism: Social and economic change* (pp. 392-397). Sydney, Australia: University of Technology.

Tomlinson, J. (1996). *The encyclopedia of extreme sports.* London: Carlton Books.

Tourism Research Group. (1988). *Adventure travel in western Canada.* Ottawa, ON: Tourism Canada.

Williams, R. (1965). *The long revolution.* Harmondsworth, Great Britain: Penguin.

Williams, R. (1977). *Marxism and literature.* Oxford, Great Britain: Oxford University Press.

Williams, R. (1981). *Culture.* Glasgow, Great Britain: Fontana.

Wooder, S. (1992, July). Multi-activity centres. *Insights,* pp. B71-81.

World Tourism Organization. (1985). *The role of recreation management in the development of active holidays and special interest tourism and consequent enrichment of the holiday experience.* Madrid, Spain: Author.

Yiannakis, A. (1992). Some predictors of tourist role preference: A logistic regression approach. In J. Sugden and C. Knox (Eds.), *Leisure in the 1990s: Rolling back the welfare state. Conference paper No. 46* (pp. 227-235). Eastbourne, Great Britain: Leisure Studies Association.

Chapter 3
Sport in the Development of Tourism

Exodus

Walking the European Alps.

The following topics are covered in this chapter:

1. The impact of increased sport participation and of an increased infrastructure on tourism.
2. The use of sport to generate and sustain tourism.
3. The various forms of sport tourism, illustrating how sport impacts tourism.

This chapter examines the ways in which sport has been used to generate and sustain tourism. After giving a brief overview of the development of sport as a segment of the tourism industry, we will look at how increased participation in sport and an increased infrastructure for sport impact tourism. Then we will analyze the various types of sport tourism, providing many examples and case studies that show sport's influence on tourism. Although problems exist with data because there are no common national, let alone international, standards, we include research evidence where estimates or measures exist. The chapter deals with both participant and spectator sport examples of tourism and with the casual amateur and the expert, and although it is primarily concerned with the international traveler, reference is included to local, regional, and national examples.

Sport as a Growing Segment of the Tourism Industry

The development of leisure and holiday time and pursuits during the last 40 years can be divided into four phases:

1. *The postwar period up to the end of the '50s.* Here, leisure and holiday time was for recreation, for relaxation after hard work. People stayed at home, went to the seaside, to the countryside, or to the mountains, not to swim, walk, or hike, but mainly to rest.
2. *The '60s.* This was a period characterized by consumption. Mobility became greater because of improvements in the means of transportation. Tourism was characterized by leaving the home, resting, and eating well.
3. *The end of the '60s up to the '80s.* New trends appeared. The concepts of development, activity, social engagement, pleasure, companionship, and self-enrichment were central in society; in other words, the recreation-oriented person wanted to participate in an active way, to observe intensively, and to enjoy consciously. Sport during holidays was becoming popular. Major sports were walking, hiking, and

swimming, but there were "new" sports as well, such as sailing and tennis. Club holidays proved successful.

4. *The '90s.* The '90s are characterized by the matching of leisure activities; the mutual benefits of an economic "marriage of convenience" between sport and tourism are clearly perceptible. The term *sport tourism* has been coined. Tourism is offering a lot of sport-oriented programs; sport is often practiced in combination with tourism (for example, bicycling and walking tours).

The Influence of Increased Sport Participation

As noted in chapter 1 and in the previous points, sport on holiday has increased in popularity since the '70s. This has resulted in a growing market for holidays with a sport content, thereby impacting tourism. Since tourism itself is still expanding and since people are now giving such importance to the body, health, and activity, sport tourism can be expected to grow still further in the near future. Furthermore, as sport changes in our society and provides a wider choice of activities, sport tourism will offer a broader range of activity programs and products.

The Influence of Increased Sport Tourism

The more sport resources—whether man-made (e.g., waterparks) or natural (e.g., beaches)—a location has, the more likely it is to attract tourism. Recognizing this, the tourism industry has developed sporting attractions and facilities in an effort to sell more tourism by diversifying its products and expanding its market. Attractions draw tourists to a destination—attractions that may be based on natural resources, culture, ethnicity, or entertainment (Mill, 1990).

Natural Resources as an Attraction

Natural coastal resources are a main reason why the Caribbean attracts a growing number of visitors. They come for the possibility of sea sailing, windsurfing, waterskiing, fishing, diving, or for "simply splashing about in the warm, translucent sea. The water is clearer for snorkeling and there are usually fewer people on the beaches than in American or Mediterranean resorts" (Jouclas, 1995a, p. 11).

Lohmann and Besel stress,

> Studies in central Europe show a marked increase in demand for opportunities to experience nature in a holiday

context. In West Germany alone there has been a growth of 20 million citizens the last few years who express a desire to experience nature-based holidays. (cited in Aas, 1990, p. 29)

Thus, we see that both coastal and landscape resources attract tourists.

Man-Made Resources as an Attraction

Besides natural experiences the culture of a country or a region also plays an important role in attracting tourists. Indigenous games, sports, and folk dances are examples of this kind of sport tourism attractions. Heritage as the preservation of culture from the past can attract tourists to visit ancient sites such as Olympia or the sports artifacts displayed in halls of fame.

Finally, entertainment has many potentialities for attractions. Sporting events such as the Olympics, the Super Bowl, and Formula One racing are good examples of major entertainment events which attract many tourists.

In 1991 the number of American visitors to Canada accounted for 1 million person trips; about 2 percent of these visitors attended a spectator sporting event (Marshall Macklin Monaghan Ltd., 1993). Of Canadian domestic tourists just over 6 million attended a spectator sporting event while on a trip (representing 5 percent of all domestic trips in 1990); two out of three of these people were on overnight trips (Marshall Macklin Monaghan Ltd., 1993).

A good example of a business using entertainment via sport to attract visitors can be found in Disney. Already world-famous for its theme parks, Disney is seeking to expand its association with entertainment and increase its identification with sport as a means of extending tourism.

Case Study 3.1

Disney's Approach to Sport Tourism
Developing Sport Facilities to Increase Tourism

Description of Context

When most people hear "Disney," images of Mickey Mouse, Donald Duck, and amusement parks come to mind. The origins of amusement parks lie in ancient and medieval religious festivals and trade fairs. Permanent outdoor amusement areas also date from antiquity. Public resorts, called pleasure gardens, for relaxation and recreation, first appeared in Europe during the Renaissance. In the United States, parks typically started as picnic grounds for public outings, but by the early twentieth century amusement parks had become profitable enough to attract the attention of big business.

In 1955 a revolution in amusement parks occurred with the first of a new themed-type of park opening in Anaheim, California. Disneyland covered 75 hectares. Five years after the death of its creator, the cartoonist Walt Disney (1901-1966), Walt Disney World, a new park covering 11,300 hectares, opened at Lake Buena Vista in Orlando, central Florida. In addition to the Magic Kingdom, the Florida resort contains many themed lands, recreation facilities (the new Wild World of Sports Complex), its own transportation system, hotels, and campgrounds. The entire resort covers an area equivalent to San Francisco. The economic and social impact of Disney World has been significant; in the first 10 years of its existence its guests are estimated to have spent US$14 billion in central Florida (Compton, 1991/92). Recently, the Walt Disney World Corporation has increased its identity with sport. According to Philip Lempert, senior vice president of Age Wave, a marketing consulting firm, "Older baby-boomers want more out of a vacation than lying on a beach. They would rather learn than laze" ("Mickey Mouse Aims Higher," 1995, p. 20).

Description of Development

Aside from owning the National Hockey League team the Anaheim Ducks and a piece of California's Angels (a major league baseball team), Disney has developed a 200-acre athletic complex at Disney World. Each accommodation complex within Disney World already has its own sports facilities, where visitors can swim, boat, rent ski boats with drivers and equipment, go on fishing expeditions and horseback rides, walk and bike on trails through the park, and play tennis and especially golf. Now with the Olympic-style project, hailed as the Walt Disney World International Sports Complex, facilities are provided for some 25 sports—everything from aerobics to fencing. The centerpiece of the multimillion-dollar project is a 7,500-seat baseball stadium that the company hopes will serve as the spring training home of a major league team. Other features include a 5,000-seat field house for basketball and volleyball, 12 tennis courts (including a center court with seating for 2,000), four baseball fields, four softball fields, track and field facilities, and a vacation-fitness center.

Organization

With 26 employees working full-time in the Orlando-based sports unit, Disney is heavily pitching its parks as sports venues. With five championship golf courses, a nine-hole executive course, four driving ranges, three pro shops, and 22 golf professionals on staff at the Walt Disney World Resort, Disney presently hosts a PGA golf tournament every year and plans over one thousand group tournaments for guests staying at one of the four Disney-owned-and-operated convention hotels. For beginners the six-hole Wee Links, a miniature championship course incorporating sand and water traps, trees, and greens, was designed for the young. Clubs, balls, and shoes may all be rented.

In addition, Disney sponsors a marathon each January through the theme park that draws nearly six thousand entries. It also produces an Indy 200 car race that runs on a specially-built 1.1-mile track next to the Magic Kingdom with temporary bleachers for up to 60,000 fans. Other sports events hosted by Disney include the World Triathlon Championship and the Disney Soccer Cup. This Cup involved six thousand children from the United States, Asia, Europe, and Latin America and was played at the Rose Bowl in Pasadena, California, the day after the 1995 World Cup championship. This event not only served as a test for future soccer investment but was part of an international marketing campaign. All participants received a free ticket to Disneyland.

A group of approximately 650 young professionals from all over the country spent one week in Orlando playing coed football and volleyball tournaments and partying at Disney's MGM Studios and Pleasure Island, a floating collection of themed bars. Along with their package of travel and accommodations, participants received a day pass to visit any of Disney's attractions.

Another attempt by Disney to market directly to adults is the Disney Institute. The "edutainment" complex at the Disney Village Resort in Orlando allows visitors to dabble in such diverse fields as entertainment (learn how to animate), culinary arts, and sport and fitness (golf and tai chi clinics). The latter, it is thought, will attract vacationers interested in improving their health through knowledge and activity.

With the complex, Disney hopes to draw everyone from major league baseball players in spring training to Little Leaguers and amateur leisure-time athletes. According to Mike Millay, Disney's director of sports events, "We feel it's going to allow Walt Disney World to become a premier sports destination. The sole purpose of such a diversity of venues is to attract a myriad of sporting events from age-group competition all the way to professional sporting events of one sort or another" (Disney considers Olympic Games bid, 1995, p. 1). The goal for the new site is to host 160 sports events each year. The Amateur Athletic Union's move to Disney in 1997 guarantees more than 50 grassroots sports events annually. As a further credibility boost, the world-famous Harlem Globetrotters basketball team has elected the Wide World of Sports as its permanent training ground (Cramer, 1997).

Why sport? Disney spokesman John Story explains that "it is the next logical step for us. People are increasingly looking to sport for their entertainment, both as spectators and participants" (Stanley, 1995, p. 18). Looking beyond the traditional theme-park goers—families with young children—Disney has started hosting sports events to try to appeal to everyone from empty nesters and senior citizens to honeymooners and postcollege singles. By hosting sport tournaments for groups such as the Sport and Social Clubs of the U.S., an organization with 80,000 21- to 35-year-old members interested in playing coed sports, Disney can lure Generation Xers to Disney World.

"They went all out to show us that it's not just Mickey Mouse anymore," said Sandy Thomas, president of the Sport & Social Clubs of the U.S. "Some of our members wouldn't really have considered going to Disney before, but they will now" (Stanley, 1995, p. 18).

The edutainment complex (with sports and fitness clinics) is directed to the same target audience as those who visit health spas such as the "Golden Door" or "Canyon Ranch." A family of three at the edutainment complex will likely spend at least US$3,500 for a week of activity, room and board included.

This case study was contributed by Lisa Delpy.

References

Compton's Interactive Encyclopaedia. (1991/92). [CD-ROM].

Cramer, G. (1997, July). It's a wonderful world. Sports Management, pp. 16-19.

Disney considers Olympic Games bid. (1995, August). Leisure Opportunities, p. 1.

Mickey Mouse aims higher. (1995, October 3). Fortune Magazine, p. 20.

Stanley, T.L. (1995, February 13). Brandweek, p. 18.

We can conclude that the number of sport opportunities the resources (natural or man-made) allow are important features for tourism. Having said this, the typology of sport tourists introduced in chapter 1 will be used as the framework for the rest of this chapter. Various forms of sport tourism will be described, illustrating sport's considerable impact on tourism.

As already noted in chapter 1 (see figure 1.2, p. 13) two kinds, or sectors, of tourism, each characterized by the combination of sport and tourism can be identified: (1) holidays with an element of sports content, and (2) nonholidays (business tourism) with an element of sports content. In both kinds, sport participation can be active or passive. At the next level of analysis it is the importance of the involvement in sport that is used to differentiate and refine the form which the sport involvement takes (i.e., the greater the emphasis upon sport and the more important it is to the touristic experience, the more likely it is to become the main intention of the trip). Active sport tourists may engage in sport activity holidays, in which sport is a main intention of the trip, or in holiday sport activities, where sport is incidental. Passive sport tourists can also be grouped according to how important sport is to the purpose of their trip. Connoisseur observers are those who have extensive passive involvement and are discriminating in the sports activity they watch as spectators or officiators. Casual observers are those who simply happen across an event rather than plan their visit to attend it.

Active Sports on Holidays

In this category two types of involvement can be identified, namely, (1) the sport activity holiday where sport is the main intention of the trip (for example, skiing holidays, participating in a sport tournament, adventure travels), and (2) the holiday sport activity where sport is incidental and not the main intention.

The Sport Activity Holiday

The primary intention and content of the sport activity holiday is sport. Two forms are (1) the single sport activity holiday, and (2) the multiple sport activity holiday.

The Single Sport Activity Holiday

This category should not be confused with the single person's sport activity holiday. With the single sport activity holiday we deal with those holidays where the main intention is to practice a single sport activity.

Winter Sports

The best-known form of this sport holiday is undoubtedly the skiing holiday. Skiing can be pursued at different levels (beginner, experienced, simply for pleasure, or in pursuit of high performance and excellence), by different age groups, and in different settings—at a ski school, a ski course, a ski club, or privately. Skiing is the classic example of sport tourism and the most popular of all winter sport activities. Every year it introduces 40-50 million visitors to the European Alps, with 40,000 ski runs and around 12,000 cable ways and lifts to support this popular holiday industry (Mader, 1988). From Britain alone it is estimated that around 653,000 people took ski holidays worth some US$321 million in 1991-92 (Mintel International Group, 1992). The ski market is now said to account for around 20 percent of the total European holiday market.

In the last 25 years the holiday market for winter sports has expanded to the extent that there are now holiday packages to suit many tastes and financial means. Skiing is no longer the preserve of high-altitude dwellers, nor is it limited to the rich and famous. Increasingly, with the provision of self-catering chalets and camp sites to complement hotels and clubs, millions of people throughout the developed world can enjoy touristic experiences of mountain beauty at the same time as learning to ski on all five continents of the world.

Cross-country skiing, sometimes known as Nordic skiing or langlauf, has also become very popular. Because this sport activity is easily learned and the equipment is less expensive than that required for downhill skiing, it is practiced by many sportists. The fact that beginners can, from day one, enjoy langlauf in a circuit of loipe (i.e., twin-grooved tracks) integrated in the countryside and free of the use of ski lifts are but two strong points of this sport (Clough, 1989).

Snowshoes are the hottest new trend in winter recreation. According to Schwiesow (1995), snowshoeing is the second fastest-growing winter sport behind snowboarding as outdoor enthusiasts search for simpler, more convenient ways to get outside during the winter.

Some other new trends are dog sledding and ice fishing. Many of the best-known winter sport resorts in the United States and Canada have at least one dog sled tour company from which to choose. Alaska is probably the best known place for dog sledding, the state's official sport (Sloan, 1995). Ice fishing is popular in Minnesota; there are plenty of companies that will rent huts by the day, week, or month (Sloan, 1995).

The model of the skiing holiday (that is, a holiday with a single sport as the primary intention—offered at different levels to different age groups and under different organizational forms) has recently been adopted by various other forms of sport. Holiday concerns, holiday organizations, (cultural) societies, and private sport schools now provide holiday courses in sailing, gliding, riding, golf, diving, cycling, mountaineering, surfing, and so forth.

Cycling

Cycling tours often follow the ski-holiday model. Nowadays there are hundreds of cycling holidays on offer, of all lengths, levels, and degrees of comfort. Some are organized by well-known cyclists, but very often people decide to organize their cycling holiday themselves. Cycle-friendly countries are growing in number. The world's most cycle-friendly country is probably the Netherlands due to its low, flat physical characteristics. Bike paths are provided all over the Netherlands from the smallest village to the biggest town. Cycle weekends are also offered by youth organizations, communities, tourist boards, hotels, and so forth.

Hotels especially are trying to reach the cycle tourists by offering half or full board, bike hire, and route maps. This is called a single-center or fixed-point holiday because the tourist is based at one hotel or campsite and takes day rides out from there to explore the surroundings. Some hotel chains offer hotel-to-hotel tours with accommodations each night in a different hotel; the luggage is transported by the hotel manager.

More sophisticated are those bicycle tours that include not only a guide, but also a bicycle technician, a medical doctor, and a support vehicle (Campbell, 1995). It is possible to take a cycling tour almost anywhere in the world. Reputable companies throughout North America and Europe operate bicycling tours in China, Africa, Vietnam, Pakistan, Sri Lanka, Bali, and Thailand, and even high-altitude regions such as the Atlas Mountains and Tibet.

Since the mid-1960s, the bicycle has divided into subspecies of racers, mountain bikes, tourers, and hybrids. All-terrain bicycling has become one of the fastest growing segments of the recreation industry. Sales of all-terrain bicycles in North America skyrocketed from 300,000 bicycles in 1984 to over 2 million in 1986 (Crandall, 1987).

Water Sports

At the January 1998 London International Boat Show, the assembled boat builders acknowledged that their industry is facing a worldwide problem, a declining interest in boating: 46 percent of sailors and 35 percent of motor boaters are now over 55 years of age, and boating magazine subscriptions are down by 20 percent in six years. The problem is not limited to Great Britain—the downward trend is acute in the United States, home of the world's biggest boat industry. In the last decade, turnover in the United States has fallen from $10 million to $8 million, and even though "recreational spending has grown by more than 50 percent in seven years, . . . boating's share has shrunk from 3.8 percent to 2.1 percent" (Groom, 1998, p. 1). In 1984, owning a boat was sixth on a wish list of American consumer preferences, but by 1996 it became the 15th.

Nevertheless, the link between water sports and holidays is increasing with sailing becoming a very popular holiday activity. The use of smaller and more easily transportable craft, such as dinghy car-toppers, jet skis, and windsurfers, has increased, and together with multihulled and chartered cruisers these crafts provide for a wide range of interests.

Cayman Islands Department of Tourism

Snorkeling in the Caymans—one of the many water activities attracting tourists to the islands.

While the Caribbean and the Mediterranean are the most popular seas, it is now possible to charter yachts in the South Pacific, the Seychelles, Australia, Alaska, Brazil, Thailand, and the Galapagos Islands (Robinson, 1984).

Martin and Mason's survey (1990) indicates that between 1.5 and 2 million people take part in water sports while on holiday in Britain. Britain has been described as a mecca for boating holidays: approximately 440,000 people take boating holidays on the country's two thousand miles of inland waterways each year; about 87 percent are U.K. residents and 13 percent are inbound tourists principally from Europe (Hoseason, 1990). A 1986 survey (Veal, 1986) found that over half of those who take part in sailing do so only when on holiday.

Also worth mentioning here are the old, great clipper ships that a century or more ago sailed around the world. The Mediterranean and the Caribbean are popular ports for such ships as the *Star Clipper*, the *Star Flyer*, the *Windstar*, and Club Med's two play boats. On some, visiting "crews" learn to navigate and handle the sails.

Valef Yachts, a Greek company, advertises "a vacation fit for a millionaire," offering its *Christina I* for around US$100,000 per week for 12 people, none of whom need to have previous yachting experience. With a crew of nine, it has a cruising range of 9,500 kilometers of Mediterranean water and includes its own private speedboat for water skiing, a small sailboat, and a Windsurfer for exploring the Greek islands (Richins, 1992).

A less luxurious vacation and one designed for the experienced sailor offers bare-boat chartering in the Caribbean. This type of charter presupposes the satisfactory completion of at least a basic sailing course and knowledge of navigational skills—training that may well be completed at home prior to the tourist trip.

White-water rafting includes, on the one hand, passive trips for tourists under the safe auspices of a guide, and on the other, rafting for experienced people over grade five rapids. Operators use a one-to-six scale for designating rivers, with five being the most difficult water for paying passengers and six being commercially unnavigable (Williams, 1995). Two main forms of rafting are commercially used, namely, passenger craft with centrally mounted oars rowed by a guide, and paddle rafting where all passengers join in. Rafting has spread across North America to the Pacific Ocean, more particularly to New Zealand and Australia. Even those with no rafting experience can enjoy white-water trips in such places as Turkey, India, Nepal, and Ethiopia.

New sports are constantly developing and tourists are continuously in search of new thrills and experiences. One of these is body-boarding, broadly practiced in Australia, New Zealand, and the U.S. states of Hawaii and California. The Atlantic coast in France is visited by an increasing amount of tourists who want to body-board and surf.

Diving is another aquatic sport that attracts thousands of people. The most popular and best places to start diving include the Red Sea, the Mediterranean, the Caribbean, Thailand, Florida, and, of course, the Great Barrier Reef of Australia. The Red Sea is extremely popular because it offers beautiful coral reefs, masses of fish, and warm, clear water. Adventurous scuba divers were some of the first holidaymakers to discover the delights of Thailand.

Sailing on land (land yachting) gives a sense of adventure and excitement wherever you are in the world. It is a sport that is easily learned and in which everyone can take part. Popular land-yachting resorts are to be found in California, Australia, and Europe, particularly on the blustery beaches of northern France, Belgium, and Holland.

Riding Holidays

Riding holidays, either wholly equestrian for real enthusiasts or with time on horseback worked into the itinerary of a more general trekking holiday, are increasingly popular. Riding holidays fall into two broad categories: trailing (that is, overnighting along the way) and the more sedate trekking. Two-week holidays offer a one-week horse-riding class, followed by trailing.

Some tour operators specialize in adventure treks, others in the gentler alternative, trekking on ponies; some provide ranch holidays with a choice between a working ranch (mere riding) or a ranch where campfires, rodeos, and square dances inject an element of fun (Atkins, 1995).

Masterclass Holidays

"Masterclass" holidays designed for ordinary sport players to realize their dreams of playing with, and being coached by, their heroes are another form of single sport activity holiday. They confirm the high value that some people place upon developing their sporting prowess even while on holiday. One example is playing tennis at Newk's ranch in Texas with John Newcombe (who won Wimbledon three times) and some of his legendary contemporaries such as Ken Rosewall, Marty Riessen, and Fred Stolle (Low, 1992).

Cricket

The Barbados Tourism Board has devised a unique cricket holiday coached by their own legendary master, Sir Garfield Sobers, described on his retirement as arguably the greatest cricketer of all time. Here, the idea is for a squad of enthusiasts to be coached every morning on the famous Kensington Oval in Bridgetown and to play games against local sides in the afternoon (Heald, 1992).

Golf

Tennis and golf resorts are competing with each other to offer the finest facilities and the most expert professionals to improve visitors' games. That golf provides an incentive to travel has been understood in Europe since the 1930s, but only in recent years have resort areas such as the Spanish Costa del Sol recognized the economic benefit to be gained from the mass migration in winter of Britain's golf enthusiasts (Stoddart, 1994).

Florida, in the United States, is renowned for its golf courses. Florida attracts not only visitors who come just to play golf, but also travelers who fit in a game of golf between conference sessions or business meetings (Jouclas, 1995b). The Meon Travel Group promotes so-called "Longshot Golf Holidays," consisting of tuition holidays, tournament holidays, and group golf holidays with destinations in Portugal, Spain, Gran Canaria, Majorca, Ireland, Tunisia, Bermuda, Dubai, and South Africa.

An American company, Fairway Systems, has developed a system to book a round of golf in Honolulu using a credit card. The service provides the caller with a choice of courses in the area, reveals the best times to play, determines which courses have free slots, and matches a player up with a group of players (Wheat, 1995).

But golf tourism is not confined to the Northern Hemisphere: "emerging economies" in Southeast Asia are now investing heavily in courses, hoping to attract Japan's wealthy golfers, and Thailand promoted 1993 as the "Visit Thai Golf Year."

Racquet Sports

Apart from golf, the Iberian peninsula has also specialized in racquet sports. The Barrington Sports Club at Vale do Lobo, an exclusive resort in the Algarve, is patronized mainly by British aspirants to squash fame (Jones, 1992). Another resort where racquet sports are the centerpiece is Nueva Andalucia, near Marbella in Spain. Alongside 360 apartments and penthouses are 22 squash and racquets courts, plus facilities for badminton and table tennis, as well as a gymnasium and fitness center, jogging track, bowling green, 10-pin bowling center, a pistol range, putting green, and three swimming pools.

Walking

Walking remains one of the least commercialized and most informal active recreations, often casual and unorganized in nature. Yet its popularity is evidenced by the huge number of guidebooks available, most of which are commercial publications, and the increasing number of travel firms offering package tours.

Fast and convenient forms of transportation have brought real adventure-type walking holidays to a growing number of people, so that a trek in the Himalayas is no longer reserved for Sir Edmund Hilary. Indeed the path to Everest has become so popular that as long ago as 1981 it required a special expedition to clean up the debris around the base camp (Tuting, cited in Ryan, 1991). Perhaps even closer to the ultimate example of sport tourism by walking was Ffyona Campbell's 11-year walk around the world, completed by her return to Scotland in 1994. She set out from John O'Groat's in 1983 to become the first woman to traverse the globe on foot, traveling through America, Australia, Africa, and Europe, at times without even a backup team in support.

Adventure Sports

Adventure sports is one of the fastest growing segments of the travel business (Weiler and Hall, 1992): witness the proliferation of commercial operators, brochures, advertisements, specialist magazines, equipment manufacturers, and suppliers throughout the world. Based in natural, often rugged, outdoor locations, these trips let participants interact with their environment in a variety of adventurous activities and single sports activities such as rock climbing, hiking, kayaking, hang gliding, mountain biking, and the like. When these trips are practiced under extreme conditions (e.g., Heli skiing, river rafting), they are considered to be adventure sports holidays. They indicate a "quest for excitement"; they provide an opportunity to produce pleasurable forms of tension and excitement, which provide an important contrast to the routines of daily life in (unexciting) modern societies. It is the element of (perceived) risk that differentiates the adventure sports and the single sport activity participants. It is not the actual sport necessarily that changes, it is the situation, the circumstances, and especially the environmental challenge. So, white-water rafting down low-grade rivers will be considered here as a single sport activity while white-water rafting down grade five rivers will be considered as adventure sports.

Hall (1992) advocates using the Speciality Travel Index, which "provides a comprehensive coverage of thousands of unusual travel opportunities worldwide" (p. 6), including many sports activities, such as hunting holidays, trekking with Sherpas, hang gliding, extreme skiing, big wave surfing, river rafting, and so forth. However, we should not try to define only new kinds of sport under the umbrella of adventure sport. For many decades youth organizations have arranged adventure holidays; many commercial providers nowadays offer this same "product" but with a different name. Adventure holidays are selling better even though they are often working with the same content.

Experienced leisure travelers constantly seek new levels of vacations, and organized travel adventures provide extraordinary experiences under safe auspices, offering European hunting holidays, trekking with Sherpas in Nepal, rafting a river, Nordic skiing in Alaska, and so forth.

British companies, such as Exodus and Explore Wordwide, that specialize in arranging active and unusual trips (walking tours, biking adventures, and overland expeditions), are good examples of adventure-oriented travel in more than 80 countries. By leading small groups the companies aim to cause as little environmental damage and cultural disturbance as possible. This is achieved mainly by utilizing local resources and services and by making itineraries individual enough to be a sustainable alternative to the juggernaut of mass tourism. Exodus grade their active holidays which might involve a gentle 10-day walk in Andalucia (Grade G), or a 19-day trek to Everest Base Camp (Grade C) (Exodus Walking Holidays 98/99).

Another example of adventure holidays are the short trips offered by Safari Drive Limited. The *Daily Mail* describes Safari Drive's adventure holiday "Adrenalin Pump" in Zimbabwe:

> Taking just five days off work, people visit Zimbabwe and experience a walking safari, canoeing down the Zambezi River and white water rafting below Victoria Falls . . . On the luxury front, the hotels at the beginning and at the end of the trip are four-star, while the overnight accommodation are tents. And as to the touring . . . the group chooses how tough the terrain will be and whether or not to take the easy option of the boatman doing the steering. (Watts, 1995, p. 7)

There are also hundreds of small adventure companies all over the world providing various nature sport activities in the neighborhood. These organizations offer "standard activities" such as kayaking, canoeing, float journeys, adventure journeys, mountaineering, trekking, speleology, and mountain biking. Besides these standard activities, special events can be organized based on the wishes of the customer (for example, balloon trips, funny carts, motorized events, helicopter droppings). Sometimes special programs (for example, Outsider Special Outward Bound Program) are offered to companies, combining sport activities with teamwork and teambuilding. Different mobile attractions such as a climbing wall, a mountain bike circuit, a speleo-box, a rope-walk, an archery installation, and a net labyrinth can be hired, providing schools and youth organizations the possibilities to arrange adventure holiday weeks.

Finally, the "in things" for the truly adventurous are bridge jumping and bungee jumping, innovated in 1987 by A.J. Hacket with his historic jump from the Eiffel Tower. Nowadays there are nine official bungee jumping operations spanning Australia, Europe, and America.

Of the adventure activities, clearly the most popular and one of the best ways to get out into the countryside is adventurous walking with all its variants such as backpacking, hiking, rambling, trekking, tramping, and snowshoeing.

Trekking

A well-known type of adventure travel is trekking—a type of travel that can entail anything from climbing mountains to rafting to snowmobiling. A classic form of trekking takes place in the Himalayas where thousands of trekkers gather on and around Mt. Everest to climb it during a trip lasting several weeks. New routes have recently been added, for example, in Uzbekistan or Tadjikistan—two of the newly independent republics of the former Soviet Union—and in the Amazon jungle and the Andes in South America (Madigan, 1995). Other popular treks are found in Portage Glacier Lake in Alaska, the Kalimantan and the jungle in Borneo, the Sinai in Egypt, the Dordogne in France, the Himachal Pradesh in India, the High Atlas in Morocco, the Abel Tasman and Kahurangi National Parks in New Zealand, the Stromboli and the Etna Volcano Hike in Sicily, the Bernese Oberland in Switzerland, the Wild Pamirs in Turkistan, and in the national parks of the United States. Trekkers also enjoy the long-distance walking paths (Grande Randonnées or GR) crossing Europe from north to south and from west to east.

Sport Tours

A little different interpretation of the sport activity holiday comes in the form of sporting tours, or the visits of amateur and professional teams to engage in sport competitions against foreign clubs. In the European context these "friendlies" often take place between teams from twinned towns and are the main attraction for many weekend tourist trips. For example, in the Netherlands, the provincial tourist board for Gelderland partly funds a private company that offers off-season holidays for sport teams from abroad. Visiting teams are provided with training facilities and the opportunity to take part in friendly matches with local teams (Glyptis, 1991).

Sometimes also the sports departments of local municipalities organize sports tournaments in another region or in another country, combining two offers, namely, sport and tourism. Also sport associations and private companies specialize in sport tours.

Case Study 3.2

The New York City Marathon
Sports Tours Creating Tourism

Description of Context

The New York City Marathon is a huge event that transforms the city into a sports-lover's paradise for one day. The 26-mile, 385-yard road race (or 42.195 kilometers) unites New York's five boroughs in the shared mission of urging on 28,000 friends and foreigners for every step of their journey from the Verrazano-Narrows Bridge over New York Harbor to the fabled finish in Sylvan Central Park.

Description of Development

The "running boom" was a mere whisper before race director Fred Lebow and his staff, volunteers, and sponsors celebrated the U.S. Bicentennial in 1976 with an event that perfectly encapsulated the striving, questing, adventuresome spirit of America along with all of its variety and bigness. The marathon became New York's most enticing advertisement for itself, and nobody who had ever laced up a running shoe wanted to be left out of the show. The prospect of covering 26.2 miles on foot in a single afternoon may seem impossibly daunting, but those granted an entry into the marathon don't take the privilege lightly. For many, it is the supreme goal of the year, and they arrive prepared, often with hundreds of hours of training behind them.

The 1994 race was the 25th celebration of the New York City Marathon. Before moving to the open streets of Staten Island, Brooklyn, Queens, the Bronx, and Manhattan in 1976, the race began in 1970 as four loops (and change) of the entire Central Park roadway. Back then, the entire marathon budget was US$1,000. Only 55 of the 127 starters were up to completing the 26.2-mile test that September day. The winner, a firefighter named Gary Muhreke, had signed up almost as an afterthought, but the distinction of being the New York City Marathon's inaugural champion subsequently made him a local "celebrity" within the New York running and marathon circles (New York Times, 1994).

Organization

Every year the organizing committee gets about 100,000 requests to start, of which only 28,000 are allowed by lottery. The New York City Marathon has become the marathon of choice for recreational runners, famous for its friendly crowds. However, New York is not the most popular marathon: Boston and Chicago are more popular ("New York, de toeristische marathon," 1994).

Many Europeans come to the race on four-to-seven-day package tours bought from travel agents who secure in advance the crucial official entry numbers, which are very difficult for people overseas to obtain any other way. The packages, which include air fare, lodging, bus transport around town, and in many cases a Broadway show and sight-seeing trips, are priced in the neighborhood of US$1,200 to $1,400.

Evaluation

The participants come to run, but they stay to shop, to go to museums, to eat bagels, to see shows, and to party. For about 11,700 foreigners who made up more than 40 percent of the runners in the 1994 New York City Marathon, the race was only one part of what amounted to a mini-Olympic festival and an adventure vacation. The French contingent (2,200 members) was the largest among foreign groups. At the start on the Verrazano-Narrows Bridge there were more French participants than at the start of the Reims Marathon (which after the Paris Marathon is the second most important marathon of France). Germans were the second-largest group with 1,660 entrants and the Netherlands third with 1,160. One Dutch group, sponsored by a radio station that provided the athletes with handsome black-and-red jogging suits, filled all the economy seats of a Boeing 747 ("The 1995 New York City Marathon," 1995). Although West Europeans dominated the foreign entrants, there were representatives from every state of the United States and from 105 countries; it wasn't too long ago that there weren't even that many nations on the globe.

The New York City Marathon is a good example of a single sport activity holiday: the main intention of the holiday is indeed to enjoy the experience of having participated in the New York City Marathon.

References

New York, de toeristische marathon [New York, the touristic marathon]. (1994, November 4). Het Nieuwsblad, p. 32.

New York City Marathon—the 25th running. (1994, November 7). The New York Times, p. D1.

The 1995 New York City Marathon. (1995, November 12). The New York Times, p. S13.

The most popular sport tours in Britain involve cricket, rugby, hockey, and golf. Tours from Britain to foreign clubs can be arranged:

> One example of a sports tour was that organized by the Indian ministry of external affairs which subsidised the Air India flights from Britain for a cricket team made up of journalists from London's Fleet Street, until recently the headquarters of the national press. (Evans, 1995, p. 17)

Michael Evans (1995) reports that

> The best way to see India is with a cricket bat in your handluggage. The sight of a bat places you on a different level from all the other tourists and back-packers who go to India for their holidays or for spiritual regeneration. For the Indians, cricket is a religion. Anyone who can flick a ball with a wrist or twirl a bat practises all year round in parks or on dusty sidestreets, trying to emulate their cricketing heroes. (p. 17)

Sport Festivals

Finally, the many sport festivals in which amateurs take part while on holiday have to be mentioned as single sport activity holidays. Good examples are the Czech Slet and the World Gymnastrada (an international recreative gymnastic event that occurs every two years).

The first national festival, or slet, in Bohemia was held in 1882, but this was three years after immigrants to the United States had held a slet in

New York. Ten slets were held in Czechoslovakia prior to 1941when they were dissolved by the Germans because of their strong nationalistic nature. Revived in 1948, the 11th slet involved 98,000 schoolchildren and 273,000 men and women who participated in mass exercise displays that lasted for two weeks. The festival took place in the huge Strahov Stadium in Prague, which has a field area of 300 by 200 meters and seats 250,000 spectators (Van Dalen and Bennett, 1971). Members used the 1948 slet to express their own nationalism, which displeased the new Communist premier of Czechoslovakia. The Sokol's slet was replaced by a Spartakiade, which was first held in 1955 and took place every five years until the end of the Communist regime (Sokol Rally in Prague, 1994). With their freedom the Czech people revived their cultural tradition and the 12th slet took place in Prague on 5 and 6 July 1994, involving 23,000 participants from around the world (Kluka, Jansa, and Rehor, 1997).

The Multiple Sport Activity Holiday

With the multiple sport activity holiday we deal with those holidays where the main intention of the holiday is to practice several sport activities. Sport camps, the more luxurious club formula, sport cures, and hotels with sport and exercise facilities can be identified here. In this book, adventure tourism is considered to be also a multiple sport activity holiday. In fact, some adventure tourism holidays involve several sports. Many others, on the other hand, are single sport activity holidays as described earlier.

Sport Camps

Multiple sport activity holidays vary from fitness training camps for everyone to multiple water sport holidays for the specialist. Municipalities, sport administrative bodies, and sport federations in several countries all over the world provide sporting opportunities (mainly for school children) during holiday periods. The Hapoel Sport Association in Israel organizes sport vacation camps in which workers and their families have a four-to-eight-day active holiday. The camps are located in the countryside and feature sport facilities and proficient guides. Special attention is given to suitable food for the active vacationer. As we discuss in the next section, the commercial sector has also capitalized on the development of sport camps—but camps created according to the club formula.

The Club Formula

One of the most well-known of the club-formula camps is Club Med, a 46-year-old concept that has grown into a US$1.3 billion empire with 98 villages in 40 countries on five continents. All Club Med villages are situated in beautiful locations and offer their visitors not only numerous activities organized by congenial hosts (Gentil Organisateurs or GO) but also a varied cuisine. This formula has proved to be one of the most successful offerings in international tourism (Redmond, 1991).

Case Study 3.3
Club Méditerranée
The Club Formula Using Sport to Attract Tourism

Description of Context

Club Med is one of the biggest tour operators in the world with a yearly number of clients of 1.6 million. These clients, or G.M.'s (i.e., Gentil Membre), stay in one of the 98 Club Med villages all over the world, either in a cabin, a luxurious bungalow, or a hotel, or are onboard one of the two luxury ships (Direction des Ressources Humaines Club Med, 1994).

The Club Med concept differs from what other tour operators offer. Club Med wants to give people a relaxing journey to a heavenly spot, far away from the life and stress of everyday. In these magical places, social differences disappear and people are supposed to feel totally free. They can choose from a broad offer of activities, drinks, and food, and everything is included in the price, apart from some extras for which one has to pay with beads. Also typical for Club Med are the G.O.'s, or Gentils Organisateurs. These animators (i.e., activity leaders) spend a lot of time with the clients, making sure they are comfortable and offering them almost any service they want.

Description of Development

In 1950, the Belgian Gérard Blitz started the small company Club Méditerranée in order to give people the chance to return to nature. The Club Med villages at that time were rather primitive and consisted of tents or cabins. During the following years more villages, as well as ski resorts, were built and the firm became a French limited liability company.

From 1963 on, the company has been led by Gilbert Trigano, a very enthusiastic Frenchman who has dedicated his life to Club Med. Under his skillful leadership, Club Med has opened villages all over the world, characterized by luxury and a broad offer of all kinds of social and recreational activities and sports activities. This diversity led the company in 1982 to split up its commercial and administrative functions into different geographic regions (Europe, Africa, America, and Asia/Indian and Atlantic Ocean) and two juridical structures (Club Med S.A. and Club Med Inc.) that operate completely autonomously.

Meanwhile, several other smaller companies operating on the tourist market were bought so the market share of Club Med increased. In order to satisfy the needs of different target groups, Club Med also further diversified its offer. Examples of these offers are the club hotels, the City Club, and the less expensive alternative "Club Aquarius." Recently, Club Med also started to organize expensive cruises on two luxurious ships, the *Club Med I* and *II*.

Organization

The operations within the different villages all over the world are lead by the "Chef de Village," or the director of the village. This person has some 120 G.O.'s and 300 other people of different nationalities under his supervision. Since the people at the bottom of the organization are in direct contact with the clients, it is very important that they are selected and trained in an adequate way.

As in many other firms, the main objective of Club Med is to gain as much profit as possible. Therefore, it has to try to sell as many journeys as possible and to satisfy its clients so that they come back for another trip or promote the Club Med offer among friends and family.

In order to realize this, Club Med tries to improve the quality of the services it offers by training the G.O.'s as well as their supervisors, the Chefs de Villages. Moreover, marketing studies were done in order to trace the specific needs of the target groups from the different countries. Based on this market information, standardized programs were developed for every village.

Although anyone can book a Club Med holiday, most of the clients are younger single people looking for adventure and fun. However, families with children are also welcome since Club Med organizes specific activities in so-called Mini Clubs for children of different ages. During the next few years, Club Med also wants to focus on developing a specific offer for the growing number of active, older people who have a lot of time and money.

Now that Club Med has become one of the biggest companies on the club holiday market, it is interested in extending into air travel. It has bought the travel rights of Minerve and Air Liberté, which together have the same capacity and power as Air France.

Another plan of Club Med is to build another 40 villages all over the world as well as Aquarius villages.

A new formula that will be fully developed within 20 years is the system of the memory card. The client chooses at home what kind of journey he wants (sun or snow for instance) and the organization decides upon a holiday destination for the client. A big advantage of this system is that one does not have to take any luggage because everything is available at the village.

The yearly return of Club Med amounts to US$600 million, with an annual profit of US$30 million.

Evaluation

The story of Club Med is one of success and increasing profits. At this moment, annually 1.6 million clients use Club Med for their holidays. This figure is still increasing: 7 percent of the clients are from France, 10 percent from Italy, and 25 percent from Japan. It is a typical example of what we have described as multiple sport activity holidays. We have chosen to highlight Club Med because it is the most successful organization in this sector and because it has set the trend for other companies (for example, Centre Parcs and Club Robinson).

References

Direction des Ressources Humaines Club Med. (1994). *Club Med.* Paris, France: Club Med.

Originally designed to appeal to young singles who wanted an activity-based opportunity to meet and interact with others, Club Med has evolved toward attracting families who want sport facilities in desirable holiday locations together with high-quality accommodations. Club Med's success in attracting visitors in large numbers has led others such as Club Aldiana, Club Escolette, Club Mark Warner, Club Valtur, Sunsail Clubs, and Club Robinson to emulate the formula. Club La Santa in the Canary Islands markets itself as "The World's No. 1 Sports Resort," offering what it describes as world-class facilities for over 20 sports including handball, volleyball, and tennis as well as a stadium with facilities for all Olympic track-and-field events except hammer throwing.

These upmarket clubs catering mainly to adults are a sophisticated version of the sport-based summer camps for children that have been popular in the United States for decades. Now not only young people but everyone can improve their sporting skills during their vacation.

During the past few years this club formula has experienced a revival in western Europe. Club holidays with sport opportunities in a so-called year-round, weather-independent club (for example, Center Parcs, Gran Dorado, Sun Clubs) have been created all over Europe.

Established in 1967 in Holland, Sporthuis Centrum created a new type of second or third holiday for higher income customers who wanted an active, short stay. Its main emphasis has been on the provision of very comfortable, well-designed accommodations in villas set in wooded, rural areas with the provision of an extensive range of active leisure facilities based around the centerpiece of a subtropical, indoor, free-form swimming pool.

Center Parcs opened its first club in 1967and now manages 12 clubs in four different countries with a level of occupation of more than 95 percent all year around. Clerbout (1990) explains this success in terms of

1. Changes in holiday habits due to (a) the economic crisis, in consequence of which holidaymakers choose destinations that are not so far from home; they still want to go on holiday but for shorter periods and are more conscious of prices and values, (b) a trend toward shorter breaks taken more often, (c) an increase in demand for more active holidays and animation, (d) a greater need for freedom, and (e) special arrangements for specific target groups.

2. An emphasis on family life that requires (a) different types of accommodations (for from 1 up to 12 people), (b) child-friendliness (baby-sitting, special animation for children—all infrastructure is child-friendly), and (c) special arrangements for families.

3. The recreational infrastructure, for example, (a) weather-independent, subtropical swimming pools, (b) beautiful facilities in quiet surroundings, (c) a multitude of sport and recreational facilities.

4. Professional management.

5. Specific sport courses.

6. The integration of business (for example, meetings, seminars) and holidays.

Sport Cures and Fitness Clinics

The sport cure is another form of multiple sport activity holiday that should not be forgotten. It is useful for people who are ill or convalescing (an example is Bad Salzuflen, Germany). More recently, the fitness clinic has become popular for healthy people who want to increase their vitality and tone up their bodies. A fitness clinic features daily physical training according to a special plan drawn up for each person on the basis of a medical examination (Larner, 1992). Generally this form of sport cure proves to be very expensive and, therefore, is an activity for the wealthy rather than the ordinary person.

A good example is the Lenkerhof resorts in Germany, which comprise a spa center and the Lenkerhof Spa Hotel. They offer sport facilities and activities during all seasons: outdoor and indoor swimming pools, sauna, mountain bike, cross-country and downhill skiing, tour skiing, walking, tennis, paragliding, curling, ice skating, river rafting, and so forth.

Hotel Holidays

Hotels are also developing programs on the multisport activity holiday market. The world's major hotel chains, such as Hilton, Forte, and the like, now feature specially styled breaks. Hilton, for example, offers "Action Breaks," which they describe as action packed weekends for anyone who loves a challenge. Their Action Extra breaks in Britain include ballooning, hang gliding, tandem skydiving, golf, trout fishing, rally driving, falconry, and much more. Although hotels with sport and fitness facilities and special programs are not a particularly new phenomenon, their current expansion is unparalleled.

Holiday Sport Activities

The category of holiday sport activities is used when sport occupies a minor but still significantly important part of the leisure activities during a holiday.

Two kinds of holiday sport activities can be identified: (1) the incidental participation in organized sport provided during holidays and (2) participation in private or independent sport activity on holiday.

Organized Holiday Sport Activities

Organized holidays that have a sport ingredient mixed with other activities range from impromptu games of volleyball on the beach to the kinds of holiday where an organized day on horseback is followed by a day on the beach or in town. In 1963 the way was paved by Marcel Meier from the Magglingen Physical Training College in the Swiss tourist resort of Engelberg. Sport activities during holiday periods, such as gymnastics, swimming, games, fitness exercises, folk dancing, gymnastics using apparatus, and walks in the forest, were provided under the guidance of coaches. Other examples in this category include the "Team Holiday" (that is, exercise teams with potential for individual decision and organization) held in Ruhpolding, Germany, since 1965, the venture known as "Dolce-far-Sport" operated in Lezerheide-Valbella, Switzerland, since 1969, and since 1970 the venture "Job Join In, Keep Fit" and the "Pro-fit-Sport-Holiday" in Switzerland (Sprecher, 1971). In some parts of Austria game festivals (i.e., Spielfest) are held during holidays.

South African Tourism Board

Golf is an increasingly popular holiday activity that South Africa now offers at Lost City and many other challenging courses.

Today in Belgium the tourist communities (for instance, at the seaside) are competing to provide the best "sport for all" program for their visitors on holiday. People take part on a come-and-go-as-you-please basis, free of charge, or for a reduced price in a sport activity, for example, beach recreation or even catamaran sailing.

Some praiseworthy initiatives were started in the 1980s by municipalities with an interest in promoting tourism:

1. The Flemish biking route was established. This is a 641-kilometer, signposted loop through the five Flemish provinces of Belgium. People can start or end wherever they want. They may also pass the night in hiking huts, at camp sites, and even at hotels.

2. Sport- and game-lending services were installed at seaside resorts.

3. Physical fitness activities guided by "sport for all" leaders were started on the beach (for example, aerobics and gymnastics).

4. Sport governmental bodies initiated sports, for example, BLOSO's (Commissariaat-Generaal voor de Bevordering var de Lichamelijke Ontwikkeling, de Sport en de Openluchtrecreatie) program "With BLOSO in the Breakers" (for example, sea swimming, sailing, and windsurfing).

5. In cooperation with BLOSO, local tourist information services, and local sport councils, a number of "Volkssportroutes" (routes with traditional folk games and sports) were installed. The objective of this initiative was to promote local tourism and the wealth of these traditional Flemish sports and games on a larger scale. Thirteen different "Volkssportroutes" were developed in different Flemish regions. Each of these routes can be followed by bike or by car and consists of a number of traditional sports, situated in the neighborhood of local pubs. The description of the games, the route, and some local places of interest can be obtained at the local tourist information services.

Now almost every tourist resort in many countries has elaborated such recreational programs to attract tourists, providing cycling tours, folk games routes, open-door activities in holiday resorts, opportunities to rent a bicycle at train stations, specific sport promotional campaigns, walking, sport courses for people staying at home, and, in cooperation with sport federations and clubs, special offers for tourists, and so forth.

Handbooks and leaflets containing practical instructions are distributed to holidaymakers. In some countries a series of television programs have been used to promote participation in sport during holidays. Games and sport facilities have been established (for example, cycling paths and swimming pools). Specific storage facilities have been provided for surfboards and mountain bikes, and now even special beach patrols have been trained for controlling surfers as in Australia and the United States.

Several communities, regions, provinces, and so forth in countries all over the world have set up touristic bicycling routes. Cycles can be hired at a fair price from many Austrian, Belgian, and French railway stations and returned to any manned station. In Copenhagen the city has launched a "free" bike scheme. Bikes are placed in lockers around the city center. A coin releases them. The bike can be left in any other locker and you get your coin back.

Another product on the holiday sport activity market is the cruise vacation: once notorious for the high life and relaxation of the wealthy, the cruise vacation also has entered the activity market. Different cruise lines now offer a full array of sports and activities including snorkeling, scuba diving, aerobics, and jogging.

Cruise liners, like clubs, now compete to have the ultimate features. The *Queen Elizabeth II* offers a computerized golf course and putting range on deck together with a resident professional; and it advertises "free access to the Golden Door Spa at sea." P&O's luxury liner, the *Oriana*, launched in 1995, claims in its Crystal Pool to have "the largest pool on the high seas . . . Large enough for serious lap swimming" (Peninsilar and Oriental Steam Navigation, 1994, p. 6), and as if one large pool is not enough it has two other pools besides.

The fabled Royal Caribbean Cruise liners are promoted as " Spas at sea." They offer not simply the latest exercise equipment with workout classes professionally designed "for every fitness level" but "a full program of sports events from ping-pong to a triathlon" and a Golf Ahoy! program that enables avid golfers to tee off at some of the best courses in the Caribbean.

Cruise liners in the ports of popular diving resorts such as the Bahamas offer their passengers an introduction to the sport of snorkeling. Participants are loaned equipment and given an instructional lecture prior to a guided lesson in shallow water. As snorkelers gain their confidence they are formed into groups to engage in short tours to deeper water, to view local wrecks, and to feed the tropical fish. This represents a very different level of participation from the diving holidays offered in the Comores—a scattering of tiny Indian Ocean islands—where fully certified (PADI) diving courses are offered as pure sport holidays.

In 1981 the German city of Kiel's form of sport for holidays was the extensive Kiel holiday pass, a proposition put forward by the Institute for Sport and Sport Science of the University of Kiel. This leisure-time sports promotion, held in the large university sports forum, comprised almost 30 different sport activities and was held during the summer holidays. The two thousand children and parents who took part daily were professionally coached by three full time university lecturers and 40 student leaders. Financial support came from the town of Kiel and the university. The most popular sport activities were swimming, trampoline, and table tennis (De Knop, 1989).

Independent Holiday Sport Activities

Participating in sport activities during holidays is not new, yet it can still be a novelty. Almost any type of sport activity can be done independently on holiday, so here we discuss several that might not be as familiar internationally.

Ever since people have gone on holiday to the seaside or to the mountains, they have swum or gone for a walk. Holidaymakers at camping sites have played "jeu de boules." At the beach the sport holidaymakers played volleyball on a pitch marked in the sand with the big toe.

First Choice Holidays' *1995 Lakes and Mountains* brochure included an activities panel for each of its 35 resorts in Europe and North America that provided information to help holidaymakers obtain fishing permits, hire a bicycle, know where to swim, sail, or play tennis as well as find suitable space to pursue the more traditional activity of walking.

During the 1994 Tour de France, the French National Geographic Institute (IGN) distributed 200,000 free maps of France showing the Tour's circuit. This is only one of the initiatives employing maps specifically related to sport. The IGN nowadays offers a catalogue consisting of sport touristic maps: hiking maps, canoe-kayak maps, cyclist maps, mountain bike maps, and wall-climbing maps. Besides the description of the "routes," they also provide touristic and cultural information as well as useful tips (such as where to rent a bike and precautions to take). Shell France, the multinational oil company, is providing maps to its clients describing hiking routes, mountain-biking routes, and canoe-kayak rivers.

Fit for Fun has made a map of "Active Germany" that gives an overview of summer sports facilities in one hundred locations all over Germany. It is focused on outdoor sports on land, in and upon the water, and in the air.

Sometimes specific infrastructure is used for holiday activities. Waterparks are a good example. Waterparks are no longer confined to America. In central Bangkok, where building space is limited, Paradise Garden combines luxury pools, cascades, and other typical features that have been built on the rooftop of a department store one hundred feet above street level. In China there is a waterpark in almost every large city, and Latin America, despite poor economic conditions, claims to operate more waterparks outside the United States than any other area. Essentially focused on family entertainment, these parks provide water-based fun experiences that closely resemble beach and sea activities.

Justifying them as tourism developments—at a time when outbound visits to the sunnier coasts of Spain showed a rapid increase—the English Tourist Board provided grants toward the construction of numerous leisure swimming pools in resort locations throughout the country. In the Netherlands, downtown Rotterdam boasts the only nonresidential Centre Parcs operation in its Tropicana, a massive leisure pool built on the banks of the River Maas to encourage tourism in the city center (see the case study on page 144).

The Netherlands is a watery land. There is enough space for all kinds of water sports. Recreation areas, surf beaches, landing stages, and other recreational facilities open to the public are found on the shores of the lakes. Near these water areas, sportsmen and sportswomen find a lot of camping sites and hotels.

Case Study 3.4

Queenstown: The Adventure Capital of New Zealand
Independent Sport on Holiday

Description of Context

Queenstown is situated 283 kilometers from Dunedin and 187 kilometers from Invercargill on the shores of Lake Wakatipu in the Southern Alps of New Zealand's South Island. With its associated districts of Arrowtown and Wakatipu, Queenstown now has a permanent population of approximately 10,500 (Queenstown Promotion Board, 1995a) and can accommodate approximately 15,000 visitors. In round terms it currently hosts 400,000 international and 200,000 domestic visitors a year. The average length of stay is between 2.5 and 3 nights. Altogether, the district supports 1.3 million person nights per year with average occupancy levels, year round, in all types of accommodation, an enviable 75 percent. The town likes to describe itself as "The Adventure Capital of New Zealand—and the World." The location and scenery draw holidaymakers from all over the world to this magnificent area.

Description of Development

The district was first settled in 1860 as a gold mining center (Barriball, 1994). At a public meeting in 1863 the small settlement on the shores of Lake Wakatipu was said to be fit for a queen, a claim that gave the town its name—reflective, perhaps, of an aspiration to host a visit from Queen Victoria, the reigning monarch of colonial New Zealand. The Remarkables range, rising to a height of 2,343 meters, is the highest of the three ski areas surrounding the town that helped to make it famous as a holiday destination. Aside from domestic tourists, the town's main visitors come from Australia, Japan, North America, and the United Kingdom. Over 70 percent of the Japanese visitors in the winter of 1995 came to ski, 67 percent of the Australian visitors, 30 percent of the American tourists, and almost half of all other overseas visitors, demonstrating the district's international reputation as a modern ski destination (Advanced Business Research Ltd., 1995) though the slopes have been used by local skiers since the early days of this century.

The magnificence of the surrounding landscape (mountains, lakes, rivers, forests, and farmlands in close proximity to each other) and the variety of natural amenities have led to the development of an outstanding range of outdoor adventure activities offered by mainly thriving commercial businesses. What other town of 10,000 inhabitants boasts that it has 15 jet-boating companies, five tandem parapenting operators, five white-water rafting businesses, three heli-ski companies, three 18-hole golf courses, accessibility to five 2-to-5-day walking tracks, and the world's highest, as well as its first, commercial bungee

Plunge a thrilling 143 feet at the Kawaru in New Zealand—the world's first commercial Bungee Bridge.

jump (from a helicopter at a minimum of one thousand feet high)? Altogether, 14 sensational adventure activities are on offer including skydiving, river surfing and sledging, kayaking, jet skiing, and hang gliding. Sixteen recreations and sports from fishing to bowls, swimming, sailing, tennis, squash, and trail biking, as well as horse treks, ice skating, windsurfing and paraflying can all be pursued in and around Queenstown. No less than 75 commercial companies are listed in the directory *New Zealand Outside* (Hobbs, 1996), based in and immediately around Queenstown and 68 percent of its 65 major annual events are sport oriented.

Though this massive development of sports-oriented tourism is not one the local district council has gone out of its way to cause, it "plays on it," but with a strong recognition of the priority that it has to give to the local environment's sustainability. The Queenstown Lakes District Council states, "The challenge for the Council is to chart a course of growth and prosperity while maintaining a satisfactory environment" (1995, p. 4). With a resident population growing six times faster than the New Zealand average, and expected to more than double, and the number of visitor nights forecast to more than double in the next 20 years, the major challenge the council identifies is to "continue to offer a quality product . . . without damaging the environment or the community" (Queenstown Lakes District Council, 1995, p. 29).

Organization

In its 10-year vision statement, the Queenstown Lakes District Council declares that its program is designed to make the Queenstown district "the best alpine destination in the South Pacific" (Queenstown Lakes District Council, 1995, p. 13). Not that it necessarily means to attract more visitors than anywhere else— rather, "it means that this district will be the quality destination of choice" (Queenstown Lakes District Council, 1995, p. 13). Although preservation of the environment is the most critical general objective, this does not mean that tourism growth cannot occur. Indeed, it is recognized that tourism supports almost all of the jobs and services presently available and that it will provide jobs and wealth "for the whole community in the foreseeable future" (Queenstown Lakes District Council, 1995, p. 3).

Evaluation

Attracting increasing numbers of residents, visitors, and businesses suggests that Queenstown is desirable to live and work in, as well as a holiday destination. The visitor survey by Advanced Business Research Ltd. (1995) showed that on a scale of 1 (very satisfied) to 5 (very dissatisfied), mean scores ranged from American visitors at 1.3 to the Japanese at 1.8. At least some of both the foreign and domestic tourists were on a repeat visit to Queenstown (80 percent of New Zealanders had been before; just over one-third of the Australians; 15 percent of the Japanese; 12 percent of the Americans; and 16 percent of all other groups). Eighty-three percent of the Japanese and 93 percent of the Americans said they would recommend Queenstown.

According to the Visitor Survey, visitors crossed the spectrum of age groups though the Japanese were predominantly young (86 percent were under 30 years of age). The attraction of the town to younger people (especially in winter) was confirmed by other national groups (45 percent of the domestic visitors were under 30, 43 percent of Australians, and 57 percent of other national groups)—indeed all except the Americans where only 17 percent were under 30 and a high 44 percent were 55 or over. This predominance of older or younger visitors was reflected in the activities undertaken or intended to be undertaken. The Japanese were the most active in sports and adventure, and the Americans markedly less so.

Queensland provides a good example of what we have identified as active sport on holiday where people participate independently in organized holiday sport activities.

References

Advanced Business Research Ltd. (1995). *Queenstown—July—September 1995.* Queenstown, New Zealand: Author.

Burton, R. (1995). *Travel geography.* London: Pitman.

Dykes, M. (1994). *New Zealand's South Island.* Auckland, New Zealand: Reed.

Hobbs, M. (1996). *New Zealand outside: Annual and directory.* Christchurch, New Zealand: Southern Alps Publications Ltd.

Queenstown Lakes District Council. (1995). *Queenstown Lakes district strategic plan: Shaping our future. Final draft.* Queenstown, New Zealand: Author.

Queenstown Promotion Board. (1995a). *Queenstown fact sheet.* Queenstown, New Zealand: Author.

Queenstown Promotion Board. (1995b, July). X-Press. *Newsletter from Queenstown,* p. 2.

Passive Sports on Holidays

This category encompasses the people who devote more or less time during holidays to passive sports. Two types of involvement can be identified, namely, (1) connoisseur observers who have extensive involvement in the sport activity they watch as spectators or officials, and (2) casual observers who simply enjoy watching an event and who usually happen across it rather than plan their visit to attend it.

Connoisseur Observer

Of great importance for connoisseur observers are the megasport events. These events have been around for centuries. All megasport happenings have certain commonalities: they are loaded with tradition, have profound historical significance, have developed a certain mystique, and in some cases have taken on mythical qualities (Rooney, 1988). These mega-events have in recent years been hyped and promoted in the media.

Major sporting events such as world championships and multisport festivals attract huge numbers of visitors, players, officials, spectators, and media, and towns and cities throughout the world seek to host them to boost their tourist attraction. Individual or group travel to sports events of national or international significance are thus a good opportunity for travel organizations to book flights and hotel accommodations (for example, French, Spanish, and Dutch interest in Wimbledon; Swedish interest in soccer at Wembley; and worldwide interest in the Olympic Games).

The Olympic Games are but the tip of the iceberg. They have spawned many similar festivals that also regularly attract thousands of visitors. Several kinds of imitations exist, based on

- geographical regions, (e.g., Asian Games, African Games, Pan-American Games),
- physical disabilities (e.g., Special Olympics),
- religious affiliation (e.g., Maccabiah Games),
- career or profession (e.g., World Student Games, Law Enforcement Olympics),
- political affiliation (e.g., Commonwealth Games), and
- sexual orientation (e.g., Gay Games). (Preston, 1990)

Three types of megasport events can be distinguished on the basis of geographical or spatial criteria, or both, namely,

- events which occur periodically at different places over both regular (e.g., the Olympics, World Cup Soccer) and irregular time spans (e.g., the British and U.S. Golf Opens),
- events with a long-term attachment to a specific place (e.g., Wimbledon tennis), and
- sports franchises with a general spatial stability (e.g., the Asian Games). (Rooney, 1988)

World Cup Football (Soccer) and the Olympic Games

World Cup Football (soccer) and the Olympic Games vie to obtain the largest number of spectators for a "single" sporting event, though of course neither actually is a single event! For the 1994 World Cup, 490 elimination games were held, each attracting thousands of spectators, before the 24 final-phase games were played in the United States. The sheer cost of tickets for such events virtually ensures that those who attend can rightly be classified as connoisseurs of the sport they watch. The 1992 Summer Olympic Games in Barcelona attracted 420,000 spectators, many of whom traveled hundreds of thousands of miles at considerable cost to witness a particular event (*Olympische Spelen te Brussel?*, 1994).

The Masters

In golf, the Masters evolved slowly at first, then became established as a mega-event after World War II. A great name, a great facility, the best players, excitement, and extremely astute management and promotion have made the Masters. The ticket situation nowadays is impossible. The waiting list was stopped when it reached five thousand in 1978, because those at the end would have a 50-year wait for the prestigious badges.

As the tournament grew in prestige so did its economic and social impact. Georgia (United States) is a relatively small place with limited lodging facilities. Thus the relative impact on the local economy is substantial—in the vicinity of U.S.$25 to U.S.$30 million for the tournament week. Hotels triple their workforce, and room rates double. During Masters week, hotels make as much money as they would in a normal six-week period. Hertz triples its fleet by bringing in cars from all over the Southeast. The Green Jacket restaurant on Washington Road directly across from the main entrance to the Augusta National Golf Club grosses U.S.$200,000 during the week, about 300 percent more than its normal revenue. Other restaurants experience similar booms. Homeowners in Augusta, Georgia, move out, renting their dwellings for U.S.$1,500 or more for the week (Getz, 1991).

The Kentucky Derby

The Kentucky Derby's first race was held in 1875, and, although beginning like the Masters in a modest fashion, developed by the end of World War I into a stable and profitable event. The Kentucky Derby has gradually evolved from a one-day to a ten-day event. The Kentucky Derby Festival is a commercial spin-off of the race itself. It includes a parade, marathon, balloon race, auto event, and jazz festival. Approximately 750,000 people attend these and other festival activities, helping to promote business throughout the Louisville area. A study concluded that the festival had an economic impact of nearly U.S.$18 million annually (Kentucky Derby Festival, 1985).

Pre-Wimbledon Ladies Warm-Up

Even comparatively small towns can host international level sports events and thereby elevate their tourism earnings if they have the necessary facilities. Eastbourne, a resort community of some 80,000 in southeast England annually hosts the pre-Wimbledon ladies warm-up tournament the week before the prime event on the world's tennis calendar. Attracting an audience of over 30,000 spectators, including 2 percent from abroad, the tournament generates over 70,000 visitor nights and U.K.£2.2 million (U.S.$3.3 million) in revenue for the town. Three out of four spectators attend regularly, in this way demonstrating their level of commitment and loyalty as connoisseurs of the game.

Using Facilities to Attract Major Events

The enormous economic and regenerative potential of these megasport events has induced cities throughout the world to provide sporting facilities to host major events and attract both connoisseur and casual observers. Indianapolis, Indiana (United States), was famous initially for its "500 motor race," said to be the largest one-day sporting event in the world attracting upwards of 450,000 spectators. In 1984, the city of Indianapolis built the U.S.$77.5 million 65,000-seat Hoosier Dome (now called the RCA Dome) to bring new activities and more visitors to the city (Law, 1993).

The RCA Dome, which succeeded in attracting the Colts (American) football team, previously based in Baltimore, is also used for other sports, and in 1991 it hosted the World Gymnastic Championships. Two-thirds of the spectators came from outside the state as did most of the competitors, officials, and press personnel, spending U.S.$37.2 million during the event (Law, 1993).

Other cities have similarly used sport as a catalyst to attract visitors. The Sky Dome, famous for its retractable roof, opened in Toronto in 1989 and was projected to attract more than five million spectators plus several million visitors and tourists in its first season (Huntley, 1989). And in New Orleans the Louisiana Superdome, despite a loss on its current account (Nebel, 1986 cited in Collins, 1991), has provided the necessary momentum for the development of the city's downtown area as a tourist center (Bale, 1989). These enormous projects have been justified as tourist attractions and have an obvious economic and touristic perspective by providing new or enhanced sport facilities for the local community.

Smaller Events

Doubtless the increased media attention created by international sporting events has induced travel and increased the number of visitors to more distant places. The last Grand Prix from Adelaide in South Australia was transmitted directly to around 750 million viewers in 75 countries and attracted around 32,000 interstate and international visitors (Collins, 1991). Burns, Hatch, and Mules' (1986) appraisal shows that the city's confidence in hosting the event achieved economic as well as social benefits. A follow-up survey of those who paid for corporate boxes at the track confirmed that the race had contributed to Adelaide being seen as a place worth visiting as well, perhaps, as a place in which to invest.

Sport tourism is not confined to exotic or remote regions, nor limited to highly prestigious events. National, premier, and even local teams have their avid supporters who in any one season travel frequently to watch their team or idol play.

It does not always have to be a big event or a well-known team to attract foreign supporters. Consider, for example, the one hundred Norwegians who have formed a supporters club for a small Scottish soccer team, Stenhouse Muir. This town team has never won a major trophy. Yet representatives from the Norwegian Supporters Club make regular visits to Scotland to watch their team play.

Sports Museums and Halls of Fame

Sports museums and halls of fame provide a different example of passive sport tourism likely to attract the connoisseur. Nowadays, in many countries several sport museums can be found. They can be located in the capital of the country or simply in the trophy rooms of famous sport associations or sport clubs. The outstanding example is the United States of America where hundreds of sport halls of fame can be found. Although sport has no monopoly of this American obsession, it dominates it. Another significant point is that many of the general or "nonsport" halls of fame (for example, agriculture, art, business, drama, literature, music, politics, and technology) actually do include sporting displays within their precincts.

Case Study 3.5

The Olympic Museum in Lausanne

A Sports Museum Providing Connoisseur Observers an Opportunity for Passive Sport on Holiday

---

Description of Context

The Olympic Museum is probably the best-known sport museum in the world. It is built on the shores of Lake Geneva, close to the place where for a time Pierre de Coubertin even dreamed of building a modern Olympia. In his opinion, the true secret of Greek beauty lay in a virtually perfect and indisputable harmony between landscape and architecture, and between architecture and man. Today we would probably say it has a respect for proportions and the environment. It was with this spirit in mind that the architects—Pedro Ramirez Vazquez of Mexico and Jean-Pierre Cahen of Lausanne—did everything in their power to ensure that the museum was harmoniously integrated within the landscape.

The aim of the museologists was to make visitors aware of the breadth and the importance of the Olympic movement—to show them, by means of images and symbols, that this is not purely a matter of sports competitions but rather a philosophy of life whose roots are deeply embedded in our history.

The museologists also wanted visitors to rediscover the emotions experienced during the Olympic Games, to relive the beauty of effort and physical movement, the strength of will and the joy of victory, and the pleasures of celebration and ceremony.

Description of Development

The Olympic Museum was inaugurated on the 23rd of June, 1993. Two years later 368,828 people had visited it. In 1995 it received the European Museum of the Year Award. The construction of the museum began on 9 December 1988. It required 11,000 cubic meters of concrete building material and approximately 250,000 hours of work. It employed 450 people and more than 70 companies.

Organization

The museum is more than just a space for exhibitions: it is a cultural center for concerts, Olympic Weeks, conferences, exchanges, and picture contests. It consists of (a) exhibition rooms, (b) a study center and library, (c) a video shop, (d) education rooms, (e) a congress room for 180 people, and (f) five meeting rooms.

One gallery retraces the history of the Olympic movement. It brings back to life the ancient games at their zenith during the fifth century B.C. It evokes the life and the ideas of Pierre de Coubertin by integrating them within the course of events of the last century.

The first floor is basically devoted to a presentation of the Olympic Games of the modern era, from their beginnings in 1896 to our day, and to the practice of Olympic disciplines. Giant video screens make it possible to share the decisive moments in the life of a champion, during training, victory, or defeat.

An exhibition room is reserved for philately and numismatics. It presents over 12,000 stamps—the Olympic collection itself (stamps and postmarks) and President Samaranch's famous stamp collection, which he has donated to the museum. The museum exhibits several interesting examples of Pierre de Coubertin's writings (books, brochures, and articles) in the rooms reserved for philately. The museum presents the complete collection of almost six hundred Olympic coins minted by the host cities of the Olympic Games.

Audiovisual systems play a special role at the Olympic Museum. It is a veritable kingdom of video and interaction with computers and screens of all kinds. Interactive terminals allow the visitor to travel at will through the Olympiads and through time, choosing whatever is of particular interest to him or her. A simulation room is already being studied where visitors have an opportunity to appreciate the athletes' exploits by measuring their own performances against those of the champions.

Since Stockholm paved the way in 1912, the host cities of the Olympic Games have, on each occasion, commissioned artists to promote them by means of posters. Even if several are created, only one is considered to be the official poster. The museum possesses the complete collection of these.

The Olympic Museum has the largest and most complete data bank in the world on the Games and Olympic memorabilia. The library holds more than 15,000 volumes on the Olympic movement, the International Olympic Committee, the Games and Olympic disciplines, the practice of sport in general, and its evolution as a phenomenon of society.

The photographic department contains some 250,000 illustrations in both black and white and color, of which approximately 100,000 concern the Olympic Games. The audiovisual and multimedia department, including a film library, possesses archives with a total of seven thousand hours of projection time. The archives and documentation department preserves the archives of the Olympic movement (documents, correspondence, and files).

Evaluation

A visit to the Olympic Museum is a good example of passive sport on holiday where the connoisseur observer planned a visit to the museum to enjoy the history of the Olympics. In figures, the global impact of visitors to the Olympic Museum is valued at SFr. 100 million (about U.S.$67 million) for the Lausanne region. Average daily expenses per visitor are about SFr. 44 (about U.S.$30) for an average stay of four days. The largest part of the money spent comes from outside the region of Lausanne. Only 4 percent of visitors live in Lausanne, while 43 percent come from the rest of Switzerland, and the remaining 53 percent come from abroad (Olympic Magazine Redaction, 1996).

References

Dumond, F. (1994). *Discovering the Olympic Museum—Visitor's guide.* Lausanne, Switzerland: International Olympic Committee.

Olympic Magazine Redaction. (1996, November). Economic impact of the IOC and the Olympic Museum. *Olympic Magazine, 11,* p. 43.

The International Association of Sports Museums and Halls of Fame (IASMHF), founded in 1971, already advertised in the early 1980s a tour of 32 facilities, from California to Newfoundland (Redmond, 1981). Similar tours could be arranged covering sports museums in Europe, Australia and New Zealand, Brazil, and Japan. The foundation of an international committee of sport museums within the International Council of Museums (ICOM) was on the 1997 agenda in Lausanne.

Casual Observers

Connoisseur observers were defined as those who have extensive passive involvement in the sports activity they watch as spectators. The overriding objective of the holiday is the sport event. Casual observers simply enjoy watching an event and happen across it while on holiday rather than plan their visit to include it. So, the difference between them is not what they are observing but more in what they see, their level of interest, involvement, and knowledge of the sport.

People on holiday sometimes attend specific or traditional sports of the country they visit (for example, American football and baseball in the

United States, hurling in Ireland, bull fighting in Spain, or cricket in India) and thus become casual observers of sport while on holiday. Let us provide an example: Kerala is a small state situated in the southwest corner of the Indian triangle. It is a land of rivers and backwaters. Among its water sports, the Snake Boat Race is very popular and attracts many tourists to the southern state. Another boat race, the Nehru Trophy Boat Race, attracts hundreds of casual observers a year.

Some cities, for example, Vienna, provide the possibility to include a visit to a sports event in their city trip package. A more recent trend is the visit to newly constructed sport facilities or to sport heritage sites dedicated to significant sporting events, for example, the Olympic Stadium in Barcelona.

Active Sports During Nonholiday Time

Active sports tourism during nonholiday time involves travel away from home and work locality for noncommercial or business/commercial reasons, during which one participates actively in sports activities.

Involvement in this category ranges from professional coaches, officials, and players on tour—the West Indies cricket team in India or the Ryder Cup golf players—to the business executive who fits in a game of tennis at the end of an intense strategy meeting. The significant level of travel generated or resulting from participation in elite-level athletics was highlighted by Jackson and Reeves (1998).

Table 3.1 Evidence of the Sport-Tourism Relationship*

Sport commitment	Senior athlete	Intermediate athlete	Junior athlete	Average
Training in UK	38	31	12	
Competition in UK	24	20	40	
Total in UK	62	51	52	55
Training abroad	4	28	14	
Competition abroad	34	2	10	
Total abroad	38	30	24	30
Total commitment	100	81	76	

*The results are from the case studies of three elite British athletes. The data are in days spent in the activity.

Adapted, by permission, from G. Jackson and M. Reeves, 1998, Evidencing the sports-tourism interrelationship: A case study of elite British athletes. In *Leisure management issues and applications*, edited by M.F. Collins and I.S. Cooper (Wallingford, Great Britain: CAB International).

Whilst the level of travel for competition on a domestic and international basis was expected, the volume of travel for week-to-week training and additional travel for warm-weather training purposes exceeded expectations. (p. 268)

Case Study 3.6

The World Medical Tennis Society Conference and Tennis Tournament
A Business Society Including Sport in Its Conference Program

Description of Context

The World Medical Tennis Society Conference and Tennis Tournament is held annually in a different country each year. The conference was held in Eastbourne (UK) in 1993 and timed to coincide with the first week of the All England Lawn Tennis Championships at Wimbledon; the whole event was spread over eight nights.

Description of Development

The World Medical Tennis Society started 25 years ago when American and French doctors met in Monte Carlo; the society now numbers 50 member countries. Its founder and Honorary Life President is Dr. Stan McCampbell of America. The objective of the society is to promote peace and friendship through medicine and tennis.

Organization

At each conference, directors from all attending countries meet under the chairmanship of the current president, who is in office for two years, and they elect the future vice-president who automatically becomes president two years later. The national directors plan the venues for the next five to six years from the list of countries willing to organize the event.

There is an executive secretary (based in America) who liaises between countries and sends out summaries of each meeting and tournament. The organizing country forms its own committee, appoints its tournament director, decides on location, and organizes courts, balls, printing, publicity, transport, match draws, and results. A location must have 18 to 20 courts of the same surface, a nearby lecture theater, and in places with uncertain weather, alternative indoor courts. The organizing country also selects and advises on accommodations and the center for the medical conference, finds speakers, and arranges the lecture program. The 22 tennis events are arranged in age groups with a consolation plate in each group for first-round losers.

Preliminary information is handed out about two years ahead of time and final details on the medical and tennis programs, social events, accommodations with prices, and conference fees are sent to the director of every member country 6 to 12 months ahead of time.

The host country must plan the financing of the tournament and conference. Each individual member is responsible for his or her travel costs to the conference plus accommodations and the conference fee. The host country obtains as much sponsorship as possible to lower the conference fee and attract as many members as possible.

Evaluation

The 1993 U.K. conference was a great success for the 230 members from 18 countries who attended. It thus provides an excellent example of a business society fitting in a sport tournament in a conference program. An excellent medical program was complemented by superb weather for the tennis. Social events included a welcome supper, midweek "1812 Overture" evening with fireworks display and barbecue, and finals night dinner dance and prize distribution. Two tours were arranged to surrounding places of interest.

Financing the event was difficult as promised sponsorship was withdrawn at the last minute because of government restrictions on pharmaceutical companies' spending, and because of the worldwide recession. Because virtually all of the organizing was done on a voluntary basis, costs were kept to a minimum. The conference also benefited from generous hosting by the local community council. A small profit was made that will be used to expand the small national medical tennis association in the United Kingdom.

The organizing committee of three persons local to the tournament venue was more efficient than a large committee spread over the country would have been. Many of the overseas guests visited Wimbledon during and after the conference and took the opportunity to make pre- and postevent tours of Great Britain and France.

Like sport tourists on holiday, business tourists vary widely in the amount of time spent on sporting activity. To professional players, sport is their business and when they are not playing, they are training. Whether playing or training, the many teams and individuals who spend considerable periods away from home are, to all intents and purposes, sport tourists. Extensive travel over long periods of time—the England Cricket Team spent four months on an international tour in 1994-95—is not unusual.

Exercise facilities offered by hotels for their clientele should also be considered as contributing to this type of sport tourism. Redmond (1988) refers to an article on this trend from the magazine *Travelling on Business,* which not only describes an explosion in the hotel industry in the area of physical fitness facilities but also concludes that

> as long as the general interest in fitness remains at its current high level, and as long as at least one hotel can claim some advantages by providing this very expensive amenity, fitness facilities in hotels will be an important consideration for any hotel with an eye to capturing the business. (p. 5)

This statement is born out by the specific renovations of all the major hotel chains around the world (for example, Hilton, Trusthouse Forte, and Westin) in recent years (Redmond, 1988).

Increasingly, hotels have had to invest in sport and fitness facilities if they were to compete with other developments (such as the club formula) to attract active tourists. Redmond (1991) comments on this trend:

> Comprehensive health and sports facilities are becoming mandatory for any resort worthy of the title; and urban hotels which are restricted by space considerations from providing the extensive sports facilities necessary for qualification as a fully-fledged resort, are nevertheless now providing exercise facilities far beyond what would have been expected a few years ago. (pp. 109-110)

However, a cautionary note has to be sounded: leisure facilities attract guests to a hotel and thereby increase room sales; yet the evidence that guests actually use these facilities is sparse! Furthermore, Hales and Collins (1988), in a research study on the process of investing in hotel leisure facilities in the United Kingdom, suggest that the belief in the success of this new formula is often based more on faith than hard evidence:

> The conclusion that the provision of hotel leisure facilities must happen in order to cater for some inevitable guest demand has been made more on the basis of faith than a detached examination of the available evidence. (p. 47)

Leisure in general and health and fitness in particular form important aspects of the total holiday package offered nowadays to customers. Hotels are therefore trying to attract seminars and business conferences by offering golf courses and tennis courts besides business facilities. Incentive weekends are also introduced.

Many business visitors to Miami play golf at the Doral Country Club, which is close to the international airport. The Doral has one of the most fearsome courses in the United States, called the Blue Monster because of the profusion of lakes which cover more area than its fairways.

The Boca Raton Resort and Club, 45 miles north of the airport, is also popular. It has two 18-hole championship golf courses, 34 tennis courts, five pools, a marina, a private beach, and 963 guest rooms. Orlando's many excellent facilities include the Grenelefe Resort and Conference Center and Bay Hill, which is home to the PGA Tour's Nestlé Invitational.

Golf has been allowed to take root in the world's most populous nation. China's government is encouraging golf to attract more foreigners to invest in China: in 1995 China had 12 golf courses—by the end of the century there will be 40 more (Evans, 1995).

In the south of Japan, the Miyazaki Prefecture has established a world-class international convention and leisure resort complex, Seagaia. This resort's aim is to attract the most prestigious global conferences and has set its sights on hosting the summit of industrialized nations in the year 2000. Recently, the new center hosted Toyota's world convention for its executives from 130 countries (Seagaia brochure). The Seagaia provides a state-of-the-art mix of venues and hospitality on one site, including two golf courses and the world's largest all-weather domed waterpark (Ocean Dome), which complements the Hotel Ocean 45 and the World Convention Center (Summit), the main hall which can accommodate 5,000.

Passive Sports During Nonholiday Time

This category of sport tourists includes those who observe sports while traveling for reasons other than to take a holiday. The best-known example is the travel of sport managers, coaches, journalists, and so forth to participate in megasport events. The world championships of gymnastics in Rotterdam (the Netherlands) had 450 participants from 42 different countries, 400 delegates attended from the mass media, and 500 volunteers came from all over the country. The Olympic Games held in Barcelona in 1992 counted even more journalists than participants. Finally, we include in this category those who, while attending a business conference, make time to go to a sport event.

Case Study 3.7

The Hong Kong Dragon Boat Festival— International Races

A Sport Festival Attracting Passive Sportists During Nonholiday Time

Description of Context

The Chinese tradition of dragon boat racing, which dates back to the Chou Dynasty, has been for centuries a major international Chinese festival. Of all the festivals celebrated in Hong Kong, the Dragon Boat Festival (Tuen Ng) is perhaps the most known outside Hong Kong. Now, the Hong Kong Dragon Boat Festival—International Races attracts teams of expert rowers from all over the world to compete in the annual races. The Hong Kong Dragon Boat Festival is a good example of passive sport during nonholiday time in view of the tremendous international business conducted in Hong Kong. Many business people take the opportunity while they are in Hong Kong for business matters to visit the Hong Kong Dragon Boat Festival.

Description of Development

The dragon boat races are said to have originated in the fourth century B.C. to commemorate the death of the statesman-poet Ch'u Yuen, who drowned himself as a protest against a corrupt government. During Tuen Ng in Hong Kong, slender boats with dragon heads and tails, raced to the beat of drums in honor of their village, their company, or just for the fun of it all. Although dragon boat races have been held for more than two thousand years, it was only in 1976 that the international races were introduced. This feature of the festival is a separate event from the local races, which are still held by various fishing and boat communities in different parts of the territory. Since 1976 the event has grown and now attracts Olympic rowers, canoeists, other world-class champions, and tourists.

Hong Kong's dragon boat races—a traditional sporting attraction appealing to many tourists.

Organization

The first International Dragon Boat Races were organized by the Fishermen's Society of Hong Kong and the Hong Kong Tourist Association. Nowadays the Hong Kong Tourist Association, in conjunction with the Urban Council of Hong Kong, is the organizer.

The Hong Kong Dragon Boat Festival takes place every second weekend of June. Several races are held during these two days. A race starts every 15 minutes.

Each year, sponsored teams from the business and hotel communities participate in a series of "charity races." The money raised from this event is donated to Hong Kong's Community Chest, the government-appointed body responsible for organizing and coordinating fundraising for its member agencies. The winner of each category competes in the Hong Kong Championship Race.

In the past, dragon boats varied in size from 12 to 37 meters long and in capacity from 20 to 48 rowers. This is still true of the local races. However, strict specifications now regulate the international races, which have a set course. The boats must measure 11.58 meters long, 1.07 meters wide, and 0.46 meters deep. The crew must include a steersman and a drummer.

Evaluation

The Dragon Boat Festival has become one of the major tourist attractions in Hong Kong (Höfer, 1995). Its share of the total tourism account has increased considerably in recent years. It can be considered a good example of passive sport on nonholiday where business people attend a specific sport festival of the country that is visited.

References

Höfer, H. (1995). *Insight Guides Hong Kong.* Hong Kong, Hong Kong: APA.

Summary

Sport is a growing segment of the tourism industry: the demand for active sport holidays increases, the demand for second holidays is on the increase, and several types of activity holidays are provided as a year-round tourist product. However, although the number of people who participate in sport activity holidays is on the increase, they still remain a minority. The number of people who are looking for a more recreational, not so intensive, sport activity is much higher and is still growing. The trend in sport tourism is to practice several activities and to look for variety.

Two sectors characterized by the combination of sport and tourism can be identified, namely, holidays with an element of sport content (active or passive), and trips for business reasons (nonholidays) with a sport content (active or passive). Sport activity holidays range from a camping holiday to staying at a five-star hotel that boasts two 18-hole golf courses, a health center, a well-stocked salmon stream, and six tennis courts.

It has also been illustrated that sport holidays can contribute to opportunities in tourism. Sport is however not just an important element of the touristic product. Mass sport events can generate a considerable tourist flow arising from the attention given by the mass media to the city, the area, or the country where the event takes place.

Just as sport participation and tourism are diversifying, so the sport tourism market profile will become increasingly diverse.

References

Aas, O. (1990). Is easy access to a scenic landmark of importance? A study of visitors' attitudes towards proposed management actions in the Briksdal Glacier area, Norway. In A.J. Veal, P. Jonson, and G. Cushman (Eds.), *Leisure and tourism: Social and environmental change* (pp. 29-38). Sydney, Australia: University of Technology.

Atkins, C. (1995, May 7). Days on the trot. *The Sunday Times*, pp. 4-5.

Bale, J. (1989). *Sports geography*. London: E&FN Spon.

Brian, K. (1995, September/October). Putt it there. *Voyager*, pp. 38-42.

Burns, J.P., Hatch, J.A., and Mules, T. (Eds.). (1986). *The Adelaide Grand Prix: The impact of a special event*. Adelaide, Australia: Centre for South Australian Economic Studies.

Butwin, D. (1995). Wind on the water. *Hemispheres, November*, 98-109.

Campbell, S. (1995, February). The wheel thing. *BBC Holidays*, pp. 30-35.

Clerbout, I. (1990). *Clubtoerisme: Een pilootstudie naar het profiel van het clienteel en mogelijke redenen van succes* [Club tourism: A pilot study into the profile of the clientele and possible reasons for success]. Unpublished licentiate dissertation, Vrije Universiteit Brussel, Brussels, Belgium.

Clough, J. (1989). Lauglauf. *Leisure Management, 9*(10), 57-58.

Collins, M. (1991). The economics of sport and sport in the economy: Some international comparisons. In C. Cooper (Ed.), *Progress in tourism, recreation and hospitality management. Vol. 3* (pp. 184-214). London: Belhaven Press.

Crandall, D.A. (1987). 1988 Outlook for recreation. In U.S. Travel Data Center (Ed.), *Proceedings of the Thirteenth Annual Travel Outlook Forum* (pp. 236-240). Las Vegas, NV: U.S. Travel Data Center.

De Knop, P. (1989). The reciprocal development of sport and tourism. In M. Blagajac and O. Urednik (Eds.), *Programmes of sport recreation in the process of work and tourism* (pp. 185-204). Rovinj, Yugoslavia: International Council for Sport Sciences and Physical Education.

Evans, L. (1995, April 30). Of all the tee-offs . . . . *The Sunday Times*, p. 14.

Evans, M. (1995, February 18). Hot games and curry for lunch. *The Sunday Times*, p. 17.

Explore Worldwide Ltd. (1995). *Explore. Small group exploratory holidays. You'll see more.* Aldershot, Great Britain: Author.

Getz, D. (1991). *Festivals, special events and tourism.* New York: Van Nostrand Reinhold.

Glyptis, S.A. (1991). Sport and tourism. In C. Cooper (Ed.), *Progress in tourism, recreation and hospitality management. Vol. 3* (pp. 165-183). London: Belhaven Press.

Grossman, C.L. (1995, November 3). For golfers, greens in paradise. *USA Today,* p. 13E.

Hales, C., and Collins, P. (1988). Hotel Leisure: A spring in the step or a leap in the dark? *Leisure Management, 8*(8), 46-52.

Hall, C.M. (1992). Adventure, sport and health. In C.M. Hall and B. Weiler (Eds.), *Special interest tourism* (pp. 141-158). London: Belhaven Press.

Heald, T. (1992, January). Perfect pitch in Barbados. *Observer Magazine,* pp. 35-37.

Hoseason, J. (1990). Boating holidays—Opportunities in Britain. *Insights,* pp. B1-4.

Huntley, C. (1989). Skydome opens in Toronto. *Leisure Management, 9*(7), 39-40.

Jackson, G., and Reeves, M. (1998). Evidencing the sports-tourism interrelationship: A case study of elite British athletes. In M.F. Collins and I.S. Cooper (Eds.), *Leisure management issues and applications* (pp. 263-275). Wallingford, Great Britain: CAB International.

Jones, S. (1992, January). Smash hits. *Observer Magazine,* pp. 38-40.

Jouclas, S. (1995a, March). Easy in the islands. *High Life,* pp. 11-18.

Jouclas, S. (1995b, May). Mad about golf. *High Life,* pp. 79-82.

Kentucky Derby Festival Inc. (1985). *Economic impact study 1984.* Louisville, KY: Author.

Kluka, D.A., Jansa, P.G., and Rehor, P. (1997). The Sokol Movement: Nation building in the Czech Republic, the United States, and Canada. *International Council for Health, Physical Education and Recreation SD Journal, 36,* 1, 46-51.

Larner, C. (1992). Luxuriously healthy. *Leisure Management, 12*(3), 20-21.

Law, C.M. (1993). *Urban Tourism: Attracting visitors to large cities.* London: Mansell.

Low, R. (1992, January). Masterclass holidays. *Observer Magazine,* pp. 32-33.

Mader, U. (1988). Tourism and the environment. *Annals of Tourism Research, 15*(2), 274-277.

Madigan (1995, Summer). Roam the Earth. *Daily Mail Holiday Action,* pp. 78-79.

Maisonneuve, M.L. (1995, July 19). La déferlante des stages. *Sud Ouest,* p. 6.

Marshall Macklin Monaghan Ltd. (1993). *Spectator sporting activities in Canada from a tourism perspective.* Ottawa, ON: ISTC-Tourism Canada Directorate.

Martin, B., and Mason, S. (1990). Water leisure: Riding a wave. *Leisure Management, 10*(4), 28-32.

Mill, R.C. (1990). *Tourism: The international business.* Englewood Cliffs, NJ: Prentice Hall.

Mintel Marketing Intelligence. (1992). *Leisure intelligence—3.* London: Author.

Olympische Spelen in Brussel? [Olympic Games in Brussels?]. (1994, December 12). *Het Laatste Nieuws,* p. 1.

Orban, D.M. (1993). New destinations and innovative itineraries led the way for cruise industry. In J.R.B. Ritchie and D.E. Hawkins (Eds.), *World travel and tourism review. Vol. 3* (pp. 193-194). Wallingford, Great Britain: CAB International.

Parsons, G. (1995, Summer). The deep. *Daily Mail Holiday Action,* pp. 16-18.

Peninsilar and Oriental Steam Navigation. (1994). *Oriana: The maiden season (1995).* London: Author.

Preston, B. (1990). The pursuit of happiness. *West, November,* 26-34.

Pybus, V. (1995). *Adventure holidays.* Oxford, Great Britain: Vacation Work.

Redmond, G. (1981). The world's sports museums. *Sports International, 5,* 31-34.

Redmond, G. (1988, June). *Points of increasing contact: Sport and tourism in the modern world.* Paper presented at the 2nd International Conference of the Leisure Studies Association, Brighton, Great Britain.

Redmond, G. (1990). Points of increasing contact: Sport and tourism in the modern world. In A. Tomlinson (Ed.), *Sport in society: Policy, politics and culture. Conference papers No. 43* (pp. 158-169). Eastbourne, Great Britain: Leisure Studies Association Publications.

Redmond, G. (1991). Changing styles of sports tourism: Industry, consumer interactions in Canada, the USA and Europe. In M.T. Sinclair and M.J. Stabler (Eds.), *The tourism industry: An international analysis* (pp. 107-120). Wallingford, Great Britain: CAB International.

Richins, J. (1992). Yachting holidays, an experience with island adventures. In B. Weiler and M. Hall (Eds.), *Special event tourism* (pp. 185-197). London: Belhaven Press.

Robinson, B. (1984). *Where to cruise.* New York: W.W. Norton.

Rooney, J.F. (1988). Mega-sports events as tourist attractions—A geographical analysis. In Travel and Tourism Research Association (Ed.), *Proceedings of the 19th Annual Conference* (p. 93). Montreal, PQ: Travel and Tourism Research Association.

Ryan, C. (1991). *Recreational tourism.* London: Routledge.

Schwiesow, D.R. (1995, November 3). Snowshoeing: Making tracks toward popularity. *USA Today,* p. 11E.

Sloan, G. (1995, November 3). Dog sledding: Even amateurs can mush. *USA Today,* p. 11E.

Sokol Rally in Prague. (1994, June DAY). *Prague News,* 12-13.

Sprecher, H. (1971). *Kurortsport—Angebot sportlicher Bestätigungen für Feriengäste* [Health clinic—Sport for tourists]. Unpublished master's thesis, ETS, Magglingen, Switzerland.

Stoddart, B. (1994). Golf international: Considerations of sport in the global marketplace. In R. Wilcox (Ed.), *Sport in the global village* (pp. 21-34). Morgantown, WV: Fitness Information Technology Inc.

Tabata, R. (1992). Scuba diving holidays. In B. Weiler and C.M. Hall (Eds.), *Special interest tourism* (pp. 171-184). London: Belhaven Press.

Taylor, D. (1994, August). Fun in the saddle. *High Life,* pp. 94-100.

Van Dalen, D.B., and Bennett, B. (1971). *A world history of physical education.* Englewood Cliffs, NJ: Prentice Hall.

Veal, A. (1986). *People in sport and recreation 1980. Summary of data from the 1980 General Household Survey for England and Wales.* London: Centre for Leisure and Tourism Studies, Polytechnic of North London.

Watts, D. (1995, Summer). Pump it up. *Daily Mail,* p. 7.

Weiler, B., and Hall, C.M. (Eds.). (1992). *Special interest tourism.* London: Belhaven press.

Wheat, S. (1995). Marking golf's card. *Leisure Management, 15*(5), 26-28.

Williams, G. (1995, March). River thrills. *High Life,* pp. 83-86.

Chapter 4
Tourism in the Development of Sport

An inside view of Tropicana in Rotterdam, The Netherlands.

© Joy Standeven

The following topics are covered in this chapter:

1. The use of tourism as a catalyst for sports development.
2. The concept of sports development.
3. The ways in which tourism resources, places, programs, and events have contributed to sports development.
4. How elite sport tourists contribute to sports development.
5. Sports development as a spin-off at home.
6. The constraints that inhibit sports development being initiated by tourism.

The use of sport as a catalyst for the development of tourism is now extensive, as chapter 3 has demonstrated. The use of tourism in the development of sport is considerably less common, except when viewed historically as in chapter 1. Much of the activity of sport takes place entirely independent of tourism and vice versa. However, this book (see figure 1.1 on page 5) argues for a two-way interaction, or reciprocal process, between sport and tourism. But the role of tourism in developing sport does not yet feature in research or promotion to any appreciable extent.

This chapter reviews ways in which tourism, touristic cultural experiences, and tourist facilities contribute to the development of sport in our contemporary world. We begin by examining the concept of sports development from the participants' viewpoint.

Sports Development

By *sports development* we mean the learning of a sport, whether being initiated to a certain sport or improving one's skill in sport. Because the impact of tourism on sport really occurs at the individual level, we have chosen to focus this chapter on the impact of tourism on individual sports development rather than on the impact of tourism on the development of sport overall (i.e., the historical evolution of sport). Obviously, over time, the trends in individual sports development affect the overall historical evolution of sport.

The Canadian model of sports development identifies recreational sport, organized competitive sport, and high-performance sport as three stages of sports development (Best, Blackhurst, and Makosky, 1992). In Great Britain the Sports Council's (1993) model identifies four categories of experience—foundation, participation, performance, and excellence. The advantage of the Sports Council's segmentation model is that competition is not seen as an essential component either of sport itself or of an aspiration to improve performance. This model therefore fits our definition of sport and avoids the problems inherent to stage-based models (Pearce, 1994).

Figure 4.1 shows a diagram of the four categories of experience with an emphasis on the pathways that exist for movement between the different "levels." This model of sports development is a framework of experience rather than a stage or linear model; an individual can move in a variety of directions.

Foundation

Foundation is defined as the development of movement literacy. It includes the learning of basic movement skills and is the only aspect of the model to be closely tied to the age of the individual. So far as the U.K. Sports Council is concerned foundation experience should be provided in the primary school (i.e., by age 11). The opportunity to learn sports is often used as an argument to justify the provision of physical education in schools through-

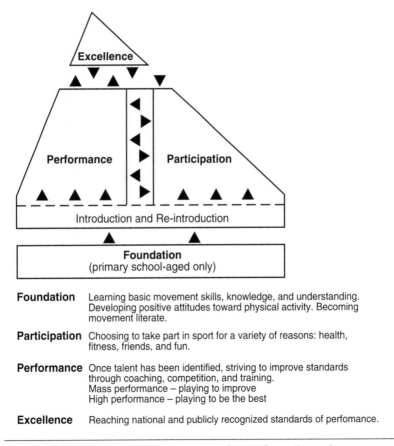

Foundation   Learning basic movement skills, knowledge, and understanding. Developing positive attitudes toward physical activity. Becoming movement literate.

Participation   Choosing to take part in sport for a variety of reasons: health, fitness, friends, and fun.

Performance   Once talent has been identified, striving to improve standards through coaching, competition, and training.
Mass performance – playing to improve
High performance – playing to be the best

Excellence   Reaching national and publicly recognized standards of perfomance.

Figure 4.1   Model of sports development (Sports Council, 1993).

out the world. But, all too often the physical education lesson is in jeopardy of being displaced by greater concentration on subjects considered more important to secure a child's professional future (De Knop, Wylleman, Theeboom, De Martelaer, Van Puymbroeck, and Wittock, 1994).

Introduction/Re-introduction

The physical education curriculum in secondary school (usually from about the age of 12) will introduce young people to specific sports. De Knop et al. (1994) add, "If one wants to give a child a sufficient opportunity for physical movement, it is often necessary to have him (or her) engage in sports as an extracurricular activity" (p. 284). Regular opportunities are clearly best provided locally through youth clubs or adult clubs with junior sections.

Although some young people continue an involvement in sport into adulthood, there are many who need an introduction, or a re-introduction, to specific sports at some later date. This part of the model identifies the need for basic skill acquisition when starting a sport at any age. The overall increasing interest in activity holidays and holiday activities (see chapter 3) provides a very effective way of introducing all, not just young, people to sports activities.

Companies such as Mark Warner in London and Union Nationale des Centres Sportifs de Plein Air (UCPA), with offices throughout France, offer, as part of their package holiday price, instruction that is clearly designed to lead holidaymakers through a progressive sports development opportunity.

Apart from those who are introduced to sport through a holiday program, there are those who first try their hand at home, some through programs such as "Learn to Play," sponsored jointly by the West Country Tourist Board and the Sports Council (South West) in England, and others who simply get out and have a go. Following a basic introduction there are those who aspire to a sports holiday specifically to increase their skill level. Holidays can provide the safe, learner-friendly environment unconstrained by time that is often of paramount importance to the early stages of learning a sports skill.

Participation

Three broad categories of recreational participants can be identified:

1. People who simply enjoy the activity without feeling the need to improve.
2. People who participate for health and fitness reasons, some of whom may wish to improve their technique in order to take part for longer or go further.
3. People who participate for social contact.

Careful reference to the model (see figure 4.1) shows the possibility of moving from introduction/re-introduction straight into "performance" for the sportist who seeks to improve his or her standard. Others may simply enjoy the participation experience. Movement can occur in both directions between performance and participation. However, if the aim is to attain excellence, the model implies that this is rarely, if ever, achieved without the coaching and training of "performance sport." Hence there is deliberately no arrow direct from participation to excellence, though it is possible to move from excellence to participation.

Performance

At this level of involvement the emphasis is on striving to improve standards once talent has been identified. Coaching and training are essential to this process. Many, though not all of these participants, are likely to be interested in some objective measure of their attainment or in competition. Such enthusiasts generally need high levels of provision in terms of facilities, coaching, and equipment. At this level, participants would normally be regularly involved in their sport and use tourism as a means of boosting their attainment.

Excellence

At the peak of sports development are those sportists with the interest and ability to achieve publicly recognized levels of excellence. Considerable previous experience and coaching is a normal prerequisite and facilities are required that meet recognized high standards. Sometimes it is the lack of appropriate facilities reasonably close to home that drives athletes to become sport tourists. The touristic experience that develops excellence is usually fashioned as a training camp for squads and teams, a series of matches on tour, or an individual challenge.

Development can occur from active sports participation as a holiday or nonholiday experience, from passive sports experience in the tourist context, or "at home." Sports development "at home" can benefit from, or be dependent on, facilities, programs, and even instruction intended primarily for tourists. The touristic experience that can give rise to sports development may be a visit to natural resources—landscapes, seascapes, and airscapes—or to cultural and man-made resources (see figure 2.4 on page 64). Sports development can arise from both independent and organized activities.

Sports development is a broad concept covering all levels of all sports. We have identified six particular ways in which tourism and its resources can be the catalyst for sports development.

1. Development of the sport activity itself based on tourism resources.
2. Participants' sports development as a result of visiting tourist resources.
3. Development of participation resulting from specially designed programs and/or instruction intended for tourists.

4. Development of interest leading to participation as a consequence of attending a sports event.

5. Development inspired by visiting sport tourists.

6. As a spin-off from 2-5, development of sports experience "at home" based on tourism infrastructure.

Development of Sport Activity Based on Available Tourism Resources

Specific land, sea, and airscapes can be the source of sports development. In chapter 1 we noted the evolution of skiing and climbing from utilitarian activities to sports in the nineteenth century that were tied to the physical resources of mountains. In recent years, the challenges of air, land, and sea have resulted in enthusiasts redefining the boundaries of sports experiences and even inventing new sports or developing "old" ones. The legendary explorer and mountaineer Sir Edmund Hillary, when asked why he climbed Everest, is reputed to have replied, "because it is there." In other words, the existence on our planet of that particular landform presented both a personal challenge and an opportunity.

In this section we deal with sports development that has taken place in our contemporary world simply because specific natural resources exist and have challenged people (most often as tourists at a distance from their home environment) to conquer them. These are the same geographical resources that make destinations attractive to tourists. We believe that as long as there are physical challenges to conquer and as long as man can aspire to go further, deeper, higher, and faster, new sport forms will evolve, most often based on tourism.

Skiing, especially downhill, has not simply developed by attracting increasing numbers of devotees; it has developed as a sport form. "As skiers became more familiar with the types of terrain that were ski-able, extreme steep skiing grew among those who saw skiing as a personal challenge" (Tomlinson, 1996, p. 122). Steep skiing takes place on slopes of 60 degrees or more and involves dropping off large cliffs and flying through the air. The European Alps, the North American Rockies, the South American Andes, and the Southern Alps of New Zealand attract adventurous skiers from around the world to this form of sport development.

It is debatable whether the desire to conquer the physical challenges presented by the natural world leads to the development of the necessary equipment, or whether the evolution of technology and equipment have themselves been the source of much sport development. Doubtless, there is an interplay here.

Until the early '80s, racing and road-style pedal bikes limited the terrain available to cyclists. Then Mike Sinyard of the fledgling company Specialized took four Ritchey's (California designed bikes) to the factories of Taiwan (Crowther, 1996). The new style of bikes (mountain bikes) that emerged are so rugged and versatile that they have opened up remote wilderness landscapes and terrain previously accessible only to tourists on foot. And this development is now a new event on the Olympic agenda.

The existence of Hawaii's massive waves, coupled with high winds, led to groundbreaking modifications to sailboards. The addition of footstraps enabled boardsailors to maintain control and stay on their boards longer. This has led to spectacular leaps and stunts that are now part of the windsurfer's repertoire. The quality and size of Hawaii's waves, unparalleled anywhere else in the world, were also the genesis of surfing and have provided the challenge that has led to its development as a sport.

The existence of thermals (rising warm air currents) is the basis for many air sports. Since new records for both distance and altitude were set above Hobbs, New Mexico, and Horseshoe Meadows, California, they have become favorite spots that provide the challenging conditions for the extremes of the sport of hang gliding (Tomlinson, 1996). Pilots will travel hundreds, even thousands, of land miles seeking the best thermals needed to lift off and to gain altitude. Gliding, the sport of flying without engine power, and soaring, without engine power or loss of altitude, also depend on a pilot's ability to find and use thermals. Sky diving, and more recently, sky surfing, using a board shaped like a snowboard, now involve complicated stunts such as rolls, flips, and spins. Although equipment and technique are indispensable, without the presence of thermals these sports could not have developed. Using the same air qualities that have stimulated the development of sports, aircraft in increasing number and size carry enthusiasts to the best performance sites.

Land, sea, and air sports continue to develop as a consequence of the world's physical resources. On these same resources tourism depends—however, those resources are finite. Therefore, a key to maintaining the relationship between sport and tourism must be sustaining the environment on which both depend for their development; we deal with this aspect of sport tourism in chapter 7.

Historic, cultural, and man-made resources are vital to tourism. To regenerate a city or ailing resort, or simply to add another dimension to their tourist provision, towns and cities worldwide have built new facilities, some to simulate the natural resources that may be distant or uncomfortable (usually due to climatic conditions) to use. Artificial ski slopes, leisure swimming pools, and artificial climbing walls now take their place alongside more traditional arenas, stadiums, tracks, and courts. They not only provide the sites for tourist participation but, in some instances, actually lead to the development of a new sport form.

Artificial climbing walls (ACWs), for example, have not simply enabled a whole number of new sport tourists to learn to climb, they have also created a new sport (Morgan, 1998). The first purpose-designed climbing wall in the United Kingdom was built in 1964. In the early 1980s climbing walls became popular in France (Robinson, 1996). There, reconfigurable walls and holds were developed "to facilitate competition climbing, and they gave impetus for the ensuing worldwide growth of the sport" (Robinson, 1996, p. 31). Indoor climbing is claimed to be one of the fastest growing sports in Britain, the United States, and New Zealand (Major, 1994; Morgan, 1998; Robinson, 1996) and, like artificial slope skiing, is attracting sufficient interest to be a commercial proposition. Easy to access in urban areas and not subject to inhospitable weather conditions or hazards such as falling rocks, ACWs are rapidly increasing. Modern climbing appeals to men and women of any age, though in Britain it is said there are two distinct user groups: committed sport climbers who compete on vertical and overhanging walls, and adventure climbers attracted by the risk of the natural environment (Morgan, 1998). Demand for instructional courses at all levels is consistently oversubscribed, and the development is encouraging people to travel considerable distances to participate.

In New Zealand the push to develop more walls came from climbers themselves, who as sport tourists had seen what was available overseas. Now there are at least 9 walls operating around the country and two more under construction (Wane, 1995). The United Kingdom currently has 24 purpose-built commercially-oriented climbing walls (Morgan, 1998). The first international climbing competition on an ACW took place in 1987 when the former Soviet Union began holding speed climbing events (Tomlinson, 1996). The first World Championships were held in 1991 in Frankfurt, Germany, the same year in which the International Olympic Committee recognized the sport.

Unlike ACWs, artificial ski slopes and leisure swimming pools have not generated new sport forms, but provision of these facilities, designed to attract tourists, contributes to participants' sports development. We shall now examine the ways in which both natural and man-made tourist resources provide the sites for sports participation that contribute to sports development.

Sports Development as a Result of Visiting Tourist Resources

As we just saw, the mere existence of tourist resources—land, air, sea, and man-made—can cause the evolution of sports forms themselves. Now we turn to sports development that is a direct result of people traveling away from home to use those resources. We use the most basic classification of tourist resources (see chapter 2), dividing them between natural and man-made installations.

Sports Development From Visits to Natural Resources

Sports that are tied to the geographical pattern of physical resources—land, sea, and air—are prime cases for sport tourism because most participants will have to travel outside their home area. On holiday or as a break while on a business trip, an active participation experience will be the root from which sports development can grow. At whatever level of involvement and for whatever period of time, a sport development opportunity exists. These *participants* may be divided into four categories:

1. Those who are introduced to a sport through taking a trip with a sporting content.
2. Those who have started to participate and who choose a sport-related trip in order to develop their competence.
3. Performers who use sport tourism experiences to refine their skills, and some who use the experience to pit themselves against other participants.
4. Those at the level of excellence who retain their skill and fitness through sport tourism experiences.

Learning to snorkel, scuba dive, or rock climb are all examples of sports development due to visits to natural tourist resources. However, a classic case of a touristic cultural experience being used in the development of sport is the ski holiday. Unless people travel away from home, the majority of potentially interested skiers could not develop the sport. Its appeal to an estimated 85-90 million people worldwide also accounts for the enormous commercial interest shown by tour operators and ski resort developers (see chapter 3). Without doubt, skiing is a prime example of the symbiotic nature of sport tourism.

Because skiing can be easily packaged and made reasonably affordable, its commercial appeal is obvious. Moreover, as the basic skills can be mastered comparatively quickly by people of almost any age without exposure to high risk, it gives immediate pleasure and the possibility for further development. These are the characteristics that make skiing a prime example of tourism for the purpose of sport, and, at the same time, a sport that depends for its development on touristic experience.

Ski operators show a particular commitment to teaching the skill of skiing: ski school is typically available at all resorts designed to cover all levels of ability. In addition, many companies now provide their own ski guides, hosts, or leaders who, as experienced skiers, are there to offer advice and guide the independent skier around the slopes. Short of accidents, there can be little excuse for active participants not increasing their skiing ability.

For the vacationer there are ever-increasing opportunities to ski on all five continents of the world—in Australia, New Zealand, Japan, Chile, Israel, India, Russia, Turkey, and Morocco to name only a few of the less well recognized countries. Indeed 35 nations met in Japan at the 15th International Interski Congress (Vine, 1995, p. 26). The development of skiing can be directly related to its promotion as a sport tourism experience. Goodall and Bergsma (1989) believe that although considerable variation exists between ski resorts: "the average inclusive tour skier is probably indifferent as to the country in which the resort is located" (p. 2). In other words, the choice of where to ski is not dominated by a desire to notch up touristic experience, but rather by the possibility of combining the most suitable skiing terrain with other factors such as accessibility and cost. For most participants, the sport activity is of key importance; that it most frequently embraces tourism is a subsidiary consideration. But, of course, it cannot be denied that skiing has proved to be a highly lucrative part of the tourism industry, which has led many small communities, and some larger ones, to capitalize on it as a destination attraction.

Tourist demand to use natural outdoor environments for physical activity has led to increased built amenities and other forms of infrastructure in support of access and usage. Car parks, toilets, accommodation and catering facilities, signposts, path creation, and more specialized development for some activities such as mountain lifts and marine jetties are increasingly common even in remote places. These developments have occurred worldwide, on a massive scale, and have been largely tourist-led and tourist-targeted. They have, however, provided additional facilities for local communities.

The province of New Brunswick in Canada has developed a network of 20 Day Adventure Centers in wooded rural areas specifically targeted to provide outdoor activity experiences first to residents and second to visitors.

Case Study 4.1

New Brunswick, Canada

Sports Development From a Day Adventure Outdoor Program

Description of Context

New Brunswick, Canada, covers an area of approximately 71,560 square kilometers and has a population of 760,600. The province is bounded on three sides by the Atlantic Ocean and has an abundance of rivers, a varied terrain, and vast woodlands. Traditionally the economy of the province relied heavily on forestry, agriculture, and fishing; however, more recently tourism has become an important component of this economic mix. The tourism sector now represents about 5 percent of the provincial GDP. Over the period from 1992 to 1994 tourism revenues in the province rose from Can$574 million to Can$676 million (US$390 to US$460 million) and employment in the sector went from 21,600 to 24,000 man years.

The desire for continued growth in this sector, coupled with the knowledge that outdoor activity-based tourism has shown growth rates in excess of 20 percent annually in Canada, prompted the New Brunswick government to pursue the possibility of becoming a leader in this field. New Brunswick recognized that it had the natural resource base necessary for prominence in outdoor activity tourism, but it also recognized that the infrastructure and the trained human resource base were not well developed within the province.

In response to these shortcomings the Department of Economic Development and Tourism undertook a year-long planning exercise which resulted in the creation of the "Day Adventure Program." Four central areas were identified as the focus of the program. These include the development of an in-province marketing campaign, the construction of the Day Adventure Centres, the development of a point-of-sale network, and human resource training.

Description of Development

The Day Adventure Centres comprise a cluster of buildings each of which is leased to a qualified outdoor activity operator. The Centres are to be built, owned, and operated by local developers under the terms of a franchise agreement established by the Department of Economic Development and Tourism.

To qualify as a Centre, the owner must submit a site plan, a full business plan, and meet the requirements as set out in the franchise agreement. To be located in a Centre, the activity operators must cover the four central areas which are the focus of the program. In addition, the Department of Economic Development and Tourism must review the interpretive components of each operation to determine eligibility.

New Brunswick was weak in the "stay-at-home" holiday market and the program has been viewed as a way to strengthen this part of the tourism market. The basic premise is that once the public has the opportunity and the skill level to pursue outdoor recreation activities they will be more inclined to stay in the province. Target groups are primarily New Brunswick domestic tourists, and secondly, visitors, encouraging them to extend their stay in the province by providing them with accessible, activity-based, all-inclusive program options. This is expected to increase the short-term economic impact of tourism; moreover, it should affect its long-term impact by encouraging visitors to return to pursue the activities in subsequent years.

Organization

The intent of the focus is to construct a network of 20 Centres of like physical appearance throughout the province that group at least five outdoor adventure operations in a single, easily accessible and visible site. The creation of this infrastructure is seen as necessary because the few existing outdoor activity operations in the province were often difficult to locate and they lacked the resources to construct facilities in high-profile locations or to market effectively on an individual basis.

In addition to being able to purchase programs directly from the operators at the Day Adventure Centres, clients can get vouchers and information from a variety of other locations in the province. These locations include Provincial Tourist Information Centres, major attractions, national parks, branches of major banks, and several large hotels.

The available activity options vary greatly and are suited to a number of different skill levels and interests. Examples of the 50 activity options currently involved in the program include such sports as kayaking, hunting, sailing, biking, hiking, horseback riding, canoeing, and deep-sea diving. The experiences can range from a half-day to four-day excursions. The price per individual participant can vary from Can$15-$200 (US$10-$140) according to the length of program and its content.

Evaluation

The Day Adventure Program has proven to be a new and exciting initiative for the Province of New Brunswick. Since its inception, ghost visits, and other evaluation techniques, have pointed to the overall success of the program. Each year the initiative continues to grow and expand, fostering increasing participation, infrastructural development, and economic benefits.

This case study was contributed by Cynthia Stacey.

Sports Development From Visits to Man-Made Resources

One can develop sport skills by visiting a man-made sport facility, such as a man-made ski facility or an indoor pool. In Britain, as in many other parts of the world, more people have learned to swim in swimming pools than in a sea, river, or lake. But in addition to man-made resources that simulate natural features, the development of many sports depends on the availability of built facilities. Appearance can be deceptive; the development of golf skills depends to a large extent on access to suitable courses. Track and field athletes and tennis and bowls players also depend on man-made resources to develop their sporting prowess. For our two detailed examples we take skiing and swimming.

Man-Made Ski Facilities

Again, the sport of skiing provides a good example of sports development through the use of artificially constructed facilities. In Britain alone there are upwards of 120 artificial ski slopes and tracks, the vast majority using a nylon brush matting surface. The slopes in Great Britain vary in length from a short 30 meters up to 410 meters and many include ski tows. These artificial facilities allow for a full range of ski activities at foundation and participation levels, and some include provision for downhill, cross-country, and freestyle disciplines. Most operators offer graded instruction and private lessons as well as free practice sessions. Equipment hire is readily available. The widespread provision of artificial slopes makes it possible for

Thomas Lepisto

Downhill skiing near Ottawa, Canada. Sport tourists look for the best skiing terrain that is accessible and affordable.

most interested participants to reach a slope within less than an hour's journey from their home.

The largest artificial ski centers in Britain attract more than 150 skiers per hour at peak times, demonstrating their popularity. There is ample evidence that artificial ski slopes have contributed enormously to the development of the sport in Britain. The most ambitious project representing the latest trend in non-alpine skiing development, is the Snowdome, an indoor facility that has made year-round skiing and snowboarding on actual powder snow a reality. Developed as a tourist attraction, it is also a sports development opportunity.

Case Study 4.2

The Snowdome, Tamworth, England
Sports Development From a Man-Made Tourist Facility

Description of Context

Tamworth is a prosperous commercial town in the United Kingdom's West Midlands. Rich in history and culture, the community covers more than 3,094 hectares and is home to some 70,000 people. The town can trace its history back to the ninth century and is proud of its heritage. Dominating the town is the twelfth-century Saxon castle which until recently was the only major tourist attraction of Tamworth. The town has excellent road and rail links and 30 million people live within a two-hour drive.

Description of Development

In spring 1994, Tamworth opened the Snowdome, a *Prosnow* (a brand of artificially made snow) indoor ski slope at a cost of UK£8 million (US$12 million). The municipal authority welcomed the innovation for its potential to put a small town on the tourist map. The location of the Snowdome in the center of the country was chosen by the developer with a keen commercial eye and a strong belief in sport tourism. While most of the three thousand users each week live within 50 miles, other visitors have traveled hundreds of miles as tourists to enjoy the experience.

The 150-meter-long by 30-meter-wide slope has a gradient which varies between 11 and 18 degrees. A uniform 16 centimeters of real snow covers the slope which is maintained in near perfect skiing condition by regular grooming and a sub-zero temperature base. The air-conditioned building, resembling an aircraft hangar, is maintained at five degrees Celsius.

Organization

Tamworth Borough Council has split its tourism and sports interests into two separate departments under two different strands of its organization. The Tourism Department promotes the Snowdome, seeing it as a "tourist attraction" for the town. The Leisure Department is responsible for the facility managed under contract by Snowdome Leisure Ltd. The contract ensures that real sports development opportunities are secured for Tamworth residents.

All residents of the Borough are eligible to become members of Tamworth Leisure Club at no cost to themselves. The production of a valid membership card gives reduced price access for almost all leisure facilities and activities run by the Borough Council as well as a range of other benefits. Residents on low incomes receive bigger reductions.

By securing town center land for leisure development and by instituting the concessionary pricing scheme, the Leisure Department has brought about a successful private-public sector partnership and ensured that tourist development has not, and will not, interfere with excellent provision and service to the local community.

The objective of the Snowdome's management is to attract as many current skiers as possible who want to develop their standard of skiing, and to introduce the sport to a wide range of interested people.

The facility is open 364 days of the year and offers recreational skiing at all times. All skiers must be able to do linked snowplough turns and ski in control, or else they must take lessons from one of the Snowdome's qualified instructors. Four beginner level instruction classes are offered from the introduction of complete beginners up to linked snowplough turns; intermediate and advanced courses are also programmed.

Evaluation

Membership has increased and research on the use of the facility indicates its immense popularity. On average around half of the users are members and half are casual recreational skiers who may or may not visit a second time. About one-fifth of the users are new to skiing, and there is a retention rate of 55-65 percent. Some 12,500 people are members, of whom 60 percent live within a 40-mile radius, the majority in Birmingham, Dudley, and Wolverhampton. The remaining 40 percent are widely distributed from Lockerbie in Scotland to the county of Devon in the southwest. The facility has proved a highly successful tourist attraction with a new hotel being built for its visitors. Given its weekly usage figure, around three thousand, the Snowdome is a successful example of a tourist-oriented, man-made resource being used for sports development.

"Les Alpes de Tamworth," an indoor ski center, (Fyfe, 1994) is a new generation of sport tourism experiences for recreational skiers and snow-boarders, beginners and participants who want to learn or improve their skiing. Other Permasnow (a brand of artificially-made snow) slopes exist in Australia and South Africa (Brunner, 1990). Japan currently boasts the biggest indoor ski slope in the world, the Ski Dome at Minami Funabashi on the outskirts of Tokyo (Wilson, 1995/1996). The man-made mountain has two high-speed quad chairs serving both easy and more difficult runs almost a quarter of a mile long and with a vertical drop of some 250 feet. The development of skiing can be directly related to its promotion as a sport tourism experience dependent on touristic places both natural and man-made.

Indoor Pools

Aware of their market drifting to the sunnier shores of the Iberian peninsula, holiday towns in Britain and elsewhere in northern Europe could no longer be content to sit back and wait for the sun to shine—all too often it does not! So to complement the beach and provide an inclement weather attraction that would extend the length of the holiday season, resorts constructed indoor leisure swimming pool complexes and justified their investment as a means to revitalize their tourism revenues. But these complexes, like the German Alpamare, Amsterdam's Miranda, and Tokyo's Summerland pools, have greatly increased swimming provision for local residents. For one English resort, the stated objective was "to produce a leisure complex that would prove a valued amenity for local residents whilst being an attraction to staying visitors and day trippers" (Standeven and Tomlinson, 1994, p. 60). A summer season survey in 1990 found that one in four users were either staying visitors or day trippers to the resort, while three out of four were local citizens. Here, as in many similar towns, swimming opportunities for the local community increased as a spin-off from a tourist-led development.

Further, research has found that the free-form leisure pool has widened the swimming market in the United Kingdom, particularly at its foundation level, and contributed to bringing into the activity more new users and less habitual swimmers, creating a broader interest in swimming (Gratton and Taylor, 1990; Standeven, 1993). Doubtless, tourist attraction is an additional motive at Wild Blue, Japan's new UK£190 million (US$285 million) indoor beach created as an alternative for those of Yokahama's population who cannot take a holiday away from home (Terry, 1995).

Leisure pools have been found to create significant tourist demand (Gratton and Taylor, 1990) and have been used by cities as part of their regeneration strategies. Center Parcs, noted for its modern, upmarket versions of the holiday village (see chapter 3), developed a unique operation in downtown Rotterdam as part of the city's urban renewal program and Center Parcs only nonresidential facility.

Case Study 4.3

Tropicana, Rotterdam, the Netherlands
Sports Development From Facilities Built for Urban Regeneration

Description of Context

Indoor leisure water complexes first became popular in Germany in the late 1960s and proved a valuable tourist attraction. Seaside resorts introduced them to extend their season, the club-type holiday villages have made them their centerpiece, and cities have developed them as an attraction within an economic regeneration program. There are now around 250 leisure pools in operation in Europe.

Rotterdam, the Netherlands' second largest city, lies about 19 miles from the North Sea and has a population well in excess of one million. The navigable River Maas led to the city's economy becoming almost completely dependent on shipping, handling the transfer of ocean freight to canal barges for transport to the industrial centers of Belgium and Germany. Badly damaged in World War II, a new inner city has been designed and rebuilt. Like other industrial cities, Rotterdam has sought redevelopment to attract tourism while at the same time offering its citizens high-quality sports installations.

In keeping with its standard criteria, Center Parcs locates its installations in regions with a high population density and spending power within a two-hour drive. Between five and eight million inhabitants live within the catchment area of Tropicana.

Description of Development

Tropicana has a 10,000-square-meter surface area and houses a subtropical swimming paradise, including a 700-square-meter artificial wave pool connected by lagoons, waterfalls, Jacuzzis, and a running stream to an outdoor pool maintained at a constant 29 degrees Celsius. Wild-water rapids bring swimmers back from the outdoor pool to the 17.5-meter, dodecagonal, glass-dome-covered pool, the characteristic trademark of Center Parcs, used to protect the tropical paradise from the climate of northern Europe. Hot whirlpools, a special toddlers' pool, water slides, a Turkish steam bath and cold-plunge pool, and a huge 590-square-meter sauna and solarium are complemented by eight catering facilities, three of which are accessible to swimmers. The prestigious revolving five-star restaurant situated high above the main entrance completes one revolution every hour thus enabling visitors to enjoy the touristic sites of the city and a surrogate experience of the water complex. Floatation tanks offer relaxation using salt water three times more concentrated than the Dead Sea and maintained at 34.5 degrees Celsius.

One of the most noticeable features of this enormous facility is the extensive use of tropical greenery. Banana trees, orchids, papayas, mangoes, oranges, dates, and olives add realism to the tropical atmosphere. Design, construction, fittings, and maintenance are of the highest quality making this arguably the best indoor water leisure complex in Europe open to the public.

Organization

One hundred and fifty full- and part-time staff supervise and manage the facility, tasks made more difficult by its garden setting which deliberately conceals lagoons, streams, and Jacuzzis to make the complex attractive and stimulating.

Tropicana is open 364 days each year. Despite its massive size, the maximum number of bathers admitted for any four-hour session is 1,500. Once in the complex visitors are free to use any part of the facility they choose. Treatment sessions are on a bookable basis, but for the remainder the participants control their own recreational program of fun and relaxation. Special provision is made for adults who want peace and quiet in that children are excluded for the first hour each weekday morning and only 150 tickets are available each day, thus guaranteeing a relaxing, uncrowded space.

Special theme nights are organized using a laser show coordinated with music. The pool is lit in a myriad of colors with underwater and dome lighting, and smoke cannons and wind machines high above it add to the effects.

Evaluation

Center Parcs' commitment to provide an excellent physical environment is a major contributing factor to the success of Tropicana. Tropicana caters to all ages of people who enjoy relaxing and playing in water. It attracts in excess of 600,000 users each year.

The complex does not provide for the athletic swimmer, who is best served by conventional rectangular pools. Tropicana is a successful tourist attraction in its own right and is a facility which by its design is ideal for developing interest and confidence in swimming. It is a good example of a facility built as a tourist attraction for city regeneration that serves as a sports development opportunity for tourists and residents alike.

Effects on Local Sports Development

Holiday and business visitors may base their choice of destination accommodations on the leisure facilities offered, though they do not necessarily make use of them during their stay. In consequence more reliable and sustainable markets have had to be explored. This has led hotels, holiday camps, and other private tourist concerns to open the doors of their centers to local community users. Apart from providing sport development opportunities at the upper end of the market there is a chain reaction, since usage pressure may be relieved on local public facilities. Both directly and indirectly, then, facilities provided for tourists have made a significant contribution to the facilities and opportunities for sports development available to local residents.

However, some authors raise serious questions as to who benefits from such development, claiming the main beneficiaries are those in the sports and media industries and affluent residents (Whitson and Macintosh, 1993). However, even constituencies less likely to benefit can still favor the hosting of mega-events (Reasons, 1984). Calgarians, who hosted the 1988 Winter Olympic Games, gained an ice hockey arena, speed skating oval, luge and bobsled track, and ski jumps, facilities to attract elite athletes rather than the average citizen (Reasons, 1984). Nevertheless, this limited number of athletes gained benefit from the use of high-performance training centers that they would not otherwise have had, and at least some of the practice facilities have been well used since (Hiller, 1989). But as Hiller goes on to point out, although the provision of facilities for elite athletes is very desirable—at any rate from the point of view of the athletes themselves—such provision should not be portrayed, as it often is, as something inevitably likely to benefit the average citizen.

Tourism-Generated Sports Development Through Programs and Instruction

Activities for young people during their school holidays have a long pedigree in many countries, with some of the most sophisticated examples occurring in the United States summer camp programs, which are said to cater to 11 million children every year. The concept of the summer camp as a special program has now been emulated worldwide. Superchoice is a wholly owned subsidiary of the company that operates Center Parcs. It has now opened its first two Summer Camp Adventure Centres in the south of England. The camps are intended for young people to develop their sporting interest and skills during vacations.

The German Federation of Sport (Deutscher Sportbund) operates Trimm Dich ("Keep Fit") campaigns targeted at different groups and adopting an appropriate theme. In holiday periods specially organized campaigns, "Trimm on Vacations," are designed to use the holiday period to boost sports recruitment. Similar developments are found in southwest England's "Learn to Play" schemes targeted at overseas and "high-spend" tourist markets (West Country Tourist Board and Sports Council, 1992). Intended primarily for tourists, and offering a package including accommodations and activity programs in bowls, golf, and tennis taught by professional coaches, the scheme also reaches out to local residents and provides them with expert instruction that might not otherwise be available.

Another policy in the same English region encourages sports clubs to be more welcoming to the casual tourist visitor. This is similar to Beekse Bergen, a profit-making safari park in the Netherlands funded by two municipal authorities with facilities including waterskiing, rowing, sailing, windsurfing, and tennis. Local sports clubs are permitted free use of the water sports and tennis facilities provided they offer free lessons for visitors at specified times (Glyptis, 1991).

Sport development arising from an instructional holiday can be bought, at a price, from the tennis ranches in America, Spain, and Australia. In Tucson, Arizona, the Westin La Paloma resort offers back-to-basics and stroke-of-the-day clinics. The Harry Hopman Tennis Academy at Saddlebrook advertises five hours of intensive daily instruction with 4:1 student-pro ratio in a four-star resort atmosphere. A week at John Newcombe's Tennis Ranch at New Braunfels in Texas cost almost US$4,000 in 1992. Fifty aspirants, mainly Americans, willingly paid for this unique sports development opportunity (Low, 1992). Each day included extensive coaching sessions from one or more of the former tennis stars who coach at the ranch and matches, filmed on video for postmatch analysis. Sold as a holiday, the whole focus of Tennis Fantasies is sports development.

Golf, like tennis, benefits from an upmarket, mobile clientele who travel considerable distances in order to develop their game. Richard Brain, for several years the teaching professional at the Southern Hills Country Club in Tulsa, Oklahoma, estimated that he traveled around the globe 26 times in search of the perfect golf swing. In his post in Singapore he taught golf to a

Courtesy of The Harry Hopman Tennis Academy

The Harry Hopman Tennis Academy in Saddlebrook has one teaching pro for every four students.

range of students, many of whom traveled to Singapore from throughout Asia for their lessons (Stoddart, 1994). Still today, the opportunity to develop their game spurs many golfers who find access to play difficult while at home to seek holiday venues that cater to their interest. One of the major attractions of the Spanish coast to British holidaymakers is the provision made for golf enthusiasts. Great Britain has some way to go before reaching the golf participation levels recorded in Canada, Japan, or Australia. Europe has approximately 3,000 golf facilities and a population of 320 million. This generates a ratio of 106,000 people per golf course. In contrast, the United States has approximately 12,500 facilities and a population of 240 million, a ratio of 19,200 people per course (Henley Centre, 1991). It is hardly surprising that access to courses is not easy in the United Kingdom, especially in England. The attraction of playing abroad and receiving high quality tuition is sufficient to generate a large market of golfers seeking to develop their game. Having survived a downturn in the golf market in the early 1990s, major operators in Europe now aim to create a network of clubs to enable their members to access golf courses worldwide through their local club (Muirden, 1998).

La Manga Golf Club, on the Costa Calida, Spain

Sports Development From an Independent Golfing Holiday

Description of Context

Golf enthusiasts, though little more than beginners, can be attracted to take a golfing holiday with the specific purpose of developing their level of play. Players aspiring to such a holiday must normally obtain a handicap prior to registering at a foreign golf resort. Beginners who intend to take a course of instruction would not be expected to have a handicap.

Description of Development

La Manga Golf Club is situated on the Costa Calida, between the Mediterranean and the sea of La Manga del Mar Menor in Spain, 60 miles west of Alicante. It lies in 1,400 acres of sun-guaranteed, semitropical countryside near Cartagena and is typical of a number of Spain's high-class resorts designed to appeal to visiting golfers. Surrounded on two sides by the sparkling waters of the Mediterranean Sea, amidst olive trees, lemon trees, and bougainvilleas, the resort has been developed to cater to players of all standards, including beginners, and their families.

Seventy-two luxury apartments cluster around a picturesque village setting with shops and several restaurants. Individual villas are situated right on the side of the palm-fringed fairways, giving visitors uninterrupted opportunities to learn from watching other enthusiasts. The resort offers programs for children between three and twelve years of age where they can enjoy a selection of supervised fun and games.

Organization

La Manga, described as a "golfers paradise," is a British-owned, Hyatt-managed spectacular resort with three golf courses, two beaches, numerous swimming pools, bowling greens, and 18 tennis courts. At the Principe Felipe five-star hotel, a luxury double room in 1994 cost around 155,400 Pesetas (UK£775 including tax or US$1165) for seven nights including breakfast and green fees. A more modest arrangement, of interest to less affluent players, are the private villas suitable for four people to rent for about UK£100 (US$150) per day. The golf club is run separately from the accommodations, but discounted green fees are available. On the 18-hole course a round takes the amateur golfer, on average, five hours, thus making it possible to play one round in the morning and a second in the afternoon.

La Manga aims to attract golfers at all levels of play, inspiring golfers and their families to take a holiday at the club. For those who buy a tuition package the aim is to improve their game.

Evaluation

The La Manga golf course was rated as equivalent to some of the best private golf courses in Britain. It was easier to book and choose tee times, rounds were less rushed, and the course was less crowded. The golf was seen as good value for the money and the warm sunshine an added bonus. The standard of tuition offered was very good. Golf players rated the experience as "brilliant." Families were somewhat less enthusiastic. The size of the complex necessitated the use of a car to reach all the facilities and the bus provided for the purpose was too infrequent.

As an independent sport activity holiday, sports development was a success. Players improved their standard of play significantly as a result of the special opportunities and quality of instruction available.

Major Events Used to Stimulate Sports Development

Towns and cities everywhere have seized on tourism as a means of establishing a new economic base and increasing their revenues (see also chapter 5). Portsmouth, in southern England, in seeking to change its industrial and naval dockyard image chose to establish maritime heritage as its theme. Famous ships from the history of sea warfare are all accessible to visitors in the historic waterside area of the dockyard. In addition to its large marina with berthing for nine hundred craft, Portsmouth offers sporting activities including swimming, fishing, sailing and windsurfing, bowls, tennis, and golf for visitors who wish to participate.

The city has also deliberately sought top-line sporting attractions as a means of encouraging tourism and to create spin-offs to sports development for residents. Each year a number of major events are hosted including the National Windsurfing Championships, the Tour of Britain Professional Cycle Race, an international triathlon, and the Great South Run. The athletic events produced a 100 percent increase in membership of the local joggers' club from 400 to 800 in two years and a four-fold increase in the local triathlon club, demonstrating the power of events to attract people to sport.

Sports development, as one of three reasons for seeking to host major events, has resulted in the Sports Council in Great Britain setting up a Major Events Support Group (MESG) to assist with U.K. bids for international sporting events (Maloney, 1996).

In 1994 the south of England captured a stage of the world-renowned Le Tour, the preeminent cycle race in Europe formerly known as the Tour de

France. One of Brighton's stated aims in its bid to attract the race to the town was cycling development. A program concentrating on a school's cycling package and community cycling days was initiated. Most recently, as part of its portfolio of events, Brighton has hosted the BMX World Championships.

A further benefit from hosting major events is the opportunity provided to recruit and train a large number of volunteers to assist with management, administration, and officiating. Such volunteers are generally drawn from the ranks of people involved in sport at a basic level, and direct participation in a major event can increase their motivation and ultimately lead to improving their skill level.

Use of Major-Event Facilities for Local Sports Development

Facilities built for prestigious events such as the Olympic Games or the World Student Games have often been legitimated on the grounds of the benefit they will ultimately provide for their local community and the sports development they will foster. In 1976, Willi Daume, president of the Organizing Committee for the Games of the XXth Olympiad held in Munich in 1972, commented on the difficulties of providing facilities for world-class competition with adequate provision for spectators while retaining the good will and enthusiasm of all those involved in the games—from the Organizing Committee down to the taxpayer (Daume, 1976). Given the size and technical requirements of the facilities, their subsequent use is an important factor. Writing a postevent report, Daume said, "I maintain that the Olympic cities usually gain a great deal from the Games, in idealism of course, but also materially. Munich certainly did so. The city acquired exemplary sports facilities and after the Games they became the city's" (p. 155).

Kariel (1991) reviewed the impact of the XVth Winter Olympic Games in 1988 in Calgary and concluded that the facility legacy left first-class sport facilities, providing support for numerous regional, national, and international competitions. In addition he noted that the games increased sport participation and sport-mindedness among Calgarians and increased the positive image of Calgary, broadening its range of attractions, making it a city more desirable to visit (Kariel, 1991).

Commenting two years after the Barcelona '92 Olympics, the city's Deputy Mayor for Sports and Tourism considered that sport for the citizens of Barcelona and the Olympic project had a positive relationship (Truno, 1994). From its selection in 1986 as the host city of the XXVth Olympiad, "the Games were used as a huge civil campaign . . . as a way of creating awareness of sport as a socially accepted value" (Truno, 1994, p. 177). This resulted in building sports installations in schools, in siting the major Olympic installations in four strategically selected "corners" of the city of Barcelona, and in using 16 other sites in the province of Catalonia. In this way the Olympic project was shared with a whole region and the new facilities were designed with the "day after" in mind (Truno, 1994). One aspect of the post-Olympic years was the development of specific holiday recreation programs.

Yet in constructing arguments in favor of civic investment the point has too often been disregarded that the facilities required for high-level competition are both too large and too sophisticated for general community use (Whitson and Macintosh, 1993). Victoria, Canada, host to the 1994 Commonwealth Games, recognized this, and in consequence the athletics facilities were smaller in terms of spectator accommodation than those built in Edmonton 20 years earlier, and the aquatic facility was designed to be highly versatile.

In Sheffield, England, host to the 1991 World Student Games, many existing sports facilities were upgraded as practice venues for the waiting athletes, and a new arena, a pool complex, and a velodrome were built. Second only in size to the Olympics, these games, with around seven thousand athletes from about 140 countries taking part in 11 sports, presented a city in decline with an opportunity for regeneration. Case study 4.5 describes how Sheffield responded to this challenge.

Case Study 4.5

Sheffield, England
Sports Development From Facilities Constructed for Hosting a Major Event

Description of Context

Sheffield, the fourth largest city in England, was well known as the center of Great Britain's steel industry. In 1971 this industry employed 80,000 of Sheffield's total working population of some 300,000. During the 1980s the decline, and eventually the almost total closure, of the steelworks devastated the city and led to unemployment reaching a record level of around 16 percent in 1985. Between 1971 and 1984 the city lost 75,000 manufacturing jobs. By 1990 unemployment was still at 9.5 percent, well above the national average of 5.6 percent (Critcher, 1992). Economic regeneration became an imperative, and the city council chose sport as the vehicle through which to change the city's nineteenth-century industrial image.

Description of Development

The city made a bid and was chosen to host the 1991 World Student Games (WSG), or Universiade. Ten thousand athletes took part in 11 sports (athletics [track and field], basketball, diving, fencing, gymnastics, hockey, soccer, swimming, tennis, volleyball, and water polo). At the time the games were awarded to Sheffield the city did not have the necessary facilities. In a presentation to government seeking financial aid to host the WSG, it was claimed, "The magnificent sports and entertainment facilities will be given a great start in life by the games. They then have a key role in the plan for developing sport, leisure and tourism as key components of our citywide strategy" (Critcher, 1992, p. 195).

From the outset the city had a long-term plan for the facilities that it intended would benefit local residents. In all there were 17 newly built constructions including a tennis center, a theater, hockey fields, the Ponds Forge International Sports Centre, an athletics stadium, the Leisure Centre, and Sheffield Arena. Provision for the World Student Games was the justification for extensive facility investment.

The facilities revenue costs are financed by the city council through admissions income and sponsorship arrangements, and the shortfall is made up from the Recreation Department's budget which is largely derived from community taxes and grants from central government.

Organization

In creating a Sports Development Unit in the early 1980s, Sheffield was in the forefront of new strategic thinking. A decade later the unit accounted for the work of 40 people fulfilling different community sports development roles. The council's Leisure Services are also responsible for the development of performance and excellence in sport, the development of an events program, and the furtherance of sports education in the city's schools and colleges.

A huge range of activities are programmed in the city's sporting venues to cater to the needs of the resident population. Ponds Forge (the 50-meter WSG pool, a leisure pool, and dry sports center) operates a menu of 50 activities that drew 0.5 million attendees in 1994. A total of 17 clubs operate at the center. The Don Valley Athletics Stadium had sports events on 136 days in 1994, apart from daily fitness training sessions and regular usage by the winter bowls club, the athletics club, an athletics coaching scheme, and junior coaching in American football.

Two particular programs deal with performance and excellence levels of sports development. One provides for the sports-talented students at the city's tertiary college to be brought together from various campuses to receive specialist coaching. The second is a concerted attempt to attract national governing bodies of sport to relocate to Sheffield and develop a high-level institute of sport in the city.

In keeping with the overall policy, the Sports Development Unit aims to increase participation at all levels in a number of sports and specifically in diving, gymnastics, and trampolining.

Evaluation

The total number of swims in the city has increased. Had Sheffield not developed its new facilities, it is estimated that in swimming alone the Recreation

Department's income would be 43 percent below its 1993-94 level. This situation would have placed a heavier burden on the city's budget; thus, it is concluded that the community is economically advantaged.

Competitive squads swimming training has risen by more than 500 percent between 1991 and 1995 with the provision of the new pool. By 1994 the recreational diving lesson program attracted around five times more participants per week; the performance program had 40 participants per week and the elite diving squad had 9 divers. The program had produced a senior national diving champion and taken medals at world, European, and Commonwealth events. In one upgraded wet and dry facility, usage has risen from its pre-WSG level of 100,000 annual admissions to 400,000. The stadium program is considered to make it the busiest in England for community recreation and events.

Over the last couple of years, the Events Unit has been successful in attracting eight major events to Sheffield: two world championships events; two World Cup Swimming meets; two international athletics meetings; and two European aquatic events. Most recently, Sheffield has won the honor to become the headquarters of the new United Kingdom Sports Institute, a prestigious facility that will be developed at a cost of UK£68 million national lottery funding (Copley, 1997).

In the national economic climate a revenue deficit for the department is unavoidable. The city is containing this and assesses that its new facilities are not only contributing to economic regeneration but are also reducing the losses that would have been incurred with the pre-1991 mix of recreation facilities. In most respects this represents a very successful sports development achievement. The disadvantage may be that some residents now have to travel greater distances to the upgraded facilities.

References

Copley, J. (1997, December 17). Sheffield wins race to forge new breed of sporting heroes. *The Daily Telegraph*, p. 5.

Critcher, C. (1992). Sporting civic pride: Sheffield and the World Student Games of 1991. In J. Sugden and C. Knox (Eds.), *Leisure in the 1990s: Rolling back the welfare state. Publication 46* (pp. 193-204). Eastbourne, Great Britain: Leisure Studies Association.

As multisport events grow in size in terms of the number of countries and athletes who take part (in Atlanta for the games of the XXVIth Olympiad, there were over 10,700 athletes from 197 countries) (Stevens, 1996) and the number of tourists expected, the challenge of providing world-standard venues increases. Sydney, Australia, host to the XXVIIth Olympiad, has confronted the problem ingeniously. The Sydney International Aquatic Centre was designed to meet the city's long-term needs but be capable of efficient modification for the Olympic Games. The pools and technical facilities were opened to the public in 1995, five years before the games! To avoid the "white elephants" seen in some previous Olympic venues, the pool design allows for the spectator seating and the VIP and media facilities to be temporarily expanded for the games by the removal of the current wall to extend the area up the earth bank behind. A temporary roof and walls will be added for the Olympic Games and removed afterwards to return the facility to its present size and community use. Creative design can make facilities versatile and allow for tourist use, even for the world's most prestigious event, yet still benefit the local community as a sports development venue.

Mixed Sports Development Results of World Cup Soccer in the United States

An event many regard as second in importance only to the Olympics is World Cup Soccer. The 1994 event was held in the United States and was expected to boost the development of soccer in a country where baseball, basketball, and American football are much more popular. Reports a year after the event indicate two contrasting responses ("Youth Soccer in the U.S.," 1995). Some 2.6 million children now play soccer in leagues organized by the United States Youth Soccer Association (USYSA) and the American Youth Soccer Association (AYSA). Sparked by the World Cup, membership in the USYSA increased some 9 percent to reach 2.1 million, while the AYSA saw its membership grow 14 percent to 500,000 participants. Some small-time professional indoor soccer leagues started as well ("Youth Soccer in the U.S.," 1995).

However, the euphoria of the '94 cup did not have as great an impact at the top professional level. A year after the event, soccer had yet to make a big breakthrough in the United States and those involved in the game feared that interest may have diminished. The plan to start a countrywide elite professional outdoor league was delayed to 1996 at the earliest, and this was dependent upon attracting investors, finding adequate stadiums and local franchise control, as well as the television coverage that baseball prospers from ("Youth Soccer in the U.S.," 1995).

The development of an American professional outdoor league began with the American Professional Soccer League (A-League), which was formed in 1990 and granted Division II international status in 1993-1994. Expanded from 7 teams in 1996 to 24 teams in 1997, it is recognized as the official development system for Major League Soccer (MLS), inaugurated in 1996. The 10-team MLS (the top professional level or Division I) in the United States calls up players from the A-League of United Systems Independent Soccer Leagues (USISL). Together MLS and USISL confirmed their commitment to the development of soccer in North America by planning one MLS/A-League exhibition game in each of the 24 A-League cities over the 1996-1997 seasons (USISL, 1997).

The Influence of Elite Performers and Coaches on Sports Development

Ease of travel in the last 15 years has led more and more amateur and professional athletes to cross international borders to train and to gain experience (and rewards) not available in their home country (Craven, 1994). Teams at all levels of play go on tour to gain experience and elevate their profile. A case study follows of the Women's Cricket World Cup, a minority sport, but one in which development has occurred as a direct result of international travel by the game's elite players.

Case Study 4.6

1988 Women's Cricket World Cup Tour, Australia

Sports Development From Elite Performers
in a World Cup Tour

Description of Context

The Women's Cricket World Cup is now held every four years in a different country. Although there are historical records of women playing cricket as early as the eighteenth century (the first recorded women's match in England was in 1745), women's cricket is considered to be a minority sport. The rules for the event specify that the World Cup tournament must be played within a period of two weeks.

The International Women's Cricket Council approves the timetable and program. Meetings are convened to decide the rules of the event and to agree on the next venue to host the World Cup.

Description of Development

The Women's Cricket Association was formed in England in 1926, and the first tour to Australia took place during the winter of 1934-35. British-born millionaire Sir Jack Hayward supported England's women cricketers on their first tour of the West Indies in 1969-70 and then proposed a women's World Cup with his sponsorship. First staged in England in 1973 (two years before the men's first World Cup event in 1975), the cup has since been held in India (1977-78), New Zealand (1982), Australia (1988), and England in 1993. Overall the number of teams participating has increased.

The concept of the World Cup is aimed to enhance the relationships between countries and promote women's cricket. As a minority sport, women's cricket depends on touring to elevate its profile. Touring markets the game to a wider audience primarily through media exposure and opportunities to spectate at elite matches. Underlying, but vitally important, aims include attracting sponsorship to enhance the development of women's cricket, to promote women in sport, and to promote sport to women.

Organization

The 1988 World Cup, staged in Australia, was sponsored principally by Shell Australia, part of the huge multinational oil company. The 1988 Cup was organized by the Australian Women's Cricket Council.

Each team plays every other team within the two-week period. Each match consists of 60 overs and lasts one day. Four points are awarded for a win and two for a tied match. The venue for each match is different, requiring teams to travel. In Australia this was extensive, with matches held in Perth, Sydney, Canberra, and Melbourne. The final took place on the Melbourne Cricket Ground, one of the most prestigious grounds in the country, between the two leading teams, Australia and England; Australia won.

Each team must raise its own sponsorship for travel and equipment. Players are not paid and in order to play have to arrange leave from their jobs both for training and for the competition itself. This often has to be taken as "holiday" leave.

The host country is responsible for organizing and financing the whole event and all the costs incurred once the overseas teams arrive. The costs involved for the accommodation of approximately 140 people, together with venues, transport, and official functions for the two-week period are considerable.

Evaluation

Australia has had success with World Cup Cricket since it obtained increased funding and a continued commitment from both government and corporate spheres. The Australian Sports Commission increased its funding by 1,750 percent between 1982 and 1988, from Aus$5,000 to $88,000 (US$3,800 to $63,000) and Shell committed support for at least three years after the 1988 Cup.

From 1988 to 1993 the number of registered women players increased by 50 percent, from six to nine thousand, as a consequence of the wide exposure of the game. The Kanga Cricket Program, conceived by the Australian Cricket Board, was taken up by 81 percent of primary schools throughout Australia based on modified rules. Another progressive move has been the trend for women's and men's clubs to amalgamate

The individual player will find that her actual experience of "touring" and the general perception of touring are remarkably different. "Tours are fun, and there are games . . . but the sightseeing potential of travelling tends to be overshadowed by the rigors of training, playing, attending functions" (Larsen, 1988, p. 18). Yet the opportunity to travel presented both by national and international tours is judged one of the best things that can ever happen in the career of a player, coach, or administrator.

Hosting prestigious competitions that attract elite participants and spectators as sport tourists also has the potential for sports development "at home," as the Australians have successfully shown.

References

Larsen, L. (1988). Cricket bags on tour. In The Organizing Committee (Ed.), *The Shell Bicentary World Cup 1988–Women's Cricket Programme.* Sydney, Australia: Shell (Australia)/Australian Women's Cricket Council.

Increasingly, clubs, associations, and even national teams import foreign master coaches, often at great expense, to train their elite athletes. The lack of adequate training facilities at home led Britain's ice dance champions Jayne Torville and Christopher Dean to hold many of their practice sessions in Obersdorf, Austria. The opportunity to spectate and "rub shoulders" with model performers, even in training, can lead to sports development amongst fans in the local community as they aspire to emulate their visiting models.

The All England Lawn Tennis Club, in conjunction with the United Kingdom's Lawn Tennis Association (LTA), provides a good example of sports development occurring from the presence of elite performers. The LTA has sponsored a free coaching program, "Love Tennis," at tennis centers nationwide intended to increase awareness of the game and encourage new participants. In 1995, Love Tennis introduced 22,000 new players to the game for an investment of £125,000 (US$187,500) (LTA, 1996). As part of this program, on the middle Saturday of the Wimbledon Championships, some of the world's top players go to the local park to coach more than three hundred young people from beginners to more proficient players.

Sports Development as a Spin-Off "At Home"

Public and commercial sector providers need to be more active in following up sport tourists' experience "at home." At the individual level there is an obvious market with clear potential for development—research in Belgium (Claeys, 1982) has found that as many as one in four of the "sports population" seems to be active only during his or her holidays. In England and Wales the General Household Survey (Veal, 1986) found that more than half (55 percent) of those who took part in sailing did so only when on holiday. Similarly, 80 percent of those who swam outdoors, 40 percent who went fishing, 38 percent who played bowls, 34 percent of table tennis players, 30 percent of those who swam indoors and of those who played golf, 28 percent of tennis players, and 25 percent of those who walked did so only while on holiday. This represents a large number of people who seem to be sufficiently interested in activity to undertake it while on vacation, but who do not engage in it during the rest of the year.

Constraints That Inhibit Sports Development Being Initiated by Tourism

A number of inhibitors to sports development being initiated by tourism fit into two categories:

1. Lack of resources to engage in sports development.
2. The fragmented nature of the sport tourism industry.

Lack of Resources

The world's resources are finite and man's physical capabilities limited. But as long as there are air, land, and seascapes to be explored, new sports will develop and new records will be achieved. As in the past, much development in the forms of sport will depend on tourism, that is, on traveling to the locations that offer the challenge or provide the best conditions to meet it. This will demand a level of personal resources.

Effects on the Traveler

The personal decision to participate or not in sport is influenced by external constraints that tend to modify individual motivation (Rodgers, 1977). According to Rodgers the decision to participate also involves a set of "personal filters" that include adequate sports literacy, level of sports skill, basic motivation, social contact with sporting friends, awareness of opportunity, self-evaluation of the social accessibility of a particular sport (this may be related to age, health, and commitments to others), physical access to facilities, availability of free time, and sufficient disposable income. Given a favorable assessment of each of these factors, the individual is highly likely to decide to participate. A number of surveys have examined some of these regulators.

Research in Norway and Britain in the 1970s found that nonparticipants in sport blamed their passivity on lack of free time (Rodgers, 1977). Other more recent studies support this in Britain (Coalter, 1993; Kay and Jackson, 1991; Tucker, 1990), in Canada (Shaw, Bonen and McCabe, 1991), and in Brazil (Bramante, 1998). Coalter's study concluded that a decision to participate in sport was facilitated more by time availability than by money (Coalter, 1993). However, in Kay and Jackson's (1991) earlier research, 56 percent indicated financial constraints as opposed to only 45 percent who indicated time constraints.

Tucker (1990) asked respondents what they would do if they had more free time. More than 30 percent chose holidays abroad and weekend breaks from home, while 20-25 percent wanted more time for sport and exercise.

An examination of travel unsurprisingly identifies some of the same constraints on participation. In 1960 Lansing and Blood (cited in Boniface and Cooper, 1994) suggested five main barriers: expense of travel, lack of time, physical limitations (such as ill health), family circumstances, and lack of interest. More recently, Boniface and Cooper (1994) concluded that

> at the individual scale, a certain level of discretionary income is required to allow participation in tourism, and this income, and indeed, the type of participation, will be influenced by such factors as job type, life-cycle stage, mobility, level of educational attainment, and personality. (p. 16)

In Canada, 7 out of 10 respondents (69.9 percent) said they would engage in travel if leisure time increased over the next 5 to 10 years (Reid and Mannell, 1993). Over half of the Canadians (56.4 percent) also wanted to participate in more recreational activities and sport. Mintel International Group (1995) found that only 35 percent of United Kingdom consumers claimed to have no interest in taking any type of activity holiday.

Although a number of factors interrelate and influence both sports participation and tourism, it is evident that free time and sufficient disposable income are two key ingredients. Given the propensity to travel (short or long distances and durations), holidays are clearly an occasion when people feel they have the time to participate in sport, thus removing the major barrier.

Effects on the "At Home" Participant

Conversely, tourism's ability to enable sports development "at home" depends on whether those people whose interest has been stimulated have adequate resources, particularly time, to follow up their activity. Perhaps tourism's strongest contribution to sports development is in the provision of sports facilities, but while such facilities are all important, of themselves they will not guarantee sports development any more than the provision of facilities has ever done. Whitson and Macintosh (1993) draw attention to the less affluent who are too often the "losers" when world-class facilities are developed:

> Thus, the development of the world-class city can be said to widen gaps between the affluent residents and tourists for whom attendance at world-class entertainment is part of their lifestyle, and those whose lives mostly take place a long way from downtown, except perhaps as service workers. (p. 237)

From an East European perspective tourist growth has been substantial since the dismantling effect of glasnost, so sports development might be thought to have gone hand-in-hand. But instead of increased tourism generating sports facilities for the community, it is doing the reverse. To take Hungary as an example, in 1991 overseas tourism increased by 56 percent and visitor spending by 71 percent (Evans, 1995). Yet Evans comments, "The commodification of spa and leisure centres in Hungary is converting local amenity to tourist facility, with obvious impacts on access and pricing policies, including the place of sport and recreation in education and community provision" (p. 60). Thus to view tourism as inevitably beneficial in terms of the provision of facilities is to oversimplify the situation.

Research in Ontario, Canada, suggests the need for a more proactive approach. In Simmons' (1993) view, "tourism development that is beneficial to tourists, the environment and to host communities cannot be achieved without greater community awareness of tourism and involvement of destination area residents in its planning" (p. 665). In his view there has been too much focus on visitors' needs, and tourism developers have failed to see the host communities as consumers of the wider processes of tourism development. Thus planning for a touristic experience should also involve considering "what priority should be given to the host community needs from tourism *vis à vis* tourist needs" (Simmons, 1993, p. 664). This is a view supported by Whitson and Macintosh (1993), especially in terms of facility development for mega-events. They suggest, "We need to establish public discussions in which the buying public is not the only public that counts, and the polarizing effects of world-class status are held up for reflection and examination" (p. 238).

The Fragmented Nature of the Sport Tourism Industry

The separation of sport and tourism into two distinct sectors of the leisure industry has been a major problem. In 1991, Glyptis (1991) called for "sport and tourist authorities (in the UK) to talk to one another, and to forge real working partnerships to establish coherent policies, programmes and pro-visions" (p. 181). A more recent review revealed an increasing amount of sport tourism activity not matched by any significant liaison among the agencies responsible for sport and tourism policies in England (Weed and Bull, 1997). Moreover, the separation of sport and tourism's organizational structures (e.g., separate government departments at national, regional, and local levels) remains common in many countries of the world (see chapter 9).

However, in this and previous chapters, a large number of the naturally evolved links between sport and tourism has been discussed. In particular, we identified the extensive infrastructure (see table 2.3 on page 71) and showed the potential for a close relationship between sport and tourism because of their shared resources. At the local level, examples of some developers, owners, and managers forming constructive liaisons between sport and tourism operations have been noted. Sport has been used to generate and sustain tourism (see chapter 3). Yet many organizations still jealously guard their independence to protect their market share. To use holidays as a way of bringing people into sport and sustaining their sporting interests is reason enough to further the fledgling links between sport and tourism.

Summary

This chapter has used a number of examples to illustrate how tourism can be a catalyst for sports development. This validates our basic model, which claims that the sport-tourism relation is interdependent and reciprocal. It is not simply that significant aspects of tourism are sport-related as shown in chapter 3, but that, as this chapter has evidenced, the interaction between sport and tourism increases the forms of sport, the number of sports participants, their sports literacy and enjoyment, and the range of sports facilities. Nevertheless, as Glyptis and Jackson (1992) have claimed, "the reciprocal process of tourism being harnessed in the cause of sports development is . . . rare" (p. 41).

Two major contributing factors that inhibit the process of tourism being used in the development of sport have been identified. First, both the world's and each individual's resources are finite and unevenly distributed. Second, the responsibilities for development and coordination of policy are dispersed and fragmented. This chapter has demonstrated the potential that exists to exploit tourism for the benefit of sports development.

References

Best, J.C., Blackhurst, M., and Makosky, L. (1992). *Minister's Task Force on Federal Sport Policy: The way ahead.* Ottawa, ON: Minister of Supply and Services.

Boniface, B., and Cooper, C. (1994). *The geography of travel and tourism.* Oxford, Great Britain: Butterworth-Heinemann.

Bramante, A. (1998). Leisure lifestyles in a developing country: Reasons for non-participation. In M.F. Collins and I.S. Cooper (Eds.), *Leisure management issues and applications* (pp. 49-64). Wallingford, Great Britain: CAB International.

Brunner, C. (1990). Snowfake, *Leisure Management, 10*(4), 57-63.

Claeys, U. (1982). *Sportbeoefening in Vlaanderen opnieuw bekeken* [Sports participation in Flanders re-studied]. Leuven, Belgium: SOCK.

Coalter, F. (1993). Sports participation: price or priorities? *Leisure Studies, 12,* 171-182.

Craven, J. (1994). Cross-cultural impacts on effectiveness in sport. In R.C. Wilcox (Ed.), *Sport in the global village* (pp. 433-448). Morgantown, WV: Fitness Information Technology.

Crowther, N. (1996). *The ultimate mountain bike book*. London: Carlton Books.

Daume, H.C.W. (1976). Organizing the Games. In Lord Killanin and J. Rodda (Eds.), *The Olympic Games* (pp. 153-156). London: Book Club Associates.

De Knop, P., Wylleman, P., Theeboom, M., De Martelaer, K., Van Puymbroek, L., and Wittock, H. (1994). *Developing an effective youth sport policy*. Brussels, Belgium: VUB Press.

European Community (1992). Item 2444, *Sports Information Bulletin, 30*.

Evans, G. (1995). Tourism and leisure in eastern Europe. In D. Leslie (Ed.), *Tourism and leisure—Culture, heritage and participation. Vol. 1* (pp. 59-79). Eastbourne, Great Britain: Leisure Studies Association.

Fyfe, L. (1994). Real snow, real fun. *Sport, 2*(3), 20-21.

Glyptis, S.A. (1991). Sport and tourism. In C. Cooper (Ed.), *Progress in tourism, recreation and hospitality management. Vol. 3* (pp. 165-183). London: Belhaven Press.

Goodall, B., and Bergsma, J. (1989). The skiing holiday market in the Netherlands and the United Kingdom: The role of the mass tour operators. In D. Botterill (Ed.), *Tourism and leisure. markets, users and sites. Conference papers No. 40* (pp. 1-16). Eastbourne, Great Britain: Leisure Studies Association.

Gratton, C. and Taylor, P. (1990). Leisure vs. conventional pools. *Leisure Management, 10*(1), 42-44.

Henley Centre. (1991, November). Golfing economics—a fairway too far? *Leisure Futures*, pp. 5-10.

Hiller, H. (1989). Impact and image: The convergence of urban factors in preparing for the 1988 Calgary Winter Olympics. In G. Syme, B. Shaw, D. Fenton, and W. Mueller (Eds.), *The planning and evaluation of hallmark events* (pp. 119-131). Brookfield, VT: Avebury.

Kariel, H.G. (1991). La region de Calgary et les Xve Jeux Olympiques dhiver. *Revue de Geographie, 3*, pp. 73-77. (Grenoble).

Kay, T. and Jackson, G.A.M. (1991). Leisure despite constraint: The impact of leisure constraints on leisure participation. *Journal of Leisure Research, 23*(4), 301-313.

Lawn Tennis Association. (1996). Personal communication. July 25.

Low, R. (1992, January). Masterclass holidays. *Observer Magazine*, pp. 32-33.

Major, R. (1994). When climbing the wall is pleasurable. *Leisure Manager, Spring*, 10-13.

Maloney, A. (1996). Attracting major events. *Sport, 5*, p. 5.

Mintel International Group. (1995). *Activity holidays in the UK*. London: Author.

Morgan, D. (1998). Up the wall: The impact of the development of climbing walls on British rock climbing. In M.F. Collins and I.S. Cooper (Eds.), *Leisure management issues and applications* (pp. 255-262). Wallingford, Great Britain: CAB International.

Muirden, M. (1998). On the fairway. *Leisure Management, 18*(1), pp. 20-22.

Pearce, P.L. (1994). Tourist-resident impacts: Examples, explanations and emerging solutions. In W. Theobald (Ed.), *Global tourism* (pp. 103-123). Oxford, Great Britain: Butterworth-Heinemann.

Reasons, C. (1984). It's just a game? The 1988 Winter Olympics. In C. Reasons (Ed.), *Stampede city: Power and politics in the west* (pp. 123-145). Toronto, ON: Between the Lines.

Reid, D.G. and Mannell, R.C. (1993). Future possibilities: The changing patterns of work and leisure. In A.J. Veal, P. Jonson, and G. Cushman (Eds.), *Leisure and tourism: Social and environmental change* (pp. 361-365). Sydney, Australia: University of Technology.

Robinson, D. (1996). Peak performance. *Leisure Management, 16*(6), 31-32.

Rodgers, B. (1977). Urbanism, sport and leisure. In M. Smith (Ed.), *Leisure and urban society. Conference papers No. 6* (pp. 48-58). Eastbourne, Great Britain: Leisure Studies Association.

Shaw, S.M., Bonen, A., and McCabe, J.F. (1991). Do more constraints mean less leisure? Examining the relationship between constraints and participation. *Journal of Leisure Research, 23*(4), 286-300.

Simmons, D. (1993). Local input into destination area tourism planning. In A.J. Veal, P. Jonson, and G. Cushman (Eds.), *Leisure and tourism: Social and environmental change* (pp. 661-665). Sydney, Australia: University of Technology.

Sports Council. (1993). *Sport in the nineties—New horizons.* London: Author.

Standeven, J. (1993). Aquatic facility usage trends in UK and Europe. In E.M. Murphy (Ed.), *Tomorrow's pools today* (pp. 32-43). Melbourne, Australia: Sport and Recreation Victoria.

Standeven, J., and Tomlinson, A. (1994). *Sport and tourism in south east England.* London: South East Council for Sport and Recreation.

Stevens, T. (1996). Olympic gains. *Leisure Management, 16*(7), 34-37.

Stoddart, B. (1994). Golf international: Considerations of sport in the global marketplace. In R. Wilcox (Ed.), *Sport in the global village* (pp. 21-34). Morgantown, WV: Fitness Information Technology Inc.

Terry, L. (1995). In brief. *Leisure Management, 15*(8), 8.

Tomlinson, J. (1996). *The ultimate encyclopedia of extreme sports.* London: Carlton Books.

Tow, S. (1997). Sport tourism—The benefits. *Journal of Sport Tourism, 3*(4). Available at http://www.mcb.co.uk/journals/jst/archive/vol3no4/benefits.htm. World Wide Web.

Truno, E. (1994, October). *L'Esport per a Tothom a les Grans Ciutats.* Paper presented at the 2nd European Congress Sport for All in Cities, Barcelona, Spain.

Tucker, D. (1990). Time limits. *Leisure Management, 10*(12), 24-25.

United Systems of Independent Soccer Leagues (USISL). (1997). USISL story. Available at http://www.e-gram.com/~usisl/html/usis.

Veal, A.J. (1986). *People in sport and recreation 1980. Summary of data from the 1980 General Household Survey for England and Wales.* London: Centre for Leisure and Tourism Studies, Polytechnic of North London.

Vine, D. (1995, Summer). Holiday action. *Daily Mail,* p. 264.

Wane, J. (1995). Off the edge. *Pacific Way, October,* 59-66.

Weed, M.E. and Bull, C.J. (1997). Integrating sport and tourism: a review of regional policies in England. *Progress in Tourism and Hospitality Research, 3*(2), 129-148.

West Country Tourist Board and the Sports Council (South West). (1992). *Tourism and sport: A joint policy statement*. Exerter/Crewkerne, Great Britain: Author.

Whitson, D. and Macintosh, D. (1993). Becoming a world class city: Hallmark events and sport franchises in the growth strategies of western Canadian cities. *Sociology of Sport Journal, 10*, 221-240.

Wilson, A. (1995/96). Ski the world. *Sky Life, Winter/Spring*, 42-46.

Youth soccer in the U.S. (1995, March 2). *Sports Industry News*, p. 48.

Part II

The Impact
of Sport Tourism

Chapter 5
The Economic Impact of Sport Tourism   169

Chapter 6
The Sociocultural Impact of Sport Tourism   203

Chapter 7
The Environmental Impact of Sport Tourism   235

Chapter 8
The Health Impact of Sport Tourism   271

Chapter 5

The Economic Impact of Sport Tourism

Michael F. Collins and Guy A.M. Jackson

World Rugby 7s in Hong Kong.

Hong Kong Tourist Association

The following topics are covered in this chapter:

1. The economic significance of sport and tourism.

2. Economic features of sport as a main holiday purpose—sport activity holidays.

3. Economic features of sport, especially major facilities and events, as an attraction for visitors.

4. Economic features of sport as part of a regeneration strategy for cities and regions.

This chapter attempts to present an overview of the economic impacts of the sport-tourism relationship. It is structured around a number of the headings identified by De Knop (1990) as important in recognizing the economic significance of sport tourism. The scope of the economic parameters of the sport-tourism relationship is made evident by considering (a) sport and tourism as economic activities, (b) sport as a main holiday purpose—sport activity holidays, (c) sport, especially major events and facilities, as an attraction for visitors, and (d) sport as part of regeneration strategies for cities and regions.

Sport and Tourism as Economic Activities

Sport and tourism each contribute a great deal to the global economy. As a combination of the two, sport tourism has significant impact economically. However, the impact of sport tourism is difficult to quantify. In this section, we look at the economic impacts of sport and tourism individually and then discuss the economic impact of sport tourism as a combined entity. Much of the data used is from Great Britain; this helps us trace the relationships between the economic impact of sport, tourism, and sport tourism. Many of the conclusions can be extrapolated to the developed countries worldwide.

Economic Impact of Sport

The first study of the impact of sport was undertaken in the United Kingdom using 1985 data (Henley Centre for Forecasting, 1986) and surprised the U.K. government, and even some sporting interests, by demonstrating its significance as an economic activity, involving 1.1 percent of

Michael F. Collins and Guy A.M. Jackson are with the Recreation Management Group at Loughborough University.

Gross National Product (GNP) and employing some 370,000 people. Perhaps more surprising was that the commercial sector was the largest component (circa 50 percent), and much of that activity and employment was in the gambling, catering, transport, and building sectors generated by sporting demands.

The Council of Europe then sought to coordinate a nine-nation study to identify sport's economic significance more widely across Europe. This showed results similar to the U.K. research, with contributions to the gross domestic product (GDP) ranging from 0.8 percent in Portugal to 2.1 percent in the Netherlands (Jones, 1989). Five years later another study was prepared; table 5.1 shows that sport in these states contributed between 0.6 and 1.8 percent of GDP (excluding the unlikely high figure for Switzerland explained in the footnote to the table). Sport in these countries involved finance totaling US$93 billion and compares relatively well with tourism, which accounted for 4 to 5 percent of GDP. Thatcher's United Kingdom showed a noticeably lower level of government support than most states comparable in size and level of development. However, while it remains significant, a slow retreat of state funding for sport is noticeable in most countries.

Table 5.1   Financing of European Sport (1990 Prices)

Purchasing Power Parities (PPP) per head of population (US$)[3]			
	Total	% Sport in public sector	Sport as % GDP
Switzerland[1]	1337[1]	6	3.5[2]
Finland	350	29	1.1
Sweden	342	23	1.8
United Kingdom	294	16	1.7
Germany	271	27	1.3
France	268	38	1.1
Belgium	241	32	1.2
Spain	236	14	1.7
Italy	224	19	1.0
Denmark	164	39	0.6
Portugal	116	35	0.6
Hungary	18	47	0.8

Notes. [1]Affected by very high figures for household spending derived from a newspaper estimate; if equal to United Kingdom and Finland, then total would be 345 to 350$ (7.2% of GDP) and public share would be 22%. [2]Very rough and variable base to estimates. Source: Andreff et al., 1995. [3]Purchasing Power Parities are a measure that removes the effects of inflation and exchange rates to allow comparisons.

Economic Impact of Tourism

Tourism is a much larger economic nexus than sport, and one where the economic impacts have been studied in considerably more detail. As with tourism generally, some of the most convincing arguments for exploiting the sport-tourism relationship are those in favor of its positive impact on local economies, although as we shall see, there are also environmental and sociocultural costs and benefits.

Tourism, and therefore sport tourism, is generally thought to be responsible for such well-documented economic impacts as

- increasing national income (through tourist spending on government revenue from direct and indirect taxation),
- generating employment, and
- improving a nation's balance of payments.

Further indirect contributions come through the tourism multiplier when money recirculates through spending on meals, transport, entertainment, attractions, and gifts.

Tourism's impact is not, however, consistent across all areas and is determined by variables such as (a) the level of development of the economy concerned, (b) the extent of dependency on imported goods, and (c) the degree of sophistication of the tourist economy in that place.

Recognition of tourism's impacts has grown, particularly in light of the recent economic recession, because of tourism's resilience to what are worldwide economic downturns. In economic terms, tourism has relatively elastic demand. These features have made tourism an increasingly attractive area of investment locally, regionally, and nationally in the West and the developing world, as traditional industries have stagnated and declined. Tourism including sport has been harnessed in alleviating regional imbalances in wealth, particularly in areas with limited alternative employment opportunities.

In broad economic terms, the World Travel and Tourism Council estimates that in 1994 the industry worldwide generated US$340 billion in gross output and invested US$693 billion in new facilities and equipment. Thereby it contributed US$654 million in tax revenues and created jobs for 204 million people, or one in nine of all those in employment. This all amounted to around 10 percent of global GDP (English Tourist Board, 1995).

Individual countries also showed the economic significance of tourism. For the United Kingdom, for example, tourism's share of GDP in 1993 stood at 3.8 percent and represented 6.8 percent of consumer spending when staying visitors only are considered; this rose to 10 percent when day-trippers are included (English Tourist Board, 1995). All these figures have experienced consistent growth over the last two decades. Tourism employs some 1.5 million Britons (7 percent of people in paid employment), and the industry is comprised in the majority of a large number of small firms, especially in the hotel, catering, and attraction sectors.

The United Kingdom has been a major beneficiary of recent growth in tourism generally and is the sixth largest attractor of international tourists, but it is also the fourth largest generator of tourists, which represents a significant economic outflow. Recent U.K. balance of payments deficits on tourism rise toward UK£3.5 billion (US$5.25 billion). While the more fragile economies of southern Europe, and those benefiting from winter sport tourism in addition to the summer influx, continue well in credit from tourism, the problem of invisible trade deficits from tourism remains an even more significant problem for Germany than for the United Kingdom.

Other potentially negative economic impacts from tourism include tourism's utilization of scarce resources, particularly land and water; increases in property prices which disadvantage local residents; tourism income benefiting national or global rather than local suppliers; and low paid and/or seasonal work for the indigenous population. Some commentators also see tourism as a dangerous avenue of development because it can distract labor from traditional forms of employment, from developments seen as more valuable, and from secure employers (this has become a problem with farming in the Alps, for example).

In reality, tourism (including sport tourism) creates both positive and negative economic impacts for the destination area, and longer term considerations should serve to minimize the latter and maximize the benefits that we know tourism can bring to host communities.

Economic Impact of Sport Tourism

What is now clear is that sport is increasingly playing a role in the tourism product of many countries. A good example is Longleat (the newest U.K. Center Parcs), which showed that nearly 25 percent of all building contracts, worth UK£385 million (US$557.5 million), was spent locally on jobs, goods, and services. Eight hundred and seventy jobs out of the one thousand created were permanent, of which 92 percent were local or within 15 miles. UK£36 million (US$54 million) of goods and services were purchased locally. Two hundred and fifty thousand visitors were attracted to the area with an additional spend of UK£31 million (US$46.5 million) (PAEC, 1991).

We are handicapped, however, in quantifying sport tourism's contribution and potential by a lack of definitive statistics; the necessary data lie frustratingly buried within the increasing body of sport and tourism statistics. Even at the national level, estimates are rough and generally lack empirical data.

Tourism surveys rarely detail "trip purposes" in sufficient detail to allow confident estimates of the exact economic significance of sport tourism. Equally, sport participation statistics rarely identify nonresident activity, except occasionally in surveys of individual centers, and activities are grouped very broadly. Some recent surveys do at least allow us to identify the proportion of trips of a generally sporting nature (playing or spectating) and increasingly permit their separation from broader outdoor interests such as sight-seeing or casual swimming. We shall now attempt to estimate the scale of sport tourism in the state we know best, the United Kingdom.

The United Kingdom Tourism Survey has in the past reported 26 percent of respondents stating "sport" as a main trip purpose, where walking and swimming are included (British Tourist Authority/English Tourist Board [BTA/ETB], annual). Mintel International Group Ltd. (1993) found that special interest and activity tourism accounted for 20 percent of all holiday trips in Britain and 25 percent of expenditure on them. Clearly then, irrespective of definitional problems, we are dealing with a market of significant economic value. Equally we know that only a proportion of these figures reflects dedicated activity-oriented tourism with sport as a primary trip purpose.

More conservative estimates have been generated: studies on motivations for holidays of four or more nights have found that outdoor sports were a "main" reason for some 4 percent of domestic and 5 percent of overseas British tourists (BTA/ETB, 1987); however, higher figures were reported for sport as a partial reason for the holiday, and we know that sports will be a greater influence on short break trips and destination choices, where estimates range from 10 percent to 40 percent of the market being sports activity related in a broad sense (BTA/ETB, 1988; MEW Research, 1993). Incidental or casual sports activity should be excluded from estimates of value and volume wherever possible.

The true volume of sports-related activity holidays for the United Kingdom probably lies between these two broad magnitudes. Our own preliminary estimates support the contention that the field represents a significant niche, and clearly more extravagant claims could be made. Although space limitations preclude setting out all the details of our assumptions, we estimate the market value to be of the order of UK£2.61 billion (US$3.9 billion) in the United Kingdom, as shown in table 5.2.

Thus, using arguably conservative assumptions, sport tourism is worth around UK£2.61 billion (US$3.9 billion) to the U.K. tourism industry. However, because of the large volumes of tourists involved, this figure is highly sensitive to the assumptions made. Mintel International Group Ltd (1995) estimates that a higher proportion of U.K. domestic holiday tourism is generated by sports activity. Increasing the proportion of UK domestic holiday tourism generated by sports activity to the one in seven figure often quoted would inflate the overall value to UK£3.54 billion (US$5.3 billion).

However, the value of sport tourism cannot be confined to activity holidays, though they are the major contributors. Tourism also plays a part in generating sport spending on clothing, footwear, and equipment specifically for touristic purposes. The sport sector is complex in most economies

Table 5.2 The Value of Sport Tourism and Activity Holidays in the United Kingdom

Item	Value (£million)
Sports tourism	
1. Short & long domestic holidays (excluding incidental sport)	1,640
2. Independent[1] overseas tourists	142
3. Day visits	831
Total	2,611

[1]Not "inclusive package" tourists, visiting friends and relatives, or business travelers.

with contributions made by government (local and national) as well as the private (commercial) and voluntary sectors. To separate and trace the flows for sport tourism as against sport is not feasible given our inability to identify nonresident activity. However, an estimate of 10 percent of all consumer expenditure on sports goods being for touristic purposes might seem reasonable given the following assumptions.

Water sports have high capital costs when boats are included (and many expensive yachts "tour" the seas to a mooring in foreign ports). In the United Kingdom in 1991, swimming was the fifth highest spending sport, reflecting the importance of fashion wear on the beach and in the pools (Sports Council, n.d.). If only one-fifth of this was tourist related, then a substantial UK£26 million(US$39 million) was spent (Sports Council, n.d.). Much more than one-fifth of spending on ski clothing, footwear, and equipment is generated by tourism, with tourists also buying apparel and equipment for walking, golf, tennis, cycling, and other sports. Consumer spending on sport and related goods in the United Kingdom was estimated as UK£9.75 billion in 1992 (equal to US$14.62 billion) (Henley Centre for Forecasting, 1992). Of this, UK£4.07 billion (US$6.1 billion) was on equipment, clothing, and footwear. Some UK£407 million (US$610 million) of this we suggest represents the part tourism played in generating sports spending.

Thus, for the UK in the early 1990s we estimate the market value of sport tourism to be of the order of UK£3 billion (US$4.5 billion), representing activity holiday spending of UK£ 2.6 billion (US$ 3.9 billion) plus UK£407 million (US$610 million) sport-related spending. If popular quasi-sports activities such as "walking" and incidental sports participation while traveling for other primary purposes (arguably inseparable in market terms) are added, the value of the sector is further considerably enhanced. Nor have we included those "serious" sport tourists—high-level athletes—who can spend up to a third of their year "on the road" attending competitions and training camps, and for whom their travel is a means to an end, and not at all leisurely (see Jackson & Reeves, 1998).

These volume and value figures from the United Kingdom, and the opportunities and problems they identify, are mirrored throughout Europe and for most developed economies. In France, for example, countryside tourism by 4 million staying and 5 million touring holidaymakers generates 51.7 million bed nights and some FF 18 billion (UK£2 billion; US$3 billion) a year from its eight major European customer states alone (Davidson, 1995). After the most popular activity (cultural visits), come swimming and hiking for British (40 percent) and German (30 percent) visitors, and other outdoor elements for Scandinavians. Delpy's (1997) claim that 25% of tourism receipts in North America are related to sports tourism is considerably more ambitious. If correct, this would amount to a market worth US$350 billion annually in the United States, with a predicted growth rate between 8% and 10%.

Although presented in summary form, even these broad estimates reflect both the substantial potential that sport tourism has as a niche market of growing significance, and the problems in quantifying it. The remainder of this chapter outlines the economic features of some key parts of the sport tourism system—activity holidays and major events and their associated facilities.

Sport Activity Holidays

In the previous section we considered sports-related tourism generally and included tourism for spectating, sports-related day excursions from home, and other forms in our calculations. Similar problems exist in estimating the volume and economic value of dedicated activity holidays as for sport tourism more generally. Nonetheless, some attempts have been made. There is also some difficulty in using this data to review the importance of sport within activity holidays more broadly defined, a matter rarely considered in detail. Europe-wide, Smith and Jenner (1990) estimated that by the turn of the last decade activity holidays, where sport or a specific activity was the main purpose of the trip, accounted for around 10 percent of all holidays in Europe and that by 1995 the figure would be around 13 percent.

The authors surveyed the data for several nations, and again found the difficulties created by not separating sport activity holidays from those that contained some element of activity outdoors, inconsistency in separating (or not) domestic and overseas holidays, and focusing on particular groups or activities. For the United Kingdom, the figure of 12 percent of domestic holiday tourists engaging in sport activity holidays is often used (BTA/ETB, 1992). Roughly comparable figures for Sweden suggest that 8.4 percent of domestic holiday tourists took dedicated activity holidays, although a further 7 percent engaged incidentally in "active options" while on holiday. Broader figures for Germany, including both domestic and international tourism, suggest that 18 percent of the German population take sporting opportunities into account when choosing holidays and destinations and 7 percent of all tourists can be classed as "real" sport tourists (Studiënkreis für Tourismus, 1990). Thus, within this necessarily limited sample, there is some consistency in the magnitude of importance of activity holidays in the overall market.

If we take more specific estimates for an individual country, a more distinct picture emerges. For activity holidays specifically, the Economist Intelligence Unit assessed the U.K. market (Ogilvie & Dickinson, 1992) to generate around three million holiday trips annually, with people targeting European destinations spending an average of UK£500 to UK£600 per head (US$750-900), and long-haul holidaymakers, a smaller proportion, generating spending between UK£1,500 and UK£2,000 per head (US$2,250-3,000). This estimate, based on consultation with tour operators, was clearly focused upon outbound tourism from the United Kingdom, at a time when total outbound tourism generated just over 30 million trips annually (Burton, 1995). Thus, activity holidays taken abroad by Britons are estimated as making up about 10 percent of the total outbound market.

Support for such figures comes from Leisure Consultants' (1992) study, which estimated that three million activity holidays were taken abroad by Britons annually, generating spending of roughly UK£2 billion (US$3 billion). In 1994 international tourism by the British reached an all-time high of almost 40 million trips (Cooper & Latham, 1996). Based on our 10 percent estimate, 4 million would be activity-based holidays. However, Leisure Consultants estimates that only around half of activity holidays are primarily of a sports nature, which would value the U.K. market for sport activity holidays overseas in 1994 at around two million trips annually and UK£1.33 billion (US$2 billion) in expenditure overseas.

Leisure Consultants (1992) believes that seven million domestic trips by Britons are activity holidays and, if about half of these are primarily of a sports nature, domestic sport activity holidays in the United Kingdom would generate 3.5 million trips and UK£500 million (US$750 million) in expenditure. We should note that Leisure Consultants' study considered only "organized" trips, that is, those requiring some industry input, and excluded those arranged by individuals and sports clubs and those that lacked tuition; hence they underestimate the total market value. What is clear from this limited review is that, although there is no consensus on volume or value, dedicated activity holidays have considerable significance, and this has increased recently. In very broad terms, using conservative volume figures, the sector appears to account for at least 10 percent of holiday tourism in northern European countries. From best estimates, "pure" sports activities appear to generate roughly half of these holidays, the rest being comprised of social, intellectual, cultural, and incidental sports activities.

In the case of the United Kingdom, this would value organized domestic active sport holidays as annually generating around UK£1.64 billion in spending (US$2.46 billion), based on the British Tourist Authority's 1994 total domestic tourism spend of UK£32.8 billion (US$49.2 billion) (Cooper & Latham, 1996). However, the Mintel (1995) study makes a clearly more extravagant claim, estimating the domestic sport and recreation sector market volume at 12.7 million trips with an estimated value of UK£2.6 billion (US$3.9 billion). We note a significant difference in these estimates, which may be accounted for by the definition imposed on "activity holidays" and "sport and recreation" and the relative importance of sport within the trip. To this has to be added the relatively small proportion of all overseas tourists to Britain whose primary purpose is sports activity, which we value at around UK£140 million (US$224 million).

Economic Impact of Day Visits

The definition of tourism with which we are working includes leisure-based day visits. Data problems exist in this sector too, but a survey conducted by the Office of Population Censuses and Surveys provides a guide and demonstrates the importance of sport within the day visit market (Baty & Richards, 1991). Of the 630 million round trips in 1988-89, 18 percent were sports related (outdoor and indoor), generating a spend of UK£829 million (US$1,243.5 million) (Baty & Richards, 1991). This study valued sports spectating at UK£80 million (US$120 million) whereas a study by Mintel International Group Ltd. (1989) virtually doubled this figure. Again differences in value and the age of the data exemplify the difficulty we have in estimating the economic impact of sport tourism activity.

Infrastructure as an Economic Indicator

The industry infrastructure also provides useful indicators of the increasing size and scope of this sector. These involve the organizations of tour operators, venue owners, activity instructors, event and tour organizers, and so forth. U.K. provision is described as fragmented, not only because of the variation in interest group types, but also because many operators in the sector are small independent family firms or partnerships with modest turnovers (Collins & Randolph, 1994).

Leisure Consultants (1992) identifies one thousand organizations offering activity holidays to the U.K. market, two-thirds serving the domestic and one-third the overseas market, mostly exclusively. Interestingly in this context, two-thirds deal in sports. However, again there is variation in the data: Algar (1988) puts the overall number operating in the activity holiday sector at nearer three thousand, a figure supported by Mintel International Group Ltd. (1995), and Ogilvie and Dickinson (1992) identify three hundred tour operators alone offering activity holidays in their portfolios.

Skiing as an Example of Economic Impact

There are other facets to the significance of this sector and its economic value that should be recognized. A particular case of concentrated sports holiday activity and investment is skiing. This is a good example of how interest in active tourism and its supply of facilities has grown spectacularly in recent years. The economic benefits of developing tourism, described at the outset of this chapter, have been well recognized around the globe, and in states with beaches and mountains, winter tourism serves not least to smooth any seasonality in tourism receipts.

Skiing is a worldwide market, with resorts developing in all continents and competing with its Alpine birthplace and heartland. As a high-priced activity, it is susceptible to trade cycles and is under ever greater scrutiny from environmental interests. However, the basic thrill of pitting oneself against gravity and the elements at speed, in settings of natural grandeur at great distance from the everyday city life of millions, seems certain to sustain the sport's growth in the foreseeable term. Global warming leading to the shrinking of the season and the snowfields is the great long-term threat.

Increasing Recognition of Economic Benefits of Sport Tourism

There are other macroeconomic factors likely to foster continued expansion in the active holiday market. These include that many providers of sports facilities have not understood or realized their tourist potential. Beyond individual facilities, whole areas can benefit from active tourism in the same way as they can, or have done, from tourism more generally. Despite the example of the Alps, this too has yet to be fully recognized. Europe-wide, active tourism is likely to be further fueled as this potential is increasingly recognized for the hitherto relatively underdeveloped (particularly inland) areas of some major tourist-receiving countries, which are now looking to diversify their product away from reliance on beach or snow tourism. Most indications, therefore, are for the continued expansion of sport tourism and activity holidays.

Major Sport Facilities and Events as an Attraction for Visitors

As Leisure Consultants (1992) shows, the sporadic participation in sport by holidaymakers and day-trippers is growing, but participation is growing even more on the specific, dedicated sports holiday or trip. Events, large and small, for display and competition, focus the interest of tourist and resident alike. Repeated events like league matches in soccer, American football, baseball, and so forth demand purpose-built facilities, and their volumes of attendance make them desirable attractions for regeneration programs, as we shall see in the next section.

Most sports events are quite modest, involving a few hundred participants and spectators, few of whom stay overnight. Yet a regular events program adds noticeably to a city's or a region's economy, or the events can be of substantial national or international nature, attracting extensive TV coverage and associated sponsorship and advertising, and involve merchandising of club or team-branded goods and souvenirs. Table 5.3 gives some European examples of the scale of finance behind different sports events and illustrates the great differences in the scale of prime televised events and of the minority sports that are valuable to their host cities but make smaller impacts; the figures also emphasize some differences because of the size of the host nation's market.

At the top of the hierarchy come mega-events, defined by Ritchie (1984, p. 3) as

> major one-time or recurring events of limited duration, developed primarily to enhance the awareness, appeal, and profitability of a tourist destination in the short and/or long term. Such events rely for their success on uniqueness, status or timely significance to create interest and attract attention.

On a more modest scale, some facilities and events produce healthy profits from ticket sales, catering, stadium advertising, and increasingly from executive business boxes. Even technically bankrupt British soccer clubs can have their finances rescued by lotteries and merchandising of clothing and souvenirs for fans. Although the operation of some urban sports facilities has to be subsidized from the public purse, the associated travel, shopping, eating, drinking, entertainment, and souvenir spending of visitors from out of town or overseas produces a valuable indirect income and job generation, which is taken, and sometimes assessed, as justifying it.

Some of this new income to the host community is then re-spent on paying employees, on consumption, on maintenance, on buying more materials, on insurance, and so forth, and in local taxes; and some "leaks" out of the locality to pay regional or national taxes, employees, shareholders, HQ offices, and so forth. This is the "multiplier effect." This first round of spending then generates further, diminishing rounds, but tracing such money flows is difficult and laborious beyond the first round. The smaller the area concerned with the event, the larger the leakage is likely to be. What we do know is that the multiplier effect significantly increases the value of financial injections from outside the local economic system, whether through mega-events or other forms of tourist-related initiatives.

Methods Used to Examine the Impact of Major Events

In this section we discuss three different-sized events as examples, but first we need to look at the evaluation methods for examining the economic,

Table 5.3 Support for Major Events and Facilities in Europe in 1991–93 ($million at 1990 Purchasing Power Parities)

France	$m	Portugal	$m	Sweden	$m	Switzerland	$m
Paris-Dakar rally	92.0	Cycling championships	0.5	Euro '92 football	42.6	Zurich athletic meet	4.2
Prix d'America trotting	36.1	Junior football championships	0.5	Fallen ski meeting	9.7	Gymnastic festival	3.4
Roland-Gar, tennis	32.9	Basketball championships	0.5	O ringen orienteer	3.6	Wrestling festival	2.4
Pr de l'Arc de Tri	31.0	Trampolining championships	0.3	Stockholm Open tennis	3.6	Engadin ski marathon	1.0
Tour de France cycling	21.6	Judo championships	0.1	Scand. Masters golf	3.1	Berne Grand Prix	0.3
Grand Prix de France motor	8.8			World handball championships	3.1		
PSG/Mars D1 football	1.0			World table tennis championships	1.8		
PSG/Monaco D1 football	0.7			Gothb'g horse show	1.7		
				Stockholm women's marathon	1.1		

Source: Andreff et al., 1995.

physical, and social impacts of events, for in the enthusiastic search for arguments in support of hosting events or building facilities, technical errors, assumptions, borrowed evidence, and political overruling have often had a large part to play. Some events have been roaring successes, others have notable "downsides" in their side effects, and some are unmitigated failures.

The most common method for measuring the impacts has been cost-benefit analysis. Its purpose and method is described in its title, but there are two major limitations to it, in that there are a large number of nonmonetary costs and benefits, and that there are a large number of technical points on which there can be errors. One method of taking nonmonetary cost more fully into account is the Planning Balance Sheet (Litchfield & Margolis, 1961). In addition to costs and benefits described in money, it shows for each item and each group affected positively or negatively the size of the group and the degree of effect. This method has the benefit of demonstrating three aspects that are very important to strategic managers or politicians in decision making, that is, salience (the weight and nature of the effect), severity of impact, and the distribution of the effect. Unfortunately, it has not been widely adopted.

Getz (1991) criticizes many studies for failing to show the losers and gainers, who—as we shall see—are not always the same people or groups. Crompton (1995) also points out that many promoters of events use whatever data suit them to support their advocacy for an event or development. He quotes the case of the San Francisco Giants being wooed by San Jose, whose mayor was trying to persuade the citizens to agree by referendum to raise US$265 million in public funds for a new stadium and claimed the franchise would deliver economic benefits of "somewhere between US$50 million and US$150 million," whereas San Francisco's budget director could document only a US$3.1-million loss of benefits, or one ten-thousandth of the city's gross economic product, as a result of the transfer of the franchise out of the area. Crompton makes several criticisms of misapplications of economic impact studies, amongst other things, for using inappropriate multipliers of sales or employment, omitting costs, and including spending by visitors who would be in the city anyway.

Mega-Events: Olympic Games and World Cup Soccer

At the apex of mega-events are the Olympic Games and the soccer World Cup, which have grown massively in scale of finance and impact, mainly due to the growth of global TV rights, associated sponsorship, and sales of souvenirs and branded products. The Olympics are not just a global quadrennial sports event, but, summer or winter alike, a major tourist attraction (Ahn, 1987; Heinemann, 1992; Ritchie, n.d.).

© Stephen Slade

World Cup soccer match—United States vs. Colombia.

The total impacts are substantial—Montreal 1976 was reckoned to generate between US$77 million and $135 million, or US$124 million and $216 million including multiplier effects, probably exaggerated at the estimated 1.6 times. In a similar vein, the estimated total impact of the Los Angeles games was US$417 million in value-added terms (Pyo, Cook, & Howell, 1988). It is also clear that pre–Olympic Games studies have consistently overestimated attendances, due to public fears of overcrowding and overcharging ("gouging") by hotels, restaurants, taxis, and others, often prominently voiced in the press and on TV. Other regular tourists and business travelers stayed away, so that, even in the financially successful Los Angeles games, six to eight thousand hotel beds stayed empty and the organizing committee reckoned US$331 million (a huge sum if true) may have been lost.

What the figures also do not reveal is the extent of municipal debt and written-off capital in Olympic Games prior to 1984, when Los Angeles showed how to minimize these by refurbishment of existing facilities, private partnership funding, reuse of sports and communications centers, and resale of residential units. These practices have been followed since. The Atlanta 1996 Games Committee (1993) estimated that it and its partner marketing company would generate US$2.4 billion of new investment in Georgia, and that visitors would spend US$2.7 billion. (ACOG used the Department of Commerce multiplier of 2.3 mentioned by Wang and Irwin [1993].)

Also on the global scale, table 5.4 shows how the enormously successful (in sport and publicity terms) 1976 soccer World Cup increased Argentina's

Table 5.4   World Cup Glory—At a Price? Argentina, 1976

- US$2 billion resources, but US$8 billion debt to World Bank/International Monetary Fund
- Cup cost US$1 billion for TV Center, refurbished stadium, new stadia, housing, modernized hospitals, and transport
- Income US$35 million from TV, US$6 million from FIFA, US$8 million from sponsors, etc., but much leakage because most were multinationals (Adidas, Atlas, Bosch, Coca Cola, Ericson, Mercedes, Osram, Seimens)

national debt and channeled benefits to multinational sponsors based in Europe, North America, and Japan. During the 1994 World Cup in the United States, when TV rights and visitor spending were multiplied many times over that of Argentina, Japanese visitors alone were estimated to have each spent US$2,780 during an average 9.2 day stay, or US$900 million directly (and more contentiously, using regional multipliers, an estimated US$1.8 billion indirectly) (Nogawa, Hagi, Suzuki, & Yamaguchi, 1995). Japanese interest in soccer is booming with the advent of the professional J-League, to back amateur leagues.

Why are such events popular with cities and governments? Basically, they form a shop window to the world, to announce the arrival of a little-recognized state or culture, as in the Seoul Summer Olympic Games (Ritchie, n.d.), or to bring a city out from the shadow of the national capital or its provincial competitors, as in the Barcelona and Los Angeles Olympics, the Adelaide Grand Prix, the Calgary Winter Olympic Games, or the Victoria, British Columbia, Commonwealth Games; or it is to provide a boost to tourism and external investment or reconstruction, as in the Albertville and Lillehammer Winter Olympics.

Intermediate Events

Now we shall examine an event of intermediate scale. Table 5.5 illustrates the Americas Cup sailing races in Fremantle in 1986-87. This was a case of a prolonged media exposure of Western Australia, an event managed very successfully, with good international attendance, but one which still failed to bring as many interstate Australian visitors as predicted. As with the case of Sheffield (table 5.7), this event left the region with a much improved hotel infrastructure, but equally as important, a human infrastructure experienced in running major events, which was marshaled to run the World Swimming Championships four years later. The Americas Cup study remains one of the few that attempted a "before and after" evaluation, and the bold figures in the panel indicate the effects of the visitor shortfall.

Table 5.5   World-Class Event: The Americas Cup 1986–87

- 13 international and 4 Australian sailing syndicates, each employing 40–50 people, contested the Cup.
- The Commonwealth World government granted Aus$30 million, listed as income.
- Several new hotels and restaurants were developed in Fremantle in time for the event; new roads, sewers, car parks, and boat ramps were built; public buildings and coastal dunes were restored.
- 1.2 million visitors were predicted—146,000 international, 360,000 interstate, and 506,000 country, in addition to the 190,000 regular tourists expected at this summer time.
- Centre for Applied and Business Research estimates of benefits were Aus$389 million direct and Aus$514 million induced/multiplier effects, with postrace estimates in italics:

Aus$ million	Induced	Production	Household income	Job/yrs FTE
Visitors spend	211	316	139	9,250
Sailing syndicates	39	62	20	970
Construction	60	102	33	1,350
Operations	79	120	52	2,850
Total	389 *289*	600 *454*	244 *170*	14,420 *9,500*

- In fact, there were more international but 43% fewer interstate visitors than predicted. There was some loss of domestic TV and live interest as the races proceeded, and the cost of travel and accommodation was perceived as high.
- The Western Australia Tourism Commission sustained a strong international promotional campaign to ensure hotel occupancy.
- There was good exposure for both Perth and Fremantle, resulting in great interest in high technology industries (focused around Murdoch University) and in new business investment; general and tourism infrastructure were much modernized.
- EventsCorp set up and ran 1991 World Swimming championships.

Sources: Centre for Applied and Business Research, 1986, 1987; Selwood and Jones, 1993.

Steve Tow of New Zealand's Hillary Commission presents some details from events hosted in New Zealand (Tow, 1997). The 1990 XIV Commonwealth Games were held in Auckland. The total benefits of the Games to New Zealand were forecast to be NZ$325 million, with the majority of the benefits accruing to the host city. The total economic impact of the 1994

Auckland stopover of the Whitbread Round of the World Yacht Race was estimated at NZ$16.2 million (Tow, 1997).

Smaller Events

The third case study is of the 1994 Europa Cup, a two-day athletics (track-and-field) event hosted by the city of Birmingham, England, in its newly refurbished Alexander Stadium (see table 5.6). The city's Convention and Visitor Bureau had been energetically implementing the Council's policy of targeting leisure visitors through events, as well as using new facilities like a new indoor arena and conference center to reimage the city. The convention bureau's chief executive was quoted by Bramwell and Rawding (1994) to have noted that

> tourism is labour-intensive and brings in money from outside. It is also being used to regenerate the fabric of the city. It has brought enormous developments in the amenities, attractions, and services for the community, so their quality of life has improved" (p. 432).

Even with grants from the Sports Council and the Foundation for Sport and the Arts, there was some concern as to how attractive the event would be. In fact, outcomes exceeded expectations, with two-thirds of visitors coming from outside the region, three-fifths staying overnight, and half attending both days. There was an on-site spend of UK£260,000 (US$390,000) and spending in the city amounted to UK£150,000 (US$225,000) (Train, 1994).

Further examples of smaller sports events generating significant economic impact come from New Zealand (Tow, 1997). Rugby is the major men's winter team sport and the match in Dunedin during the weekend of July 7–8, 1994 was an event of enormous interest since the opposing team was from South Africa which had recently returned to the sporting community (see Chapter 6). The game takes only 80 minutes to play but was predicted to generate NZ$13 million into the local economy. For an even smaller event the Wellington City Council through its Capital Development Agency invests NZ$360,000 in the Wellington Street Race. A study in 1993 estimated that the 7,266 visitors from outside Wellington spent NZ$2.48 million representing a return of NZ$6.8 for every NZ$1 invested (Tow, 1997).

Increasing Economic Gain

Having held a successful event, what next? The following options present themselves for further economic gain:

1. Extend the duration or the frequency of the event.
2. Change the season, if possible, to increase attendance.

Table 5.6   The Europa Athletics Cup, Birmingham, England, 1994

- 16,000 spectators, 67% from outside region
- 11% first visit to city
- 50% of outsiders visited both days, and 58% stayed overnight (3,000)
- 1,000 shopping trips were generated
- Improved image of the city as an athletics host
- No bad side effects were evident

City expenditure £000		Income projected £000	
Stadium + seats	97	Car parking	7
Media/host/prom	43	Tickets/commission	25
Contingency	10	Promotion	5
Total	150	SC, FSA grants	32
			69
		Deficit	81

Actual Spending

	Regional visitors per head £	Outsiders per head £	Total £000
Tickets	9.07	12.88	186
Car parking	0.79	1.01	12
Travel	1.45	3.49	11
Souvenirs	2.36	3.86	29
Food/drink at Cup	2.69	2.93	22
Total direct on event			260 (60%)
Food/drink elsewhere	5.10	12.87	42
Accommodation	1.07	31.18	93
Shopping in Birmingham	5.98	14.38	9
Entertainment in Birmingham	0	7.83	2
Other	6.24	10.54	8
Total in city			154 (40%)
Grand total	12.62	32.41	414

Source: Train, 1994.

3. Organize lead-in, follow-up, or satellite events.

4. "Mimic" the event for other age groups or regions (as the EC is devising for Europe).

5. Transform the event from purely sport, as TV and merchandising has done with the Olympics.

6. Increase media penetration.

7. Create profitable legacies (for example, coins, stamps, videos, catalogs, guides, clothing, lotteries, sports medicine facilities, coaching centers).

Clearly, all events generate economic activity; some like the Olympics attract high-spending long-haul visitors; others may bring kudos but have a very different visitor profile (like the World Student Games), and many local sports events may have low-income students and young people, who borrow accommodations or camp. Some attract TV, large-scale sponsorship, and corporate hospitality; others need grants, patronage, and much volunteer help to run, and may leave city officials and sports governing body members drained of energy and enthusiasm for months. All may be shown to be sporting successes. The political decision to bid for an event needs a clear picture of the profile of participants and spectators; the judgment of its benefits needs better data and more careful assumptions in

Cyclists in Southern England. Tourism spending can be increased by hosting events such as Le Tour (formerly le Tour de France).

the calculation than is often given. Both are often clouded by the rhetoric of officials, promoters, agents, consultants, or journalists, whose vested interest is in boosting the city or the event by a "good story."

Sport and Tourism as Part of Regeneration Strategies for Cities and Regions

Some noneconomists would claim that the fashion for justifying new facilities is overdrawn and merely moves benefits about; for every major sports event represents spending that is lost elsewhere. In a global sense that is, of course, true, but first, it is true as well for locating new pharmaceutical or biotechnology plants, and second, while cities and regions are in competition for new jobs and investment, sport can help improve their image and environment and help those ends.

Roche (1992) sees mega-events as "quintessentially" part of postindustrial and postnation-state modernization. In the twenty-first century health issues will grow in importance for aging populations (Ermisch, 1990), and in a world where physical activity at home, at work, and while traveling has been largely replaced by robots, machines, or telecommunications, and sport represents the main way of getting vigorous and much of moderate exercise, it will grow in importance both in local communities and while people are on holiday (Morris & Collins, 1992).

In the developed economies of the Organization for Economic Cooperation and Development (OECD) states, there has been a marked shift from manufacturing to information and biotechnology services (financial, producer, governmental, and consumer—including leisure). Even so, this has lead to a growth of early retirement and unemployment for middle-aged people, even those who have retrained, and a lower pay and skill level for some of the redeployed. The leisure industry, especially tourism, has been accused of providing overwhelmingly low-skill, low-quality, and markedly seasonal jobs—characterized scornfully by Prime Minister Thatcher on one occasion as "mickey mouse" jobs. Roche (1992) sees these as characteristics of an immature industry, which will decline with the development of year-round attractions, better marketing, and better training in response to a more sophisticated and demanding clientele. Much recent evidence supports this view.

For governments in the 1960s and 1970s, especially in the third world, tourism was about earning hard foreign currencies. For cities in the developed economies in the 1980s and 1990s, it is about job creation in tourism, culture, and sport directly, or by using these and other services to "reimage" the city to make it attractive for employers to locate there. This is particularly true of "rust belt" coal, steel, and textile towns and ports, which were bypassed by the bulk carrier revolution in shipping. The United States, with major regional cities and the scatter of baseball, basketball, and football franchises, provides examples of sport-based development, often on the edge of the central business district on sites of run-down housing, industry, railway yards, or dock warehouses, creating new "visitor destinations." This can be seen in Boston, Philadelphia, and Indianapolis.

World Student Games in Sheffield

Elsewhere the scale of such developments is more modest. Our first example in this section is of the World Student Games in Sheffield, England, in 1991 (see table 5.7). This competition is as large in competitors (ten

Table 5.7   Short-Term Civic Failure and Medium-Term Sporting and Economic Success: The World Student Games in Sheffield, 1991

Pre Bid:
- 1986 feasibility study reports "no event deficit . . . low capital costs"
- 1987 political commitment made; bid won; operating company (city/chamber of commerce) formed; negative financial report suppressed
- UK£147 million for new competition (£50 million pool, arena, velodrome) and practice areas, housing, open space improvements, and two new hotels

Post Bid:
- Problems
  1. Company collapses, city takes back
  2. Capital costs escalate to UK£400 million
  3. Little government support or matching EEC money
  4. No network TV interest, slashes sponsorship
  5. Severe public and media criticism
- Official impact study positive but no cost-benefit analysis
- Only one-third of jobs created locally, cheaper in wider region
- 1991 event a sporting success with much volunteer help, but poor media coverage

Post Event:
- No research on impacts, but city estimates Games were worth UK£31 million
- Deficits of revenue UK£10 million, of capital UK£400 million over 20 years
- No political accounting for failures
- Joint public/private Visitor/Conference Bureau seeks major events
- 10 World and 6 European Championships and 190 other events in four years; 5.7 million spectators in 1994
- Research at European Swimming and UK Special Olympics suggests UK£1.7 million spending in city

Sources: Bramwell, 1993; Bramwell & Rawding, 1994; Dobson and Gratton, 1995; Foley, 1991; Roche, 1991.

thousand) and journalists (seven thousand) as the Olympics and when held in the Eastern bloc countries generated great spectator and television interest, being a nursery or rehearsal for the next Olympiad.

Sheffield bid for the games in 1986 as part of a strategy to replace thousands of jobs lost in steel and metal working. It is not clear how well the city politicians understood that the host's costs were greater and the likely spending of supporting spectators smaller than at the Olympics. This matter was exacerbated by a lack of governmental and (both North American and British) TV support and consequently reduced sponsorship, but above all by poor management and cover-ups of problems. The event was a genuine celebration, but the aftermath of debts and recrimination left a sour taste in the electorate's mouths and impoverished the image of the city's managers rather than enhancing it.

A few years on, there has been a series of successful major events and a strong continuing marketing effort, through the jointly funded Sheffield Visitor and Convention Bureau (a public/private sector partnership), which city officials claim has brought advertising and visibility beyond anything that Sheffield could have purchased—for instance, TV coverage worth UK£85 million (US$127.5 million). They reckon the benefits now outweigh the costs of the games sevenfold, and this has begun modifying the criticisms, with more people now seeing the games' facilities as assets to the city (Bramwell & Rawding, 1994; Bramwell 1996).

Dobson and Gratton (1995) comment that

> sport has brought the public and private sectors together to work for Sheffield and the strategies for urban governance to utilise sport as part of "The Way Ahead" for Sheffield. However, the degree to which this commitment to sport has benefitted the community's quality of life, patterns of sporting participation and social regeneration remains unanswered. (p. 5)

Facilities and Events Helping to Rejuvenate Birmingham and Other Cities

Ironically, Birmingham had failed in bids for the two previous Olympics, but gained in sports facilities and civic reputation while doing so. Using its substantial financial resources as the nation's largest municipality after the abolition of the Greater London Council, it developed an indoor arena with 20,000 seats, a 50-meter pool, and a refurbished stadium, as well as a major convention center and concert hall. It has a major events planning unit, and the benefits of events are illustrated by the example of the Europa Cup in the last section. The failed Olympic bid process cost UK£5 million (US$7.5 million), but it has been estimated that the media coverage worldwide was worth UK£25 million (US$37.5 million), without the hassle of running the event! (Roche, 1992).

In Britain, Birmingham, Glasgow, Sheffield, and Manchester in turn sought to use sport as part of their regeneration attempts. London, lacking a metropolitan council since 1974, lagged behind and could not make a credible Olympic bid; but the owners of Wembley Stadium plan to rebuild it, using National Lottery money. Having been awarded the next Commonwealth Games, Manchester is seeking an equally large stadium and hopes to bid for the 2004 Olympiad. In all these cases, sport brings the prestige event, but the visitors bring the tourist spending that is the largest part of the (desirable) economic impact, being not diverted spending but spending attracted at the cost of some city distant in the state, or in another continent.

1992 Summer Olympic Games in Barcelona, Spain

A recent example which demonstrates how to use sport intelligently as a tool for raising a provincial profile to global scale and for regenerating a flagging industrial base is Barcelona and the 1992 Summer Olympic Games (see table 5.8). Barcelona provides a contrast with Sheffield.

Several of Spain's provincial capitals are keen to demonstrate that they are not overshadowed by Madrid. Barcelona had outworn railway and dock areas and, as with other cases we have cited, the need was to find new investment for jobs and to attract visitors, but the city wanted to proclaim

Table 5.8   Barcelona and the 1992 Summer Olympics

The Games were run by HOLSA, a company owned 51% by the federal government and 49% by the city. There were 422,000 visitors.

Investment: Allocations of a total of $5.4 billion	%
City Olympic facilities/villages	33.6
Olympic facilities elsewhere	9.1
Other sports facilities	3.9
Cultural facilities	2.1
Roads	33.1
Airport	3.5
Public transport	1.5
Hotels	5.1
Communications/other services	4.5

Operating expenses: Allocations of a total of $1.08 billion

Expenditure	%	Income	%
Technology	5	Tickets	6
Sites	25	Accommodation	2
Media	10	Sponsors	22
Organization	14	Licenses	4
Ceremonies	5	Lotteries, coins, stamps	20
Promotion/advertising	9	Services	33
Security	3	State transfers	10
Housing/transport	18	Asset sales	1
Test events/ParaOlympics	8		

Other effects:

Positive	Negative
• Unemployment decreased from 128,000 in 1986 to 78,000 in 1993	• Rentals increased by 339% 1986–92
• Hotel beds grow by 38% 1990–92	• 48% of population feel "apathetic" about developments
• New beaches attract 2.5 million users	
• New sports facilities jointly managed by clubs, federations, or companies	

Sources: Truno, 1994; Tsubota, 1993; Varley, 1992.

that Catalonia is a good area for investment. The same year a world trade fair expo was held in Seville to reinforce the same message for that region.

The 1992 games were a roaring success—as a sporting event and as a cultural spectacle, with record TV coverage, payments, and sponsorship. But the city had also concentrated many years of future investment into just five through a short-term rebuilding program including renewing its railway station, improving its airport links, opening up its waterfront to public use, sweeping away dereliction, and developing high-class housing and craft and tourist businesses in part of its old town. This aspect is important, for although to the economist the time shifting of investment is handled by discounting for inflation, in daily affairs the effect of so much bustle and renewal is disproportionate on the confidence of citizens and visitors alike. It is even more important to mayors wanting to be reelected or to leave their stamp on the city, literally.

Avoiding the "white elephants" of isolated sports areas and competitors' housing, like those left on Montreal's site by the St. Lawrence River, and learning from Los Angeles and Seoul that housing and other facilities must be sold off or reused, the Barcelona Olympic village provided two thousand flats, three parks, offices, and a conference center that all became part of the city's fabric.

1994 Winter Olympic Games in Lillehammer, Norway

In the Lillehammer Winter Olympiad, the same result was achieved by using much prefabricated housing, for few of the 50,000 visitors who descended on the 25,000 inhabitants would return. After the games one ski jump and one ice rink were dismantled, and part of the village became commercial offices and part a second exhibition gallery for the small town. But the coup was to have the major telecommunications center reused as a center for telecommunications training, a function that a small town so near the Arctic circle would have found difficult to wrest from larger, more southern towns in normal circumstances.

The costs of US$1.17 billion considerably outweighed the revenue of US$0.8 billion as the local organizers openly admitted in the games brochure (Lillehammer OOC, 1994): "anticipated revenues are substantially lower than the forecast costs. The Games are primarily expected to yield general spin-offs for the Olympic region and the country as a whole." But apart from the psychological benefits mentioned above, the purpose was to have the small ski resorts appearing on the world stage as worthy competitors with the Alpine countries, still investing in ski technology and promotion, and it was fully achieved.

Smaller Scale Results of Using Sport Tourism for Local Regeneration

In a much more small-scale, everyday fashion, sport and sport tourism have been seen as part of regeneration strategies, even in towns with no hallmark event or flagship facility. A case in point is Batley in West Yorkshire (see table 5.9), which needed to overcome structural unemployment and major health and environmental problems. Batley has obtained, in competition, a substantial government grant from the City Challenge fund, and it will be fascinating to track how fully it achieves its aspirations to regenerate the area using sport and sport tourism. This will be particularly so since it has to compete with Leeds, the regional center, and Bradford, which have both had major successes in attracting day visitors and short-stay tourists, but have arguably saturated the area with visitor attractions. One dimension of success in tourism is to create a distinctive sense of place, which Batley will have to do.

Table 5.9   Part of a Vision: Sport and Regeneration in Batley, West Yorkshire

- Traditional textile employment collapsed leaving 34% jobless, very high levels of ill health, crime, poor schooling
- One of five aspects of City Challenge bid was for "people services" including sport—UK£37.5 million, seeking to attract UK£120 million, i.e., leverage of 4:1
- The people initiative for education and training, health and recreation seeks to spend UK£6.1 million, and to "lever in" UK£14 million including:
  1. Improving Mount Pleasant rugby league ground for regional excellence and community fitness and health
  2. Employing a recreation development officer
  3. Providing an indoor tennis center, and helping clubs to manage park courts
  4. Providing a synthetic multigames area, mainly for young people
  5. Providing new, safe play areas for children

Source: Fytche, 1995.

As part of regeneration strategies, there has been a growth in "place marketing" of destinations that have no tradition of tourism (Ashworth & Voogd, 1990; Kotler, Heider, & Irving, 1993), and within this trend there has been clearly a greater use of sport to attract tourists and commercial investment, as well as more generally contributing to the reimaging of cities in economic decline. Only a few things have been written about sport in this context, some overclaiming the benefits, some criticizing the imbalance of beneficiaries and sufferers, but increasingly there is an emphasis on the value of high-quality facilities and major events in attracting leisure and business/conference tourists and day visitors (for example, see Bramwell & Rawding, 1994).

One of the problems in the United Kingdom is that almost all the development funds have been combined in a Single Regeneration Budget, which can only be accessed through a bidding system. Apart from any issues of the wastefulness of this compared with a planned approach, it leads, naturally, to each bidder proposing his or her most dynamic projects and the areas most likely to take off. This systematically disadvantages the most run-down and needy areas, and increases spatial and community disparities, in opposition to European Union (EU) objectives (Oatley, 1995).

Summary

We have seen that sport and tourism are major economic sectors showing steady growth; sport tourism comprises between 10 percent and 20 percent of holiday taking, with the exact percentage dependent on the importance of sport within the tourist trip.

The availability of data and research both lag behind the market, and it is difficult to measure the overall value of activity holidays and sport tourism more broadly; given the different reference definitions in use, estimates vary widely even within the United Kingdom, whose data and its limitations we know best, with total impact ranging between UK£3 billion (US$4.5 billion) to UK£3.9 billion (US$5.9 billion).

Events and their purpose-made facilities, from local to global, can leave debts, displace homes and jobs, and damage the environment, but they can also generate numerous jobs and substantial income.

Sport has become an element in the armory of politicians, planners, and economists seeking to regenerate local economies whose manufacturing job base and built fabric is obsolescent, or places which have tourism as their major hope for development (Kotler et al., 1993).

The desire to do active things while on holiday or day trips seems certain to motivate more holiday takers, and therefore the conclusions of Leisure Consultants that activity holidays will grow in domestic and international markets seem well founded. Nonetheless, this chapter demonstrates that there is much still not known about the demand and supply sides of this business and that it is easy to exaggerate the benefits of a new event or facility through lack of competent research or political chicanery.

Also, it is easy to lose money and public credibility on events and to have to go on subsidizing facilities long after their flagship starter event has passed. In a world where citizens are ever more aware of the need for sustainable development, greater care has to be taken in all settings, whether Alpine slopes (May, 1995) or housing overlooked by refurbished or new stadia (Bale, 1993; Churchman, 1995). Likewise, people will mobilize if they think some are going to lose their homes or that all the benefits are going to corporations or politicians (Lipsitz, 1984; Whitson & Macintosh, 1993).

The impacts of sport tourism can be wider: the 1995 Rugby Union World Cup was expected to give South African tourism a mighty boost after many years of isolation under apartheid (Scott, 1995), and the Australian stock market is hoping for an injection of confidence in the last days of the millennium leading to the 2000 Olympic Games (Miller, 1995). KPMG Peat Marwick (SOCOG, 1997), Sydney Olympic Games Organizing Committee's consultants, claim that during the period 1994–2004 hosting the Games could add A$7.3 billion to Australia's Gross Domestic Product, create 150,000 full- and part-time jobs, and bring an extra 1.32 million visitors from overseas and an extra 174,000 domestic visitors to Sydney. Much of the growth in employment will be due to tourism. The Sydney Olympic Committee for the Olympic Games (SOCOG) has budgeted for a small profit. The estimated costs of staging the Games is

US$960 million (1992 dollars), and projected income is US$975 million (1992 dollars). The KPMG study also indicated that Australia will have a legacy of world class sporting facilities that will attract sporting competitions for years after the Games, and the Games will dramatically improve Australia's profile in business and tourism.

This analysis suggests that sport tourism must be considered a sector of some significance in the economy of many countries. Yet the economic benefits attributable to sport tourism have to be offset against the costs involved—and these are not limited to financial costs. Any benefits must be seen in the context of the sociocultural, environmental, and health impacts involved. If sport tourism is developed for economic gain without regard to its other impacts, there is a very real danger that its true costs will greatly exceed its economic value.

References

Ahn, J-A. (1987). The role and impact of mega-events and attractions on tourism development in Asia. In Association Internationale d'Experts Scientifique du Tourisme. (Ed.), *The role and impact of mega-events and attractions on regional and national tourist development* (pp. 133-185). St. Gall, Switzerland: Association Internationale d'Experts Scientifique du Tourisme.

Algar, R. (1988). Adult activities: Residential holiday programmes. *Leisure Management, 8*(2), 51-53.

Andreff, W., Bourg, J-F., Halba, B., & Nys, J-F. (1995). *Les jeux economiques du sport en Europe: Financement et impact economique* [The economic games of sport in Europe: Financing and economic impact]. Paris: Editions Dalloz.

Ashworth, G.J., & Voogd, H. (1990). *Selling the city.* London: Belhaven Press.

Atlanta Committee for the Olympic Games. (1993). The Economic Impact on the State of Georgia of Hosting the 1996 Olympic Games. Leaflet: Atlanta, GA: The Committee.

Bale, J. (1993). *Sport, space and the city.* London: Routledge.

Baty, B., & Richards, S. (1991, May). Results from the Leisure Day Visits Survey 1988-89. *Employment Gazette,* pp. 257-268.

Beioley, S. (1991, May). Activity holidays. *Insights,* B61-78.

Bramwell, W. (1993). Planning for tourism in an industrial city. *Town and Country Planning, Jan/Feb,* 17-19.

Bramwell, W., & Rawding, L. (1994). Tourism marketing organisations in industrial cities. *Tourism Management, 15*(6), 425-434.

Bramwell, W. (1996). Event tourism in Sheffield: A sustainable approach to urban development. In Bramwell, B., Henry, I., Jackson, G., Goytia, A., Richards, G., and van der Straaten, J. (Eds.), Sustainable tourism management: Principles and practice (pp. 147-170). Tilburg, The Netherlands: Tilburg University Press.

British Tourist Authority/English Tourist Board. (1987). *Holiday Motivations Survey.* London: Author.

British Tourist Authority/English Tourist Board. (1988). *The short break market.* London: Author.

British Tourist Authority/English Tourist Board. (1992). *The U.K. Tourist: Statistics 1991.* London: Author.

British Tourist Authority/English Tourist Board. (1994). *Short break destination choice.* London: Author.

Burton, R. (1995). *Travel geography.* London: Pitman.

Centre for Applied and Business Research (1986). *America's Cup—Economic impact.* Nedlands, Australia: University of Western Australia.

Centre for Applied and Business Research (1987). *America's Cup Defence Series 1986-87: Impact on the community.* Nedlands, Australia: University of Western Australia.

Churchman, C. (1995). Sports stadia and the landscape. *Built Environment, 21*(1), 6-24.

Collins, M. (1991). The economics of sport and sports in the economy: Some international comparisons. In C. Cooper (Ed.), *Progress in tourism, recreation and hospitality management. Vol. 3* (pp. 184-214). London: Belhaven Press.

Collins, M.F., & Randolph, L. (1994). Business or hobby? Small firms in sport and recreation. In A.J. Veal, P. Jonson, & G. Cushman (Eds.), *Leisure and tourism: Social and economic change* (pp. 433-438). Sydney, Australia: University of Technology.

Cooper, C. & Latham, J. (1996). Foreign affairs. *Leisure Management, 16*(2), 28-30.

Crompton, J.L. (1995). Economic impact analysis of sports facilities and events: Eleven sources of misapplication. *Journal of Sport Management, 9,* 14-35.

Davidson, R. (1995). Rural tourism in France. *Insights, May,* A145-154.

De Knop, P. (1990). Sport for all and active tourism. *World Leisure & Recreation, 35*(3), 30-36.

Dobson, N., & Gratton, C. (1995, September). *From 'city of steel' to 'city of sport': An evaluation of Sheffield's attempts to use sport as a vehicle for urban regeneration.* Paper presented at the Recreation in the City conference, Staffordshire University, Stoke on Trent, Great Britain.

English Tourist Board. (1995). The role of tourism in the British economy. *Insights, March,* F31-33.

Ermisch, J. (1990). *Fewer babies, longer lives.* York, Great Britain: Joseph Rowntree Foundation.

Foley, P. (1991). The impact of major events. A case study of the World Student Games and Sheffield. *Environment and Planning, C9,* 65-69.

Fytche, I. (1995). *Sport and urban Regeneration. Facilities Factfile No 2.* London: The Sports Council.

Getz, D. (1991). Assessing the economic impacts of festivals and events: Research issues. *Journal of Applied Economic Research, 16*(1), 61-77.

Glyptis, S.A. (1982). *Sport and tourism in western Europe.* London: British Travel Educational Trust.

Hall, C.M. (1994). *Hallmark tourist events.* London: Belhaven Press.

Heinemann, K. (1992). The economic impact of the Olympic Games. In International Olympic Committe (Ed.), *Proceedings of the 32nd Session of the International Olympic Academy* (pp. 147-156). Lausanne, Switzerland: International Olympic Committee.

Henley Centre for Forecasting. (1986). *The economic impact and importance of sport in the UK. Study 30.* London: The Sports Council.

Henley Centre for Forecasting. (1992). *The economic impact of sport in the UK in 1990.* London: The Sports Council.

Jackson, G.A.M., & Glyptis, S.A. (1992). *Sport and tourism: A review of the literature.* Unpublished report to the Sports Council, London.

Jackson, G.A.M., & Reeves, M. (1998). Evidencing the sport-tourism interrelationship: A case study of Elite British athletes. In M.F. Collins & I.S. Cooper (Eds.), *Leisure management: Issues and applications* (pp. 263-276). Wallingford, Great Britain.

Jones, H.G. (1989). *The economic impact and importance of sport: A European study.* Strasbourg, France: Council of Europe.

Kotler, P., Heider, D.H., & Irving, R. (1993). *Marketing places: Attracting investment, industry and tourism to cities, states and nations.* Glencoe, NY: Free Press.

Leisure Consultants. (1992). *Activity holidays: The growth market in tourism.* Sudbury, Great Britain: Author.

Lillehammer Olympic Organizing Committee. (1994). *Games Official Visitor Guide.* Lillehammer, Norway: The Committee, Lillehammer.

Lipsitz, G. (1984). Sports stadia and urban development: A tale of three cities. *Sport and Social Issues, 8*(2), 1-18.

Litchfield, N., & Margolis, J. (1961). Cost benefit analysis in urban government decision making. In H.G. Scaller (Ed.), *Public expenditure decisions in the urban community.* Washington, DC: Resources for the Future Inc.

May, K. (1996). Grand Tour. *Leisure Management, 16*(12), 23.

May, V. (1995). Environmental impact of the Winter Olympic Games. *Tourism Management, 16*(4), 269-275.

MEW Research (1993). *Short break destination choice.* Unpublished manuscript, English Tourist Board, London, Great Britain.

Miller, R. (1995, February 25). Game for a short punt in the run up to the Olympics. *The Times*, p. 38.

Mintel International Group Ltd. (1989). *The day visit market. Vol. 2.* London: Author.

Mintel International Group Ltd. (1993). *Leisure destination survey: Motivations and behaviour of British leisure visitors in the UK.* London: Author.

Mintel International Group Ltd. (1994). *UK sports market.* London: Author.

Mintel International Group Ltd. (1995). *Activity holidays in the UK.* London: Author.

Morris, J.N., & Collins, M.F. (1992). Health through exercise: A law of nature. *World Health*, Jan/Feb, 6-7.

Nogawa, H., Hagi, Y., Suzuki, S., & Yamaguchi, Y. (1995, August). *Measuring the economic impact of sport tourists during the 1994 World Cup, USA: A case study of Japanese sport tourists.* Paper presented at the International Federation of Student Sport (FISU/CESU) conference, Fukuoka, Japan.

NOP Market Research Ltd. (1987). *Holiday survey.* Exeter, Great Britain: National Opinion Polls.

NOP Market Research Ltd. (1989). *Activities by the British on holiday in Britain.* London: British Tourist Authority/English Tourist Board/National Opinion Polls.

Oatley, N. (1995). Competitive urban policy and the regeneration game. *Town Planning Review, 66*(1), 1-14.

Ogilvie, J., & Dickinson, C. (1992). The UK adventure holiday market. *EIU Travel and Tourism Analyst, 3,* 37-50.

PA Cambridge Economic Consultants (PAEC). (1991). The economic impact of holiday villages. Salisbury, Great Britain: Rural Development Commission.

Pyo, S., Cook, R., & Howell, R.L. (1988). Summer Olympic tourist market—Learning from the past. *Tourism Management, June,* 137-144.

Redmond, G. (1990). Points of increasing contact: Sport and tourism in the modern world. In A. Tomlinson (Ed.), *Sport in society: Policy, politics and culture. Conference papers No. 43* (pp. 158-169). Eastbourne, Great Britain: Leisure Studies Association Publications.

Remans, A. & Delforge, M. (1992). *Sports structures in Europe.* Brussels, Belgium: Council of Europe.

Ritchie, J.R.B. (1984). Assessing impact of Conferences: Research Issues. *Journal of Travel Research, 23*(1), 2-11.

Ritchie, J.R.B. (n.d.). *The Seoul Olympics as a tourism mega-event: Understanding and enhancing the long term impacts.* Unpublished manuscript, Korean National Tourist Office—University of Calgary, AB.

Roche, M. (1992). Mega events and micro-modernisation: On the sociology of the new urban tourism. *British Journal of Sociology, 43*(4), 563-600.

Roche, M. (1994). Mega events and urban policy. *Annals of Tourism Research, 21,* 1-19.

Rooney, J.F. (1976). Mega-sports events as tourist attractions: A geographical analysis. In Travel and Tourism Association Conference (Ed.), *Proceedings of the 19th Travel and Tourism Association Conference* (pp. 93-99). Montreal, PQ: Travel and Tourism Association Conference.

Scott, C. (1995, March 21). Rugby's World Cup will kick off a tourism boom. *The Daily Telegraph,* p. 33.

Selwood, H.J., & Jones, R. (1993). The America's Cup in retrospect: The aftershock in Fremantle. In A.J. Veal, P. Jonson & G. Cushman (Eds.), *Leisure and tourism: Social and environmental change* (pp. 656-660). Sydney, Australia: University of Technology.

Smith, C., & Jenner, P. (1990). Activity holidays in Europe. *EIU Travel and Tourism Analyst, 5,* 58-78.

Sports Council (South West)/West Country Tourist Board. (1992). *Tourism and sport: A joint policy statement.* Crewkerne/Exeter, Great Britain: Author.

Sports Council/Cumbria Tourist Board/Northumbria Tourist Board. (n.d.). *Sport and tourism: A statement of intent.* Durham/Windermere, Great Britain: Author.

Standeven, J.& Tomlinson, A. (1992). *Sport and tourism in south east England.* London: South East Council for Sport and Recreation.

Studiënkreis für Tourismus. (1990). *Reiseanalyse* [Analysis of the holiday]. Starnberg, Germany: Author.

Sydney Organizing Committee for the Olympic Games (SOCOG), (1997). Internet: http://www.sydney.olympic.org/summary/fs.htm

Tow, S. (1997). Sport Tourism—The benefits. *Journal of Sport Tourism,* 3(4). Internet: http://www.mcb.co.uk/journals/jst/archive/vol3no4/benefits.htm

Train, P. (1994). *Tourism and economic impacts of staging a special event: The Europa Cup—Birmingham, 1994.* Unpublished MSc. dissertation, The University of Technology, Loughborough, Great Britain.

Truno, E. (1994, October). Sport for All and the Barcelona Olympic Games. Proceedings pp. 176-183. Paper presented at the Second European Congress on Sport for All in Cities, Barcelona, Spain.

Tsubota, R. (1993). *Comparative analysis of the 1992 summer and winter Olympic Games.* Unpublished master's thesis, dissertation, The University of Technology, Loughborough, Great Britain.

Varley, D. (1992). Barcelona's Olympic facelift. *Geographical Magazine, LXIV*(7), 20-24.

Wang, P., & Irwin, R.L. (1993). An assessment of economic impact techniques for small sporting events. *Sport Marketing Quarterly, II*(3), 33-37.

Weed, M., & Bull, C. (1996, July). *The search for a sport-tourism network.* Paper presented at the World Leisure and Recreation Association Congress, Cardiff, Great Britain.

Whitson, D. & Macintosh, D. (1993). Becoming a world class city: Hallmark events and sport franchises in the growth strategies of western Canadian cities. *Sociology of Sport Journal, 10,* 221-240.

Wilkinson, J. (1991, May). *The role of sport as an economic regenerator.* Paper presented at the meeting of the British Urban Regeneration Association, London.

Withyman, M. (1994, September). Out for the day. *Insights,* pp. B19-34. 5.

World Tourism Organization. (1985). *The role of recreation management in the development of active holidays and special interest tourism and consequent enrichment of the holiday experience.* Madrid, Spain: Author.

World Tourist Organization. (1988). *Special interest tourism.* Madrid, Spain: Author.

Chapter 6
The Sociocultural Impact of Sport Tourism

Hiker with children of Northern India, near Ladakh.

The following topics are covered in this chapter:

1. Selected theoretical contributions that aid our understanding of the relationships that can arise between tourists and their hosts.
2. The positive sociocultural impacts of sport tourism.
3. The negative sociocultural impacts of sport tourism.
4. The issue of violence surrounding sport tourism.
5. Sport and tourism for all—the issue of social equity.
6. The issue of cultural homogeneity.

Sport tourism inevitably affects more than the economy; tourists by their presence impact on the host population and, at least in some respects, hosts have an effect on their visitors. Pearce has noted the increasing amount of research in tourist-resident impacts and has suggested that it would not be difficult to cite more than two hundred articles dealing with this area of interest alone (Pearce, 1994). For a fuller review, Pearce's work should be consulted, though very few pieces refer directly to sport tourism.

Underpinning this chapter is a strong emphasis on ethical behavior, which is clearly important in a discussion of impacts. But as Pearce (1994) notes, these are not the only reason for considering sociocultural impacts. Many sport tourism activities require the services provided by members of the destination community—thus they have the potential to bring about social benefits by creating employment that would not otherwise exist. For prestigious events such as the Olympic Games and other international championships, the provision to host large crowds usually involves infrastructure and environmental improvements. So over and above new employment, which may well be a short-lived benefit, there remains the wider improvement to the destination that is inherited as a legacy by the local community. Other less tangible benefits can be seen in the preservation, perhaps even the revival, of cultural customs, events, and pastimes, which, but for tourism, might have long since died out.

But sociocultural impacts can have wider significance. Pearce (1994) identifies some major economic and political repercussions of ignoring these impacts. For example, communities may withdraw their support for tourism and those who promote it, and this may lead to open hostility between tourists and residents. Unnecessary delays may occur in the construction of tourist facilities. Shortages of appropriately qualified personnel may be created by people unwilling to provide their services.

In 1982, Travis reviewed literature concerned with the sociocultural and political impacts of tourism and found that, by a ratio of nearly 3.8 to 1, tourism generated negative impacts (Travis, 1982). So far as sport tourism is concerned, Bale (1992) noted some negative impacts, particularly those associated with traffic congestion and crowding. All too often, stadia and arenas are sited in city center locations and this can simply exacerbate the problems of overcrowding and result in a reduction of the quality of life of the host community.

Probably the most serious negative impacts arise from the increase in crime and the behavior of some visiting sport tourists. Black marketeering of tickets in short supply, theft, vandalism, and hooliganism are examples of harmful actions. Sport tourists themselves may suffer from the elevated price of tickets bought through the black market. Of much greater concern is the possibility of trouble among supporters if they purchase tickets for the wrong areas in the grounds. Where fans of opposing sides are not segregated, authorities find control more difficult and spectators' behavior is more likely to cause problems.

The growing popularity and consumption of sport tourism can be seen as a form of cultural consumption, yet not everyone can expect to benefit. We shall examine those sectors of the community for whom special provision is made. The issue of equity is addressed since it is clear that even in affluent countries only a minority of the population actually make sport tourism trips.

A different kind of problem concerns adventure holidays, which are often based in the more remote regions of the world. Travel companies whose business largely depends on offering novel, off-the-beaten-track holidays, have become increasingly conscious of the need to protect the cultural, just as much as the natural, environment.

There is a further question as to whether sport tourism provides an opportunity for cultural innovation, or whether it merely fuels the spread of a homogenizing global culture. Does sport tourism lead to the positive celebration of cultural differences, or is cultural identity homogenized? If cultural differences are eroded and we finish up with many similar destinations and experiences, then will not part of the attraction of sport tourism have been destroyed?

The next part of this chapter provides a conceptual background to our topic. We shall then look at some specific examples of how the links between sport and tourism result in positive sociocultural effects, and finally, we shall consider some examples of negative sociocultural impacts.

Conceptual Background to Sociocultural Impacts

We have selected just two examples from the wealth of material dealing with the sociocultural impacts of tourism to provide a conceptual background for the sport tourism examples that follow. Research into tourist-resident relations in the 1970s proposed stage-based models that saw the relationship proceeding through a series of steps. For example, Smith (1978) saw the development of tourism evolving through seven stages of expanding community impact as tourist numbers increased. Stage-based models can be criticized for the apparent rigidity of categories and for implying too neat a sequence of steps that are often difficult to identify in field-based studies. For our purposes, although we are aware of the criticisms of stage-based models, we have selected two that we believe offer a useful way of understanding sport tourism's social impacts. Smith (1978) concentrates on the tourist's impact, Doxey (1975) on the host's response.

Impact of Tourists

It is a truism that the smaller the host community and the greater the number of visitors, the more the impact will be likely to be felt by the hosts. Smith (1978) developed a typology of seven types of tourists based on their numerical strength and their adaptations to the cultures they visit and argued that their impact went hand-in-hand with their increasing numbers (see table 6.1).

"Explorers" Smith (1989) saw as few in number, self-sufficient, and able to fully accept local conditions. By definition, true explorers are not tourists; they are more akin to anthropologists living as active participant-observers among "their" people. Early climbers perhaps fit this description, but nowadays it would be difficult to cite a sport tourism example.

"Elite" tourists, according to Smith (1978), differ from explorers because they are "touring." They have been "almost everywhere" and look for something different. Such a group might choose a canoe adventure on the

Table 6.1 Smith's Typology of Tourists

Type of tourist	Number of tourists	Adapt to local norms
1. Explorer	Very limited	Adapts fully
2. Elite tourists	Rarely seen	Adapts fully
3. Off-beat	Uncommon but seen	Adapts well
4. Unusual	Occasional	Adapts somewhat
5. Incipient mass	Steady-flow	Seeks Western amenities
6. Mass	Continuous influx	Expects Western amenities
7. Charter	Massive arrivals	Demands Western amenities

Reprinted, by permission, from V.L. Smith, Ed., 1989, *Hosts and guests: The anthropology of tourism*, 2nd ed. (Philadelphia: University of Pennsylvania), 12.

Zambezi River in Zimbabwe, where two nights are spent in camp en route. This group adapts easily to local norms.

"Offbeat" tourists include, for example, those who take a major four-week trek in Nepal; they seek to do something beyond the norm. They may be found in rather larger groups and they "put up with" rather than fully adapt to the touristic conditions.

The "unusual" tourist generally seeks an unusual experience within a more predictable package—for example a two-day white-water rafting experience as part of a regular sight-seeing tour in Alaska. They use facilities commonly used by the locals and take an interest in local culture but prefer their "safe" box lunch.

"Incipient mass" tourists are present in greater numbers, although they more often travel as individuals than as package tourists. These visitors prepare their own itineraries and like Western amenities. They are the kind of tourists who enjoy guided walking trails in countries similar to their own, traveling in heated or air-conditioned buses, and staying in modern hotels.

"Mass" tourists, as their category implies, impact in very large numbers. They hold middle-class values and generally enjoy comparatively high incomes. They expect Western amenities; they are the kind of tourists who expect a trained, multi-lingual guide. Although these tourists are always present, their impact is more noticeably seasonal. The "club formula" tourists, identified in chapter 3, have a great impact because of their sheer numbers.

"Charter" tourists travel en masse for their holiday—for example, skiing—and are treated as though they had standardized tastes and demands. Arriving in large batches at their foreign airport, their onward transportation is organized by destination, their individuality lost within the group, which is identified only by the destination name for which they are bound. This group demands Western amenities.

The inverse relationship between touristic impact upon a culture and local perceptions of visitors is shown in figure 6.1 (Smith, 1978). When the frequency of the different tourist types is taken into account, it approximates a pyramid in which the number of tourists increases from top (explorer) to bottom (charter). An inverse triangle superimposed on this depicts the role of the host culture as it is penetrated by the increased flow of tourists. At the apex of the tourist triangle, explorers make only a tiny impact; their presence is hardly noticed by the host culture. As the number of tourists increases to group four (unusual tourists), the breadth of their impact is now felt right across the host culture. Charter tourists, by their very number, can so dominate a host community to the extent that the hosts perceive their culture as overwhelmed (the base of the triangle). This typology can be seen as particularly relevant when examining the interaction of sport tourists with their hosts.

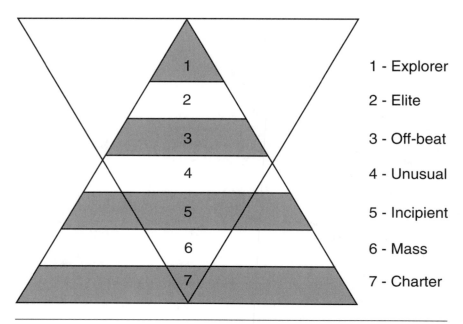

Figure 6.1   Touristic impact upon a culture and local perceptions of visitors.

Reprinted, by permission, from V.L. Smith, Ed., 1989, *Hosts and guests: The anthropology of tourism,* 2nd ed. (Philadelphia: University of Pennsylvania), 15.

To a host population, tourism is often a mixed blessing. Smith's (1978) model shows an inverse relationship between the volume of tourists and their level of adaptation to local cultural norms. But the model takes us beyond numbers to consider the different types of people who will choose the different kinds of sport tourist experience and the likely direction of impacts on the tourists or their hosts. On the whole, as the number of visitors increases so does the potential for negative impacts on the host community, which can create tension between the two groups. As long as the number of visitors remains small the potential for positive impacts is heightened. By this model, then, a breakdown in host-guest relationships can largely be attributed to an increase in the volume of visitors.

However, visitor volume is not a fully adequate explanation for all cultural impacts. Elite tourists, although fewer in number, could be more harmful than mass tourists since the elite tourist, interested in other cultures, may insert himself or herself more deeply into a culture. The mass tourist's interest is more superficial.

The Host Response

Particularly concerned with attempts to measure the social impact of visitors on a community's culture, Doxey (1975) developed the "Irridex" (irritation index), a model of the relationship between tourism growth and community stress (see table 6.2). Like most theoretical models it can be criticized for oversimplifying the relationship. Nevertheless, it provides a useful way of analyzing host-guest relations.

Assuming that tourism is a new development, the local community is generally pleased to welcome the visitor, a state which Doxey calls "euphoria." Doxey's idea that the local host community initially accepts visitors is supported by both Butler (1980) and Keller (1984). Generally speaking, the potential benefits of tourist arrivals are perceived by the hosts to outweigh any possible disbenefits. Investment and improved employment prospects are expected to flow from the development and provide a source of income that did not previously exist. In any case the first tourists tend to arrive in small numbers and adapt well to the local community.

As the number of tourists increase, citizens of the host community recognize that relatively few people actually derive benefit. They then become increasingly aware of the problems created by tourist development and their response, according to Doxey (1975), changes to "apathy." Visitors are taken for granted and contact becomes more formal. Further tourism growth changes the relationship again, so that the local community finds itself marginalized in its own home area. At this point "annoyance" sets in, and infrastructure improvements are required to maintain the tourist experience and an equilibrium in the visitor-host relationship. Tourism development continues and infrastructure improvements come too late or are too few. "Antagonism" of the local community can be expressed as irritation or lead to an open expression of hostility toward the tourists.

Table 6.2   Doxey's Irridex

Stages	Characteristics	Symptoms
Stage 1	Euphoria	Visitors welcome; little planning or formal development
Stage 2	Apathy	Visitors are taken for granted; contacts become formalized and generally commercial
Stage 3	Annoyance	Saturation point is approached; locals become concerned about tourism; planners make attempts to improve the infrastructure
Stage 4	Antagonism	Openly expressed hostility from the locals toward the tourists; planners make remedial attempts to limit the damage; promotion is nevertheless increased to offset the deteriorating image of the destination

From Doxey, G.V., 1975. Adapted with permission.

Summary of Models

In summary, we have introduced two theoretical models for their value in examining the relationships that occur between sport tourists and their hosts. We shall see the application of these models in the next sections of the chapter as we examine some positive and negative sociocultural impacts of sport tourism.

Smith's (1978) classification of seven types of tourists deals particularly with their level of adaptation to local norms and has been described in detail for its application to the role of the host culture as it is penetrated by an increasing flow from "explorers" to "charter" tourists. Doxey's (1975) Irridex describes the host community's changing attitude toward tourist arrivals from the first euphoria of welcome through apathy and annoyance to antagonism.

These categorizations should not be seen as immutable types. There are many types of tourists, and residents of host communities, who may vary in their responses—the same individual can adopt one "position" in one particular situation and a different one elsewhere. Nor will the host-guest relation necessarily proceed evenly step-by-step as these models imply. Nevertheless, they are useful ways to extend our understanding of the sociocultural impact of sport tourism and have been introduced for that purpose.

Positive Impacts

Sport tourism benefits the host community and the sport tourist in many ways. Here we consider several positive outcomes: positive impact on land use, psychological benefits to the host community, promotion of cultural understanding, preservation of traditions, and the promotion of racial equality by means of international sanctions imposed by the sporting community.

Positive Impacts on Rural Land Use

Access to the countryside to enjoy recreational activities is valued by millions of tourists worldwide, and the tourism stemming from such recreation can, in turn, strengthen rural economies. For example, Murphy (1985) noted that tourism to national parks (often with a recreational intent) contributes to their continued existence.

For centuries travelers have passed through the countryside on their journeys, but more recently the countryside has become a destination in its own right. Research carried out in the United Kingdom in 1987 showed the importance the British attach to countryside recreation, (Harrison, Burgess, & Limb, 1987) and a recent review for *Time* magazine confirmed the countryside's popularity for active holiday pursuits in Europe (Usher, 1996).

Changing patterns of land use, in particular the reduction in hectares needed for farming, have increased the importance of diversification and encouraged farmers to seek alternative uses for their land, with potential for new jobs. From the 1970s onward the countryside became a real alternative to the beach for holidaymakers. By the mid-1980s an average of 48 percent of the populations of EC countries chose either rural or mountainous areas for their main holiday. These areas have increased in popularity even more alongside the trend to take second holidays and short breaks. Writing about Europe, Davidson (1992) comments,

> Consequently, operators in European rural tourism have come to recognise that accommodation in itself is no longer sufficient to satisfy the demands of their clientele. Farm tours, nature studies, cycling and walking tours, cultural activities, craft courses, health-related activities, and a wide range of water and land-based sports help attract customers into the European countryside. (p. 143)

Austria provides an example of a declining farming sector where, in the 20 years following 1960, the number of workers in agriculture more than halved (Davidson, 1992). In the Tyrol, farmhouses offering accommodations have organized themselves into *bauerlicher gastering* (farmhouse circles) to promote farm tourism in their province. Recognizing the rise in interest in activity holidays, the Tyrol farmhouse circle now offers walking and cycling tours where guests stay at different farms each night, their luggage is transported for them, and they are provided with the services of a guide. These activity holidays have been developed particularly to attract summer tourists, a market which in recent years has shown decline in Austria (Davidson, 1992).

A complementary benefit is achieved by the diversified employment opportunities created for local people. Payne (1995) noted the employment of local people as porters for sport tourists in the Himalayas, and Koloff (1993) referred to it in connection with a beach resort development which required labor for its construction and continuing operation in a region of Australia previously dependent on coal mining and steel production.

In Britain, changes to land use have attracted similar ideas for generating tourism to rural areas, including walking routes, sport, and other active recreations (Talbot-Ponsonby, 1988). Extra grants have been paid to farmers through the government's Farm Diversification Grant Scheme to cover the costs of making land available for non-agricultural uses, such as the creation of new circular walking routes, including the signposting and publicity required (Byrne and Ravenscroft, 1989). Schemes like this have encouraged an enterprising group of farmers in mid-Wales to combine to provide a single sport tourist attraction involving three sports (quad trekking, clay pigeon shooting, and golf), together with accommodations, on land they no longer require for agriculture.

The use of sporting events as a tool in the development of tourism in rural areas in Australia is also seen as a positive social development. Tourism generated by activity holidays and sports events has a major role to play in rural development in this country where vast tracts of uninhabited land abound (Harding, 1988).

Positive Impacts on Urban Land Use

Sport tourism can have a positive effect in urban areas. Usually this is seen in the construction of new infrastructure and in the resulting economic development.

In common with many other cities that have hosted major sporting events, Barcelona used its staging of the 1992 Olympic Games to launch its tourism strategy for the new millenium and, alongside it, a program of regeneration projects. Described as the "four critical elements" in the city's long-term development plan were enlarging the airport, increasing the number of quality hotels, creating conference and congress facilities, and integrating the entire package. These major reconstructive efforts were the cornerstone of the program designed to revitalize the old city (Stevens, 1990). In the metropolitan region three areas of focus were the sea front, the inner city, including the historic center, and the creation of jobs in the suburbs. Work on these projects would aid the overall reconstruction. Stevens (1990) summed up the long-term effects of the Olympics on the city:

> The full impact of the Games should be considered in a wider context. The Games have led to the upgrading of telecommunications, have stimulated investment in development and transportation projects throughout the city and have provided an unprecedented platform for promoting Barcelona in the future. (p. 48)

Such significant improvements to the infrastructure can bring positive social benefits to the host community that last well into the future and strengthen a region's economy, a process to which Fremantle, Australia, as host of the America's Cup (Selwood and Jones, 1993), and Indianapolis, called "Sports City USA" due to its Hoosier Dome stadium and a whole range of sporting venues (Herron Associates, 1991), also attest.

Denver's bid to host the 1976 Winter Olympics was the catalyst that led to federal funding in support of airport and motorway improvements, which were crucial factors in the growth of the Colorado ski industry and the boom that benefited Denver in the 1970s (Whitson and Macintosh, 1993). However, in spite of these developments, the citizens of Colorado opposed state spending on the Olympic facilities, and the Games were transferred to

Innsbruck. This demonstrates the importance of local community support for projects, as Pearce (1994) has noted.

Sports stadia, museums, halls of fame, and other constructions become tourist attractions and bring into generally urban areas tourists who would not otherwise be there. Thus sports facilities may encourage investment in other business enterprises (Baade and Dye, 1990).

Psychological Benefits to the Community

Organizing major events, for example the Olympic Games, can bring benefits to the host nation such as prestige and improved national morale (Ritchie, 1988). In addition to the pleasure of hosting visitors from around the world, hosts have the opportunity to share their national heritage and culture of which they are inestimably proud. Lillehammer provides a relevant example.

Host to the 1994 Winter Olympic Games, the town faced a social impact of gigantic proportions. The local Norwegian community numbered no more than 23,000, but for one short period Lillehammer would more than double its number, and in that time it had many objectives to fulfill. Not only should it mount an impressive and economically sound Games, it was also charged with engineering an event that would unify the Norwegian nation, an event in which everyone would participate and of which everyone would be proud (Klausen, 1992). As written in the design manual for the Lillehammer Olympic Games, "The Winter Games shall give a strong and uniform view of Norway, establish our position as a winter sports nation, strengthen respect for our values and international role, and promote Norwegian industry and its products" (Klausen, 1992, p. 1).

The organizers of this event, which was more remarkable than many similar events due to the small size of the local host population, were charged with reversing Smith's (1978) typology. Lillehammer was to receive huge numbers of visitors, active and passive sports holiday tourists together with active and passive sports nonholiday tourists, and blend these groups together in their shared interest and send them all away with a strong impression of the Norwegian image.

In his assessment of the impact of hallmark events, Ritchie identified the strengthening of regional traditions and values as positive effects, together with increased awareness of the area as a tourist destination (Ritchie, 1988). Elliott (1995) confirmed the increased awareness of the West Indies as a tourist destination following England's cricket test tour there in 1995. Research among Lillehammer residents and the Norwegian population also bears out Ritchie's thesis. It was found that before and after the Games there was a significant general tendency for ethnocentrism to increase (Kolstad, Rundmo, and Svarva, 1995): "Glorification of the nation and self complacency seemed to reach a peak in Norway during and just after the Games. Pride in being Norwegian increased significantly during the Games" (p. 91).

Cyclists at Khardung La in Northern India: the highest motor-able road in the world.

Cultural Understanding

Another social benefit from sport tourism can be its use as a means of fostering better understanding, giving foreign visitors the opportunity to get to know a country, its people, and its culture (Collins, 1991). Tours less prestigious than major international events will usually have the advantage of bringing visitors into closer contact with their hosts.

By way of example, we use a Fleet Street journalist's account of his experiences as a member of a corporate Fleet Street XI cricket tour to India (Fleet Street until recently was the London headquarters of much of the British press). For Evans (1995), "the cricket provided an insight into a different world" (p. 17). In his report, he described the pungent smell of curry, the sacred cows, the congested cities, the Mad Max buses—"fearsome-looking three-wheeled vehicles with huge, brightly painted bonnets always over-flowing with customers and belching black smoke"—and the tradition of gift giving at the end of each match (Evans, 1995, p. 17). The stark contrasts that are India were this sport tourist's main impressions. This cricket tour, Evans stated, enriched his understanding of a very different culture.

Preservation and Revitalization of Traditions

Sport tourism can also be beneficial by encouraging the preservation and regeneration of traditions. For example, sports museums, a favorite tourist destination, record sport as a cultural form from the past to make it, not simply a tradition, but an active and effective cultural element of the present (Williams, 1977). As another example, the Maine Windjammers Association on the northeast coast of the United States has been able to maintain its fleet of old sailing vessels by using them for tourist trips, thus preserving both the ships and the maritime characteristics of which they were a part (Ryan, 1991).

Other cultural artifacts that may owe their continuation to tourism can be found in traditional sports now used mainly as tourist attractions. In chapter 2 we referred to the Rose Garden, a country resort outside Bangkok, where displays of cultural events such as sword fighting and Thai boxing take place daily. Sofield (1991) has indicated the continued importance of the *naghol* ritual in Vanuatu, a South Pacific island nation, where young men plunge from a high wooden tower to be snatched from certain death by a flexible vine rope attached to their ankles—this is the precursor of modern bungee jumping. To avoid commercialization of the event, local chiefs formed a council to manage it and so maintain its authenticity (Getz, 1994). Some would claim that by staging events for visitors, by restructuring or shortening performances to best accommodate tourist excursions, their authenticity is jeopardized (MacCannell, 1996). But at the very least, tourism provides the rationale for keeping many cultural traditions alive that might otherwise be lost.

Sanctions of Sports Teams Used Positively

Refusals to allow countries to host or even participate in major sports events can be seen to have positive sociocultural and political impacts. Morne du Plessis, the manager of the victorious 1995 South African World Cup rugby team, claimed that the sports boycott, which effectively excluded South African sports teams from all international competitions throughout the late 1970s and 1980s, was "the most effective tool" used *for* the betterment of South Africa's race relations. Rugby was a game appropriated by the white Afrikaners as their sport, in contrast to soccer, which had a largely black following, and cricket, which was too English (Bose, 1993). To exclude the Springboks (South Africa's rugby team), which won its first international match against Britain in 1903 and won every Test series it played for the next 50 years, from competing "really hurt us," (Hamlyn, 1995) said du Plessis. He went on to say,

> We thought it was unfair to involve politics in sport, but if you look back on it now, hell, it was effective. It first of all made us wonder how a world could be so united in a feeling against us. It made me wonder, you know, they can't all be wrong. (p. 22)

The creation of one multiracial South African Rugby Football Union did not take place until 1992. In 1995 the new nation proudly hosted the World

Cup and although only one black player, Chester Williams, was on the world-beating team, their popular success became the symbol for national unity that their competition slogan, "One Team, One Country," implied. As Edward Griffiths, the South African Rugby Football Union's chief executive acknowledged, "It will be facile to pretend that four weeks of (international) rugby can unify the country. It's our responsibility to go out into the community and make the spark lit here turn into a flame" (Hands, 1995, p. 42).

Only time will tell. It could take many years before those involved in sport at the community level see this dream turn into a reality. International sport tourism at the elite level can be invested with enormous meaning and has the potential for massive sociocultural impact.

Negative Impacts

An important difference between tourists and their hosts is that while one is on holiday, the other is at work (Krippendorf, 1987). This places them in "diametrically opposite positions" and, at least in part, may account for the development of negative relationships between them. By definition, tourism demands consumption at the site of production. This can lead to the almost inevitable congestion that occurs at many tourist attractions. In this section of the chapter, we discuss the downside of the tourist-resident relation, namely, the negative impact of sport tourism on land use, the lack of understanding of the host's culture, and difficulties in preservation of culture and traditions.

Negative Impacts on Rural Land Use

The development of recreational activities in rural areas to ameliorate the decline in the use of land for agricultural purposes has been seen as a social benefit amongst Western societies. But in some more agriculturally-based societies rapid social change has negative impacts. The increasing availability of and dependence on tourist-related employment may alter the job structure and the balance of the local economy (Pearce, 1994). For example, working at the local beach providing water sports can be more attractive than working on the family smallholding, a situation which can be observed in the Caribbean. In this way, traditional farming communities may lose vital labor to more attractive employment in sport tourism. And, perhaps the decline of the West Indies cricketing talent may be attributed to the overcrowding of beaches and parks by tourists, that has made traditional, spontaneous cricket games dangerous (Hill and Ludgren, 1977, cited in Pearce, 1994).

The creation of parks for outdoor recreation can have negative impacts as evidenced in Canada. Creating the parks at Forillon and Gros Morne necessitated evicting a number of previous residents and provoked considerable local opposition (Archer and Cooper, 1994). Local people were similarly disadvantaged by the construction of hotels along part of the Mediterranean coast. The hotels retained the beach adjacent to their property for the sole use of their visitors, denying easy access to the sea to local residents (Archer and Cooper, 1994). A similar case was noted in Australia (Koloff, 1993), and in Cuba, golf course development was criticized for its failure to appreciate the displacement of local people (Wheat, 1995).

Some sport tourists prefer to own their own accommodations and seek to purchase holiday homes. This can escalate property prices and land values to the detriment of local residents' interests as occurred in the Snowdonia National Park in Wales (Coppock, 1977), in Whistler, a ski resort in British Columbia (Ritchie, 1988), and in the Lake Macquarie region of Australia (Koloff, 1993).

Another source of tension, particularly in Britain, between urbanites who wish to recreate in the country and rural landowners, relates to rights of access to private land. In Britain, 87 percent of the land is privately owned, and 1 percent of the population owns 52 percent of the land (Glyptis, 1995). In this context groups campaigning for wider access, such as the Ramblers' Association, now have a rapidly growing membership protesting against the restrictiveness of U.K. law compared with rights of access in countries such as Austria, Germany, and Sweden.

Animals have been the cause of further significant conflicts. In the United Kingdom, shooting and fishing are now increasingly major sources of revenue to many rural landowners who attract both foreign and domestic visitors to their land for sport tourism purposes (Clark, Darrall, Grove-White, Macnaghten, and Urry, 1994). But as rapidly as these recreational pursuits have gained in popularity, so has opposition grown. Hunting may be legal, but animal welfare activists now sabotage meets, and confrontations between huntspeople and antagonistic groups often result in disorder and violence. Until recently fishing has tended to be exempt from active protests, but now there is at least one anti-fishing campaign group in the United Kingdom and more are anticipated (Clark et al., 1994).

Negative Impacts on Urban Land Use

Studies of the physical impacts of tourism in urban settings emphasize such negative effects as traffic congestion, pedestrian overcrowding, noise, litter, and crime (Bale, 1992; Burton, 1995). Local residents of the surrounding working-class community opposed the siting of the Saddledome on the Stampede grounds in Calgary because they were concerned about the effects of the access roads on their neighborhood (Whitson and Macintosh, 1993). Their community-based opposition was effectively marginalized by the actions of their civic leaders, whose overwhelming desire was to host international games. Baade and Dye (1990) suggest that crowds and congestion may serve to discourage business investment in the city.

Although jobs can be created by locating sport tourism venues in the inner city, the majority of jobs do not match the skills of urban residents (Burton, 1995). The emphasis on built sports facilities such as pools, stadia, and tracks with their necessary standardization making them essentially the same as such facilities elsewhere can contribute to a sense of placelessness (Bale, 1994). Thus the importance of cultural place is diminished as destinations lose their "uniqueness."

Lack of Cultural Understanding

Because sport tourists might lack a full understanding of the culture that they are visiting, they can offend the host community or find it difficult to interact well. In this section, we look at two particular areas where sport tourists often lack understanding: dress and language.

Dress

Wide cultural differences can be reflected in dress. Appropriate dress has been a persistent issue creating tension between local residents and visitors bent on holiday activities at the beach and elsewhere. Cohen's research on two island beach resorts in Thailand (1982) identified conflicting attitudes to a dress code on the beach. Tourists saw the place as an island paradise and preferred to swim and sunbathe naked. To the local residents nudity was indecent.

Current travel brochures advise holidaymakers that some countries refuse admission to travelers not meeting their accepted standards of dress. The island of Bermuda, for example, retains a strict dress code and female bathers are not permitted to go topless. Appropriate dress is not merely a beach matter. Sport tourists trekking in Nepal are advised: "Women should note . . . wearing shorts is likely to cause offence . . . tops should be reasonably modest and not too tight." (Exodus, 1996).

Language

As sport tourism embraces ever-widening international destinations, language assumes increasing importance. Sport tourists move across national and cultural borders to engage in active sports holidays taking their language with them. Language can be a barrier to local contact, particularly where destination areas are remote, poor, and unsophisticated. If language cannot be understood, problems arise and can result in bad host–visitor relations. In his beginner's guide to trekking in the high Himalayas, Nicki Grihault (1997) warns against giving in response to the children whose knowledge of English is limited to "One pen?". He goes on to say: "Stone-hurling, demanding little monsters are created out of village children, by the arbitrary giving out of sweets, pens, money, etc." (p. 37).

Parents in such isolated regions can view the sport tourist as an unwelcome agent of cultural change as their native language and peaceful existence is overwhelmed by the tourists. On some routes in Nepal, the trekker can sleep and eat in lodges (or "tea-houses"). But in those villages, the tea house will be plastered with notices, all of them in English, advertising the hot showers, apple pie, peach wine, and other "foreign" consumables.

At the beginning of the 1996-97 ski season, British instructors who were hoping to teach at French resorts were denied the necessary teaching permits. *The Times* reported, "The instructors are casualties in the latest battle between French and British ski schools, which have fought for years over the right to teach English-speaking skiers" (August and Bale, 1996, p. 7). The French in particular are conscious of their language being under threat and in 1994 introduced laws to protect it and their culture. Shop signs and all merchandise must carry labels in French; a label in any other language can result in a company being taken to court (BBC Breakfast News, 24 February, 1997). Even Honda, the Japanese car manufacturer, has had to modify its European-wide advertisements for France. The advertisements were, for the first time, to appear in 18 countries in English, which the company believes is the continent's international language (Massey, 1997).

Craven's (1994) research into the cross-cultural experience of athletes, coaches, and administrators is one of the few analyses of the sociocultural impacts of language on sport tourists rather than on the host community. From surveys conducted in Canada, Craven (1994) noted difficulties with sport terminology and jargon in a second language. Her research highlights the problems some sport tourists experience when they are taught sport skills by a "foreigner."

Preservation of Culture and Traditions

Changes in land ownership and use can incite other forms of cultural resentment. A travel writer who had previously defended tourism and the vast caravan parks to which it gave rise "as a valuable asset to a poor region" in North Wales says, "Something has cracked in me. I have come to detest all aspects of mass tourism" (Morris, 1987, p. 11). The cause of this dramatic change of heart concerned the people developing tourism. As English, not local Welsh people, they expressed total disregard for local language and culture. Although the potential for environmental damage that goes along with tourism can cause people to reject it, the problem here might be seen as nationalism—it is, in any case, rooted in cultural values and a way of life. The concern is that local people, being swamped by "foreign" intruders, could lose sight of their own cultural heritage and uniqueness. As Glen (1995) reminds us, "Remember, language is culture is nationhood" (p. 92) and "smash the language and you smash the culture" (p. 88).

Walking, overall the most popular sport tourism activity, might be considered the least likely to cause friction between tourists and their hosts. Yet the residents of Haworth, a village in the north of England, were disillusioned by the behavior of some of their visitors. Disillusionment is a state on Doxey's (1975) Irridex scale somewhere between apathy and annoyance. The area has been popularized as the home of the Brontë family, novelists of the early nineteenth century. This part of Yorkshire is popular with hikers from local conurbations as well as those from greater distances. It was not simply a matter of footpath erosion that troubled the villagers, but of damage to the dry stone walls used in that part of the country to divide up the land. This case, rather like the one in Wales, concerned the region's heritage because the art of dry stone wall construction is fast dying out and the damage could become irreparable.

Fast and convenient forms of travel have brought adventure-type walking holidays to a growing number of people visiting some of the more remote regions of the world. As tourism has increased, so local communities have to do more—and give up more—to serve their guests. Plog (1994) notes the disadvantage of cultural conformity:

Yorkshire Tourist Board

Viewing the Ribbleshead Viaduct in Yorkshire, England.

> Natives learn that there is a proper way to act and to defer to others . . . In so doing, they give up part of their own identity and often part of a valuable ancient heritage or tradition that contributes to pride. (p. 42)

Himalayan trekkers have affected more than the finely balanced mountain ecosystem. To provide for tourists' demands for hot water, trees have had to be cut down for fuel. It is not simply that trekkers burn about 14 pounds of wood per day per person. In order for reforestation schemes to cope with this demand, the Nepalese government has had to stop local people from using wood for heating their homes, which had been their traditional practice (Tuting, cited in Ryan, 1991). Resentment, indeed antagonism, between hosts and their guests is hardly surprising when such basic customs and comfort are eroded by active sport tourists.

Australia is currently experiencing a tourist boom and many visitors include the Uluru National Park in the center of the country on their itinerary. Ayers Rock, a huge geological feature in the park, has held spiritual significance for the Aboriginals for thousands of years, long before white settlers arrived in Australia. The thriving new tourist resort developed near Ayers Rock contrasts sharply with the poverty of the local Aboriginal settlements. White tour operators promote "Aboriginality" as a drawing card for tourism to the park. Although this exploitation may be resented, some indigenous Australians can see its political advantage in terms of gaining international visibility for their plight. At Uluru and elsewhere, they have begun to produce tourist literature offering the culturally interested sport tourist the "Mutitjulu Walk" and the "Mala Walk" accompanied by Aboriginal guides (Mercer, 1994).

In summary, the instances referred to above put the sociocultural impact of sport tourism in perspective. The balance between "costs" and "benefits" is fragile and not easy to maintain. Apart from this balance, we identify three major sociocultural issues that need to be addressed. It is to these that we now turn. The first issue is violence in and surrounding sport tourism. The second, social equity and the third, cultural homogeneity.

Violence in and Surrounding Sport and Tourism

Although violence at sporting events is not solely attributable to tourists, there is considerable evidence, particularly among sport spectators, that mixing "away" supporters with "home" fans is a lethal, potentially explosive mix. Comparatively little research has been published that links spectator violence with the number of visiting supporters, although the link is more fully documented in the case of international travel (Williams, 1986;

Williams, Dunning, and Murphy, 1989). Particularly familiar to soccer in Europe, violence at sporting events is no new phenomenon, nor is it restricted to football or to the Northern Hemisphere. Lynch (1991) cites Cashman, reporting on a cricket match in Australia:

> The Sydney Cricket Ground riot began when the Australian batsman was adjudged run out. As he returned reluctantly to the pavilion there was suddenly an uproar among members who jumped to their feet and started shouting "not out" and "go back." Within seconds the anger had spread to all parts of the crowd. Moments later some 2,000 spectators had leapt the fences, invaded the pitch and mobbed the umpires. The visiting players, unable to flee the pitch, were struck with sticks and one at least had his shirt almost ripped from his back. Others complained later that they thought they were about to be murdered. (pp. 107-108)

This was not 1995, but 116 years earlier, 1879!

Lynch (1991) examined modern crowd disorder in four sports in Australia—cricket, tennis, basketball, and soccer—and concluded that as sport has been taken further into the realms of entertainment and spectacle, new types of spectators have been attracted. These people have little knowledge of the game they watch and they also lack knowledge of the historical codes of spectator behavior—this confirms our classification of this element of passive sport tourists as "casual" observers. However, to put the issue in context, some researchers in Australia offer a different point of view. One high-level study showed that between 1969 and 1984, of the incidents of public disorder recorded, only 7.5 percent occurred at sport and leisure events and these were largely contained within the sports grounds and were not generally characterized by rivalry between opposing groups of fans (Holton and Fletcher, 1988).

In Britain, hooliganism is seen as different since it most often involves rivalry between supporters of opposing teams, and violence frequently overflows from the sports stadia into the surrounding areas (Dunning, Murphy, and Williams, 1986). Perhaps the most notorious and one of the most serious incidents occurred at the 1985 European Cup Final between the English team, Liverpool, and the Italian team, Juventus. At the Heysel Stadium in Brussels (Belgium), 39 people died as a result of crowd violence amongst the English spectators. In terms of the number of deaths, an even more serious event occurred in 1989 at the English FA Cup semifinal between Liverpool and Nottingham Forest. The match was held on what was deemed to be neutral territory, so the majority of the spectators, supporters of the two clubs, would constitute sport tourists. On this occasion at the Hillsborough Stadium, 95 people died and 174 were injured as a result of being crushed against the perimeter fence. Following this disaster, English football clubs were banned from all European competitions.

Since those days, British football has undergone some major changes. All-seater stadia (stadia without any space for spectators to stand and watch a match) have become the norm, and the implementation of various recommendations has helped to achieve a generally calmer culture among spectators. This has brought about the reentry of British clubs to European competitions and the selection of Britain to host the 1996 European Football Championships, which were conducted without major incident. However, the English Football Association has expressed concern over the allocation of tickets for the 1998 World Cup finals in France (Kempson, 1998). Under the present rules, only 4,000 of the 40,000 seats will be available for English supporters. The England Travel Club alone has 20,000 members. The situation could lead English fans to purchase tickets through the black market, thus making it impossible to separate rival supporters.

Violence is by no means confined to football. At Tepotzlan, near Mexico City, the residents drove out the mayor and the town officials, including the police, and one person was reported killed in the rebellion in 1996. The reason for the uprising was a plan approved by the authorities to construct an exclusive golf resort for Mexico's elite and tourists (BBC, December 17, 1996). And Bale (1994) records indigenous Americans taking up arms in 1990 to prevent the appropriation of a pine wood containing ceremonial land wanted for golf course development.

Sport Tourism for All: The Issue of Social Equity

The European Commission (EC) produced a comprehensive study entitled *Europeans and Their Holidays* (Commission of the European Communities, 1987) that demonstrated that tourism is not for all. Almost half of the total EC population (44 percent) took no holiday trips in 1985, the year of the survey. Four groups of respondents were identified: those who went away once, those who went away more than once, those who habitually stayed at home, and "others." Those who habitually stayed at home—approximately 21 percent of the EC's total population—were those who had not taken a holiday the year before the survey, nor the year of the survey, and did not intend to take a holiday the following year, making three consecutive years without a holiday. Great differences were found in the holiday-taking habits of individual EC countries. Whereas only 16 percent of the Dutch population habitually stayed at home, this rose to 49 percent of the Portuguese. In Portugal just 7 percent went away more than once, whereas in France 27 percent did so.

Combining various sources of information, we have constructed a table (see table 6.3) to show the proportions of the populations from 21 countries

Table 6.3   Those Who Stay Home and Those Who Go Away

Country	% who stayed home	% who went away
Switzerland	17	83
Sweden	20	80
Netherlands	28	72
United States	29	71
Norway	30	70
Finland	30	70
Denmark	36	64
United Kingdom	39	61
Germany	40	60
France	40	60
Luxembourg	42	58
Italy	43	57
EC average	44	56
Finland	50	50
Greece	54	46
Brazil	54	46
Austria	55	45
Spain	56	44
Belgium	59	41
Ireland	61	39
Poland	67	33
Portugal	69	31

Compiled from Commission of the European Community (1987), Boniface & Cooper (1994); Holloway (1994); van der Poel (1993); Samuel (1996); Bramante (1998).

who go away on holiday and those who stay at home. However, data from large scale surveys on leisure participation are only available from industrial nations, which highlight the disparities existing between nations in the developed and developing world (Cushman, Veal, and Zuzanek, 1996). Many countries do not collect data on leisure and in some countries leisure and holidays are meaningless concepts.

To find out what barriers precluded holiday taking, one hundred people from each of the EC countries who did not take a holiday were asked why they had not gone anywhere (Commission of the European Communities, 1987). It was concluded that of all the variables affecting people's ability to take a holiday, socio-occupational status and the level of a family's income were the most influential. In Portugal, 67 percent reported that they did not go away because they "couldn't afford it." Other countries where financial constraint was a prominent factor included Ireland (61 percent), Greece (55 percent), Spain (50 percent), the United Kingdom (50 percent), France (44 percent), Germany (41 percent), and Belgium (40 percent). In three countries, Denmark, Belgium, and Italy, a third of the respondents who did not go away actually stated that they preferred "to stay at home"; but this was a minority response. Over the European Community as a whole, only an average of 22 percent preferred to stay at home. Closer analysis showed three-quarters of families in the top income group took a holiday, but in the lowest income group only 36 percent did so.

Assuming that holidays are desirable and that a period away from home is the best way to take a holiday, it is clear that a great many people from even some of the more affluent countries do not enjoy this social benefit. Sport tourism tends to operate in a more highly commercial environment than do some other forms of holiday, thus limiting the experience even more to the socially advantaged. Mazitelli, cited in Collins (1991), found that tourists attracted to sports events tended to be those who traveled long distances, stayed more days in costlier accommodations, and spent more per day than the average tourist; thus, they were atypical even among tourists. Alpine (1986) made a similar observation. Finally, the cost of tickets for elite sports events excludes most poor people from the live audiences (Whitson and Macintosh, 1993).

On the other hand, there are examples of more budget-conscious opportunities linked to camping, hostel accommodation, and self-catering trips, and to public intervention in the market to offer activity-based experiences to some of the more socially disadvantaged community members. Trusts, charities, and some community groups organize activity holidays for young people from poor inner-city areas with the objective of providing a life-enhancing experience from which the youngsters would not otherwise benefit. The "social tourism" movement, or "tourism for all," which attempts to provide low-cost holidays for disadvantaged groups, has been particularly strong in mainland Europe. One feature, common to most of the provision, has been the emphasis placed upon activities—at first, on educational classes, and later, on sports activities—as an essential part of the holiday experience at no extra charge (Davidson, 1992).

The Villages-Vacances-Familes in France provides some 80 establishments that offer a variety of holiday camp accommodations paid for by the state and various social organizations. These centers, which remain quite distinct from commercial tourism, were the forerunners of the highly successful commercial club-type holiday companies such as Club Med, which started life as a not-for-profit organization (Capenerhurst, 1994). The Swiss Travel Fund (REKA) also provides a means of funding holidays for low-income groups. With accommodations designed for families, the Travel Fund's centers provide recreational facilities including golf courses, swimming pools, tennis courts, skiing amenities, and children's playgrounds and emphasize an active sport tourist experience. Similar types of provision can be found in Denmark, Belgium, Greece, Italy, Portugal, and Spain (Capenerhurst, 1994) as well as in France and Germany (Bull, 1991).

A more controversial example of socially supported sport tourism can be found in the United Kingdom where there is no national policy and no central funding agency to help low-income groups in need of a holiday. However, young offenders have been sent, at public expense, on globe-trotting activity holidays with the objective of character reformation. The value of these sport tourism experiences was positively promoted in a television documentary, "The Trek," which occupied prime-time viewing in the United Kingdom for several weeks in the spring of 1995. The group was challenged to complete a four-hundred-mile trek across the deserts and mountains of Kenya with the final objective of climbing Mt. Poi, a six-thousand-foot-high peak covered in rain forest. Coalter (1990) for one, however, has criticized the assumed social "therapeutic" roles assigned to sport as a form of prevention of delinquent behavior, which he sees as a myth.

Another social-remedial type of project reported in 1995 was the Skidrow XI. This cricket team from Los Angeles comprised reformed drug dealers, criminals, and alcoholics for whom cricket was the means to help them win back their self-esteem. The team toured England throughout the summer playing matches against various teams.

Special arrangements to enable handicapped people to benefit from sport tourism activities are considered in the context of health impacts in chapter 8.

There is a case for public intervention in the market to ensure that opportunities are facilitated for a wide range of disadvantaged groups who would not otherwise benefit from a sport tourism experience. The opportunity to be a tourist, including a sport tourist, is largely confined to the more affluent populations of the Western democracies of Europe, North America, Japan, and Australia. But even in these regions, a substantial proportion of the population cannot take a holiday. Intervention in liberal market economies mainly depends on the state and voluntary organizations. Although we believe there is a case for state intervention to provide financial assistance to those who cannot afford a holiday, in the current climate of government policies (see chapter 9) we see this as unlikely. Thus, opening up sport tourism opportunities to the disadvantaged will depend, increasingly, on the initiatives of the voluntary sector.

Cultural Homogeneity

The concept of sustainability is most often applied to the impact of tourism on natural ecosystems (see chapter 7), yet the same question has to be addressed in relation to the impact of tourism on the human ecosystem. Goering (1990) observed that

> the issue of sustainability in tourism, then, seems to come down to whether the culture will adapt and yet retain its fundamental character through a period of change, or whether tourists will destroy the qualities that attracted them in the first place and in the process leave the local inhabitants worse off. (p. 24)

Tourists too often do not understand the cultural significance of their experiences (Redfoot, 1984). They seem unaware or do not care that some of these experiences are superficial or prefabricated to make them more commercially viable (MacCannell, 1996). What is often lost in this commodification of culture is a sense of local and regional cultural differences. The issue, then, is the extent to which the growing popularity and consumption of cultural events and experiences such as Formula One motor racing, international soccer, Himalayan trekking, or playing golf abroad provide an opportunity to celebrate cultural differences, or whether they merely fuel the spread of a "homogenizing global culture." If they do the latter, then will the incentive for sport tourism diminish? As Mill (1990) states, "If all cultures begin to look alike, there will be no reason to leave home" (p. 171). American author David Lodge (1992) makes a similar observation in his novel set in Hawaii:

> They're all the same, these brochures . . . same picture, same caption on every one . . . Paradise. It bears no resemblance to reality, of course. (pp. 77-78)

One key aspect of culture that sport tourism affects is language. Language is our major means of communication, but it is also an expression of cultural identity, and the way in which it is used reflects the way the world is perceived and understood by its users. This aspect of culture is under threat from increasing tourism and, specifically, from sport tourism. As long as a host society maintains its original language, it is differentiated from many of its international visitors. However, increasingly, English is becoming the language of both sport and tourism; commonly shared by the vast majority of tourists, its growing use is seen as a way of facilitating tourism.

Sport tourism in particular poses a great threat to ethnic languages because English has secured its place historically as the language of sport around the world, tied no doubt to the roots of many sports that were developed in England in the nineteenth century. Watch a major sports tournament and hear how often the score is called in English rather than in the native tongue of the host society. English is already the world language for air traffic control, the Internet, much of international business and finance, as well as many films and much of pop music. Reading (1998) argues that English will become the single language of the European Union as it moves toward a single currency and a single market. Already more documents originate in English than in any other language within the prospective single economy.

France is one nation that is fighting the trend. For example, a chain of sports retailers in France traded by the name of The Athlete's Foot, but like other companies whose signs were in English (and those shown on television were all sport-related) they must now make new signs; Anglicized words are now forbidden by French law (BBC, Breakfast News, 24 February, 1997). The Welsh travel writer referred to earlier perceived the failure to use the Welsh language as a denigration of Welsh cultural heritage. The globalization of sport and tourism can thus contribute to the erosion of distinctive languages, the dismissal of different genres of cultural expression, and ultimately lead to the homogenizing of major forms of popular culture.

Bale's (1994) detailed work on the *Landscapes of Modern Sport* is relevant to our discussion of cultural homogeneity. He writes:

> Although the "globalization of culture is not the same as its homogenization" (Appadurai, 1990: 307), the globally enforced rules of sport encourage sameness, homogenisation and placelessness to an extent not so commonly found in such global common denominators as tourism, leisure or work. (p. 8)

International governing bodies of sport and the standardizations they require result in tennis courts, running tracks, and ice hockey arenas being much the same the world over. Sport tourism experiences that depend essentially on the natural landscape for their challenge (see figure 2.4 on page 64), such as skiing, orienteering, or caving, avoid this sense of sameness and therefore offer a richer touristic experience. However, wherever the experiences sought by sport tourists emphasize achievement through competition, sport tourism will contribute to cultural homogeneity due to the necessary standardization.

Another case of sport encouraging cultural homogeneity is exemplified by New Zealanders. During the 1995 Americas Cup (Barber, 1995), Team New Zealand, with Peter Blake skippering *Black Magic*, totally outclassed the defense of Dennis Conner, the skipper of *Young America*, to win the cup 5-0 in the waters off San Diego. Back in New Zealand red socks became compulsory footwear after Peter Blake revealed that the one day in 38 starts that *Black Magic* lost, he had not worn his red socks (Barber, 1995). The prime minister, the Queen's representative, posed for photographs wearing red socks and 100,000 other pairs were sold in 10 days! Thus, red socks became an emblem of cultural homogeneity, binding New Zealanders together across the world.

A very different form of cultural homogeneity, where tourist providers have brought about a major influence even on the natural environment, is found in the Canary Islands, ancient volcanic eruptions that lie off the African coast, popular particularly as winter sunshine resorts. Their natural black sand beaches have been derived from the volcanic deposits that formed the islands. But black sand is unnatural to many of their most prolific North European visitors. In consequence, the beach at Las Teresitas on Teneriffe has been covered with golden sand imported from the Sahara desert to make it more similar and acceptable to visitors' expectations; it is claimed to be the largest artificial beach in the world at one mile long and one hundred meters wide.

Summary

The trend to increase sport touristic experiences and to provide them in faraway, often very different cultures simply increases the importance of addressing both the potential positive and the negative sociocultural impacts of sport tourism. In this chapter we have attempted an evenhanded approach so that neither the advantages nor the disadvantages of sport tourism have been overemphasized.

What are sport tourism's potentially positive impacts?

1. Sport tourism can provide a new and valuable (both economic and social) use for otherwise surplus land—thus, it can strengthen rural economies.

2. Sport tourism can strengthen national heritage, identity, and community spirit as local people join together to promote their culture.

3. Sport tourism can provide a vehicle through which visitors can come to know foreign people and their culture.

4. Sport tourism can be a stimulus to develop and improve the built infrastructure and the natural environment.

5. Exclusion of nations from sport touristic activity can be a stimulus to internal reform.

6. Sport tourism can instigate the regeneration and preservation of cultural traditions.

What are sport tourism's potentially negative impacts?

1. The attraction of more remunerative sport touristic employment opportunities can erode traditional communities and adversely affect the balance of a local economy.

2. Sport tourism can contribute to the loss of cultural identity and heritage.

3. Sport tourism can bring about modifications to cultural experiences to accommodate tourism.
4. Sport tourism can lead to crowd disorder at events.
5. Excessive violence can be related to sport tourism.
6. Sport tourism can contribute to tensions between hosts and visitors.

As sport tourists impact upon host communities, so sport tourism can be an agent of social change. Residents of the host society themselves often perceive a dilemma between their dependence upon (or wish for) the economic benefits visitors bring and their desire to withstand the impact and preserve their heritage and culture undamaged and unchanged. People themselves, it seems, value cultural differences—witness the breakup of former conglomerate states into independent, often warring ethnic groups. Achieving a balance between the potential sociocultural benefits and disbenefits of sport tourism is a global challenge that needs to be managed.

References

Alpine, L. (1986). Trends in special interest travel. *Specialty Travel Index, Fall/Winter,* 83-84.

Archer, B., and Cooper, C. (1994). The positive and negative impacts of tourism. In W. Theobald (Ed.), *Global tourism* (pp. 73-91). Oxford, Great Britain: Butterworth-Heinemann.

August, O., and Bale, J. (1996, December 14). Go-slow blocks ski instructors. *The Times,* p. 76.

Baade, R.A., and Dye, R.E. (1990). The impact of stadiums and professional sport on metropolitan area development. *Growth and Change, 21*(2), 1-14.

Bale, J. (1992). *Sport, space and the city.* London: Routledge.

Bale, J. (1994). *Landscapes of modern sport.* Leicester, Great Britain: Leicester University Press.

Barber, D. (1995, May 12). Has become all the rage in Kiwi country. *The Independent,* p. 38.

BBC Breakfast News (1996, December 17). Report. London: British Broadcasting Corporation.

BBC Breakfast News (1997, February 24). Report. London: British Broadcasting Corporation.

Boniface, B., and Cooper, C. (1994). *The geography of travel and tourism.* Oxford, Great Britain: Butterworth-Heinemann.

Bose, M. (1993). *Sporting colours: South Africa's return to international sport.* London: Robson Books.

Bramante, A. (1998). Leisure lifestyles in a developing country: Reasons for non-participation. In M.F. Collins and I.S. Cooper (Eds.), *Leisure management issues and applications* (pp. 49-64). Wallingford, Great Britain: CAB International.

Bull, A. (1991). *The economics of travel and tourism*. Melbourne, Australia: Pitman.

Burton, R. (1995). *Travel geography*. London: Pitman.

Butler, R. (1980). The concept of a tourism area cycle of evolution: Implications for managers of resources. *Canadian Geographer, 24*, 5-12.

Byrne, P. and Ravenscroft, N. (1989). *The land report: Diversification and alternative land uses for the landowner and farmer*. London: Humberts Chartered Surveyors.

Capenerhurst, J. (1994). Community tourism. In L. Haywood (Ed.), *Community leisure and recreation* (pp. 144-171). Oxford, Great Britain: Butterworth-Heinemann.

Clark, G., Darrall, J., Grove-White, R., Macnaghten, P., and Urry, J. (1994). *Leisure landscapes. Leisure, culture and the English countryside: Challenges and conflicts*. Lancaster University, Great Britain: Centre for the Study of Environmental Change.

Coalter, F. (1990). Sport and anti-social behaviour: Hits and myths. In J. Long (Ed.), *Leisure, health and wellbeing. Conference papers No. 44* (pp. 145-154). Eastbourne, Great Britain: Leisure Studies Association.

Cohen, E. (1982). Marginal paradises. *Annals of Tourism Research, 9*, 190-227.

Collins, M. (1991). The economics of sport and sports in the economy: Some international comparisons. In C. Cooper (Ed.), *Progress in tourism, recreation and hospitality management. Vol. 3* (pp. 184-214). London: Belhaven Press.

Commission of the European Communities. (1987). *Europeans and their holidays*. Luxembourg: Office for Official Publications of the European Community.

Coppock, J.T. (1977). *Second homes, curse or blessing*. Oxford, Great Britain: Pergamon Press.

Craven, J. (1994). Cross-cultural impacts on effectiveness in sport. In R.C. Wilcox (Ed.), *Sport in the global village* (pp. 433-448). Morgantown, WV: Fitness Information Technology.

Cushman, G., Veal, A.J., and Zuzanek, J. (Eds.). (1996). *World leisure participation free time in the global village*. Wallingford, Great Britain: CAB International.

Davidson, R. (1992). *Tourism in Europe*. London: Pitman.

Doxey, G.V. (1975). A causation theory of visitor-resident irritants: Methodology and research inference. In The Research Association (Ed.), *Proceedings of The Travel Research Association Sixth Annual Conference* (pp. 195-198). San Diego, CA: Author.

Dunning, E., Murphy, P., and Williams, J. (1986). Spectator violence at football matches: Towards a sociological explanation. *British Journal of Sociology, 27*, 221-244.

Elliott, H. (1995, August 3). Test series gives big boost to West Indies tourism, *The Times*, p. 19.

Evans, M. (1995, February 18). Hot games and curry for lunch. *The Times*, p. 17.

Exodus Travels Ltd. (1996). *General information for worldwide trekking holidays*. London: Author.

Getz, D. (1994). Event tourism and the authenticity dilemma. In W. Theobald (Ed.), *Global tourism* (pp. 313-329). Oxford, Great Britain: Butterworth-Heinemann.

Glen, M.H. (1995). Language, culture and heritage—Words, words, words. In D. Leslie (Ed.), *Tourism and leisure—Culture, heritage and participation. Vol. 1* (pp. 83-92). Eastbourne, Great Britain: Leisure Studies Association.

Glyptis, S. (1995). Recreation and the environment: Challenging and changing relationships. In D. Leslie (Ed.), *Tourism and leisure—Culture, heritage and participation. Vol.1* (pp. 171-178). Eastbourne, Great Britain: Leisure Studies Association.

Goering, P.G. (1990). The response to tourism in Ladakh. *Cultural Survival Quarterly, 14*(1), 20-25.

Grihault, N. (1997, October/November). Footsteps in high places. *Wanderlust, 24,* 35-37.

Hamlyn, M. (1995, May 20). Fields of dreams, *The Times Magazine,* pp. 18-22.

Hands, D. (1995, June 27). Future beckons for game and host nation. *The Times,* p. 42.

Harding, J. (1988). Sporting events as a tool in the development of tourism in rural areas. In Australian Sports Commission (Ed.), *Rural sport and regional games: Seminar proceedings* (pp. 89-92). Murray, Australia: Institute of Higher Education, N.S.W. Australia.

Harrison, C., Burgess, J., and Limb, M. (1987). Popular values for the countryside. In B. Brown (Ed.), *Leisure and the environment. Conference papers No. 31* (pp. 43-57). Eastbourne, Great Britain: Leisure Studies Association.

Herron Associates Inc. (1991). *World Gymnastics Championships impact report.* Indianapolis: Author.

Holton, R.J., and Fletcher, P. (1988). *Public disorder in contemporary Australia. A report to the Criminology Research Council of Australia.* Canberra, Australia: Criminology Research Council of Australia.

Keller, C.P. (1984). Centre-periphery tourism development and control. In Centre for Leisure Research (Ed.), *Leisure tourism and social change* (pp. 77-84). Edinburgh, Scotland: Centre for Leisure Research.

Kempson, R. (1998, January 2). FA pleads for World Cup ticket increase. *The Times,* p. 21.

Klausen, A.M. (1992). Construction of the Norwegian image: Reflections on the Olympic Design Program. In Puijk, R. (Ed.), *OL-94 og forskningen III* [Olympics 94 and research] (pp. 95-114). Lillehammer, Norway: Yenstlandsforskning.

Kliskey, A., and Kearsley, G.W. (1993). Mapping multiple perceptions of wilderness so as to minimise the impact of tourism on natural environments: A case-study of the North West South Island of New Zealand. In A.J. Veal, P. Jonson, and G. Cushman (Eds.), *Leisure and tourism: Social and economic change* (pp. 603-608). Sydney, Australia: University of Technology.

Koloff, M.L. (1993). Conflict surrounding tourism development. In A.J. Veal, P. Jonson, and G. Cushman (Eds.), *Leisure and tourism: Social and environmental change* (pp. 603-608). Sydney, Australia: University of Technology.

Kolstad, A., Rundmo, T., and Svarva, K. (1995). The consequences of the Olympic Games on the host city residents' value systems. *Corpus, Psyche et Societas, 2*(1), 85-94.

Krippendorf, J. (1987). *The holiday makers: Understanding the impact of leisure and travel.* London: Heinemann.

Lodge, D. (1992). *Paradise news.* Harmondsworth, Great Britain: Penguin.

Lynch, R. (1991). A new face of crowd disorder in Australia with the emergence of sport as mass entertainment. In D. Botterill and A. Tomlinson (Eds.), *Ideology, leisure policy and practice. Conference papers No. 45* (pp. 107-121). Eastbourne, Great Britain: Leisure Studies Association.

MacCannell,D. (1996). *Tourist or traveller?* London: BBC Educational Developments.

Massey, R. (1997, February 27). Honda stakes £300 m to put UK in the driving seat. *Daily Mail,* p. 2.

Mercer, D. (1994). Native peoples and tourism: Conflict and compromise. In W. Theobald (Ed.), *Global tourism* (pp. 124-145). Oxford, Great Britain: Butterworth-Heinemann.

Mill, R.C. (1990). *Tourism: The international business.* Englewood Cliffs, N.J.: Prentice Hall.

Morris, J. (1987, December 9). Sick of the tourist roller-coaster. *Independent,* p. 11.

Murphy, P.E. (1985). *Tourism: A community approach.* New York: Methuen.

Payne, R. (1995). Combining sport with environmental aid. *Sport, 4,* 8-9.

Pearce, P.L. (1994). Tourist-resident impacts: Examples, explanations and emerging solutions. In W. Theobald (Ed.), *Global tourism* (pp. 103-123). Oxford, Great Britain: Butterworth-Heinemann.

Plog, S.C. (1994). Leisure travel: An extraordinary industry facing superordinary problems. In W. Theobald (Ed.), *Global tourism* (pp. 40-54). Oxford, Great Britain: Butterworth-Heinemann.

Reading, B. (1998, January 17/January 18). Speaking in tongues won't do. *Financial Times,* p. 2.

Redfoot, D. (1984). Touristic authenticity, touristic angst, and modern reality. *Qualitative Sociology, 7*(4), 291-309.

Ritchie, J.R.B. (1988, July). *Alternative approaches to teaching tourism.* Paper presented at the Tourism Teaching into the 1990s Conference, Guildford, Great Britain.

Ryan, C. (1991). *Recreational tourism.* London, Great Britain: Routledge.

Samuel, N. (1996). France. In G. Cushman, A.J. Veal, and J. Zuzanek (Eds.), *World leisure participation: Free time in the global village* (pp. 77-106). Wallingford, Great Britain: CAB International.

Selwood, H.J., and Jones, R. (1993). The America's Cup in retrospect: The aftershock in Fremantle. In A.J. Veal, P. Jonson and G. Cushman (Eds.), *Leisure and tourism: Social and environmental change* (pp. 656-660). Sydney, Australia: University of Technology.

Smith, V.L. (Ed.). (1978). *Hosts and guests: The anthropology of tourism.* Oxford, Great Britain: Blackwell.

Smith, V.L. (Ed.). (1989). *Hosts and guests: The anthropology of tourism.* 2nd ed. Philadelphia: University of Pennsylvania.

Sofield, T. (1991). Sustainable ethnic tourism in the South Pacific: Some principles. *Journal of Tourism Studies, 2*(1), 56-72.

Stevens, T. (1990). Viva Barcelona. *Leisure Management, 10*(2), 46-53.

Talbot-Ponsonby, H. (Ed.). (1988). *Changing land use and recreation.* Cheltenham, Great Britain: Countryside Commission.

Travis, A. (1982). Physical impacts: Trends affecting tourism—Managing the cultural and environmental impacts. *Tourism Management, 3*(4), 256-262.

Usher, R. (1996, September 2). Some don't like it hot. *Time,* pp. 46-49.

van der Poel, H. (1993). Leisure policy in the Netherlands. In P. Bramham, I. Henry, H. Mommaas, and H. van der Poel (Eds.), *Leisure policies in Europe* (pp. 41-70). Wallingford, Great Britain: CAB International.

Wheat, S. (1995). Marking golf's card. *Leisure Management, 15*(5), 26-28.

Whitson, D. and Macintosh, D. (1993). Becoming a world class city: Hallmark events and sport franchises in the growth strategies of western Canadian cities. *Sociology of Sport Journal, 10,* 221-240.

Williams, J. (1986). White riots: The English football fan abroad. In A. Tomlinson and G. Whannel (Eds.), *Off the ball* (pp. 5-19). London: Pluto Press.

Williams, J., Dunning, E., and Murphy, P. (1989). *Hooligans abroad.* London: Routledge.

Williams, R. (1977). *Marxism and literature.* Oxford, Great Britain: Oxford University Press.

Chapter 7
The Environmental Impact of Sport Tourism

Hiking an eroded footpath in Grindsbrook Meadows in England.

The Rambler's Association

The following topics are covered in this chapter:

1. The growing concern for the environment.
2. The increasing participation in outdoor sport tourism activities.
3. The impact of sport tourism on the natural environment.
4. The impact of sport tourism on the urban environment.
5. The measures taken to minimize the influence of sport tourism on the environment.

Both sport tourism and the countryside (the environment) are aspects of life that people care about deeply—and the two aspects have a strong relationship. Sport tourism's link to the environment is both as a victim and an aggressor (Priester, 1989). In this chapter, we will discuss first the victimization of sport tourism—that is, how the growing concern in society for the natural environment threatens sport tourism. Second, sport tourism's harmfulness to the natural environment will be described. An analysis of the increasing participation in outdoor sports in general and more specifically during holidays, of the damage caused by sport tourism to the natural environment in global terms, and of the environmental impact of different sport tourism activities separately shows that sport, tourism, and sport tourism are potential aggressors of the natural environment. A number of solutions will be suggested to minimize the negative influence of outdoor sports and sport tourism on the environment. Third, the impact of sport tourism and its effect on urban environments will be highlighted.

Not only from the ecological point of view but also from the perspective of sport tourists who take part in all kinds of outdoor sports, conservation of nature is of vital importance. The more the natural environment is spoiled, the less possibility there will be for practicing both new and old forms of outdoor activities. Sport tourism is nowadays putting intense pressure on the natural environment, endangering it, and because of that sport tourism is also in danger.

The increasing participation as well as the increasing differentiation in leisure activities often intensively practiced during specific moments in time (holidays) causes a danger to the natural environment. And as many of the newer sports rapidly have become mass phenomena, there has often been no time to establish policies or to take protective action, with damage as the consequence. Some outdoor recreation activities such as hiking, hunting, kayaking, skiing, yachting, and so on depend almost exclusively on natural environments and natural resources such as mountains, forests, rivers, and seas. More people have started to practice them with damage to the natural environment as the consequence. Moreover, new outdoor activities have been invented (e.g., surfing, windsurfing, snowboarding) stressing the environment even more. If, in the future, people want to participate in sport tourism activities in a beautiful, unspoiled environment, there is an urgent need for precautionary measures. Otherwise sport tourism will destroy itself.

A Growing Concern for the Natural Environment

There is nowadays a growing concern in society for the natural environment. On earth every element is linked together in diverse and complex ecosystems that sustain life. Together these interrelated systems of oceans, reefs, dunes, rivers, wetlands, forests, bushlands, and plains support a marvelous and diverse range of plant and animal life, including the human species. After two hundred years of rapid industrial growth, this life-support system is under severe stress. Many scientists question earth's capacity to sustain an acceptable environment for human beings unless we change the way we live. Threats can be summarized as

- threats to biodiversity,
- the greenhouse effect,
- ozone depletion,
- air, water, and soil pollution, and
- overconsumption of resources (Sydney Organizing Committee for the Olympic Games [SOCOG], 1995).

With expanding populations there is an ever-increasing demand for natural environments.

Thus concern for the natural environment is becoming a hot issue. However, not everybody is always willing to keep the natural environment undamaged. In a special issue on outdoor and environmental education, the editorial board of the World Leisure and Recreation Association (1992) states,

> Because they are [i.e., the natural environments] everybody's, they are nobody's! For most people, there is no sense of urgency to conserve and sustain the environment. It becomes a problem for "someone else." It becomes a personal problem only when individual self-interest comes under threat. For some, this threat will be economic, but for others it will be recreational. (p. 5)

Furthermore, even if people are willing not to spoil nature, it is not always very clear how nature should be protected. Allison (1995), for example, writes that

> The rhetoric of ordinary language has it that landscapes are "preserved" or "destroyed." But a more serious consideration of the meaning of words tells us that neither of these words is even remotely appropriate except in a tiny fraction of cases. Landscapes change, in different ways and to different degrees. Human beings are responsible for many of the changes, but not for all of them. The changes can be evaluated as good or bad according to a wide variety of standards. The environment does not set its own standards. Ecology has no moral substance. (p. 90)

Therefore, some people will be in favor of "unspoiled environment," others will want to use nature while taking care not to destroy it, and still others will try to exploit nature without taking any precautions. Furthermore, opinions and perspectives on the protection of nature are also changing with time. Roberts (1989) indicated that a trend can be noticed from preserving the natural environment (i.e., not permitting use) to conserving it (i.e., economically exploiting it but maintaining its "naturalness"). Worthwhile to mention in this respect is the definition of conservation from U.S. President Kennedy, as cited by Roberts (1989): "the wide use of our natural environment . . . the highest form of national thrift, the prevention of waste and despoilment, while preserving, improving and renewing the quality and usefulness of all our resources" (p. 2).

In 1810 the English Lakeland poet William Wordsworth made a case for the Lake District area of Cumbria becoming a sort of national property for the enjoyment of people of "pure taste." But the whole idea of government intervention in land ownership and control for the purpose of setting aside whole areas in which people can enjoy recreation comes from the United States of America. The national park movement began with the establishment of Yellowstone National Park in 1872 by designating a wilderness area for protection in order to avert the onslaught of industrial and commercial development (Zeiger, Caneday, and Baker, 1993). In 1916 the federal government took over responsibility for the national parks. Park administrators were instructed by law to

> conserve the scenery and the natural and historic objects and the wildlife therein and to provide for the enjoyment of the same in such manner and by such means as will leave them unimpaired for the enjoyment of future generations. (Zeiger, Caneday, and Baker, 1993, p. 155)

The 1970s was the decade when people began to show increased interest in the natural environment. Significant in this respect is the establishment of the Department of the Environment in Britain, the Environmental Protection Agency/Council on Environmental Quality in the United States, and the Environmental Directorate in the Overseas Economic Community. In 1972, the United Nations held the Conference on the Human Environment in Stockholm, Sweden. Out of this conference the UN environmental program was established.

The 1980s was the decade of "green movements." In 1980, the International Union for the Conservation of Nature and Natural Resources published its "World Conservation Strategy." This strategy referred to providing facilities in the interests of social welfare for recreation and leisure time occupation. Nineteen eighty-seven was the "European Year of the Environment," an initiative of the European Community. In the same year, Jost Krippendorf's (1987) book *The Holidaymakers* was published. Krippendorf suggested that experiencing nature was one of the more important motivations for tourist travels and argued that tourism needed to be consistent with its environment. He used examples from the Swiss Cantons to show how regulations were imposed to limit tourism to what were considered to be the carrying capacities of the area.

The 1990s can be regarded as the decade of sustainable growth. Boniface and Cooper (1994) state,

> The maturing of tourism markets in the 1990s, allied to the environmentalist movement, will see changing attitudes on the part of both consumers and suppliers as commentators stress the need for sustainable growth. In particular, the realization of the negative impacts of tourism upon host environments, societies, and developing economies has prompted the search for alternative forms of tourism and a critical attitude towards mass tourism. Indeed, many argue that it is mass tourism that has caused most of the problems which are being identified with tourism generally . . . an increasing number of public agencies are drawing up guidelines for the reduction of tourism impacts and some generating countries (Germany and Scandinavia, for example) are already shunning destinations which are not "environmentally sound." (p. 241)

The 1992 United Nations Conference on Environment and Development held in Rio de Janeiro made the concept of "sustainable development" prominent. Yet in its concern to tackle threats to the global environment it failed to identify tourism as one of those threats (Holloway, 1994). Clarke (1995) described sustainable tourism as tourism that ensures that developments are of benefit to at least two generations, and that environmental, ecological, economic, historical, and cultural resources are protected from exhaustion.

Holloway (1994) notes that "a general awareness of the problems which tourism creates has led in recent years to a new movement to curtail its excesses" (p. 261). According to Holloway this movement calls for a new tourism—variously described as "sustainable tourism," "ecotourism," "green tourism," or "soft tourism"—and "that tourism must be developed as part of a properly thought-out management strategy, with collaboration between the private and public sectors, to prevent irreparable damage to the environment before it is too late" (p. 261).

Such awareness was identified in the "Charter for Sustainable Tourism," agreed to during the World Conference on Sustainable Tourism, sponsored by the United Nations, UNESCO, and the World Tourism Organization (WTO) in April 1995 on Lanzarote (Gran Canaria, Spain) (Clarke, 1995). The charter elaborates 10 principles calling on people who are involved in the planning, programming, and implementation of sustainable tourism to work together to observe the rules of "best practice." According to Clarke (1995), these principles can be summarized as working with local people to enhance resources, ensuring a long-term economic return from their investments in time, effort, and finance. Furthermore, the charter has extended the Rio Declaration (United Nations Earth Summit) by including a specific charter on sustainable tourism. Table 7.1 shows the guidelines established by the WTO.

Increasing Participation in Outdoor Sports

Recently, outdoor sports have increased in popularity both quantitatively as well as qualitatively and have become a growing segment of the touristic industry. This phenomenon is described in detail in chapter 3. According to Strasdas (1994), the increased interest for sports in the open air is due to an increasing body- and health-consciousness, a growing need to experience nature, and a continuing tendency toward individualization.

Prior to 1970s, outdoor sports enthusiasts were not very numerous—they formed only a small group of individuals looking for some renewal in their way of living. However, in the 1970s joggers became the trendsetters for a huge mass of outdoor fanatics. Immediately the sports industry took advantage of this new trend. Since then, equipment has become more attractive, more available, and more advanced, and successful marketing of this new touristic product has contributed to a mass "adventure tourism." Adventure here is synonymous with discovery, the knowledge of outdoor sports, being open for new things, and the will to explore.

Table 7.1   A Guideline for Sustainable Tourism

1. Identify and minimize product and operational environmental problems, paying particular attention to new projects.
2. Pay due regard to environmental concerns in design, planning, construction, and implementation.
3. Be sensitive to conservation of environmentally protected or threatened areas, species and scenic aesthetics, achieving landscape enhancement where possible.
4. Practice energy conservation, reduce and recycle waste, practice freshwater management, and control sewage disposal.
5. Control and diminish air emissions and pollutants.
6. Monitor, control, and reduce noise levels.
7. Control, reduce, or eliminate environmentally unfriendly products, such as asbestos, CFCs, pesticides and toxic, corrosive, infectious, explosive, or flammable material.
8. Respect and support historic or religious objects and sites.
9. Exercise due regard for the interests of local populations, including their history, traditions, culture, and future development.
10. Consider environmental issues as a key factor in the overall development of travel and tourism destinations.

Note. Holloway, J.C. (1994). *The business of tourism* (p. 262). London: Pittman. Copyright 1994 by Pittman. Adapted by permission.

In the beginning, little reference was made to a critical ecological view on practicing sports in the open air. But the increase of outdoor sports led to some local conflicts between the sports participants and the environmental protectionists. Such conflicts have since expanded to almost all regions of the world where an attractive nature patrimony can be found such as woods, mountain landscapes, rivers, rocks, caves, and so forth (Holderegger, 1990; Smidt, 1991).

The quantitative development of outdoor sports expresses itself in an increase in the number of activities and of participants, the time spent on these activities, as well as the rising costs of equipment (Strasdas, 1994). Furthermore, there was and is an increase in the number of organizations that offer outdoor activities in general and in particular as a holiday experience. Qualitatively there is an improvement in the equipment, specific training methods, adapted diets, and so forth, but there is also a differentiation or growth of a wide range of outdoor activities and an adaptation of traditional sports—for example, the evolution from traditional biking (i.e., on the street) to mountain biking (e.g., in the woods, on the beach).

Glyptis (1995) indicated that interest in outdoor recreation in the United Kingdom (i.e., countryside, active, and adventure holidays) is increasing.

Two out of five adults in England and Wales (some 18 million people) visit the countryside on an average summer Sunday. Glyptis referred to the U.K. Day Visits Survey (Baty and Richards, 1997), indicating that in 1993 alone about 900 million day visits were made to the countryside.

Clark, Darrall, Grove-White, Macnaghten, and Urry (1994) reported an expansion in the number of specific and individual leisure activities, such as organized rambling, rock climbing, cycling, orienteering, car and motorbike rallying, and activity holidays.

Similar trends have been reported in other countries as well. For example, according to estimates, since 1976 adventure travel in Canada has witnessed a yearly increase of 17 percent. Even higher growth rates are expected for the near future (Tourism Research Group, 1988).

The popularity of these outdoor sports has led to two opposite phenomena. First, there is a huge concentration of participants in some areas resulting in an intensive infrastructure to support their activities (as with skiing, for example). On the other hand, under the influence of an increasing individualization and the "back to nature" movement, outdoor activities are practiced more widely and frequently (Schemel and Erbguth, 1992). Both phenomena have led to a number of negative effects on the environment. These effects will be described next.

Damage to the Natural Environment Caused by Tourism

Davidson (1992) stated that the high numbers of visitors arriving at exotic and remote destinations that are not used to accommodating these volumes are the primary cause of environmental damage. The natural environment rarely escapes damage where large numbers of tourists are found. Thus, the concept of "carrying capacity" has been introduced in both sport and tourism (see table 7.2). It defines the maximum desirable levels of use and can be applied to any facility, such as a forest, country park, golf course, swimming pool, ski area, and so forth.

Although the idea of carrying capacity seems logical, it is misleading because there are many other factors to consider. Graefe (1993) identified five major sets of considerations that in his estimation are critical to understanding the nature of recreation impacts:

1. *Impact interrelationships.* There are no single, predictable responses of natural environments. As a result, some forms of impact are more direct than others.

2. *Use-impact relationships.* These relationships vary for different measures of visitor use. They are influenced by situational factors.

Table 7.2   Visitor Capacity for Selected Sites

Site/activity	Visitors per day/hectare
Forest park	up to 15
Suburban nature park	15–70
High-density picnicking	300–600
Low-density picnicking	60–200
Golf	10–15
Fishing/sailing	5–30
Speedboating	5–10
Waterskiing	5–15
Skiing	100 (per hectare of trails)
Nature trail hiking	40 (per kilometer)
Nature trail horse riding	25–80 (per kilometer)

From Inskeep, 1991. Cited in *"The Business of Tourism."* J.C. Holloway, 1994, London: Pittman. Copyright 1994 by Pittman. Reprinted by permission.

3. *Variation in tolerance among environments and user groups.* Some environments are more vulnerable than others, and some user groups cause more damage than others.

4. *Activity-specific influences.* The environmental impact varies according to factors such as type of transportation or equipment and visitor characteristics, such as party size.

5. *Site-specific influences.* Despite a basic tolerance level to a particular type of recreation, its effect on the use of the natural environment may still depend on the time and place of the human activity.

Roberts (1989) argued that the severity of the consequences of mechanized transport for the environment depends on the efficiency of the vehicle. He indicated that societal preferences unfortunately encourage the most inefficient use and thus the mode of the greatest impact, that is, the use of the private car; a full coach will have less impact per capita. Rocky Mountain National Park allows access via only park buses to certain locations in the park. Individual vehicles are allowed at all other places in the park.

So far, we have only indicated that tourism-related movement and activity have negative effects for the natural environment. Next is a description of the kinds of consequences that are a result of these activities. These effects concern the quality of water and air, the amount and diversity of vegetation and wildlife, the level of noise, and the aesthetic of scenery.

Holloway (1994) clearly described how the technological complexity of twentieth-century living has led to various forms of water and air pollution, which are both initiated and compounded by tourism development, and by travel in particular. Because tourism necessitates travel in the air, over land, or in water, it often increases pollution of the environment. Within this context, unacceptable levels of noise can also be regarded as a form of pollution.

The amount as well as the diversity of the vegetation also suffers in areas of high tourist intensity from the constant trampling and crushing by feet, bicycle and car wheels, and horses' hooves. This has led in some cases to erosion and to the disappearance of fragile species. Many footpaths are being widened to such an extent that the surrounding areas are suffering serious erosion. As pointed out by Davidson (1993), walkers are often responsible for destroying the vegetation at the side of paths when they want to avoid muddy conditions in the center of the paths (see chapter-opening photo). This has led in some cases to the construction of concrete or wooden paths or boardwalks to prevent further damage.

One attempt was made in 1993 to counteract the effect on the footpath across the Moors near Haworth in the U.K. Halloway reports that some 25,000 visitors had turned parts of the Bronte Way into a quagmire, necessitating flagstones being set into the track. Davidson (1993) gives the example of walkers along paths such as the Pennine Way (a long-distance walking path in the U.K.) who are responsible for trampling the vegetation at the sides of the path.

Environmental "pollution" is not limited to physical pollutants. Increasing popularity leads to expanding facilities and the despoilment of the natural landscape is as much aesthetic as physical. Holloway (1994) referred to the situation in which areas of scenic beauty attract greater numbers of tourists and as a result of the greater use lose their attractiveness. Consequently, other new areas are explored.

As Inskeep (1991) has pointed out, not all of these pressures necessarily take place in one particular area. What happens in a given location depends on the kind of tourism development and the specific environmental characteristics of that touristic area.

According to Vanreusel (1990), rising recreation pressure and the loss of quality in such areas are the main reasons people move to other recreation areas, where the same process takes place. So the relation between the environment and outdoor recreation is a vicious circle (see figure 7.1).

Some areas are more vulnerable than others. Among the most vulnerable are forests because of the constant danger of fire. Tree felling to make way for new facilities degrades local scenery and contributes to global problems. Also mountain regions can be regarded as very vulnerable. They suffer in a number of ways. Yearly about 50 million people visit the Alps, and some

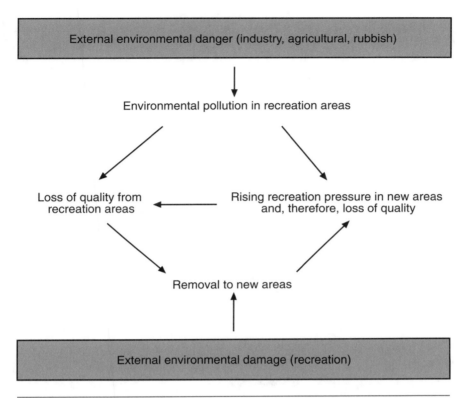

Figure 7.1   The relationship between the environment and recreation.

From Vanreusel, B. 1990. Used by permission of the publisher.

7 million passenger vehicles cross them each year, as they lay at the heart of Europe (Ward et al., 1994). Large highways, airports, and high-velocity trains provide easy access to the Alps. Due to this intensive tourism, the Alps are the most vulnerable mountains in the world. Because of hotels, ski slope infrastructure, and mountain restaurants, the landscape has changed dramatically. Perhaps the vulnerability of the Alps is best documented by the fact that potential damage to the region has led to the founding of an organization, "Alp Action." The organization, set up with the support of the Aga Khan, aims at preserving the Alps as a single ecosystem. Worthwhile to mention also is the fact that the year 1996 was dedicated to the conservation of the Alps. However, some Swiss regional authorities did not support these conservation efforts, as they feared that it would slow down the economic development of their region.

Other areas particularly vulnerable to mass tourism are the delicate ecosystems of the sea. Scuba diving and snorkeling are now immensely popular sport tourism experiences, with participants travelling extensively to explore the world's oceans. In the United States alone Monaghan reported that there were between 1.7 and 2 million divers (Tabata, 1992). Top destinations for coral reef viewing include the Bahamas, the Cayman Islands, Belize, the Red Sea and Australia's Great Barrier Reef, the largest barrier reef in the world, covering some 350,000 square kilometers. Coral reefs, like rain forests, are critical watersheds for biodiversity, yet nine out of ten of the world's reefs have been physically damaged by human activity. Some 10,000 yachts and 24,000 speedboats use Australia's Great Barrier Reef Marine Park, and in excess of one million visitor days are spent on the reef each year (Kelleher & Craik, 1993). To provide for the protection of the reef, the marine park authority has been established with its main management tools of spatial zoning of activities, together with education, incentives, prohibitions, and limitations. Visitors are prohibited from collecting specimens and divers are encouraged not to touch or trample on the fragile coral.

The Impact of Holiday Resorts on the Natural Environment

Holiday villages are developed in unspoilt rural, green, and generally wooded areas. Each village occupies some four hundred to six hundred

Australian Tourist Commission

Nine of ten of the world's reefs have been damaged by human activity, including the Great Barrier Reef of Australia.

acres of land. They cater to around three thousand to four thousand visitors at any one time with high year-round occupancy levels. This results in significant increases in local traffic and high demand on land use.

Environmental effects are more and more taken into consideration during the planning stage of new holiday resorts, which sometimes results in the cancellation of projects. For example, a proposal by the international company Rank to develop a village on a sensitive ecological site at West Wood in Kent in southeast England met such opposition from local residents on environmental grounds that the scheme was abandoned. The claim of holiday resort Center Parcs that it was very environmentally sensitive became prominent in England only after 1990 when a noticeable political shift in government interest increased the significance of environmental issues.

The Impact of Sport Tourism Activities on the Natural Environment

The environment can be damaged by different aspects of outdoor sports. In the first place, the activities and sportists themselves can have a negative influence:

- Mountain bikers can damage the flora and soil.
- The noise and light from speedboats and rally cars can rout animals.
- Campers, hikers, and boaters can dump rubbish in parks and streams.
- Boat anchors and divers' feet and hands can damage underwater coral.

Furthermore, there is the use of land, unspoiled acreage, by the infrastructure and the preparation of regions for sport tourist activities, such as the constructing of ski slopes and golf courses. Often, this results in a higher accessibility of formerly unspoilt areas. Another aspect is the equipment necessary for practicing sport. The construction as well as the use and the maintenance of this equipment (e.g., boots) can cause environmental inconvenience and damage. In addition, there is energy consumption and pollution by vehicles transporting outdoor sports participants to and from their activities. Peripheral activities like car parking and eating and drinking after or during the main activities add significantly to the pressure on the environment, often resulting in a need for extra infrastructure, transport facilities, and services. Finally, the social conflicts between recreation enthusiasts and the local population and between different sports groups can have negative effects on the environment by concentrating pressure into certain areas. As illustrated in figure 7.1, when these conflicts arise, a lot of the participants move on to less-populated areas and so the damage continues (Strasdas, 1994; Vanreusel, 1993; Wilken, 1993).

Allison (1995) argues that most of the sports that cause concern about the countryside are mere leisure activities or forms of exercise even if they also exist in a form that is undeniably sporting. As every outdoor sport has its own influence on the environment, we will now discuss in more detail some popular outdoor sport tourist activities and their impact on the natural environment.

Golf

According to Wheat (1992),

> Few forms of recreation would seem to be more benign in their impact on the environment than golf. But with the golf boom in full swing, concern is growing about the amount of land being consumed by the sport and the effect of the intensive management practices employed on courses . . . pressure is on for designers and conservationists to minimize the sport's impact on the landscape. (p. 10)

The problems about the location of golf courses and their impact on the environment have been news since the 1980s in several European countries, mainly because golf is a very space-intensive sport. A golf course with 9 holes, for example, has a use of 25 to 30 hectares and accommodates only 72 players at once, while an 18-hole course, usually using 50 to 60 hectares, accommodates 150 players at once. According to the Cobham Resource Consultants' Report to the Sports Council, golf courses in England occupy more than four hundred square kilometers, which accounts for 0.5 percent of the land area of the country. The world now has enough courses to cover an area the size of Belgium (Hodson, 1996). Golf not only consumes a great amount of land, its popularity is also constantly growing. According to Wheat (1995) there are currently about 2,600 golf courses in the United Kingdom alone and more than 900 either under construction or planned in the near future.

In an earlier report, Wheat (1992) indicated that there are about 3 million people who play golf in Britain and the number of its courses accounts for 61 percent of Europe's total facilities. She further estimated that there are about 25,000 courses worldwide, of which 15,000 are in the United States. Japan, despite its small land mass, now has over 2,000 golf courses, over 300 more under construction, and about 1,300 proposed (Wheat, 1995).

Golf has also taken its place in the tourism industry and this segment is constantly growing. Wheat (1992) referred to 200,000 golf holidays in Spain alone by north Europeans every year. There are an estimated 700,000 Britons who go abroad on golf holidays, with many courses specifically built for tourists. Other popular golf destinations have been reported as well, such as Thailand (Wheat, 1992) and Hawaii (Holloway, 1994).

However, many golf courses are built in valuable natural or agricultural areas, displacing the original flora and fauna. Ward et al. (1994) describe the environmental impact of the construction of golf courses:

> Trees have to be cut down and earth moved. Huge quantities of water are required to keep the greens and fairways playable. Herbicides and fungicide may be required to keep the grass on the courses healthy and this can lead to a build-up of phosphates wherever water drains off the course. Nearby streams and ponds affected by phosphates will suffer from a build-up of algae, resulting in the suffocation of fish and other wildlife. Golf course development has also been used as a means of circumventing planning restrictions on green belt or former agricultural land. The presence of the golf course strengthens the developer's case for permission to build additional facilities like a club house, a club shop, a hotel or apartments. (p. 89)

As the previous excerpt suggests, apart from the loss of natural scenery, golf courses require huge amounts of fresh water, which in some areas of low rainfall imposes a severe burden on local resources (Holloway, 1994). Golf was designed to be played in temperate climates where lakes and grass are natural features and was not designed for the tropics. Wheat (1992) indicated that the greatest threat posed by golf course development in Asia is high water consumption. During the dry months, in countries such as Thailand and Malaysia one course uses enough water to satisfy the domestic needs of 60,000 rural villagers (Hodson, 1996). The intense use of fertilizers and the irrigation of grasslands also cause damage to the ecosystem (Sidaway, 1992).

Mountain Biking

In comparison with other outdoor sports, mountain biking has rapidly increased in popularity. According to Clark et al. (1994), there were about 5.5 million mountain bikes in the United Kingdom by 1993. Clark et al. further report that mountain bikes account for 60 percent of all new cycles that are sold annually and that mountain biking could be regarded as the fastest growing sport in the United Kingdom.

The German Federal Institute for Ecology, Environmental and Forest planning has described the major effects of this sport on the environment. According to LOLF, the chief problem with these highly geared machines is the erosion caused by wheel slip, particularly when the ground is wet. Mountain bikers almost never use the normal paths and roads—they prefer more sensational tracks through woods, heath, and field, which often results in damage caused to the environment. Plants are run over or crushed and tree roots are damaged. This results in replacement growth of a second, less varied vegetation that is resistant to frequent mountain bike traffic. Because of undisciplined cycling on woodland and field paths, animals, especially birds in the breeding season, get startled. Moreover, in humid or wet weather, mountain bikers transform paths into quagmires. Soil erosion cannot be stopped. As the paths are hardly passable for walkers, they will leave the paths and create new tracks, increasing the negative impact on the natural environment.

Skiing

According to Ward et al. (1994) there are in the European Alps alone an estimated 40,000 ski runs with 14,000 ski lifts that are capable of handling 1.5 million skiers an hour. Fifty million people visit the Alps each year, and because of its central position in Europe, about seven million passenger vehicles cross them each year. Several authors have reported on the negative impact of the ski industry on the environment. Holloway (1994) for example indicated that substantial deforestation, which is required to make way for ski slopes (pistes), results in soil erosion. Furthermore, 60 percent of the remaining forests are affected by acid rain caused by traffic crossing the Alps.

Ward et al. (1994) stated that the construction of new ski resorts gives the greatest cause for concern with regard to the environment. By clearing trees and moving thousands of tons of earth and rocks, developers make the areas more prone to avalanches. This results in the appearance of unsightly concrete avalanche shelters along many alpine roads. Furthermore, the construction of pylons, overhead cables, lifts, and tows often detract from the slopes' appearance. Despite protective measures, Hahn (1991) has reported a strong rise in avalanche disasters over the last few years. Another factor that paves the way for avalanches is the decay of vegetation on mountain slopes caused by air pollution. The most important cause of this pollution is nitrogen oxide originating from the exhaust gas of the large number of tourist cars (Hahn, 1991).

Also, in their effort to guarantee sufficient snow, many ski resorts depend on artificial snow making machines. These machines not only put major additional demands on local water and electricity supplies (Hahn, 1991; Vandelanotte, 1990), but are also a cost to local flora and fauna since they extend the winter season artificially (Ward et al., 1994). In addition, their construction often undermines the mountainsides. Further, the chemicals that are usually added to the water to enable the production of snow above freezing point and to keep the snow longer cause damage to vegetation as well as to the quality of drinking water (Hahn, 1991). Finally, through their monotonous, throbbing noise, snow guns cause noise pollution for the people who live in the neighborhood.

Snowplows also cause damage to the environment. The soil as well as the snow gets condensed through daily flattening. Owing to the pressure, the soil becomes less pervious to water. The water flows away on the surface, with soil erosion and slumps as the consequence. Flattened snow becomes impenetrable to air. So the flora and a lot of small animals that live under the snow are liable to suffocate. The young trees and other plants that do push above the snow toward the end of the season are damaged by the snow-plows (Lauterwasser, 1989).

It is not only the infrastructure of ski areas that causes damage to the environment—the skier is also to blame. New ski forms especially—like heli-skiing, deep-snow skiing, snowboards, skisafari, snow scooter driving, and so forth—have a pernicious impact on the environment. These events mostly take place off piste beyond marked ski routes. Mountain animals, for example, need large parts of connected woods to survive. Whenever winter sportsmen enter those woods, the animals panic. Plus, the flora gets damaged by the sharp sides of the skis and young plants do not get the opportunity to grow; so the renovation of damaged woods is impossible (Vandelanotte, 1990).

Speleology

The rising interest in speleology contributes to an overuse of certain caves, for example, the initiation caves of the Belgian Ardennes and the French caves of the Ardèche region. On weekends and during the summer holiday there are a lot of sports organizations that organize speleo-holidays and initiation lessons. The concentration of visitors in a short time span changes the ecosystem of the cave. Cave formations such as stalactites and stalag-mites do not get the chance to grow, not only because of displacement of air by the many visitors, but also because parts of these formations are taken away as souvenirs. Other use-related problems include the dumping of rubbish, graffiti on the walls, and so forth (Chazaud, Collomb, and Laurent, 1992; Sidaway, 1992).

Water Sports

Today there is a lot of variation in water sports. There are more sports than ever before that involve the use of a boat of any kind (e.g., canoe acrobatics, canoe trips, wild-water canoeing, rafting, hydro-speed, use of power boats, Jet Skis). Sailing, in particular, has diversified into sports such as windsurfing, speed-sailing, and so forth. While environmental damage might not seem apparent at first sight, all these forms of water sports can have a harmful influence on inland waterways and especially on bank vegetation. Through treading and running into the banks, a lot of vulnerable plants, fringes of reeds, and swamp vegetation get damaged, resulting in erosion of the riverbanks. Also fish, mammals, and birds are disturbed by these kinds of water recreation. The use of power boats and Jet Skis causes the problem of noise pollution and wash. Noise also conflicts with other leisure interests along the banks, such as fishing and walking.

In the Belgian Ardennes, for example, water recreation creates so much damage that some managers and custodians close parts of the waterways and natural reserves. This is not surprising given the fact that the number of kayak and canoe rental agencies has doubled over the last 10 years. Many of these renters have no knowledge of canoeing or kayaking, use bad equipment, and give no guidance. The stream of one-day tourists, mainly laymen, places an extra burden on the environment because of their lack of care and understanding of nature.

Finally, the need for new marinas in coastal and estuary locations to provide berthing for the continuing growth in yachting and other water-based recreation causes the destruction of wildlife habitats.

Conclusion

Allison (1995) argues that there is a unique characteristic in the conflict that exists between sport tourism and the environment. Unlike other resource conflicts within the government where solutions can be suggested through, for example, increased expenditure (for example, the competition between health and education for scarce resources), this conflict is over a resource that is finite, namely, land. Moreover, the conflict between sport and environmental quality can be either between two general objectives or between private market mechanisms and public regulations.

When the cost of the negative effects on the environment is taken fully into account, one might at first sight simply forbid the organization of outdoor sports. However, as pointed out by Green (1990), this issue has to be put into perspective, as detailed data, which would demonstrate the results of the factors mentioned above, are currently missing. The impact of outdoor sports on the environment is relatively small when compared with the total damage the environment has suffered and with that caused by other threatening sectors, such as industry and agriculture. The increased attention of the media and the popularity of sport tourism prove, however, that this issue should be taken seriously. If the sport tourists of the twenty-first century still want to sport in unspoiled nature, they and others who have a vested interest in sport tourism must make an urgent contribution toward nature conservation. Next is an overview of the possibilities that are or have been available with regard to this purpose.

Minimizing the Influence of Outdoor Sports on the Environment

The available solutions for the sport tourism–environment conflicts are not simple and unidimensional. According to Schemel and Erbguth (1992), they are situated on different levels and make an appeal to different actors, such as

1. The sport tourist.
2. The organizer of leisure activities or products.
3. The policy makers on municipal or federal levels.

An efficient and effective environmental plan must contain different measures that will be carried out simultaneously and be applicable to the target groups mentioned above. All the measures that can be taken to reduce the environmental impact of outdoor sports can be split up into *hard* and *soft* instruments (Strasdas, 1994). Hard instruments are legally decreed commands and interdictions. Soft instruments refer to steering through information dissemination and voluntary attitude adaptation.

Hard Instruments

Often, hard instruments deal with the construction and use of sports infrastructure. The erection of new infrastructure, for example, can be stopped or reduced by making that construction a part of the district plans and making it dependent on the result of an environmental effects report (Strasdas, 1994). The Flemish (i.e., the Dutch-speaking Belgians) regulation concerning environment license or *Vlarem* is an example of a regulation that controls negative impact of infrastructures (artificial ski slopes, swimming pools, and so on) on the environment (Senten, 1992). Another hard measure is the ban to enter certain protected areas. The Flemish Forest decree, controlling the accessibility and use of Flemish woods in Belgium, can be considered a hard instrument (Schepers, 1993).

Hard instruments can also deal with specific sports activities. Environmentally unfriendly sports, such as heli-skiing or Jet Skiing, can be forbidden in specific regions by local regulations. Furthermore, some rules can be formulated for the producers of sports equipment. They can be forbidden to use certain substances or produce certain equipment that could be unsafe or dangerous to health (Strasdas, 1994).

Soft Instruments

The soft instruments are directed both to the sports participant and to the leisure industry. One of the most important measures is the environmental education of the outdoor sports participant. This can take place through different channels—for example, outdoor education at schools. Smith (1963) defined outdoor education as learning in and for the outdoors. It is not regarded as a separate discipline but more as a learning climate that offers, among other things, opportunities for real life experiences and for attaining knowledge regarding the importance, appreciation, and protection of natural resources.

For example, within the Belgian educational system, outdoor education is provided to pupils through the organization of so-called Integrated Working Periods (IWP). It is education in, for, and about the natural environment (Pasques and De Knop, 1985). The IWP is an "extra muros" activity with a typical didactical character and is integrated in the school's curricula. It is not a traditional teaching method. During one or two weeks, students and teachers combine cultural, sports, and educational activities in an educational project, which is mostly situated outdoors and in which insight into environmental issues is emphasized. Special attention is paid to dealing with natural resources. Environmentally aware leisure behavior is something that has to be taught. However, insight is not the only key to changing someone's behavior.

Opaschowski (1985) has described a number of influencing factors that can change one's environmental leisure behavior. Figure 7.2 provides an overview of these factors.

For example, information brochures with general sports and environmental tips can educate the public about an ecologically sensible use of nature. Signs with environmental tips in recreation areas can also be useful.

Outdoor sports clubs, sport federations, and sport touristic organizations can play an important part in environmental education. These organizations can contribute to the conservation of the environment by giving information sessions to trainers as well as members, distributing information brochures, or discontinuing a license because of environmentally unfriendly behavior (Strasdas, 1994). Wilken (1993) and Strasdas have suggested that the following soft measures be taken by the organizers of leisure activities or the makers of leisure products:

- The creation of a specific sports profile for every touristical sport regarding carrying capacity of the region (e.g., reserving for mountain bikes certain woods with standard trees and a less sensitive soil, while allowing walkers and hikers to go into other parts of the woods).
- Applying quota restrictions to sports facilities—for example, in the ski area of Lech am Arlberg in Austria, the sale of day passes is stopped as soon as there are 14,000 skiers in the area.
- A better use of existing infrastructure instead of new building.
- Changing or shutting down the old loaded infrastructure—for example, ski runs with a high waste of energy.
- Cleaning up polluted areas—for example, re-laying the vegetation on the ski runs.
- Linking touristical areas and recreation centers with public transport.
- Using the quality of the environment as a marketing element, by handling eco-labels (awards given to areas, facilities, and companies that take sound ecological policy measures).
- Using an eco-balance for the production of sports equipment.

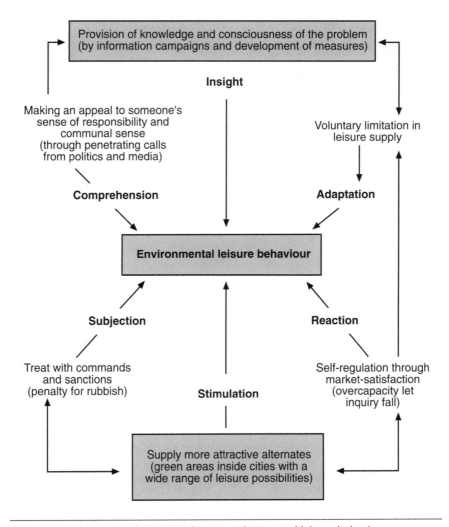

Figure 7.2   Influencing factors to change environmental leisure behavior.

From Opaschowski, H.W. 1985. Used by permission of the publisher.

Another soft instrument (which could become a hard instrument if it becomes part of a legally decreed command) is the introduction of the concept of "carrying capacity."

Holloway (1994) cites Inskeep who provides us some standards related to visitor capacity for selected sites (see table 7.2 on p. 241). However, as indicated earlier, a cautionary note is appropriate, as although the idea of carrying capacity seems logical, it is misleading because there are many other factors to be considered (Graefe, 1993).

Examples of Applying
Hard and Soft Measures

A number of these soft and hard measures were applied successfully in the so-called "Green Games" of Lillehammer, that is, the Winter Olympic Games of 1994. In *Greening Our Games*, in a section headed "A triple partnership in Lillehammer," Chernushenko (1994) states:

> Every Thursday for more than two years, representatives of the Lillehammer Olympic Organizing Committee, the Ministry of the Environment and the watchdog group Project Environment Friendly Olympics, met to discuss environmental issues, possible solutions and implementation plans. The partnership proved effective in reducing environmental harm, encouraging sponsors and donors to become positive players in greening the games, and handling media requests. Perhaps its greatest legacy was in demonstrating that industry, government and citizens groups can work effectively together to find common solutions. (p. 79)

The location of the big skating hall was changed to keep from disturbing the migration of birds from the nearby swampland. Furthermore, all the motor traffic was excluded from the Olympic region by the construction of big parking lots and regular bus and train connections with the Olympic accommodations. In all, 20 projects bore a green stamp. The most conspicuous of all was the recycling of about five hundred kilograms of lead fired during the biathlon and the separating and recycling of rubbish in the Olympic zone (Belgisch Olympisch en Interfederaal Comité 1993a, 1993b).

Organizers of outdoor sports in the commercial sector have also become more conscious of the environmental problem. The Dutch Nederlandse Milieugroep Alpen (NMGA) [Ecology Group of the Alps of the Netherlands] is very active in the field of environmental education and policy manipulation (Nederlandse Milieugroep Alpen, 1993). It tries to stimulate an ecologically friendly holiday behavior through the media. In addition, it has compiled a study pack to make youngsters aware of the specific problems in the mountain areas created by tourism.

In *Tourism in Europe* Davidson (1992) provides a vignette of the Balearic Islands (of which Majorca is the largest) headed "Balearics are going green." It states that an investment of 12,000 million Spanish pesetas (US$100 million) is being made on amenities such as beach and leisure park maintenance. The aim of the project, according to the Director of the Balearic Island Tourist Council, is a better quality of holiday for visitors and of life for residents.

Some Specific Environmental Measures

Having discussed the general principles of using hard and soft measures to control the impact of sport tourism on the environment, we now discuss how some of these measures are being used in specific areas and with specific sporting activities in order to protect the environment.

National Parks

One of the most well-known government interventions, especially in the United States, is the establishment of the national park system. According to Zeiger et al. (1993), the National Park Service in the United States has over the past 80 years been trying to ensure that the parks could be enjoyed by the public while at the same time the natural and cultural characteristics of those areas were being protected for future use. They also note that even before the National Park Service was established, the national parks and other federally reserved lands in the United States were involved in tourism. The world's first national park, Yellowstone National Park, was established in 1872. It was referred to as a potential leisure ground for the enjoyment of the traveling public.

From the late nineteenth century onwards, the parks were managed with recreation in mind. Possibilities for transportation and accommodation were improved to enable large numbers of people to visit the parks.

According to Zeiger et al., during 1990, 338,200,200 people visited the 357 U.S. national park areas. The authors expect the number of visitors to increase to about half a billion people by 2010. They indicate that, especially during the summer months when most of the visits take place, the stress on the natural resources increases dramatically. Zeiger et al. (1993) further indicate that the national parks have the potential to be destroyed as a result of their fragility and popularity. Therefore, if the symbiotic relationship between the national parks and the tourism industry is to continue, Zeiger and his colleagues suggest that several initiatives need to be organized in the immediate future, such as adjusted marketing of the parks. This marketing, combined with cooperation with the tourism industry, could reduce overuse during peak seasons and encourage off-season park visits.

The concept of national parks can be found in a number of other countries as well. Newby and Tao (1993) have reported on "reserves" that exist in the People's Republic of China. These areas provide visitors a look into China's wildlife, cultural, and forest resources. China has managed to put more than 8 million hectares (about 1 percent of its total land surface) into reserves. The Chinese government values these resources in relation to the cultural and economic development of China. The Ministry of Forestry owns about 4,100 "forest farms," of which some 160 have the potential to be regarded as forest parks or scenic areas. Newby and Tao state that, although 40 of these areas are open to the public, to date a centralized system for their management is lacking.

Adams (1990) has described the situation of national parks in the United Kingdom. With the making of the National Parks and Access to the Countryside Act of 1949, the government can designate certain areas as national parks or "Areas of Outstanding Natural Beauty" (AONB). The concept of the British national parks is in fact very different from the system in the United States. Although both kinds of parks are protected, the British parks are often areas that have been occupied and tilled by man for a long period of time, whereas the American parks are mostly untouched wilderness. As Adams states, "The British idea of a National Park is of a protected landscape, and to a large extent a protected way of life, rather than a wilderness" (p. 116). Furthermore, it is indicated that all British national parks are located in England and Wales. No parks can be found in Scotland, as planning of the designated Scottish areas has been in the hands of local councils who have been concerned more with economic development than with landscape protection.

Golf

Many national and local governments have no clear policy for the development of golf courses, thereby neglecting the environment, the landscape, and the interests of other forms of recreation. Considering golf courses' negative effects on the environment (which we described earlier), there is an urgent need for a policy that, among other things, designates the zones in which golf courses are allowed or prohibited. To that end, the European Golf Association Ecology Unit conducts research and encourages higher standards of environmental performance Europe-wide. The Ecology Unit is based on the belief that sound, scientifically-based environmental policies are good for golf (technically, aesthetically, socially, politically, and economically). Furthermore, by accepting the fundamental link between golf and the environment, the golfing world recognizes its duty to strive to preserve and enhance the natural resources with which it is entrusted (European Golf Association Ecology Unit, 1995). The Action Plan of the European Golf Association Ecology Unit focuses on a number of core themes concerned with golf course development and management—that is, development guidelines; research, monitoring, and information; and education and awareness.

Wheat (1995), however, questions whether these environmental concerns will also reach developers working outside Europe.

Mountain Biking

Conflicts between different interest groups over mountain biking policy have also created the need for regulatory measures. For example, in and around the Zonienwoud (a forest in Belgium, southeast of Brussels) a signposted track about 90 kilometers long has been constructed. Bikers who leave this track risk a fine of 10,000 Belgian francs (US$320). Elsewhere, in Flanders (i.e., the Dutch-speaking part of Belgium), other signposted mountain bike tracks from 25 to 40 kilometers in length have been constructed by the provincial working group Environment and Sport, consisting of the Flemish Administration of Physical Education and Outdoor Activities (BLOSO) and the Department of the Environment (Eliaerts, 1993).

Mountain bike clubs and federations can play an important preventive role with regard to environmental protection. By means of a code of behavior and the possibility of withdrawing a license in case of negligence, clubs and federations can insist their members take care of the environment (Informationsdienst Deutsche Sportbund, 1990).

Besides problems related to the negative effects of mountain biking on the environment, measures have been suggested or implemented dealing with managing trail-user conflicts between cyclists and other users. A hierarchy of options to manage these conflicts has been developed by Andy Julla of the Lolo National Forest in the U.S. state of Montana: good signing

Exodus

Biking in Morocco. A sudden rise in the popularity of mountain biking has made it necessary for environmental measures to be quickly established.

for routes; peer pressure related to good conduct; education of cyclists; soft-cycling trailing programs; better trail design; barriers to control speed; installation of requested walking zones; one-way-only routes; posted speed limits; patrols by peers; patrols by rangers; ban during certain times; ban on cycling on certain days; construction of separate routes for walkers and cyclists; transfer of use elsewhere; closing trails wherever it is necessary (Palmer, 1994).

However, probably the most momentous initiative in the United States dealing with user conflicts has come from the different user groups themselves (Palmer, 1994). In April 1994, the following Principles of Agreement and Action Plan was signed by both the International Mountain Bike Association (IMBA) and the Sierra Club, a powerful environmental and walking group:

- To work for wilderness, park, and open space protection.
- Mountain bicycling is a legitimate form of recreation and transportation on trails, including single-track trails, when and where it is practiced in an environmentally sound and socially responsible manner.
- Not all nonwilderness trails should be open to bicycle use.
- To create joint projects to educate all nonmotorized trail users.
- To encourage communications between local mountain bicycle groups and Sierra Club entities (Palmer, 1994).

Mountaineering

Payne (1995) described the necessity for a mountaineering group to be concerned about the environment on the slopes of K2. In the Himalayas as many as 55 million farmers depend on the productivity of the lower mountain slopes for their survival. All mountaineers have some impact on the local people and the environment—an impact that should be both fair and sustainable. Payne goes on,

> All visitors . . . can help bring benefits by following good practice such as: avoid the use of scarce resources, dispose waste in a proper manner, leave camp sites clean. (p. 8)

Sometimes recreationists themselves recognize conservation problems and take initiatives to protect the natural environment. Sidaway (1988) claims that recreationists have taken initiatives to protect geological formation; for example, climbers have accepted voluntary restrictions to protect cliff-nesting birds.

Skiing

An ecological attitude from managers as well as from skiers is fundamental to minimize the impact of skiing on the environment. Governments can, for example, oblige managers to follow specific guidelines regarding the use of snow guns. Such a regulation is in use at Vorarlberg in Austria. Also, information panels can be placed on ski lifts, slopes, and routes in the area and skiers advised to act accordingly. The government can also restrain ski behavior by specific rules. For example, in some Austrian ski areas, it is forbidden to ski more than five hundred meters outside the indicated runs. The skier can also help to decrease negative effects on the environment by choosing an ecologically friendly form of transport, by following the runs, and by avoiding skiing on glaciers or runs with only a thin layer of snow (Deutsche Sportbund, 1992; Macolin, 1987). The downhill ski course at Happo One in the beautiful Hakuba Valley in Nagano, Japan, has been severely shortened because of environmental concerns. The Nagano Olympics are the most environmentally aware yet. Caterers are using biodegradable bowls made from recycled potato pulp and plates containing recycled apple fiber. Hundreds of rare Gifu butterflies have been lured away from the finishing line by transplanting 5,000 of their favorite plants to a new location (Wilson, 1997).

Speleology

An example of possible measures to protect caves is found in Belgium where speleo-clubs have joined forces in a union of Flemish speleologists. The union has closed all the entrances to the initiation caves and only eligible clubs have a key to the gate. This is an attempt to prevent overcrowding and, at the same time, to provide for monitoring of damage or rubbish dumping. It is the duty of the instructors to report all damage so that sanctions can be imposed.

Walking

Ward et al. (1994) have described two general approaches that can be followed to try and halt damage caused by walking. One strategy is to confine tourism to areas with sufficient opportunities to control damages or available resources to construct hard-wearing surfaces. Also, parking space can be restricted, thereby restricting tourism. Another strategy is based on the use of marketing and systems of waymarking in an attempt to disperse visitors over a wider area.

Holloway (1994) reports an attempt made to counteract the effect of a footpath across the Moors near Haworth in the north of England. The path used by thousands of walkers became so muddy it necessitated inserting stepping stones in the track. Such artificial changes to the landscape as inserting flagstones creates a different "visual" landscape, but this solution is increasingly used to sustain well-worn footpaths (Holloway, 1994).

Another relevant example comes from New Zealand. There some walking tracks became so popular that new tracks were introduced: in 1988 the Kepler Track was established "principally to reduce the pressures encountered elsewhere" (Kliskey and Kearsley, 1993, p. 105).

Water Sports

As already indicated, the destruction of banks and vegetation of rivers and lakes is one of the biggest environmental disadvantages of water sports such as kayaking and windsurfing. The construction of separated areas and routes for these sports, with clearly indicated bank zones capable of resisting collision or treading, is recommended to reduce environmental damage. Therefore soil research of recreation waterways is necessary. Chemically polluted recreation water can cause illness by absorption, for example, through the isothermal suit of windsurfers (Evers, 1990). Publications can be used to inform sport participants and make them more environmentally conscious (Verkade, 1989). The Walloon district government (the French-speaking southern part of Belgium) recently proposed a number of measures imposing some restraints on water sports ("Nieuwe watersportregels," 1994). For example, the district government has the right to control the use of waterways during specific periods of the year or it can make access dependant on the minimum flow. Furthermore, the loading places for kayaks are strictly designated.

As the unlimited growth of kayak rental companies has been the cause of the growing popularity of the sport, the Dutch canoe federation wants to improve the quality of the rental companies ("Nieuwe watersportregels," 1994). Special attention must be given to the following aspects:

• Giving instructions to all the participants.
• Using sound equipment.
• Controlling the size of the group.
• Proper behavior of navigation.
• Knowledge of the elementary rules.

Through these aspects, the federation hopes to limit the threat to the environment and to prevent navigation limitations and zoning.

The Impact of Sport Tourism on Urban Environments

Sporting events can have a significant impact on the cities that host them and ultimately on the global environment. Large sport venues and residential complexes often have to be built near residential neighborhoods, which, as you might expect, results in very unhappy residents. A good example is provided by Bale(1994), who cites Tuan:

> Residents of the historic area of Brumleby in the Osterbro district of Copenhagen were distressed to discover in 1990 that the Danish national football stadium "Parken" was to

be reconstructed and enlarged and in doing so turned through 90 degrees so that it abutted much closer than previously to their precious yellow and brown painted mid-nineteenth century cottages (p. 120).

The consequences were described by Nagbol (1993) as follows:

> In particular, the shadows cast by the giant stands would now destroy the idyllic summer evenings which the residents traditionally spent eating and drinking in the sunlight. The soft, broken shadows which (like the spatial parameters of the football pitch) would be straight and hard, covering a wider expanse of the residential area, and earlier in the evening, than had hitherto been the case.

"Parken had become a landscape of fear . . . a sort of hostile space" (Bale, 1994, p. 120).

In addition, host cities must provide transport and communication systems for hundreds of thousands of athletes, officials, media and spectators. International, national, regional, and local organizers should thus be concerned that in conducting a large sporting event they should avoid long-term debts or environmental damage. The International Olympic Committee has nowadays acknowledged the relevance of environmental issues to the Olympic movement, and this was reinforced by the work of the organizing committee for the Winter Olympic Games in Lillehammer. The environmental guidelines for Sydney 2000 are described in case study 7.1.

Case Study 7.1

Sydney Organizing Committee for the Olympic Games—Environmental Guidelines (SOCOG, 1995)

Use of Hard and Soft Measures to Protect the Environment When Planning for Olympic Games

Introduction

The development of Sydney's Olympic Environment Guidelines was based on the principle adopted at the United Nations Earth Summit in Rio in 1992 and expressed in National Ecologically Sustainable Development policies.

The Australian and New South Wales governments are committed to ecologically sustainable development (ESD), a concept that aims to protect the environment with a range of initiatives to halt global warming, ozone depletion, and toxic chemical pollution, and to protect biodiversity. These policies include a commitment to

- energy conservation and the use of renewable energy sources,
- water conservation,
- waste avoidance and minimization,
- protecting human health through appropriate standards of air, water, and soil quality, and
- protecting significant natural and cultural environments.

The process that led to the preparation of Sydney's Environmental Guidelines commenced with a design competition for the Olympic Village in early 1992.

Planning and Construction of Olympic Facilities

In planning and constructing the Olympic facilities, Sydney is committed to the following policies:

- Thorough assessment of opportunities to use or adapt existing facilities, together with consideration of the long-term financial viability of all new facilities.
- Building and infrastructure design that considers environmental issues.
- Environmental and social impact assessment, with community participation in the planning process.

Australia is a world leader in research into solar technologies and other forms of renewable energy, and these skills will be incorporated into many aspects of the Olympic facilities. The Olympic Village is planned as a prototype for energy efficient, medium-density housing in Australia and internationally. It aims to achieve a low environmental impact by adhering to stringent guidelines developed in consultation with Greenpeace Australia. The use of solar-thermal cogeneration of electricity with clean, efficient backup energy sources and the use of ferries to provide transport for spectators, VIPs, athletes, and media between Sydney Olympic Park and the Sydney Harbour Zone is being seriously considered.

Water Conservation

The facilities and infrastructure required for an Olympic Games should complement the implementation of sustainable management systems for urban water resources by government. To that end, Sydney is committed to the following initiatives:

- Introduction of pricing policies that reflect the real cost of supplying water.
- Landscape design that decreases water requirements by emphasis on selection of plants appropriate to climate.

- Selection of low-water-use appliances including dishwashers and washing machines.
- Building and infrastructure design to collect wastewater for recycling.

Waste Avoidance and Minimization

Throughout the world, there is agreement on the need to minimize the amount of industrial, commercial, and domestic waste produced by society. Sydney is committed to practice the best waste reduction and avoidance possible by applying performance criteria to services, materials, and appliances.

Air, Water, and Soil Quality

The protection of human health requires high standards of air, water, and soil quality. Athletes cannot perform at their best in the absence of these conditions. Thus, Sydney is committed to the following measures to ensure a toxin-free environment:

- Improved procedures at Olympic sites to minimize toxic fume emission and outgassing from paints, carpets, glues, and pest control practices.
- Use of building techniques and interior design that minimize the need for chemical pest control and maximize opportunities for integrated pest management.

Protecting Significant Natural Environments

Sydney is committed to the following:

- Preservation and protection of the integrity of natural ecosystems adjacent to Olympic sites, including native bushland, forest, and waterways.
- Landscape programs that minimize disruption of wildlife habitat, protect indigenous plant species, and use species selected to complement existing habitats.
- Use of low-wash ferry transport to minimize impact on mangrove ecosystems.

Other Measures

Other measures are taken related to merchandising, ticketing, catering, waste management, and noise control. These include the following:

- Merchandising—for example, every company tendering for a merchandise contract is required to provide environmental information in its submission in relation to manufacture, use, and disposal.
- Ticketing—for example, ticketing systems integrating event admission with public transport.
- Catering—for example, use of recyclable or reusable packaging.
- Waste management—for example, information being carried electronically when possible to reduce unnecessary use of paper, supplemented by effective paper recycling procedures.

- Noise control—for example, adoption of noise abatement techniques that minimize disturbance for nearby residents.

This case study was contributed by the Sydney Organising Committee for the Olympic Games.

Summary

Sport tourism needs space and should have the opportunity to use the possibilities offered by the natural environment. This proposition implies that environmental protection is essential, not only for the sake of ecology but also for the sustainability of sport tourism. However, the increased participation in all kinds of outdoor sports has led to an increase in the negative effects on the environment.

It is time that outdoor sports participants and the organizers and operators (in the profit as well as nonprofit sectors) become aware of their co-responsibility concerning this problem. Appropriate steps must be taken. However, this assignment cannot be taken by sports and tourism organizations alone. A coherent global policy drawn up by a coordinating organization is necessary. The United Nations or more directly the World Tourism Organization together with the General Assembly of International Sport Federations (GAISF) could take up the initiative. A number of precautionary measures have to be taken on different action levels, fitting into a clear, global environmental policy plan. Organizers of large sport events should avoid environmental damage.

Furthermore, the need for sound research in outdoor recreation and its impact on the natural environment has never been greater. Both are prerequisites so that in the future, outdoor sports can continue to be practiced in a natural environment without causing further damage.

References

Adams, I. (1990). *Leisure and government.* Sunderland, Great Britain: Business Education Publishers.

Allison, L. (1995). Sport, planning and environment in England and Wales. In Centre for Research into Sport and Society (Ed.), *Module 3—Unit 5.* Leicester, Great Britain: Centre for Research into Sport and Society.

Bale (1994). *Landscapes of modern sport.* Leicester, Great Britain: Leicester University Press.

Baty, B., & Richards, S. (1997). The leisure day visits survey. *Employment Gazette,* May, 257-268.

Belgisch Olympisch en Interfederaal Comité. (1993a). De XVIIde Olympische Winterspelen van Lillehammer [The XVIIIth Olympic Winter Games at Lillehammer]. *Olympic News, 6,* 7-9.

Belgisch Olympisch en Interfederaal Comité. (1993b). Lillehammer '94, de groene spelen [Lillehammer '94, the green games]. *Olympic News, 3,* 11.

Boniface, B., and Cooper, C. (1994). *The geography of travel and tourism.* Oxford, Great Britain: Butterworth-Heinemann.

Chazaud, A., Collomb, P., and Laurent, R. (1992). *Speleologie, droit et environment* [Speleology, rights and environment]. Paris: Juris service.

Chernushenko, D. (1994). *Greening our games.* Ottawa, ON: Centurion Publishing & Marketing.

Clark, G., Darrall, J., Grove-White, R., Macnaghten, P., and Urry, J. (1994). The diversity and specialization of leisure and tourism. Background paper No. 13. *Leisure landscapes.* Lancaster University, Great Britain: Centre for the Study of Environmental Change.

Clarke, A. (1995). Tourist charter. *Leisure Management, June,* 34-36.

Davidson, R. (1992). *Tourism in Europe.* London: Pitman.

Davidson, R. (1993). *Tourism.* London: Pitman.

Deutsche Sportbund. (1992). Skiers protect nature. Behavioral rules from the German Ski Federation. Frankfurt, Germany: DSB Presse.

Eliaerts, P. (1993). Mountainbikers: Milieurespecterende sporters of sensatiezoekende avonturiers? [Mountain bikers: Environmentalists or sensation seeking adventurers?]. *Sport, 6,* 24-26.

European Golf Association Ecology Unit. (1995). *An environmental strategy for golf in Europe.* Oxford, Great Britain: Information Press.

Evers, K. (1990). Recreatie informatie [Recreation information]. *Recreatie, 7*(28), 9.

Glyptis, S. (1995). Recreation and the environment: Challenging and changing relationships. In D. Leslie (Ed.), *Tourism and leisure—Culture, heritage and participation. Vol. 1* (pp. 171-178). Eastbourne, Great Britain: Leisure Studies Association.

Graefe, A. (1993). Visitor impact management: An integrated approach to assessing the impacts of tourism in national parks and natural areas. In A.J. Veal, P. Jonson, and G. Cushman (Eds.), *Leisure and tourism: Social and economic change* (pp. 74-83). Sydney, Australia: University of Technology.

Green, H. (1990). Assessing the environmental impact of tourism development. *Tourism Management, June,* 111-120.

Hahn, P. (1991). Skilauf und Umwelt: Pro und Kontra [Skiing and environment: Pro and contra]. *Schule und Sportstätte, 4,* 7-8.

Hodson, M. (1996, January 21). The case against golf courses. *The Sunday Times,* p. 4.

Holderegger, A. (1990). Sport und Umwelt: Ethische Rahmenbedingungen [Sport and environment: Ethical conditions]. In SLS-ASS (Ed.), *Sind Sport und Umwelt vereinbar? Bericht zum Forum 1989 "Sport und Umwelt"* [Are sport and environment compatible? Information on Forum 1989 "Sport und Umwelt"] (pp. 24-35). Bern, Switzerland: SLS-ASS.

Holloway, J.C. (1994). *The business of tourism.* London: Pitman.

Informationsdienst Deutsche Sportbund. (1990). *Sport Schutz und umwelt* [Sport protection and environment]. Frankfurt, Germany: Author.

Inskeep, E. (1991). *Tourism planning.* New York: Van Nostrand Reinhold.

Kelleher, G., and Craik, W. (1993). How much is the Great Barrier Reef worth? In A.J. Veal, P. Jonson, and G. Cushman (Eds.), *Leisure and tourism: Social and economic change* (pp. 96-103). Sydney, Australia: University of Technology.

Kliskey, A., and Kearsley, G.W. (1993). Mapping multiple perceptions of wilderness so as to minimise the impact of tourism on natural environments: A case-study of the North West South Island of New Zealand. In A.J. Veal, P. Jonson, and G. Cushman (Eds.), *Leisure and tourism: Social and economic change* (pp. 104-119). Sydney, Australia: University of Technology.

Krippendorf, J. (1987). *The holidaymakers: understanding the impact of leisure and travel.* London: Heinemann.

Landesanstalt für Ökologie, Landschaftsentwicklung und Forstplannung. (1991). Eko-Informationen: Mountainbike—fair zur Natur? [ECO-Information: Mountain bike—fair for nature?]. *LÖLF-Mitteilungen, 2,* 52.

Lauterwasser, E. (1989). DSV Umweltplan 2000 [DSV Environmental Plan 2000]. *Ski, 89,* 10.

Macolin (1987). Protége cette nature que tu aimes [Protect this nature that you like]. *Echos de l' EFGS, 11,* 20.

Nagbol, S. (1993). Enlivening and deadening shadows. *International Review for the Sociology of Sport, 28* (213), 365-280.

Nederlandse Milieugroep Alpen. (1993). De NMGA in het kort [The NMGA in short]. *Nieuwsbrief over natuur en toerisme in de Alpen, 2,* 8.

Newby, F.L., and Tao, H. (1993). The sleeping giant awakens: Forest parks for tourism in China. In A.J. Veal, P. Jonson, and G. Cushman (Eds.), *Leisure and tourism: Social and environmental change* (pp. 641-645). Sydney, Australia: University of Technology.

Nieuwe watersportregels van kracht in de Ardennen [New water sport rules in Ardennes]. (1994, June 6). *Het Laatste Nieuws,* p. 7.

Opaschowski, H.W. (1985). *Freizeit und Umwelt: Der konflikt zwischen Freizeitverhalten und Umweltbelastung. Ansätze für Veränderungen in der Zukunft* [Leisure and environment. The conflict between leisure activities and environmental use. Measures for changes in the future]. Hamburg, Germany: B.A.T. Forschungsinstitut.

Palmer, C. (1994). Equal rights for mountain bikes. *Countryside, 70,* 7.

Pasques, J., and De Knop, P. (1985). Sneeuwklassen als onderdeel van de Ge'ntegreerde Werkperiodes (GWP) in het buitenland. [Winterclasses as a part of the Integrated Working Periods abroad]. *Tijdschrift voor Lichamelijke Opvoeding, 100,* 258-265.

Payne, R. (1995). Combining sport with environmental aid, *Sport, 4,* 8-9.

Priester, K. (1989). The theory and management of tourism impact. *Tourism Recreational Research, 14,* 15-22.

Roberts, J. (1989). Consumable packaging. In B. Brown (Ed.), *Leisure and the environment. Conference papers No. 31* (pp. 1-17). Eastbourne, Great Britain: Leisure Studies Association.

Schemel, H.J., and Erbguth, W. (1992). *Handbuch Sport und Umwelt. Ziele, Analysen, Bewertungen, Lösungsansätze, Rechtsfragen* [Manual sport and environment. Goals, analyses, validation, solutions, legal questions]. Aachen, Germany: Meyer & Meyer Verlag.

Schepers, J. (1993). Vlaamse Regering regelt de toegankelijkheid en het occasionele gebruik van de bossen [Flemish government regulates the access and occasional use of forests]. *Sportinfo Limburg, 4,* 10-13.

Senten, R. (1992). Milieuheffing voor lozing van afvalwater door zwembaden [Eco-tax on dumping of wastewater by swimming pools]. *Vlaams Tijdschrift voor Sportbeheer, 112,* 9-15.

Sidaway, R. (1988). *Sport, recreation and conservation. Study No. 32.* London: Sports Council.

Sidaway, R. (1992). *Good conservation practice for sport and recreation. Study No. 37.* London: Sports Council.

Smidt, A. (1991). Freizeitgesellschaft und die folgen [Leisure society and the consequences]. *Naturschutz und sport, 2,* 8-13.

Smith, J. (1963). *Outdoor education.* Englewood Cliffs, NJ: Prentice Hall.

Strasdas, W. (1994). *Auswirkungen neuer Freizeittrends auf die Umwelt* [Consequences of trends in leisure on the environment]. Aachen, Germany: Meyer & Meyer Verlag.

Sydney Organizing Committee for the Olympic Games. (1995). *Environmental guidelines.* Internet: http://www.sydney.olympic.org/env/index.htm.

Tabata, R. (1992). Scuba Diving Holidays. In B. Weiler and C.M. Hall (Eds.), *Special Interest Tourism* (171-184). London: Belhaven Press.

Tourism Research Group. (1988). *Adventure travel in western Canada.* Ottawa, ON: Tourism Canada.

Vanreusel, B. (1990). Over onbetreden paden: de samenhang tussen sport, recreatie en milieu [About untrod paths. The relationship between sport, recreation and environment]. *Vlaams Tijdschrift voor Sportbeheer, 100,* 42-43.

Vanreusel, B. (1993). Naar een socio-ecologische visie op sportbeoefening in de natuur [Towards a socio-ecological perspective on sport participation in nature]. In M. Buekers (Ed.), *Kwaliteit in de lichamelijke opvoeding* [Quality in physical education] (pp. 177-195). Leuven, Belgium: ACCO.

Verkade, J. (1989). Natuurgerichte recreatie, een systematische benadering voor beleid en beheer [Nature oriented recreation, a systematic approach for policy and management]. *Recreatie, 3*(27), 16-17.

von Animateuren und Animateurinnen [Formation and daily life of animators]. In H.J. Neuerburg, T. Wilken, K. Fehres, and N. Sperle (Eds.), *Sport im Urlaub* [Sport on holiday] (pp. 181-192). Aachen, Germany: Meyer & Meyer.

Ward, J., Higson, P., and Campbell, W. (1994). *Advanced leisure and tourism.* Cheltenham, Great Britain: Stanley Thornes.

Wheat, S. (1992, August). Playing a round with nature. *Geographical,* pp. 10-14.

Wheat, S. (1995). Marking golf's card. *Leisure Management, 15*(5), 26-28.

Wilken, T. (1993). Umweltverträgliche Urlaubssport-Probleme und Lösungsansätze [Environmental-friendly leisure sport—problems and solutions]. In H.J. Neuerburg, T. Wilken, K. Fehres, and N. Sperle (Eds.), *Sport im Urlaub* [Sport on holiday] (pp. 89-96). Aachen, Germany: Meyer & Meyer Verlag.

Wilson, A. (December, 1997). Japan gears up for its Olympic year. *Financial Times,* XV.

World Leisure and Recreation Association. (1992). Outdoor and environmental education: Exploring the issues. *World Leisure & Recreation, 34*(2), 5-8.

Zeiger, J.B., Caneday, L.M., and Baker, P.R. (1993). A symbolic relationship between tourism and the national parks: Future trends. In Veal, Johnson, and Cushman (Eds.), *Leisure and tourism: social and environmental change* (pp. 641-645). Sydney, Australia: University of Technology.

Chapter 8
The Health Impact of Sport Tourism

Chiva Som, Hua Hin in Thailand—Asia's first health spa.

Chiva-Som International Health Resort, Thailand

The following topics are covered in this chapter:

1. The importance and implications of health tourism for sport tourism.
2. Segments of the health tourism market that overlap with sport tourism.
3. The potentially positive health impacts of sport tourism.
4. The potentially negative health impacts of sport tourism and ways to minimize those impacts.
5. Spa tourism as a special and growing interest in sports-related health tourism.
6. Worldwide trends in sport tourism for people with disabilities.
7. Sport tourism used as a way to raise money to fight disease.

Links between health, well-being, and active leisure have been recognized for many years (Astrand 1978, 1987; Long, 1990; Williams, 1965). Likewise, travel with a view to health improvement has become popular (Mathieson & Wall, 1982; Wright, 1988). Technology, particularly that applied in the workplace, has reduced the physical demands of contemporary society with the result that everyday lifestyles have become more passive (Sleap, 1990).

Although lack of physical activity has not been indisputably established as a direct and independent risk factor for coronary heart disease (CHD), an indirect relation often exists between a sedentary lifestyle and overeating, which leads to obesity (Poole, 1984). In turn, obesity contributes to an increased risk of diseases such as impaired cardiac function, hypertension and stroke, pulmonary diseases, diabetes, several types of cancer, degenerative joint diseases, and gout (MacArdle, Katch, & Katch, 1991; Shepard, Rhind, & Shek, 1994). There is evidence that physically active people show a reduced incidence of most of these diseases and especially coronary heart problems, which seems to indicate that exercise normally lowers the risk (Astrand, 1987; Hannon, 1990). The role of physical activity in heart disease prevention is now highly publicized in the United States, Canada, Australia, and much of Europe (Sleap, 1990).

Van Andel and Austin (1984), Ingham (1990), and Fernhall (1993) support a further generally positive relationship between physical fitness and mental or psychological health.

Thanks to P. Clarijs, P. McNaught Davis, L. Wetts, and P. Wylleman for their contribution to this chapter.

Since the mid-1970s Western society has become increasingly health and fitness conscious, and this has encouraged many people to become involved in more physically active lifestyles (Clough, Shepherd, & Maughan, 1989; Fentem & Bassey, 1980; Hall, 1992; Hannon, 1990). Furthermore, the economic benefits of physical activity are becoming more widely acknowledged (Department of Arts, Sports, the Environment, Tourism and Territories, 1989; Rejnen & Velthuijsen, 1991; Shepard, 1986). This has increased interest in health tourism in several countries including the United States, Australia, Austria, Britain, France, Germany, Hungary, Italy, Israel, Japan, and Switzerland (Hall, 1992; Larner, 1992; Rea, 1987; Sargent, 1987). But not all aspects of health tourism can reasonably be embraced in our concept of sport tourism.

Hall (1992) identified five segments of the health tourism market, each progressively more specialized in terms of the health experience sought. The first two segments, namely, "sun and fun" and "engaging in healthy activities," fit our concept of holiday sport activities and sport activity holidays, respectively. The third and particularly the fourth segments ("main motive for travel is health" and "travel for sauna, massage, and other health activities [spa resort]") focus more closely on health, though they often embrace sport activities as well as spa visiting. The fifth segment, medical treatment, is the most specialized and cannot reasonably be included in the category of sport tourism.

First, we shall consider the health implications of sport tourism activities in which health is an important but subsidiary element. The two segments of health tourism in which health is the principle motive for travel will be considered as special interest health and fitness holidays and will be treated second. Finally, the chapter will include reference to sport tourism for those with special needs.

Health Implications
of Sport Tourism Activities

The "sun and fun" segment may be aligned with holiday sport activities in our typology, where sport is an incidental objective. "Engaging in healthy activities" can be linked with sport activity holidays, where sport is the overriding objective. The physical activity content in both of these types of sport tourism has potentially positive and negative impacts. On the one hand, unless the sport activities make some demands on the body's physical and psychological capabilities the potential for positive health impacts will be minimal. On the other, all physical activities contain an element of risk.

Positive Impacts

The increasing popularity of sport tourism has been documented in earlier chapters (particularly chapters 1 and 3). One important motive underlying participation is the benefit to health and fitness (Becheri, 1989; Crompton, 1979; Goodrich & Goodrich, 1987; Murphy & Bennett, 1990; Niv, 1989; Rea, 1987). Since it is acknowledged that comparatively few people engage in sufficient exercise in their everyday life to derive health benefits, the potential health enhancement that can accrue from sport tourism on holiday increases in importance.

Only rarely do people participate in sports from a single motive; more often it is the synergy that arises from a combination of several factors that elicits participation. Tourist activity is similarly prompted by a combination of several motives, rarely by one. From research amongst the Swiss, who have the highest propensity to travel (see table 6.3 on p. 224), Schmidhauser (1989) identified four main reasons people engage in tourism:

1. To compensate for the many deficits that everyday life inevitably brings.
2. To recover physically and psychologically from stress; to regain or keep physical and mental well-being.
3. To widen horizons, satisfy curiosity, or realize one's potential.
4. To reward or indulge oneself.

Deficiencies that can be compensated for by travel include deficits in sports activities, deficits in the enjoyment of outdoor recreation, and deficits in the urge for action (Schmidhauser, 1989). These results support Krippendorf's earlier study of German tourists, who gave "switching off, relaxing" as the most frequent reason for their holiday journey, but who also listed getting away from everyday life, experiencing nature, enjoying oneself, getting exercise, engaging actively in sport, broadening one's horizons, doing something for one's health, and getting fit (Krippendorf, 1987). Nogawa et al. (1996) reports relaxation at hot springs as the highest travel priority of Japanese tourists.

Some individuals increase their pleasure by subjecting themselves to emotionally stressful physical activities such as skydiving, ice climbing and extreme skiing, where the adrenaline "rush" is felt to be beneficial (Ewert & Hollenhorst, 1993). Some find involvement in sports promotes their understanding of their body and, given a sense of success and satisfaction in the physical activity, can help to reinforce a positive sense of self (Collingwood & Millett, 1971).

Physiologically, the "feel good" factor, a sense of feeling physically better and having stress diffused after exercise, is virtually a universal response of regular participants (Fernhall, 1993). In addition, physical activity is increasingly acknowledged as the most powerful antidote to modern lifestyle diseases. More and more, physical exercise at a moderate intensity is advocated for people with AIDS (Calabrese & La Perriere, 1993), cancer (Kohl, La Porte, & Blair, 1988; Shepard, 1993), diabetes, (Helmrich, Raglan, & Paffenbarger, 1994; Poortmans & Vanderstraeten, 1994), asthma (Bar-Or & Inbar, 1992), osteoporosis (Marcus, Drinkwater, Dalsky & Dufek, 1992; Pitetti, 1993), and diseases of the cardiovascular system (Sleap, 1990; Rost, 1994; Wood, 1994).

For people with mental retardation, exercise has been suggested to be very important as life expectancy is directly related to activity in this population (Fernhall, 1993). Although erroneous beliefs, misinformation, and misconceptions do circulate, health and exercise psychologists have presented empirical evidence to support an association between physical exercise and mental well-being (Ingham, 1990; Morgan & Goldston, 1987; Willis & Campbell, 1991). Furthermore, exercise has been found to lower tension and anxiety, as well as anger and hostility (Berger & Owen, 1983; Wilson, Morley & Bird, 1980).

It can be hypothesized that the positive effects of exercise on psychological well-being are related to three factors, namely:

1. Physiological factors—increased blood flow and oxygenation; reduced muscle tension

2. Psychological factors—enhanced perceptions of control and mastery of one's body

3. Social factors—increased positive feedback from significant others

While the benefits of exercise behavior on psychological and physiological well-being are possible, they are not automatic. The benefits may be reduced, eliminated, or even reversed by choosing inappropriate types of exercise or by not following good practice guidelines.

Negative Impacts

Sport tourism in the form of activity holidays and holiday activities contains an element of risk. Franklin, cited by Legwold (1985), acknowledges the value of exercise but believes professionals in sports medicine can exaggerate the benefits. This view is supported by a physiotherapist, Vivian Grisogono (1985). Murphy and Bennett (1990) record that reports of physical injury and illness as a result of exercise have increased concern for safe participation, and a recent guide to health matters that affect today's traveler stated, "Some people taking part in relatively hazardous activities, such as white-water rafting, somehow feel that if it wasn't safe, the company wouldn't suggest it. It isn't necessarily, and, yes, they would" (Ryan, 1995, p. 7). As Ingham (1990) noted, "People fall off mountains and coastal pathways, weekend parachutists discover too late that standards of quality control in the parachute-making industry have declined" (p. 234); he advises tourists to think very carefully before participating.

Travel agents within the European Community are required by law to provide information on health formalities to holidaymakers when they book a package holiday. But travel agents are not generally equipped to offer advice on the health impacts from particular physical activities, many undertaken in relatively unusual environments.

Benefits attributable to exercise are not invariably or universally experienced. For some people, physical activity can be unwise, even dangerous under certain conditions (Katzel et al., 1994). A leading insurance company in Britain reported that in its top six travel claims, heart problems occupied second and third positions (Ryan, 1995).

The trend for more and more people of all ages to engage in more adventurous activities on holiday, of which hill walking is one of the most popular and apparently safe, emphasizes the need to understand the dangers. Walkers die in fairly mundane circumstances every year. Most accidents are the result of inexperience, inadequate equipment, or an error of judgment. Although experience limits dangers it does not eliminate them (Pybus, 1995).

Many sport tourist experiences take place not only out-of-doors but in regions and temperatures in which the participant has to cope with unaccustomed climatic conditions, high altitude, extended submersion in water, heat, or cold. Sport activities performed under extreme conditions have become increasingly popular. Scuba diving, skiing, and mountaineering are sports that can impose extreme physical conditions on the body. Such conditions include changes in atmospheric pressure, the composition of inhaled air, unusual air temperatures, and excessive exposure to ultraviolet light. For the majority of people the body has the ability to adapt to these different environments provided they are not too extreme. But all too often activities are undertaken without adequate time or opportunity to engage in any intermediary experiences to acclimatize the body.

For a body at rest or barely active, altitude normally causes little problem up to 2,300 meters (7,400 feet). But as effort approaches more active levels, even at this altitude the availability of oxygen to the muscles will be decreased enough to limit performance (Cavaletti & Tredici, 1992). Apart from mountain sickness, the other two most common mountain hazards are hypothermia (when the core temperature of the body falls below 35 degrees Celsius) and frostbite, although dehydration is not unknown. While serious, mountain sickness is unlikely to occur at most normally available tourist altitudes, though there are considerable differences between individuals. Above 3,120 meters (10,000 feet) approximately two out of three people are likely to experience some of the symptoms of acute mountain sickness and around 2 percent of people will get the full-blown version (Ryan, 1995). Flying straight in to very high places such as La Paz in Bolivia (3,658 meters) can be particularly dangerous.

Hot climates can lead to dehydration of the body even without exercise, but the problem is obviously magnified by activity. Other major effects of exercising in a hot environment are exhaustion, heat stroke, and cramps. These conditions are usually caused by dehydration. The increasingly common occurrence of skin cancer, most of which is related directly to exposure to the sun, has decreased the popularity of tanning. At high altitudes, ultraviolet light rays are much stronger. Thus it is not only swimmers and sunbathers who are exposed to risk—skiers, climbers, and mountain hikers are equally in danger.

Submersion in water, even in a cool pool, can lead to hypothermia. Swimming in lakes, caverns, and underwater, as well as simply staying in the water too long, exacerbates the likelihood of developing hypothermia. Scuba divers who undertake long periods of submersion normally wear a wet suit, which is a useful protection for most water sports such as sailing, windsurfing, water skiing, and white-water rafting.

Scuba diving is growing in popularity as dive sites open up around the world and attract sport tourists to exotic locations from Hawaii to the Comores and the Great Barrier Reef. Snorkeling, which permits only brief underwater time, requires less skill and has fewer risks. Scuba diving, on the other hand, requires specialized equipment and training. The depth of a dive and the length of "bottom" time available—which are more or less inversely related—create both the attraction of a dive and its inherent risks.

Minimizing the Negative Impacts

The appropriate exercise depends on the participant's age, level of fitness, skill, preparation, and medical status (Heath, 1994). None of these factors disqualify one from participation, but they define the type and intensity of exercise that is best. Professional guidance and thorough, specific preparation and training are extremely important. Even for relatively safe outdoor activities such as trekking, thorough preparation is recommended (Eder, 1994). The greater the risk in the activity, the more imperative good management is to achieve a balance between safety and the competencies of the participants on the one hand and the real or perceived risk on the other (Hall, 1992). Anderson, cited in Hall (1992), reported on the packaging of adventure travel operations in Canada. He said, "This sense of 'dangerous adventure' is achieved, in fact, with a high degree of safety. Staff are experienced; routes are carefully selected and tested in advance regularly; safety precautions are extensive. The trips present 'danger in safety'" (p. 145).

The human body is well designed and adaptable so that, given time, the majority of people can be prepared to tolerate exercise in the most extreme conditions. Some body types do experience particular difficulties; obese people find heat very trying and may experience distress in hot and humid climates. On the other hand, these people, insulated by extra amounts of fat, can better withstand long periods in cold water. But the metabolism that makes them obese may make them poor at producing heat—thus, once their insulation is broken their condition may deteriorate very quickly.

Adequate and correct clothing can contribute significantly to safety. For example, wearing bicycle helmets has reduced head injuries among cyclists by 63 percent (Thomas, Acton, Nixon, & Battistutta, 1994). Correct equipment, properly tested, is equally as important. Mountains are often perceived as particularly hazardous areas and climbing as a dangerous sporting activity. Yet, as one guidebook states, "When practised with the appropriate equipment and precautions, climbing can be less dangerous than it may seem to the uninitiated." (Pybus, 1995, p. 97).

We shall now turn to sport touristic experiences in which health is the primary motive for participation.

Special Interest Health and Fitness Holidays

We shall divide the market into three sectors, namely:

- Health farms and hotels (spas of the athletic and pampering type) that specialize in beauty treatments together with health and fitness programs;
- Traditional spas where natural mineral spring waters are used for healing treatment;
- Thalassotherapy centers.

Health Farms and Hotels

Digel (1994), discussing sports in a changing society, notes that "people practising sports today can hardly be regarded as a homogeneous group" (p. 72). What is described as "the formerly rather closed system of sports" has disintegrated, according to Digel, and differentiation has taken place, resulting in three movements emerging from traditional sports over recent years. Fitness and health sports are identified as one of the three, and "quantitatively significant." Individualistic sports, such as trekking and hanggliding, and a "new movement culture," which attempts to replace traditional sports with activities like t'ai chi, are the other two. Elsewhere health and fitness has been described as an industry with potential for growth (Gregory, 1989). Individuals, concerned about their health, have brought about a market with high revenue earning capacity. Health and fitness clubs have become more numerous, larger, better equipped, and more popular (Gregory, 1989; Harmsworth, 1990).

Tourism for health purposes is one of the oldest reasons for traveling (refer to chapter 1). The word "spa" is used in Anglo-Saxon countries, and in Japan, as a term to indicate a spring and mineral water, as well as the place where a cure or a course of water (treatment) can be taken. The existence of a mysterious source of sparkling water in Spa, a small city in the Belgian Ardennes, has been known for many centuries, and the hot springs at Tiberius were popular with the Romans (Niv, 1989). The term "spa" is now applied widely to centers offering some form of health treatment frequently combined with physical activity and exercise.

According to Becheri (1989), traditional spa tourism expanded and significantly changed in the 1980s. Facilities now include diet therapies, physiotherapies, beauty treatments, sport and exercise, and relaxation among their offerings. Hall (1992) and Michael (1984) differentiate between spas with a "healing" emphasis traditional to Europe and "the athletic and/ or pampering variety" found in America. The increasing usage of these facilities in Europe (Harmsworth, 1990), where they tend to be linked to hotel operations, the United States (Harmsworth, 1990), Israel (Niv, 1989), and Japan (Nogawa, Yamaguchi & Hagi, 1996) warrants their consideration in this chapter.

Courteen (1997) notes the increasing pressure on hotels to introduce leisure facilities, in particular swimming pools (including sauna and steam room) and fitness gyms. In America these health-club type facilities are now offered as standard by many upmarket hotels. American spas (a term used in its widest sense there) have grown from two hundred to two thousand during the 1980s owing to the increasing interest in health and fitness, and are of two different types: the destination spa and the hotel or resort with added spa facilities. Their services are extensive, their facilities luxurious, and their market comprises mainly young, fit, and active people who want to look their best (Harmsworth, 1991; Olsen & Granzin, 1989). According to Birmingham (1995), all American states have an abundance of these facilities suited to every type of client's needs.

In the Caribbean several top hotels feature fitness and beauty treatments. Two sister hotels are particularly well-known: Le Sport on the island of St. Lucia and La Source on Grenada. Their spa/fitness centers branded "The Oasis" operate on an all-inclusive basis, so that treatments, as well as accommodation, food, sports, and entertainment are included in the holiday cost. The Athenaeum Spa at the five-star Corinthia Palace Hotel is Malta's top establishment, where guests can choose from a range of 50 therapy and beauty treatments as well as participating in exercise classes and aquarobics. In the United Kingdom, Grayshott Hall is one of the leading health and fitness resorts, set in attractive countryside an hour's drive from London. A whole range of exercise classes complements the individual treatments that include aromatherapy, reflexology, hydrotherapy, physiotherapy, and many beauty treatments. The object of a visit to any of these resorts is to feel and look healthier as a result of treatment and exercise.

Traditional Spas

Traditional spa tourism is still considered an important complement to modern medicine as well as being a very popular holiday destination in Europe.

Spa tourism never declined to the same extent in Germany as else-where due to the entitlement for employees to have time off from work for health treatment in addition to their annual leave. It has also been suggested that the German psyche is well adjusted to following strict courses of therapy that involve solid effort and sticking firmly to sched-ules (Sargent, 1987). Around 2.5 percent of the population regularly par-ticipates in thermal spring tourism according to Mesplier-Pinet (1990). In Scandinavian countries, the social security system refunds the cost of trips to the spa towns of eastern Europe if they are taken for medical purposes (Davidson, 1992). The health service cost of spa visiting in Italy had to be restricted by court action since 2 percent of domestic tourists regularly visited spas and 85 percent of the cost was government fi-nanced (Becheri, 1989; Mesplier-Pinet, 1990).

Swiss spas are usually medically oriented, which means that the majority of their guests are elderly. Luxury hotels, located adjacent to clinics, provide high-class medical treatment and recreational therapy. Where treatment is prescribed by a doctor, it can be paid for through private health insurance schemes (Larner, 1992).

Polish spas, like Swiss spas, have a therapeutic and recreational function based on their mineral waters. They provide "inpatient" and "outpatient" treatment—the former involving a stay in a sanatorium or spa hospital, the latter, tourists who come for a vacation (Groch, 1990). The number of spa tourists has increased to around 3 percent of the population (Mesplier-Pinet, 1990). Czech spas are also becoming tourist attractions.

A Japanese government white paper, reporting on the characteristics of Japanese domestic tourists, noted that 44.8 percent of travelers made relaxing at hot springs their priority (Nogawa et al., 1996). The second most popular motivation, sight-seeing, occupied 42.5 percent, whereas engaging in favorite sports was the primary motive for 34.2 percent. Souvenir shopping was the main motive for 22.6 percent. Japan is not alone among the Asian countries in terms of the popularity of hot spring tourism. Newby and Tao (1993) record visiting hot springs and swimming among the interests of Chinese domestic tourists visiting forest parks there.

France still has its traditional springs used in the treatment of a wide range of conditions with one hundred or so spas often identified by the addition of "les-Bains" to their name; for example, Bourbonne-les-Bains, which specializes in the treatment of rheumatism, bones, and joints, and Sail-les-Bains, which specializes in the treatment of skin disorders. Around 1 percent of the population regularly visits these traditional thermal resorts (Mesplier-Pinet, 1990).

Israel has established a Health Spa Authority to promote health tourism as an issue of national importance (Niv, 1989). In areas like the Dead Sea the only tourism projects to be approved for development are those associated with health tourism. And in Britain, the British Spas Federation promotes the country's 12 spa towns as tourist attractions. The United States also has real spa resorts based around Hot Springs National Park in Arkansas and Indian Springs and Glenwood Springs in Colorado. And in South America the Therms of Rio Hondo in Argentina are famous for the curing qualities of the water.

Spa bathing has reemerged as an important sector of the active holiday market. It has been estimated that around 15 million people now use more than two hundred spas and health farms in western Europe alone, once or twice each year; above 12 percent were foreign visitors (Benton, 1995). This group of modern active participants form a major sector of the activity holidays and excursions market, worth some UK£ 9billion (US$13.5 billion) (Benton, 1995). The European market's average stay at spas is between 17 and 21 days, indicating how such holidays represent a European family's annual holiday.

Thalassotherapy Centers

France's distinctive answer to the mineral spas of other European countries is thalassotherapy (a term derived from the Greek "thalassa" meaning the sea), which is based on the principle that the minerals and organisms in sea water can promote better circulation and stronger bones. The first thalasso-therapy institute was founded in the 1890s in Roscoff, Brittany. Twenty-one centers now offer courses of treatment that last anywhere from one to three weeks and are designed primarily to tone the muscles. Although the centers originally offered specialized treatment for those with recognized complaints, they are enjoyed as much today as general health and fitness packages, mixing therapy with sport activities in an attempt to give positive results in terms of health (Januarius, 1990; Mesplier-Pinet, 1990). More than 1,500 million days a year are spent at such centers (Robertson McCarta, 1991).

Sport Tourism
for People With Disabilities

Individuals with chronic diseases or disabilities have a lifestyle that is not always fully appreciated or understood by healthy individuals. Often, people with disabilities are caught in a downward spiral of a sedentary lifestyle leading to diminished physical residual functions, which can induce an even more sedentary lifestyle resulting in a further reduction in physical capacities and rehabilitation potential. This places these individu-als at risk for early development of other diseases and limitations such as heart disease, adult-onset diabetes, and hypertension.

Sport for people with disabilities is developing rapidly throughout the world, with disabled people taking part in sport in all of its diverse forms. So far as tourism is concerned, Muloin and Weiler (1993) suggest that people with disabilities have as great or greater need to enjoy travel as able-bodied persons. They identify three major barriers that have restricted travel opportunities for people with special needs: environmental, economic, and attitudinal barriers. The same three types of obstacles have limited their participation in sport and, together, in sport tourism.

Some parts of the world make far better environmental provision for travelers with disabilities than others. In many parts of the United States and Canada wheelchair users are well catered to, generally less well so in Europe. Economic barriers, where they are overcome, are more often surmounted by acts of private charity than by state involvement. Attitudinal change is again significantly demonstrated within the great tradition of American summer camps for young people; Camp Heartland in Cudahy, Milwaukee, is a special camp established for children with AIDS. Camp Heartland welcomes children who may not be accepted at other camps and through charitable donations subsidizes 100 percent of the transportation and camp costs for the children.

Therapeutic recreation with a focus on "special populations" has a high profile in the United States (Haywood, 1990). An American study in 1983 (Andrews cited in Smith, 1990) reported on a group of people with spinal injuries who completed a "healthsports" package within their rehabilitation program. A second group had no such program. The study concluded that the healthsports group displayed physical and psychological benefits and were better adapted to their disability than those who did not receive additional services.

Whereas some 30 or 40 years ago individuals with disabilities participated in sport "as a means to an end," for example the recovery of impaired bodily functions or the maintenance of health, now there is an increased tendency to take part in sporting activities at all different levels for pleasure and achievement (Doll-Tepper, 1991). Although equity has not yet been achieved, sport is becoming more available for all people with disabilities. Doll-Tepper (1991) identifies seven worldwide trends:

1. An increased interest and participation in sporting activities by people with disabilities, whether it be in rehabilitational, recreational, or competitive sports.

2. Either integrated or very specialized offers by sports clubs for the disabled as well as for the able-bodied.

3. An improved level of achievement and performance in sport by individuals with disabilities.

4. Rapid changes in technology as far as wheelchairs, orthopaedic aids, and equipment are concerned.

5. A growing public and media interest in sport for disabled persons.

6. An increasing demand for qualified teaching staff.

Calvert Trust, Keswick, UK

Wheelchair abseiling in St. John's Vale, UK.

7. Intensified endeavors to carry out multidisciplinary research on a national and international level.

In the context of increased opportunities in the United Kingdom, for example, 11 centers specially designed or adapted for the use of people with special needs have banded together to form Adventure for All, an association of the leading residential outdoor activity centers. Members aim to ensure the highest standards of safety through the employment of qualified and experienced staff; to provide a wide variety of activities and experiences; to provide courses that reflect individual requirements, responding to people's abilities rather than their disabilities; to offer a high-quality and year-round service; and to promote the enjoyment of outdoor adventure for all. Every year over 20,000 people with special needs enjoy the excitement of the outdoor experiences offered in these centers, many of them returning year after year.

In 1994 the European Commission Youth Exchange Scheme supported a two-week exchange program between the United Kingdom and Spain that enabled 15 young people and their leaders to take part in outdoor activities in each other's country. The Spanish group stayed at Keswick, the U.K. group at a mountain center at Las Picadas, about an hour's drive from Madrid. Keswick Calvert Trust has also hosted a group of disabled children and staff from Bulawayo, Zimbabwe, and exchanged staff with an Outward Bound center at Chimanimani.

One recent program offers "Mixed Ability Adventure" on tours to Nepal where "male, female, young, old, fit or flabby, handicapped or able" can participate in a three-week trek up to Everest Base Camp. No climbing experience is needed, but one does need to be fit enough to walk for 18 days. Groups consist of approximately 17 people of all ages, including the tour organizer and a doctor, who also provides medical assistance to local people in the remote areas en route (Oxventure brochure). People of all abilities participate in a wide range of adventure activities but until recently a wheelchair tourist, or even a tourist with any disability, was a rare sight in Nepal. This has now changed. In 1994, an innovative trip integrated both disabled and able-bodied athletes on an expedition paddling the Class IV rapids of the Kali Gandaki and Seti rivers. The disabled paddlers tackled exactly the same difficulty of rapids that are encountered on standard expeditions with a fully able-bodied crew" (Swearengen, 1995, p. 31).

Wheelchair racing is one of the most popular sports in the world for disabled athletes with numbers increasing all the time. The British Wheelchair Racing Association holds Annual Track Championships which attract around 80 athletes. Wheelchair rugby is another sport played at international level with 12 countries participating. Altogether the international events calendar is extensive. British wheelchair athletes participated in no less than 15 events in 1994 from the Winter Paralympic Games in Norway to the World Swimming Championships held in Malta. Berlin hosted the World Athletic Championships; the Weightlifting Championships were held in Australia, the Fencing Championships in Hong Kong and 30 teams participated in the 10 days of competition at The International Wheelchair Games. Participants in these events become avid sport tourists, as do those who participate in the many marathons now run.

Sport Tourism to Raise Sponsorship to Fight Disease

Sport tourism is often initiated in order to raise money to fight a disease. Organizers of sporting events might donate a portion of the proceeds to a cause, or participants might seek sponsors and collect money for the cause based on their completion of the event. These events might induce day-trippers to participate, or, if the events are major, they might induce people to travel internationally in order to participate.

Eight international events including the London, Boston, and New York marathons, cycling challenges in Iceland and Morocco, hiking in Jordan, and a multi-activity weekend in France are part of the 1997 challenges designed to raise money to fight cancer. The Macmillan Challenges in the

Em Hardy/NSPCC

A helping hand: Hikers on the Tanzania Trek teamed to earn over UK£40,000 for charity.

United Kingdom are strenuous activities designed for the fit and able who, through sponsorship, raise money to provide specialist care services. The seven-day Iceland Cycling Challenge requires participants to raise a minimum of UK£1,800 (US$2,700) in sponsorship. Everything is then provided (flight, accommodations, food, and bikes) to cycle four hundred kilometers over five days across moonscaped lava fields and around very active volcanoes. Described as a "Bike Ride to Hell and Back," the event expects to enlist one hundred participants. Gerrard (1997) comments, "From Ireland to China, from Iceland to Uganda, today's holiday trend is to combine a good time with a good cause" (p. 31).

The London Times recently carried an article on the twenty-six British people who walked 120 miles through the Great Rift Valley of Tanzania in six days to raise money for the National Society for Prevention of Cruelty to Children (NSPCC) (Gerrard, 1997). At the same time a group of eighteen more were nearby doing a sponsored climb of Mount Kilimanjaro. Together, the two groups raised UK£40,000 (US$60,000) for the charity. Donations are also made to local Masai eye clinics, where sight-saving operations are carried out. Sponsored hikes and bike rides now raise millions of dollars for charities in different parts of the world.

Summary

The links among health, well-being, and active leisure have been recognized for many years. This chapter discussed several issues involving the relations of health and sport tourism. These include the potentially positive and negative health impacts of sport tourism; the importance and implications of health tourism for sport tourism; spa tourism as a growing interest in sports-related health tourism; how the health tourism market sometimes overlaps with sport tourism; trends in sport tourism for people with disabilities; and sport tourism as a way to raise money to fight disease.

Regular (habitual), continuous exercise of low or medium intensity has been shown to promote health in the most appropriate way. Properly planned and adequately prepared sport tourist experiences can offer many physical and psychological health benefits. But the converse is also true. Hastily undertaken trips and sudden unaccustomed exercise without adequate preparation have potential danger.

Travel for health benefits is an increasingly popular motive, and expansion of the natural and man-made facilities used to include sports and exercise, as well as various forms of therapy, indicate the potential for more extensive health benefits to be derived from sport tourism.

References

Åstrand, P-O. (1978). *Health and fitness.* New York: Skandia Insurance Company.

Åstrand, P-O. (1987). Setting the scene. In Coronary Prevention Group (Eds.), *Exercise heart health* (pp. 5-20). London: Coronary Prevention Group.

Bar-Or, O., & Inbar, O. (1992). Swimming and asthma benefits and deleterious effects. *Sports Medicine, 14*(6), 397-405.

Becheri, E. (1989). From thermalism to health tourism. *Revue de Tourisme, 44*(4), 15-19.

Benton, N. (1995). Taking the waters. *The Leisure Manager, 13*(4), 40.

Berger, B.G., & Owen, D.R. (1983). Mood alteration with swimming—Swimmers really do feel better. *Psychosomatic Medicine, 45*(5), 425-433.

Birmingham, B. (1995). Water wonderland. *Holiday Destinations, 2*(1), 112-116.

Calabrese, L.H., & LaPerriere, A. (1993). Human immunodeficiency virus infection, exercise and athletics. *Sports Medicine, 15*(1), 6-13.

Cavaletti, G., & Tredici, G. (1992). Effects of exposure of low oxygen pressure on the central nervous system. *Sports Medicine, 13*(1), 1-7.

Clough, P., Shepherd, J., & Maughan, R. (1989). Motives for participation in recreational running. *Journal of Leisure Research, 21*(4), 287-309.Collingwood, T.R., & Millett, L. (1971). The effects of physical training upon self-concept and body attitude. *Journal of Clinical Psychology, 27,* 411-412.

Courteen, D. (1997). Healthy return. *The Leisure Manager,* December, 23-24.

Crompton, J.L. (1979). Motivations for pleasure vacation. *Annals of Tourism Research, 6*, 408-424.

Davidson, R. (1992). *Tourism in Europe.* London: Pitman.

Department of Arts, Sports, the Environment, Tourism and Territories [DASETT] (1989). *The economic impact of sport and recreation: Regular physical activity (Technical Paper 2).* Canberra, Australia: Author.

Digel, H. (1994). *Sports in a changing society.* International Council for Sports Science and Physical Education (ICSSPE). Manuscript Sports Science Series. Schorndorf, Germany: Karl Hofmann.

Doll-Tepper, G. (1991). Sport in rehabilitation and recreation. In P. Oja & R. Telama (Eds.), *Sport for all* (pp. 661-667). Amsterdam, the Netherlands: Elsevier Science Publications.

Eder, S. (1994). Trekking. *Deutsche Zeitschrift f,r Sportsmedizin, 45*(10), 399-402.

Ewert, A. & Hollenhorst, S. (1993). Adventure travel: Risky business for risky customer. In A.J. Veal, P. Jonson, & G. Cushman (Eds.), *Leisure and tourism: Social and economic change* (pp. 563-566). Sydney, Australia: University of Technology.

Fentem, P.H., & Bassey, E. (1980). The case for exercise: A statement for the Sports Council of Great Britain, In E.J. Burke (Ed.), *Exercise, science and fitness* (pp. 218-228). New York: Mouvement.

Fernhall, B. (1993). Physical fitness and exercise training of individuals with mental retardation. *Medicine and Science in Sports and Exercise, 25*(4), 442-450.

Gerrard, M. (1997). Star trekkers rewarding mission. *The Times, Weekend*, November 22, p. 31.

Goeldner, C. (1989). 39th Congress AIEST: English workshop summary. *Revue de Tourisme, 44*(4), 6-7.

Goodrich, J.N., & Goodrich, G.E. (1987). Health-care tourism. An exploratory study. *Tourism Management, 8*, 217-222.

Gregory. R. (1989). Health and fitness for the rest of your life. *Insights, A3*, 19-21.

Grisogono, V. (1985). Why bother? *Sport and Leisure, May-June*, 46.

Groch, J. (1990). Polish Carpathian spas: Their therapeutic and recreational functions. In A. Tomlinson (Ed.), *Leisure and the quality of Life: themes and issues. Conference papers No. 42.* Eastbourne, Great Britain: Leisure Studies Association.

Hall, C.M. (1992). Adventure, sport and health. In C.M. Hall & B. Weiler (Eds.), *Special interest tourism* (pp. 141-158). London: Belhaven Press.

Hannon, G. (1990). Lifestyle. In J. Long (Ed.), *Leisure, health and wellbeing. Conference papers No. 44* (pp. 177-190). Eastbourne, Great Britain: Leisure Studies Association.

Harmsworth, S. (1990, July). Health farms and spas—Their relevance to the future of hotel leisure. *Insights*, pp. A11-17.

Harmsworth, S. (1991). Body and soul. *Leisure Management, 11*(9), 31-32.

Haywood, L. (1990). Therapeutic recreation and the Elderly. In J. Long (Ed.), *Leisure, health and wellbeing. Conference Papers No. 44* (pp. 197-200). Eastbourne, Great Britain: Leisure Studies Association.

Heath, G.W. (1994). Physical fitness and aging: Effects of deconditioning. *Science & Sports, 9,* 197-200.

Helmrich, S.P., Ragland, D.R., & Paffenbarger, R.S. (1994). Prevention of non-insulin-dependent diabetes mellitus with physical activity. *Medicine and Science in Sports and Exercise, 2607,* 824-829.

Ingham, R. (1990). Leisure and wellbeing: A perspective from new social psychology. In J. Long (Ed.), *Leisure, health and wellbeing. Conference papers No. 44* (pp. 233-251). Eastbourne, Great Britain: Leisure Studies Association.

Januarius, M. (1990). Helianthal healing. *Leisure Management, 10*(1), 46-48.

Katzel, L.I., Sorkin, J.O., Colmazn, E., Goldberg, A.P., Busby-Whitehead, M.J., Lakatta, L.E., Becker, L.C., Lakatta, E.G., & Fleg, J.L. (1994). Risk factors for exercise. Induced silent myocardial ischemia in healthy volunteers. *American Journal of Cardiology, 74,* 869-874.

Kohl, H.W., La Porte, R.E., & Blair, S.N. (1988). Physical activity and cancer— An epidemiological perspective. *Sports Medicine, 6,* 222-237.

Krippendorf, J. (1987). *The Holiday Makers: Understanding the impact of leisure and tourism.* London: Heinemann.

Larner, C. (1992). Luxuriously healthy. *Leisure Management, 12*(3), 20-21.

Legwold, G. (1985). Are we running from the truth about the risks and benefits of exercise? *The Physician and Sports Medicine, 13*(5), 136-148.

Long, J. (1990). Leisure, health and wellbeing: Editor's Introduction. In J. Long (Ed.), *Leisure, health and wellbeing. Conference papers No. 44* (pp. 233-252). Eastbourne, Great Britain: Leisure Studies Association.

MacArdle, W.D., Katch, F.I., & Katch, V.L. (1991). *Exercise physiology. Energy, nutrition and human performance.* Philadelphia: Lea & Febiger.

Marcus, R., Drinkwater, B., Dalsky, G., & Dufek, J. (1992). Osteoporosis and exercise in women. *Medicine and Science in Sports and Exercise, 24*(6), S301-S307.

Mathieson, A., & Wall, G. (1982). *Tourism economic, physical and social impacts.* Harlow, Great Britain: Longman Scientific and Technical Publications.

Mesplier-Pinet, J. (1990). Thermalisme et curistes: Les contraintes. *Revue de Tourisme, 45,2,* 10-17.

Michael, J.W. (1984). The top spas of Europe. *Town and Country, April,* 126-134.

Morgan, W.P., & Goldston, S.E. (1987). *Exercise and mental health.* New York: Hemisphere.

Muloin, S., & Weiler, B. (1993). Provision of travel information for persons with specific needs. In A.J. Veal, P. Jonson, & G. Cushman (Eds.), *Leisure and tourism: Social and environmental change* (pp. 631-635). Sydney, Australia: University of Technology.

Murphy, W., & Bennett, T. (1990). Health and the individual: Pressures to participate in physical activity. In J. Long (Ed.), *Leisure, health and wellbeing. Conference papers No. 44* (pp. 41-52). Eastbourne, Great Britain: Leisure Studies Association.

Newby, F.L., & Tao, H. (1993). The sleeping giant awakens: Forest parks for tourism in China. In A.J. Veal, P. Jonson, & G. Cushman (Eds.), *Leisure and tourism:*

Social and environmental change (pp. 641-645). Sydney, Australia: University of Technology.

Niv, A. (1989). Health tourism in Israel: A developing industry. *Revue de Tourisme, 44*(4), 30-32.

Nogawa, H., Yamaguchi, Y., & Hagi, Y. (1996). An empirical research study on Japanese sport tourism in Sport-for-All events. *Journal of Travel Research, Fall, 35*(2), 46-54.

Olsen, J.A. & Granzin, K.L. (1989). Life style segmentation in a service industry: The case of fitness spas. *Visions in Leisure and Business: An International Journal of Personal Services. Programming and Administration, 8*(3), 4-20.

Oxventure. (1996). Brochure-Nepal. Oxford, Great Britain: Oxventure.

Pitetti, K.H. (1993). Introduction: Exercise capacities and adaptations of people with chronic disabilities—Current research, future directions and widespread applicability. *Medicine and Science in Sports and Exercise, 25*(4), 421-422.

Poole, G.W. (1984). Exercise, coronary heart disease and risk factors: A brief report. *Sports Medicine, 1,* 341-349.

Poortmans, J.R., & Vanderstraeten, J. (1994). Kidney function during exercise in healthy and diseased humans: An update. *Sports Medicine, 18*(6), 419-437.

Pybus, V. (1995). *Adventure holidays.* Oxford, Great Britain: Vacation Work.

Rea, P.S. (1987). Using recreation to promote fitness. *Parks and Recreation, 22,* 32-36.

Rejnen, J., & Velthuijsen, F.W. (1991). Economic aspects of health through sport. In M.F. Collins (Ed.), *Sport: An economic force in Europe,* (pp. 76-90). London: Sports Council.

Robertson McCarta. (1991). *Brittany. Touring and leisure guides.* London: Author.

Rost, R. (1994). The impact of physical activity in prevention and rehabilitation of cardiovascular and metabolic diseases. In J. Mester (Ed.), *Sport sciences in europe 1993—Current and future perspectives* (pp. 409-430). Aachen, Germany: Meyer & Meyer.

Ryan, R. (1995). *Stay healthy abroad.* London: Health Education Authority.

Sargent, P. (1987). Taking the waters. *Leisure Management, 7*(3), 35-38.

Schmidhauser, H. (1989). Tourist needs and motivations. In S.F. Witt & L. Moutinho (Eds.), *Tourism marketing and management handbook* (pp. 569-572). Hemel Hempstead, Great Britain: Prentice Hall.

Shepard, R.J. (1986). *Fitness of a nation.* Philadelphia: Karger.

Shepard, R.J. (1993). Exercise in the prevention and treatment of cancer. An update. *Sports Medicine, 15*(4), 258-280.

Shepard, R.J, Rhind, S., & Shek, P.N. (1994). Exercise and the immune system. *Sports Medicine, 18*(5), 340-369.

Sleap, M. (1990). Do you have a happy heart? In J. Long (Ed.), *Leisure, health and wellbeing. Conference papers No. 44* (pp. 31-40). Eastbourne, Great Britain: Leisure Studies Association.

Smith, V.R. (1990). An investigation into how some people with spinal injuries are able to use their free time, and to what effect. In J. Long (Ed.), *Leisure, health and wellbeing. Conference Papers No. 44* (pp. 201-208). Eastbourne, Great Britain: Leisure Studies Association.

Swearengen, A.P. (1995). Achievers—a challenge of attitude. *Action Asia* 4(4), 29-31.

Thomas, S., Acton, C., Nixon, J., & Battistutta, D. (1994). Do bicycle helmets prevent head injury in children? *British Medical Journal, 308,* 173-176.

Van Andel, G.E., & Austin, D.R. (1984). Physical fitness and mental health: A review of the literature. *Adapted Physical Activity Quarterly, 1,* 207-220.

Williams, J. (1965). *Medical aspects of sport and physical fitness.* Oxford, Great Britain: Pergamon Press.

Willis, J.D., & Campbell, L.F. (1991). *Exercise psychology.* Champaign, IL: Human Kinetics.

Wilson, V.E., Morley, N.C., & Bird, E.I. (1980). Mood profiles of marathon runners, joggers, and non-exercisers. *Perceptual and Motor Skills, 50,* 117-118.

Wood, P.D. (1994). Physical activity, diet, and health: Independent and interactive effects. *Medicine and Science in Sports and Exercise, 26*(7), 838-843.

Wright, C. (1988). *The global guide to health holidays.* London: Christopher Helm.

Part III

Present Status and Future Prospects

Chapter 9
Administrative and Policy Issues   293

Chapter 10
Conclusions and Implications:
Sport Tourism in the Twenty-First Century   321

Chapter 9
Administrative and Policy Issues

BLOSO administrative center in Belgium.

Courtesy BLOSO

The following topics are covered in this chapter:

1. The effect of the global shift toward market-based mixed economies on sport, tourism, and sport tourism.
2. Reasons why governments intervene in sport tourism.
3. The institutional framework of administrative infrastructures through which different governments supervise sport, tourism, and sport tourism.
5. Examples of policies set by governments to develop or control sport tourism.

Sport tourism depends on three types of providers: the public sector, the private sector, and the voluntary sector. In the public sector, central governments, their various agencies, local municipal authorities, and, in many states, education authorities, have assumed some responsibilities for planning, provision, and, at times, delivery, of sport and tourism services and facilities. Public provision has been traditionally rooted in the rationale of social and welfare service. In most countries the private (commercial) sector also plays a very significant role in the supply of both sport and tourism goods and experiences: it aims mainly at achieving a return on investment and profit. Concerned to serve the interests of like-minded members, the third, or voluntary sector, varies greatly from country to country. Generally speaking, it provides armies of sports club officials and heritage administrators who draw their finance from subscriptions, trusts, charities, or sponsorship. The three sectors are not necessarily discrete—partnerships are often made and prove beneficial.

However, the international trend toward market-led economies has brought about a growing emphasis on a market-oriented entrepreneurial approach to sport tourism. Although the form of government involvement varies by society and there are significant differences in the ideological commitment to sport tourism by different states (as we show in this chapter), we identify an inexorable global shift toward efficiency and income maximization and away from public involvement and welfare. The case for public sector involvement has been based on the concept of market failure. In other words, the provision and support of sport and tourism is complex and multifaceted depending on facilities, accommodation, transport, and all the other factors identified in chapter 2 (see table 2.3, p. 71) Given this complexity, it is unlikely that a country's sport or tourism policy objectives will be wholly satisfied if left only to the market mechanism. However, "the extent of public involvement depends on the economic philosophy of the government" (Wanhill, 1994, p. 308). One consequence of the trend toward free, or at least liberal, market economics has been to fragment the infrastructure and to render factors of quality, safety, and sustainability more problematic.

Sport tourism's infrastructure consists, on the one hand, of a growing number of large-scale multinational organizations (Haywood et al., 1989) and, on the other, of thousands of generally small businesses in the private, or commercial, sector (Collins & Randolph, 1993; Plog, 1994). In the United States alone, Plog claims there are more than 32,000 travel agencies, most of which fit in "the small business category" (1994, p. 51). In such a context, and lacking a strong public rationale, self-interested concern for growth and expansion can result in haphazard promotion, unrestrained competition for customers, and unacceptable pressure on resources and facilities. In the process, economies, heritage, culture, environments, and health can be damaged.

Traditionally governments have regarded sport and tourism as separate spheres for the purposes of administration. (Glyptis, 1991). There are, however, a small though growing number of examples of coordinated administration and policy making. In acknowledging the complex and interwoven problems facing the sport-tourism relationship in our increasingly globalized world, this chapter explores the different ways governments handle the relation.

Overview of Administration and Policy

Administration and policy issues have spawned a vast field of study covering the role of the state, its organizations, decisions, and actions. Other works have presented detailed theoretical analyses of the (leisure) policy process in modern states and reference to these is recommended (Bramham, Henry, Mommas, & van der Poel, 1993; Glyptis 1982, 1991; Hall & Jenkins, 1995; Ham & Hill, 1993; Henry, 1993; Houlihan, 1991; Veal, 1994; Williams & Shaw, 1988; Wilson, 1988). The purpose of this chapter is to describe briefly how administration and policy affect sport tourism and to provide illustrations of sport tourism's administrative infrastructures and some key examples of policy issues.

Administration

Administration in this particular context is understood as the arrangements of the executive part of government concerned with sport, tourism, and sport tourism.

Governments in most Westernized countries have become involved in sport and tourism primarily for the financial benefits that are seen to accrue from these activities. Involvement crosses the spectrum from direct and dominant control, formerly seen in totalitarian Eastern bloc countries, to less direct policies characterized by the United States. Some countries accord constitutional level importance to sport and tourism, but others simply develop legislation when it is needed. And while some countries have developed many levels of administrative infrastructures using local, regional, and national frameworks, others limit their interest to only one of these levels, normally national. Thus in exploring administration we shall be looking at the different ways governments organize their decision making in sport, tourism, and sport tourism.

Policy

Policy may be seen as a decision or, more often, groups of decisions that select particular goals and identify the means of achieving them (Jenkins, 1978). Policies can be stated and implemented at a variety of levels. In this context we are concerned with policies of the state that have to do with sport and tourism.

Discussing the role of the state in modern life, Ham and Hill (1993) tell us, "The state in contemporary society has a profound impact on people's lives. From the moment of birth to the instant of death, the destinies of individuals are regulated and controlled by government agencies to an extent previously unknown" (p. 22).

A major activity of government, at all levels, is policy making, a complex and varied process affected by both internal and external factors. The structure and location of the policy-making bodies are important factors influencing policy itself. Thus there is a connection between administration and policy, between the ideologies of particular administrations and the policy-making bodies they establish. Much depends on the relations they encourage, permit, or exclude as well as on the wider political, economic, or social contexts within which they operate.

In attempting to understand the role of governments and their policies for sport and tourism, it is important to appreciate the different forms of the state, rooted in different models of economic organization. The scope and level of involvement of any government depends on the type of economic system it adopts and its associated political philosophy. For the most part, the command type of economic organization consistent with communism has been abandoned with virtually all the major, and most of the minor, world states adopting some form of market-based economy. Inasmuch as one extreme form, with the state in total control, has generally been superseded, so, too, has the other extreme of a completely "free" market. The majority of states now adopt, or aspire to adopt, some form of "mixed" economy within the political philosophy of capitalism. Nahrstedt (1993) describes a clear relationship between leisure policy and the mixed economy: ". . . democratic leisure policy can only exist at a point somewhere between the extremes of a free market non-intervention and government control" (pp. 144-145). Nevertheless, governments display varying forms of organization and degrees of intervention in sport tourism.

Major reasons why governments may choose to intervene in leisure generally fall into the following categories (see Bramham et al. 1993; Harvey & Proulx, 1988; Johnson & Frey, 1985):

1. To safeguard public order.
2. To enhance national prestige.
3. To maximize economic potential.
4. To achieve sociocultural goals such as a sense of identity through leisure.
5. To protect the environment.
6. To improve the health and physical fitness of citizens.

The economic, environmental, and social impacts of sport and tourism have increasingly brought these activities within the area of state and government interest.

Governments establish the parameters within which the sport and tourism sectors operate. They influence the leisure industry in many ways: establishing financial priorities and legal frameworks; influencing disposable incomes; manipulating exchange rates and controlling the roles of different providers (Welch, 1988). Questions that governments address so far as sport and tourism are concerned include regulation of land use, planning, and protection; capital investment, ownership, support, and management of the infrastructure including the setting up of institutions that provide, assist, and supervise leisure services; facilitation of development including the recognition of professional qualifications; taxation on services and redistribution involving subsidy, social welfare, and equity; and exchange controls and consumer protection through licensing and safety regulations.

Government infrastructures change as various departments and agencies are created or disbanded and roles are transferred to other bodies. However, the institutional framework is both reflective and proactive— reflective in the sense that it represents government thinking and priorities at a period in time; proactive in the sense that it both enables and constrains policy-making opportunities. We now turn to examples of administrative infrastructures and policies recognizing that as political ideologies change so will the administrative infrastructures and the policies they affect. In chapter 10 we identify trends we perceive, but in this chapter we deal with the situation in the mid 1990s.

Sport Tourism Administrative Infrastructures in Various Countries

Global changes have forced new political alliances, in particular the 1987 Single European Act, which "has resulted in the construction of a single market bigger than even the United States" (Bramham et al., 1993, p. 234). World recession, exacerbated by the oil crisis in the 1970s, threatened America's dominance of world markets. The emergence of Japan and now of a unified Europe constitute an even greater threat. However, Europe still comprises a disparate collection of nation states each with its own administrative structures. For this reason the European states occupy a larger subsection of this chapter than the other nations referred to. We shall first identify the different administrative infrastructures that affect sport tourism within European countries, and then use Canada, Australia, the United States, and South Africa as major examples.

Europe

In the early 1980s a review of sport and tourism in five west European countries (France, the Netherlands, Spain, Sweden, and West Germany) concluded that there was a linkage between sport and tourism in the minds of participants, commercial providers, and local authorities, but that "among policy makers and administrators linkage scarcely exists" (Glyptis, 1982, p. 1). Almost ten years later Glyptis (1991) detailed the administrative infrastructure of sport and tourism in seven European countries (Britain, France, Germany, the Netherlands, Portugal, Spain, and Sweden) and showed that in only one of the seven was there real evidence of joint working arrangements between sport and tourism.

Examining leisure policies in Europe in 1993, Bramham et al. (1993) found the task of finding analysts who had a full overview of the different leisure sectors (tourism, [outdoor] recreation, sport, cultural, and media policies) in their respective countries difficult, since the study of leisure "appears to be as 'sectoralised' as the state bureaucracies" (p. 6).

In the following discussion, we identify the current administrative infrastructures that affect sport and tourism in a number of European states and show that for most governments the two sectors remain separate.

Belgium

In Belgium, sport as well as tourism is considered a cultural affair. And because Belgium has three autonomous communities, each community conducts a specific, independent cultural (and thus sport and tourism) policy. In the Flemish community the Commissariaat-generaal voor de bevordering van de Lichamelijke Ontwikkeling, de Sport en de Openluchtrecreatie (BLOSO) is the sport administrative body and the Vlaams Commissariaat-generaal voor Toerisme (VCGT) the tourist administrative body. In the past very few joint sport and tourism projects have been realized. Plans that have been made for the future suggest that awareness of the usefulness of a joint policy is growing. However, the claim by Remans and Delforge (1992) that in Belgium sport and tourism are joined at government level is evidently not the case given that even the three communities (Flemish, French, and German) are autonomously administered.

France

In France some specially constituted interministerial groups have been set up that have brought sport and tourism together, such as the Mission Interministerielle pour l'Aménagement de la Côte Aquitaine. However, this was a special commission to oversee land planning of the Aquitane coast. Generally speaking, sport and tourism have formed two separate divisions within the Ministry of Youth and Sports (Glyptis, 1991). Tourism has now lost its full-time portfolio and has been absorbed by the Ministry of Public Works, Housing, Transport, and Tourism (WTO, 1996).

Germany

In Germany there is no federal government department with responsibility for tourism, though two national agencies (one grant-aided by the federal government) promote tourism, one abroad and the other domestic. Sports policy, meanwhile, is a matter for the state governments. However, federal, state, and local governments are described as "very much an observer of the innovations in leisure developed within the commercial and voluntary sectors" (Nahrstedt, 1993, p. 143).

Great Britain

Government responsibility for sport in Great Britain has, since the establishment of its charter in 1972, been vested in the Sports Council. Three years previous, in 1969, the Development of Tourism Act of Parliament established the British Tourist Authority (BTA) whose role is concerned solely with encouraging overseas tourists to visit Britain, along with the four Tourist Boards of England, Northern Ireland, Scotland, and Wales whose concern is with tourism within their respective territories. Until 1992, these agencies reported to different government departments: the Sports Council to the Department of the Environment until 1990 when it was moved to the Department of Education and Science; the tourist authorities to the Department of Trade and Industry. During this period the two agencies produced separate guidelines and, except in relation to the countryside where a third "neutral" body (the Countryside Commission) drew them together, they had little to do with each other.

With the reelection of the Conservative government in 1992 a new Department of National Heritage (DNH) was established. The DNH was created to coordinate and direct development of the various leisure-related sectors. It gives cabinet status to sport, the arts, tourism, and broadcasting through the Minister for National Heritage. At the national level, for the first time in Britain, a connection between sport and tourism was formalized, although issues relating to the countryside and water-based recreation remained under a separate department. Since distinct subdepartments operate within the ministry it remains to be seen whether the "umbrella" organization will result in any concrete form of coordination let alone integration at the national level. With the election of a Labour government in 1997, the DNH was renamed the Department for Culture, Media, and Sport (DCMS) and embraces tourism.

Ravenscroft (1993) saw the creation of the DNH as a political maneuver designed to accelerate the transition toward a consumer-driven society. More recent confirmation of this view came from Robinson (1994) when he concluded that the direction of British government policy was to hand over responsibility for leisure to the private sector. Richards (1995) counters the argument that the creation of the DNH could be understood as a government move to win more resources for tourism by pointing to the decline in government funding that virtually accompanied the establishment of the department.

The Netherlands

In the Netherlands, the Ministry of Health, Well-Being, and Sport is responsible for sport, the Ministry of Agriculture and Fisheries for outdoor recreation, and the Ministry of Economic Affairs for tourism. Although policy-making bodies are still divided in 1998, van der Poel anticipated their coming together (van der Poel, 1993).

Portugal

Only in Portugal, of the seven countries reviewed by Glyptis (1991), was there any real sense of sport and tourism being combined through the Commission for Sport and Tourism established in 1983. Sport issues are dealt with by the State Secretariat of Sport and Tourism by the Ministry of Tourism, but the Commission was established to encourage joint ventures. This is one of the earliest examples of recognition at the central government level of the potential of sports participation as a motivator for travel, and of the potential benefits of an integrated approach to sport and tourism. The establishment of the commission was designed to avoid the duplication of effort that can arise from treating the two sectors separately. It promotes Portugal's sports facilities as an attraction for tourists seeking holiday activities and has invested in sports events with a high media profile such as the Estoril Grand Prix (Boa de Jesus, 1989).

To promote the image of Portugal by means of sport has been a deliberate marketing strategy. Sixty-four projects were reported as being under way in 1992 in the Algarve including golf courses, harbors, parks, hotels, inns, and tourist villages demonstrating an integration of sport and tourism (Davidson, 1992). In 1992, Jackson and Glyptis (1992) described Portugal's sport and tourism policy as "in many ways the most advanced level of recognition that benefits accrue from the linkage of sport and tourism" (p. 99).

Spain

In Spain, sports policy issues from the Ministry of Culture, tourism from the Ministry of Transport, Tourism and Communication (Gonzalez & Urkiola, 1993). Although both sport and tourism get great attention in Spain and sport tourism is a growing interest, sport and tourism remain largely in discrete structures.

Sweden

Sweden places sport under the auspices of the Ministry of Housing; tourism is mainly funded through the Ministry of Industry (Olson, 1993). Concluding his discussion of leisure policy in Sweden, Olson states, "In Sweden a forum for discussing common issues of mutual interest for the whole leisure sector, public and private, simply does not exist" (1993, p. 98).

Poland

Reference to East European countries has to take into account their transition from communism to market economies, which has proceeded unevenly in terms of tourism development and public policy.

Jung (1993) records recent organizational changes in Poland that have created the Office of Physical Culture and Tourism as a central body overseeing amateur and professional sport, as well as social and commercial tourism.

Canada

Fitness Canada, a program of the federal Department of Health, *Sport Canada*, a program of the federal Department of Canadian Heritage, and the *Canadian Tourism Commission* (CTC), which operates through the Canadian Government Office of Industry, act as umbrella agencies for the sport and tourism sectors in Canada. The predecessors of these current agencies came into existence in the 1960s. "Canada's poor showing in international competition and the low level of physical fitness among Canadians provided impetus for government leadership" (Minister of Supply and Services, 1992, p. 184) through the legislation of the 1961 Fitness and Amateur Sport Act. The governments of the 10 provinces and two territories work in partnership with the federal agencies and the municipal governments, who carry primary responsibility for facility development.

Canada illustrates a classic case of separation in administration of sport and tourism, yet despite this Redmond believes that Canada's investment in sport, in particular major international competitions, represents the world's most direct government involvement in sport-related tourism (Redmond, 1991). The extent of federal government involvement in sport has been clearly acknowledged in the Dubin enquiry (Minister of Supply and Services, 1992). The Task Force report, a follow-up to the enquiry, recommended that the federal government place more responsibility on the sport community for the programs and the conduct of sport in order to "dramatically reduce the administrative requirements to a negligible level" (Minister of Supply and Services, 1992, pp. 259-260). The CTC has adapted the concept of Product Clubs. Believing that products rather than destinations drive growth, Product Clubs facilitate cooperation between operators and organizations interested in the same niche market. Eco/adventure and urban tourism are two of the first Product Clubs to be established (WTO, 1996).

Australia

Australia, like Canada, is a very large country with a comparatively small population. Its land mass is roughly equal to that of the United States, but, with only 18 million people, it contains less than one-tenth of the U.S. population. Australia also parallels Canada in its colonial history and federal system of government in which six states and two territories govern many of their own affairs, including domestic tourism and sports development. The Australian Tourist Commission is the federal agency responsible for the overseas promotion of Australian tourism, while its sports counterpart, the Australian Sports Commission (ASC), is responsible for the implementation of the government's national sports policy. Australia has both a Federal Minister for Sport (with environment and territories in the portfolio) and a Minister for Tourism (since 1991) in separate commonwealth departments. Sport and tourism are also administered at the subnational level by individual state and territory governments, by various regional organizations, and by local councils. This makes for a complex web of national, state, and local government and nongovernment organizations (D. Rowe, January 17, 1996).

Of the ASC's seven divisions, the most prominent is the Australian Institute of Sport (AIS), which from its base in Canberra (with satellite operations in various states) is devoted to the development of elite national sport in Australia. Sport is also administered by national nongovernment organizations such as the Australian Olympic Committee and the Confederation of Australian Sport, the peak body of national sport organizations (both of which are partially funded by the ASC). Responsibility for coordinating the Sydney 2000 Olympics lies with the Sydney Organizing Committee for the Olympic Games (SOCOG), which was established in 1993 by an act of the New South Wales State Parliament (D. Rowe, January 17, 1996).

Australia's six states and two territories all have departments that administer sport and recreation, fostering and funding a wide variety of elite and "grass roots" sports programs. Local government is also involved in sports administration, primarily through the provision of municipal sports facilities under the rubric of community services. The administrative "spaces" between state and locally coordinated sport are often filled by regional offices of departments of sport and recreation, and regionally focused academies of sport (D. Rowe, January 17, 1996).

Tourism is administered quite separately from sport. The Commonwealth Department of Tourism is responsible for tourism at the national level, providing support for overseas tourist promotion and research data respectively through its two agencies, the Australian Tourist Commission and the Bureau of Tourism Research. At the state and territory level tourism is administered by government departments and statutory authorities, with both international and domestic tourism promoted through tourist bureaus and associations. Local governments are also involved in tourism through various tourist bureaus and information centers. As in the case of sport, various regional tourist organizations are sponsored by state governments, with representation for several local councils and industry bodies (D. Rowe, January 17, 1996).

United States of America

A third major country in which responsibilities for tourism and sport are shared between federal, state, and municipal governments is the United States of America. Its quintessential commitment to free enterprise, and therefore a free market, make it the nation showing probably the least government involvement in sport and tourism. Wilson (1988) suggests that we

> recall the federalist principles upon which the American political system is based, combine this with popular support for individualist values and take into consideration the strength of the private sector, and it should come as no surprise that the state is probably less associated with leisure in the United States than in any other democracy. (p. 79)

However, Coakley (1990) indicates a growing government interest in the political implications of sport. In 1981 the federal government in Washington gave assent to the National Tourism Policy Act, which gave birth to the United States Travel and Tourism Administration (USTTA). At the same time the federal government reduced tourism's operating budget (Ronkainen & Farano, 1987). The USTTA has operated on behalf of the federal government serving as the nation's official National Tourism Office charged with responsibility to assume a major leadership responsibility in optimizing tourism's contribution to the nation's economic goals of growth, stability, and job creation (USTTA, n.d.). The USTTA's (n.d.) funding is not intended to be some kind of subsidy to the travel industry, but rather it is used to "divert international tourists away from other countries and attract them to the United States" (p. 1).

However, as Mill (1990) comments, "Controversy still exists over the role of the government in tourism in the United States" (p. 143). The reason for the controversy, he suggests, is the argument that tourism benefits relatively few people and therefore the private sector should support it. On the other hand, the travel deficit affects the balance of trade, which therefore makes it a public and federal concern. The rising profile of government officials responsible for tourism does not necessarily indicate a similar increase in importance within the administration once the consistent underfunding of the agency is taken into account (Mill, 1990). The USTTA has recently been superseded by the privately organized USA National Tourism Organization (USANTO) (WTO, 1996). Board members of USANTO are drawn from government and the private sector, and an operating budget is being sought from both private organizations as well as state/local authorities. The US Congress has reportedly stated that federal funding will not be considered for the immediate future (WTO, 1996).

Mill (1990) goes on to show the fragmentation that prevails with approximately 50 agencies or departments, with 150 programs between them, that affect tourism, travel, or recreation in the United States. The sheer size of the country and its political organization into semiautonomous states, which differ in their management structure and the authorities and responsibilities assigned to different agencies, serve to explain the fragmentation quite apart from the states' different ideological stances that favor more or less government involvement. Theobald (1994) discusses the confusion, and reports that at the subnational level there is no accepted definition of a tourist valid throughout the country. Definitions vary from state to state.

So far as sport is concerned there is no government organization directly responsible for it. In 1978, U.S. Congress passed the Amateur Sports Act, Public Law 95-606, which affirmed the United States Olympic Committee (USOC) as the coordinating body for Olympic-related athletic activity and the rule-making body for amateur sport. The USOC was also given the responsibility for promoting and supporting physical fitness and public participation in athletic activities by encouraging developmental programs in the various sports and providing new programs (L. Delpy, September 22, 1995; G. Sage, August 29, 1996; Wilson, 1988).

Established in 1956, the President's Council (1996) on Physical Fitness and Sports "has promoted physical activity, fitness and sports for all Americans" (p. 6). The council operates within the Department of Health and Human Services, but it is a "purely advisory body" and is the only ongoing government agency solely concerned with physical fitness and sport in the United States (Wilson, 1988). Wilson notes that there have been "frequent clashes of opinion and interest between federal and local authorities" (p. 85) with regard to sport and "no real structure exists which serves to define the jurisdictional limits of the various organizations" (p. 85). Neither resources nor manpower have been dedicated to the "sport for all" function as it is termed in other countries (L. Delpy, September 22, 1995; G. Sage, August 29, 1996; Wilcox, 1993).

As far as sport tourism is concerned, over one hundred cities and regions across the United States have developed sport commissions. Sport commissions are established as either a private enterprise or a quasi-governmental or governmental entity; a majority are under the Convention and Visitor Bureau umbrella (L. Delpy September 22, 1995; G. Sage, August 29, 1996). In 1992, the National Association of Sports Commissions (NASC) was created to foster communication among America's public and private sector sports commissions and to formulate policy on major issues as needed (L. Delpy, September 22, 1995; G. Sage, August 29, 1996). Each state also has a Department of Tourism and some, like Virginia, have a specialist in sport marketing (L. Delpy, September 22, 1995).

South Africa

Although working as separate organizations in South Africa, recreation and tourism agencies there have formed a new alliance with cooperation replacing their former coexistence and even an antagonism that existed between them. Gunn (1990) sees a strong rationale for collaboration since the two fields overlap and share mutual interests, similar planning and management considerations, and research needs. South Africa's recent reentry to the world tourism scene coincided with the current growth in sport tourism and, sensibly, its agencies opportunely combined forces on a research project that was directed at identifying South Africa's market strengths, particularly in terms of sports facilities, that might boost the country's tourism appeal.

Barbados

In 1987 the government of Barbados took a policy decision to improve the island's sporting facilities (Sport Tourism, 1997). It had two main purposes. The first was to assist Barbadian athletes to improve their performance in regional and international competitions. The second was to encourage sports tourism. The government has now merged the portfolios of sports and tourism into one ministry, and the Tourism Authority has promoted a vigorous campaign marketing Barbados as an international sports tourism destination (Sport Tourism, 1997).

Summary of Administrative Infrastructures

In summary, we can state that from the foregoing we learn that administrative infrastructures vary between the states we have briefly outlined, but very largely sport and tourism remain in discrete structures. However, an increasing number of states with different political histories and ideological complexions can be identified as beginning to orchestrate some level of administrative relation between the different leisure sectors. For sport and tourism this appears to have been made most explicit in Barbados, Portugal and Poland, where single central bodies oversee the two areas. But in Belgium, Great Britain, France, and South Africa potential administrative coordination has become increasingly visible at central as well as regional (state) or municipal government levels.

We also note that although government involvement varies, the trend among most national governments at the end of the 1990s appears to be to largely divest themselves of direct responsibility for many sectors of leisure, including both sport and tourism. Insofar as administrations retain their interest, this is dependent on the economic or political advantage that they perceive is embodied in sport and tourism. The United States Travel and Tourism Administration was quite direct in expressing its funding rationale; other governments may be less open, but their support for agencies charged with responsibility to increase incoming international visitors was clear. On the other hand, domestic tourism, usually the largest sector in the Western world, has been seen as an internal matter safely left to the private sector or to "local" public agents because it could not be held to generate foreign income or international prestige.

Much the same can be said of sport. The interest that central governments maintain is strongly slanted to international elite-level performance, where a nation's athletes can be seen as visible symbols of their respective administrations. "Sport for all" is of lower political priority and has characteristically been consigned to lesser agencies, regional or municipal governments or public/private sector partnerships. Sport tourism then will attract government support to the extent that it can be seen to have potential political or economic advantages.

Implications of Administrative Infrastructures for Sport Tourism Policy

It is our contention that the structural arrangement of a government's administration is likely to have a direct bearing on resource allocations for, and limitations of, its various institutions. The relations that are enabled, and, conversely, those that are constrained, by institutional location are very relevant to the sport-tourism relation. A coordinated approach to administration will assist in exposing areas of mutual or conflicting interest and identifying "issues which need to be addressed by policy development and/or further research" (Standeven & Tomlinson, 1994, p. 2). A failure to provide adequate structural cooperation, where sport and tourism can be harnessed in a symbiotic relation, is likely to lead to inadequate policies, inefficient deployment of resources, wasteful duplication, and an inability to take full advantage of the sport-tourism connection. Henry's (1993) detailed analysis of the politics of leisure policy, with a primary focus on Great Britain, shows that the economic imperatives of the 1990s and beyond will impact on a wide range of issues, not least the professionalization of leisure services. By "professionalization," we mean a process that involves the emergence of occupational groups that control entry to status and power through the attainment (and often examination) of specialist knowledge and skills; the adoption of the principle of professional education and training. Henry submits that Britain is not unique in its policy responses:

> Thus world recession may be reacted to differently by different political groups in different cities and countries, but will nevertheless have impacts across national boundaries, as will the investment and disinvestment decisions of multi-nationals, major cultural shifts, political changes and so on. (p. 203)

Leisure services are often rendered by a nonprofessional. But leisure services are developing into unique and important social services and are more and more considered as an emerging profession. We believe that sport tourism is in the process of becoming a profession though it has not yet been fully developed (De Knop, Wylleman, De Martelaer, Van Puymbroeck & Wittock, 1993; De Knop & Standeven, in press). This book, together with the increasing body of specific literature, is a contribution to the knowledge base, but, as yet, specific education and training programs are limited and specific scientific research is rather scarce.

Whether in the public, commercial, or voluntary sectors, the economic imperatives resulting from the world recession are leading to changing policy orientations and an adaptation of professionalism within many states. Commercialization, dependent on economic efficiency, predominates. While we acknowledge the different ideological positions that separate commercial and social-welfare provision, and the different professionalisms to which they give rise (industrial semi-professions maximizing a return on investment, and liberal semi-professions securing social order) (Henry, 1993), we support the principle of interrelated administration. Only through coordination and cooperation can coherent policy in sport tourism be developed.

Alongside the demand for professionalism, the increasing popularity of sport tourism is resulting in the creation of many new organizations offering both general and specific activities, in the building of specific resorts, and in the development of new liaisons. In other words, a new subsector of industry is being created around sport tourism. Parallel to this, new job opportunities are emerging, and the further sport tourism expands, the more specific and diversified these jobs will become. Whether or not these are entirely new jobs, and not simply subdivisions or specialities of existing jobs in the broader tourism or sport field, remains a question. But if we follow Kurtzman and Zauhar (1991), they find it imperative that a new professional cadre be formed because of the specificity of the sport tourism service. It has been suggested that marketing could be the most effective starting point for liaison between sport and tourism (Standeven, 1998). The dual situation of new career opportunities within changing economic and political milieus indicates both the need, and the opportunity, for the professionalization of sport tourism, and with it the need for further textual material.

We shall now look briefly at some sport tourism policies.

Sport Tourism Policy Issues

Policies tend to take one of two directions; they focus either on restriction and control (policies of control) or on creating new opportunities and promoting development (policies of development). First we shall instance examples of development policies from different countries that have their rationale rooted in economic or social advantage. Second, regulatory policies generally directed toward adopting more sustainable approaches to life will be exemplified.

Henry's (1993) analysis of the relation between political values and central government policy shows how leisure sector policies were linked to different political administrations and their conception of the role of the state. In spite of ideological differences among the Netherlands (with its Conservative-led coalition governments), France and Spain (with their socialist administrations) and Great Britain (with its Conservative government in the 1980s and early 1990s), Henry identifies how leisure policies have reflected economic goals in all four nation-states. This illustrates the trend toward the overriding importance now attached to economic measures in policy definition in all political administrations.

Policies of Development

Several policies of development—those policies that are intended to create new sport tourism opportunities or promote sport tourism development—are evident around the world. Here we look at sport for all and tourism for all; joint policy statements made by different sport and tourism organizations; and policies made based on economics, especially policies regarding the hosting of the Olympic Games.

Sport and Tourism for All

Tourism-for-all and sport-for-all initiatives are examples of how some governments promote participation and provide financial support or subsidy to enable disadvantaged individuals and classes of the population to holiday, take part in sport, or to combine the two. Examples here include the employee policies in Germany (see chapter 8) that allow time off from work for health-restoring holidays in addition to the annual leave (Sargent, 1987); the policy in Scandinavia to refund the cost of spa trips taken for health purposes (Davidson, 1992); and the family holiday centers in Belgium that offer access to a range of activities as an essential part of the subsidized holiday package for which no extra charge is made (Davidson, 1992).

However, there are signals that social welfare policies such as these are being eroded by economic imperatives. In the Netherlands the government is said to be moving toward "consumer sovereignty" and private enterprise and away from social distribution (van der Poel, 1993). Davidson (1992) noted Ireland's and Portugal's need to limit their social tourism programs. Great Britain has not had a policy for social tourism, and the recent restructuring and refocusing of the Sports Council indicate a withdrawal from welfare policies such as "sport for all" and a move toward government disinvestment except at the international level.

Diversification of land use in Britain, and in particular the development of farm land for recreational purposes, was encouraged by the policy of grant schemes to farmers from the government (Ravenscroft, 1995). While the policy of opening up access to the countryside may have been only partially successful (Ravenscroft, 1995), it has furthered the need for sustainability now embraced in policy statements from the Countryside Commission (1991).

Joint Sport and Tourism Statements

Joint policy statements concerning sport and tourism became evident at the regional level in England in 1992, when the Sports Council (South West) and the West Country Tourist Board published *Tourism and Sport* (West Country Tourist Board & The Sports Council [South West], 1992). Given that the region is the most popular holiday destination area within Britain and that its coastal resorts face competition from more guaranteed-weather regions abroad, the regional government agencies saw the need for action. The two agencies recognized the links between sport and tourism and so published 27 statements of policy such as this one:

> WCTB and SC(SW) will encourage appropriate local authorities to give greater priority to improved sporting facilities in key resort areas and destinations, aimed at safeguarding and improving facilities for residents and tourists alike (West Country Tourist Board/The Sports Council [South West], 1992, p. 5).

Similar recognition of the sport-tourism link was evident in the southeast of England (Standeven & Tomlinson, 1994).

Economics and Sport Tourism Policies

Linking sport with tourism has been an economic policy of the Irish government since the late 80s. The partnership of the Irish Tourist Board with private and other state resources led to an investment of over IR£1 billion in new product development from 1989 to 1994. A range of quality facilities have been developed such as new and improved hotels, leisure centers, golf resorts, activity holiday centers, and products based on Ireland's history and culture (Dwyer, 1993). As in Portugal, tourism chiefs were charged to dramatically increase earnings from tourism, and, speaking in 1992, the Irish Minister of Sport and Leisure confirmed the tourism aspects of sport as important: "The economic future of the North and South is tied up with making sport a tourism attraction—the country could become 'a prestigious destination for sporting activity tourism'" (Sugden, Knox, & Tomlinson, 1992, p. 5).

With similar economic aims, the Tunisian government's policy has been to invest in sports facilities with the objective of developing tourism, attempting to increase its market by 2.5 million visitors between 1981 and 1991 particularly by attracting what it perceived as high-income tourists (Fozzard, 1988).

During its period of economic expansion, Japan maintained a six-day working week with little opportunity or need to create resort locations. The exception was the development of high-quality and astronomically high-cost golf clubs and recreation venues such as hot springs for the Sunday pursuits of business executives. Having attained world power status, working hours have been decreased from about 2,500 in 1960 to just under 2,000 in the mid-1990s. By law the working population are now expected to be employed for 1,774 hours per year (H. Nogawa, December 21, 1997). The reductions are accompanied by a concomitant increase in leisure time (Allanson, 1993). With this change has come a change in tourism policy. Rather than culture, the government is placing policy emphasis on health, activity, and family recreation combined with travel.

Compared to other developed countries, Japan is short of parks and sports facilities. Policy attempts have therefore been made to encourage the development of recreational facilities to provide for new more leisurely and healthy lifestyles, to increase the leisure repertoire of individuals, and to satisfy popular demand (Harada, 1994).

Poujol (1993), discussing policies in France, finds that the planning of professional qualifications in the leisure field is "the one area in which a more conscious approach to policy has been adopted" (p. 22). In the field of sport, almost all professional education is regulated by law.

Bids to Host Olympics

Competition to host the Olympics now costs bidding cities multimillion-dollar budgets. Even so, cities throughout the Western world continue to vie to become hosts. Henry (1993) describes Barcelona's Olympic bid, and the promotion of city marketing, as a spectacular feature of Spanish leisure policy in the early 1990s, given the vast sums of money required. According to Henry this illustrates "the degree to which economic development goals have displaced those of social or community development" (p. 208). A highly topical example of policy directed toward the opportunities created by sport tourism is found in the following case study of Sydney's bid to host the 2000 Olympic Games.

Case Study 9.1

Australia's National Tourism Strategy and the Sydney 2000 Olympics

Bidding to Host the Olympics as a Policy of Development

Sydney's successful bid for the 2000 Summer Olympic Games has provided the focal point for short- and medium-term debates about the future of Australia's tourism industry.

When the federally-funded Australian Tourism Commission established a series of special interest theme years from 1993 to 1997 in order "to develop a more diverse range of tourism products" (Australia, p. 18), the first to be launched was "The Year of Sport." The various tiers of government have facilitated and sometimes contested the staging of several sports megaspectacles (e.g., in motorcar and bike racing) over the last decade, with tourism consistently used as the justification for public investment in sports infrastructure, disruption to everyday local life, and exemptions in planning and other regulations.

The most striking example of a tourism-led Australian sports mega-event is the Australian Formula One Grand Prix, which was first secured by the South Australian State Government for Adelaide and has since been acquired by Victoria for Melbourne on more favorable terms to the race organizers. Any criticism of the mounting of these sports mega-events is met with the response by government and business that they generate local economic activity and, in particular, that international media coverage is a very inexpensive and compelling form of tourist advertising.

This use of tourism as a justification for sport and media developments coincides with the "export" of Australia's sporting and recreational facilities, space, and climate. For example, energetic marketing overseas of water sports on the Great Barrier Reef and the frenetic building of golf courses (and, it is proposed, even baseball pitches) in Queensland primarily for Japanese sports tourists have not only generated greater revenue for the sport-tourism combination, but have also caused new policy dilemmas for governments in terms of environmental controls, foreign ownership rules, visa regulations, and so on.

Sport as local event, amenity, and media spectacle is now widely regarded as a component of the tourism industry, with the Sydney 2000 Olympics positioned as an unprecedented opportunity to develop this new synergy in the Australian leisure complex.

The pivotal role that Sydney 2000 is expected to play in the future fortunes of Australian tourism (and other forms of business) is readily apparent in almost every forum where economic development is addressed. For example, a discussion paper for the New South Wales Tourism Masterplan (1994) identifies sport as an "emerging speciality tourist market" (p. 23) and stresses the projected favorable impact of the Olympics on the state's economy. In a rather different publication, Ansett Australia's in-flight magazine *Panorama*, an editorial states,

> The Olympic Games are the world's greatest sporting event and are also one of the world's biggest travel drawcards. The Games and the associated international publicity build-up during the next five years also represent a golden opportunity for Australian tourism to attract those visitors to see other parts of Australia during their trips down under (McMahon, 1995, p. 4).

The decision to stage almost all Olympic events within the Sydney metropoli-

The pool for the 2000 summer Olympic Games. Sydney's Aquatic Centre houses the most modern and extensive swimming facilities in the world.

tan area has resulted in contention. This Sydney-centric nature of the Games organization has been permitted in spite of the support received from national government and the underwriting of the Olympics by the New South Wales State Government rather than the local councils of metropolitan Sydney. Various other cities and regions are attempting to secure some of the tourist and other commercial benefits of the Games by offering themselves as pre-Games practice and acclimatization "base camps" for visiting international squads.

In summary, we see that in Australia there is a deep faith in the economic potential of tourism, that sport has emerged as both a significant promotional tourist "theme" and as a specialist tourist market, and that the Sydney 2000 Olympics have already substantially fused conceptions of tourism and sport for both commercial activity and government policy. The outcome of this convergence in administrative and policy terms has been intensified pressure to articulate the modes of organization of different tiers of government and also to exacerbate competition between cities, regions, and states. It has also presented a series of policy dilemmas concerning the environmental, social, cultural, and fiscal impact of integrating hitherto largely separate spheres of leisure and commerce.

This case study was contributed by David Rowe.

Policies of Control

Policies of control—those policies that focus on restricting or controlling sport tourism—are often environmentally focused. However, some policies of control are used to control overambitious development and to safeguard the public.

Environmental Policies

Policies of restriction and control are most often environmentally driven— for example, the policy in Lech am Arlberg in Austria, referred to in chapter 7, where the sale of day passes is limited to 14,000 skiers.

The French use the policy of zoning in their national parks to protect the environment. Tourism and recreation are encouraged in the outer zone, the second zone is subject to regulations on environmentally sensitive activities, and the inner zone is generally reserved for research and often includes a nature reserve from which the public is excluded (Boniface & Cooper, 1994).

Unsurprisingly, the enormously high density of population in the Netherlands (over 14 million inhabitants in a small country of about 33,000 square kilometers of land and 7,000 square kilometers of inland and coastal waters) has led that government to adopt some of the strictest outdoor recreation planning policies in Europe (Kroon, 1989).

In spite of its vast open spaces, America was one of the first countries to demonstrate its concern for the environment when it established the world's first national park in 1872. A major, current problem within the parks relates to their overuse by active tourists during peak seasons of the year. To help rectify this damaging situation requires changes in the policy of funding to enable the National Park Service to "actively participate in the marketing process and work directly with the tourism industry to change problematic public use patterns" (Zeiger, Caneday, & Baker, 1993, p. 157). The continuance of the mutually advantageous relationship between tourism and outdoor recreation in the national parks depends upon a policy that allows a greater return of the franchise and user fees to the National Park Service rather than to the General Treasury of the United States (Zeiger, Caneday, & Baker, 1993)

Belize, a small Central American country, obtained its independence from Britain only in 1981; it has a small population of around 200,000. Between 1984 and 1989 its tourist arrivals almost doubled from 88,430 to 172,830. With tourism revenues amounting to US$9 million in 1988, the country recognized tourism as its second most important sector (to sugar production) (Maguire, 1993). Belize is described as having an extraordinarily diverse natural resource base including a coral reef with abundant coastal islands, rainforests with scenic rivers and waterfalls, and unexplored limestone caves. Its coral reef, second in length only to the Great Barrier Reef in Australia, is said to offer some of the finest diving in the

Hundreds of thousands of tourists flock each year to the Grand Canyon National Park in Arizona, resulting in the need for policies of control.

world, the only aspect of tourism for which Belize had previously been known (Maguire, 1993). The government has recognized the dynamic nature of tourism development and the sensitivity of the natural environment, and in its new policy statement identifies the need to incorporate the reef, atolls, rivers, lagoons, forests, and caves into a National Parks Plan in order to protect them from overuse (Maguire, 1993).

In the United Kingdom, the government has stated its concern for the potentially negative effects that the growth of sport tourism could have on the countryside (Sports Council, 1990).

Policies Driven by Revenue

Portugal's early enthusiasm for sport tourism led to hasty actions that created regional imbalances of development and income. As a consequence, the Portuguese government had to adopt planning policies to attempt to control development and even out its perceived benefits (Jackson & Glyptis, 1992).

Policy driven by approaching (sport) tourism as a revenue-producing activity is criticized by Richter (1991). And her criticism is directed toward the United States. She notes,

> Unlike much of the industrialized world, the United States and its policy has not moved beyond the profit motive to a consideration of leisure in the promotion of health, reduction of crime, reward of labor, or the importance of travel as an information medium (p. 155).

Social Behavior Policies

The other main area of policies of control relates to social behavior, an example of which would be safeguarding public order. The death of 39 spectators at the European Cup Final at the Heysel Stadium in Brussels in 1985 forced the British government to take action since British football hooligans (many of whom were casual sport tourists) were the cause of the disaster. The week following the riot, a statement by the Prime Minister to the House of Commons outlined a five-point policy plan that included altering the law on crowd safety and hooliganism, strengthening and clarifying police powers, and granting the courts a wider range of sentencing options (Houlihan, 1990). There was even a proposal that in some cases a ban might be imposed on visiting spectators (by definition, sport tourists).

Summary

Sport tourism is, and will continue to be, of interest to central government for so long as it can be seen to deliver economic or political advantage or to require restrictive regulations. In spite of a global ideological shift toward market-based mixed economies, government administration and involvement in sport tourism varies between states. Although some governments are seeking to integrate sport and tourism and have established administrative frameworks to do so, the majority have not defined any formal connection. Separation of the two special interest areas, fragmentation into private/commercial and public concerns, and differentiation within the hierarchical tiers of worldwide political systems indicate that the relationship between sport and tourism will be characterized by negotiation and conflict as hitherto unconnected groups come together. The creation of new agencies or departments may not be necessary if there is a commitment from the different "players" involved—including a state's agencies—within the existing situation.

The implications for policy integration include the need for policy makers (local, regional, and national) to become more closely involved and recognize the links, issuing guidelines to enable sport and tourism agencies to work more closely together. Policy makers need to develop a joint strategic approach and establish infrastructures that facilitate linkages between operators in the different sectors. If direct funding is impractical or undesirable, governments and official agencies at least need to create a favorable fiscal environment that encourages both tourism and sporting activities. Legislation must be in place to regulate safety and guarantee quality of experience for visitors and the local community alike. Professional qualifications, and a scheme that defines their mutual recognition between states, are also needed. Providers should be encouraged to consider the needs of both the local and tourism market in the design and promotion of their facilities. Examples of "best practice" need to be identified and knowledge shared—in particular, examples of tourism genuinely helping to provide or sustain local community sport initiatives should be recognized.

The potential benefits of a coordinated administrative approach to sport tourism should, by this stage, be evident and will be necessary to solve the problems the relation implies. Yet a recent paper from England concludes, "Sadly, (this review) has established that although sport-tourism activity by policy makers is rising, examples of genuine collaboration by sport and tourism bodies are few and far between" (Weed & Bull, 1996, 1998). It may be that this situation is replicated elsewhere. It would appear, therefore, that there is now a need to establish administrative bodies with clearly defined policy roles at the local community, county, region, province, state, and supranational levels—and to establish these bodies in such a way that coordination is an essential requirement of their operation.

References

Allanson, N. (1993). Land of the rising sun. *Leisure Management, 13*(7), 24-25.

Australia. (1992). *Tourism: Australia's passport to growth: A National Tourist Strategy.* Canberra, Australia: Commonwealth Department of Tourism.

Boa de Jesus, M. (1989, August). *Sport and tourism in Portugal.* Paper presented at the Congress of Federation Internationalle d'Education Physique (FIEP), Waterford, Ireland.

Boniface, B.G., & Cooper, C. (1994). *The geography of travel and tourism.* Oxford, Great Britain: Butterworth-Heinemann.

Bramham, P., Henry, I., Mommas, H., & van der Poel, H. (1993). Leisure policies in Europe: An introduction. In P. Bramham, I. Henry, H. Mommas, & H. van der Poel (Eds.), *Leisure policies in Europe* (pp. 1-11). Wallingford, Great Britain: CAB International.

Coakley, J.(1990). *Sport in society.* St. Louis: Times Mirror/Mosby.

Collins, M. & Randolph, L. (1993). Business or hobby? Small firms in sport and recreation. In A.J. Veal, P. Jonson, & G. Cushman (Eds.), *Leisure and tourism: Social and environmental change* (pp. 433-438). Sydney, Australia: Centre for Leisure and Tourism Studies, University of Technology.

Countryside Commission. (1991). *Visitors to the countryside.* Cheltenham, Great Britain: Author.

Davidson, R. (1992). *Tourism in Europe.* London: Pitman.

De Knop, P., Wylleman, P., De Martelaer, K., Van Puymbroeck, L., & Wittock, H. (1993). New professions in sport and tourism. In J. Mester (Ed.), 2nd European Forum—*Sport Sciences in Europe 1993*: Current and Future Perspectives (32-54). Aachen, Germany: Meyer & Meyer.

De Knop, P., & Standeven, J. (in press). Sport tourism: A new area of sport management: *European Journal of Sport Management.*

Dwyer, D. (1993). Irish vision. *Leisure Management, 13*(4), 34-37.

Fozzard, A. (1988). Tunisia: National report. *International Tourism Reports, 4,* 20-39.

Freeman, W.H. (1992). *Physical Education and Sport in a changing society.* Toronto, Canada: Maxwell Macmillan Canada.

Glyptis, S. (1982). *Sport and tourism in western Europe.* London: British Travel Educational Trust.

Glyptis, S. (1991). Sport and tourism. In C. Cooper (Ed.), *Progress in tourism, recreation and hospitality management. Vol. 3* (pp. 166-183). London: Belhaven Press.

Gonzalez, J. & Urkiola, A. (1993). Leisure policy in Spain. In P. Bramham, I. Henry, H. Mommas, & H. van der Poel (Eds.), *Leisure policies in Europe* (pp. 149-174). Wallingford, Great Britain: CAB International.

Gunn, C.A. (1990). The new recreation-tourism alliance. *Journal of Park and Recreation Administration, 8*(1), 1-8.

Hall, C.M., & Jenkins, J.M. (1995). *Tourism and public policy.* London: Routledge.

Ham, C., & Hill, M. (1993). *The policy process in the modern capitalist state.* London: Wheatsheaf Harvester.

Harada, M. (1994). Towards a renaissance of leisure in Japan. *Leisure Studies, 13,* 277-287.

Harvey, J. & Proulx, R. (1988). Sport and the state in Canada. In J. Harvey & H. Cantelon (Eds.), *Not just a game.* Ottawa, ON: University of Ottawa Press.

Haywood, L., Kew, F., Bramham, P., Spink, J., Capenerhurst, J., & Henry, I. (1989). *Understanding leisure*. London: Hutchinson.

Henry, I.P. (1993). *The politics of leisure policy*. London: Macmillan.

Houlihan, B. (1990). The politics of sports policy in Britain: The examples of football hooliganism and drug abuse. *Leisure Studies, 9*(1), 55-71.

Houlihan, B. (1991). *The government and politics of sport*. London: Routledge.

Jackson, G.A.M., & Glyptis, S.A. (1992). *Sport and tourism: A review of the literature*. Unpublished Report to the Sports Council, London.

Jenkins, W.I. (1978). *Policy analysis*. London: Martin Robertson.

Johnson, A. & Frey, J.H. (Eds.). (1985). *Government and sport*. Totowa, NJ: Rowman & Allanheld.

Jung, B. (1993). Elements of leisure policy in post war Poland. In P. Bramham, I. Henry, H. Mommas, & H. van der Poel (Eds.), *Leisure policies in Europe* (pp. 189-210). Wallingford, Great Britain: CAB International.

Kroon, H.J.J. (1989). Political and social aspects of forest recreation: The Dutch case. In B.J.H. Brown (Ed.), *Leisure and the environment. Congress paper No. 31* (pp. 150-163). Eastbourne, Great Britain: Leisure Studies Association.

Kurtzman, J. & Zauhar, J. (1991, June). *Tourism Sport*. Paper presented at the symposium of the North American Society of Sport Management, Ottawa, Canada.

Maguire, P. (1993). Ecotourism development policy in Belize. In A.J. Veal, P. Jonson, & G. Cushman (Eds.), *Leisure and tourism: Social and environmental change* (pp. 624-630). Sydney, Australia: Centre for Leisure and Tourism Studies, University of Technology.

McMahon, G. (1995, September). Speaking personally. *Panorama*, p. 4.

Mill, R.C. (1990). *Tourism: The international business*. Englewood Cliffs, NJ: Prentice Hall.

Minister of Supply and Services. (1992). *Sport: The way ahead. Minister's task force on federal sport policy*. Ottawa, ON: Author.

Nahrestedt, W. (1993). Leisure policy in Germany. In P. Bramham, I. Henry, H. Mommas, & H. van der Poel (Eds.), *Leisure policies in Europe* (pp. 129-148). Wallingford, Great Britain: CAB International.

New South Wales Tourist Commission. (1994). *New South Wales tourism masterplan: Discussion paper for Direction 2010 Workshops*. Sydney, Australia: Author.

Olson, H-E. (1993). Leisure policy in Sweden. In P. Bramham, I. Henry, H. Mommas, & H. van der Poel (Eds.), *Leisure policies in Europe* (pp. 71-100). Wallingford, Great Britain: CAB International.

Plog, S.C. (1994). Leisure travel: an extraordinary industry faces superordinary problems. In W.Theobald (Ed.), *Global tourism* (pp.40-54). Oxford, Great Britain: Butterworth-Heinemann.

Poujol, G. (1993). Leisure Politics and Policies in France. In P. Branham, I. Henry, H. Mommaas, H. van der Poel (Eds.), *Leisure Policies in Europe* (pp. 13-40). Wallingford, Great Britain: CAB International.

Chapter 10

Conclusions and Implications: Sport Tourism in the Twenty-First Century

Exodus

View from the Tour du Mont Blanc Trail.

The following topics are covered in this chapter:

1. A summary of contemporary sport tourism.
2. The growth and diversification of sport tourism in the twentieth century.
3. The need to maximize the benefits and minimize the disbenefits of sport tourism.
4. The separation of sport tourism into the discrete areas of sport and tourism.
5. The conflicts of interest prevalent in sport tourism.
6. The need to increase access to sport tourism while ensuring its sustainability.
7. The need to manage the process of integrating sport and tourism.
8. Changes expected in sport, tourism, and sport tourism in the twenty-first century based on the changing context of society.

According to the World Travel and Tourism Council (WTTC), by the year 1992 tourism had become the world's largest industry (World Travel and Tourism Council, 1993). Employing around 130 million people, or almost 7 percent of all employees in 1992, tourism is the world's largest employer (WTTC, 1991). According to the World Tourism Organization (WTO), 595 million international tourists were recorded in 1996, a year in which tourism spending topped US$425 billion (World Tourism Organization, 1997). By the year 2000, international tourist arrivals are expected to reach 650 million, an increase of almost 50 percent in the last decade of the century alone (Savignac, 1994). The WTO's new forecast *Tourism: 2020 Vision* predicts tourist arrivals will grow by an average 4.3 percent a year over the next two decades, while receipts from international tourism will climb by 6.7 percent a year (WTO, 1997). This forecast anticipates that by 2020 1.6 billion tourists will be visiting foreign destinations annually. China is expected to become the world's number one destination (followed by the United States of America, France, and Spain) and it will also become the fourth most important generating market, according to the study. However, the study concludes that international tourism in 2020 will still be the prerogative of only 7 percent of the world's population, up from 3.5 percent in 1996—"but still just the tip of the iceberg" (WTO, 1997, p. 2). Tourism is, then, a hugely significant industry in global terms, although its fragmentation, diversity, and lack of comparable data make it difficult to assess precisely its true worldwide impact (Plog, 1994).

Sport, too, has become a global product and massive business. The growing popularity of just one sport, basketball, attracts annual revenues of US$1.1 billion from television and almost three times that much from merchandising (Glendinning, 1996). In Formula One motor racing, the German driver Michael Schumacher was on a US$25 million retainer with Ferrari in 1997 and will likely negotiate for much more in coming years (Glendinning, 1996). For the 1998 soccer World Cup to be held in France it is estimated that attendances will generate in the region of US$60 million. The final match alone will bring in a little over US$4 million (Nicholls, 1997). At the World Athletic Championships to be held in Athens in 1997, prizes of US$100,000 are guaranteed to world record breakers. These are huge sums of money by any standard. Atlanta, in its bid to secure the XXVIth Olympiad, spent US$7 million, while Athens' failed bid cost the city US$22 million (Broom, 1994). For television rights to Sydney in 2000 and the Salt Lake City Winter Games of 2002, NBC has contracted to pay US$1.25 billion, and US$2.3 billion for the American rights to the Summer Games of 2004 and 2008 and the Winter Games of 2006 (Jennings, 1996). As we move toward the twenty-first century, we note a growing symbiosis between sports cultures and the values of commerce.

Sport tourism, as we have shown throughout this book, has become an increasingly significant niche tourism market. Around one in four to one in five holiday takers can be considered sport tourists; that amounts to a fifth, or more, of the market (see chapters 1 and 5). There are few definite statistics available for sport tourism's market value since it is rarely separated from general tourism, but a conservative estimate for the United Kingdom identifies the sector to be worth in the order of UK£3 billion (US$4.5 billion) (see chapter 5). In one of the few studies focused on sport tourists themselves, Nogawa, Hagi, Suzuki, and Yamaguchi (1995) estimated that Japanese visitors to the 1994 World Cup in the United States spent US$900 million directly, and perhaps as much as US$1.8 billion indirectly. If our estimates for the United Kingdom are assumed to be reasonable, and 10 percent of all tourism is sports-related tourism, then in global terms the niche tourism market in 1992 was worth in the order of UK£18.6 billion (US$27.9 billion), based on the World Tourism Organization's statistics of international tourism receipts (Savignac, 1994). We have no comparable estimates for the part tourism plays in generating sport spending, but it is assumed that this is also significant.

Previous chapters have described the many multifaceted connections between sport and tourism and discussed important issues arising from the links between them. In terms of popular participation and for many commercial providers, sport and tourism have become inextricably linked, yet only recently have these links begun to be documented (De Knop, 1990;

Jackson & Glyptis, 1992; Kurtzman & Zauhar, 1993; Redmond, 1991; Standeven & Tomlinson, 1994; Weiler & Hall, 1992). This book's analysis of their growing interdependence has attempted to reveal the significance of the sport-tourism relation and identify the key opportunities and problems emerging from greater integration.

The purpose of this concluding chapter is to summarize these opportunities and problems in the context of our contemporary situation, and draw from this review implications that will raise the level of consciousness about prospects for the future of sport tourism. We believe it is important to review extant opportunities and problems, since changes in the future are rooted in existing social conditions and people's efforts to reshape these conditions to fit their vision of what sport tourism should be. As Coakley (1990) points out in his discussion of sport,

> This means the future of sport will not just happen according to some predicted pattern. Instead, it will be shaped by people making choices about what they want sport to be in the future. Those choices will be limited by existing social conditions and guided by people's perceptions and evaluations of what sport is today. (p.370)

This situation we find equally the case for our predictions of the future of sport tourism.

In this chapter we will, therefore, do two things. First, we will summarize the position of sport tourism today through a discussion of the main themes and key issues that have permeated our book so far. Second, we will identify the changes we believe can realistically be expected as sport tourism moves into the twenty-first century.

Sport Tourism Today: A Summary

Throughout history people have traveled for a variety of purposes—for survival, as religious pilgrims, to explore, to trade, to fight, and to educate themselves. But travel alone does not make tourism. The pursuit of pleasure is an essential component—and this requires freedom from obligations such as work and an adequate means of support to indulge in travel. Transport networks, however primitive, are also essential. These conditions have existed for centuries, and in chapter 1 we traced the earliest forms of sport tourism to the ancient Olympic Games in Greece more than two millennia ago.

However, sport tourism as we know it today really began to emerge in the latter half of the nineteenth century. The industrial revolution, along with the development of comparatively inexpensive transportation and the rise of the middle classes, created the social conditions that gave birth to mass tourism (Theobald, 1994). Just as people traveled from place to place for pleasure so, too, they took part in day-to-day activities but gave them a new meaning, transforming them into sports. Our outline of different sports in chapter 1 was admittedly selective, but it demonstrated that the interaction between sport and tourism that we see in the modern world has in fact been in evidence for close to two centuries.

In the 1950s, as an outcome of the Second World War, the advance in aircraft technology led to the development of the jet engine and an increasingly viable commercial airline industry. Faster, and relatively cheaper, long-distance travel stimulated the development of the package tour and the growth of international tourism. In the context of a broadening tourism market, sport tourism has expanded and become increasingly important and widespread (Holloway, 1994; Ogilvie & Dickinson, 1992; Smith & Jenner, 1990; Weiler & Hall, 1992).

Throughout this book we have contended that neither sport, tourism, nor sport tourism can be adequately described as industries, for they are more than this. Like Davidson (1994), we argue that tourism should be viewed as a social phenomenon, an experience or a process involving people. And we say the same about sport.

Since sport, tourism, and thus sport tourism can have different meanings for different people, and no universal definitions have yet been adopted, it is not easy to define precisely our area of interest. The wide definitions we have used (see chapter 1) are legitimated by the diverse models of sport, tourism, and sport tourism that have developed around the world as a result of the process of value differentiation. In chapter 2 we examined analytically the nature of these experiences in order to construct a model of the sport-tourism interaction.

The three dimensions of the nature of sport that led us to define it as a cultural experience of physical activity are (1) it needs to present an environmental or interpersonal challenge, (2) it needs conditions imposed upon that challenge, and (3) the challenge, conditioned by its equipment, rules, and conventions needs to demand a physical response (cfr. Haywood, 1994) (see chapter 2).

As with sport, tourism can be identified as a cultural experience, but of place not activity. MacCannell (1976, 1996) maintains that the experience of the destination needs to be an authentic interaction with the place. Sport tourism thus becomes a cultural experience of physical activity tied to a cultural experience of place. This definition led us to propose a two-dimensional typology of the nature of sport tourism. In terms of the sport experience dimension, this took account of the nature of the environmental or interpersonal challenge present. For the tourism dimension, it took into account the natural or man-made resources that define the nature of the place experience. Combining these dimensions produced a grid of eight segments within which different sport tourism experiences were located (see chapter 2). It is our contention that although the sport activities and touristic locations may shift, sport tourism will continue to be based on a two-dimensional experience of physical activity tied to an experience of place.

As well as offering a typology of the nature of sport tourism, we have provided a typology of sport tourists based on the relative importance of sport within their touristic experience (see chapters 1 and 3), and a model of the sport-tourism relation (see chapter 1).

Rather than continue to review each chapter separately, we will use a theme-based approach for the remainder of this summary. This enables us to bring together commonalities that can be identified in different chapters in order to provide a more comprehensive perspective on contemporary sport tourism.

Four Main Themes

Four main themes have permeated this book:

- increased participation in diversified provision, though sport tourism for *all* is far from a reality;
- the need to maximize the benefits and minimize the disbenefits of the economic, sociocultural, environmental, and health impacts of sport tourism;
- missed opportunities that have resulted from the discrete administrative and policy communities of sport tourism; and
- conflicts in interests and values, in the role of state departments, and in the management of the sport-tourism relation.

We will deal with each theme in turn.

Growth, Diversification, and Democratization of Sport Tourism

A main emphasis throughout this book has been the growth of sport tourism, and the potential for continuing development, from the intensifying symbiosis between sport and tourism. Almost every chapter contains descriptive examples drawn from around the world, both general and specific, which demonstrate ways in which tourism has been increasingly generated via sport. We are now at the point where approximately a fifth to a quarter of all holiday taking has some element of sporting activity associated with it.

More limited but nevertheless significant examples have been detailed, predominantly in chapter 4, where activity holidays and even holiday activities can be a way of bringing people into the sports experience, some for the first time and in a one-off situation, others in a more sustained way. Thus tourism can be identified as a catalyst for sports development.

Our review of the ways in which sport has been used in the development of tourism (see chapter 3) concluded that just as sports participation and tourism are diversifying in terms of activities, destinations, and accommodation types, so the sport tourism market profile is becoming increasingly diverse. In chapter 1 we outlined economic, political, and attitudinal changes in the twentieth century that created the conditions that encouraged participation in sport tourism and favored democratization.

However, not everyone has the same opportunities to participate, even in the most developed economies, as we showed in chapter 6. Nor is every sport available in accessible touristic settings. Moreover, different regions and countries experience different impacts, be they positive or negative, as a result of sport tourism. Thus, we must exercise caution in our claims about the democratization of sport tourism. Growth is indisputable in terms of the number of participants. Diversification is equally incontrovertible in terms of the number and range of sport and destination experiences now available. Democratization is beginning to be evident as a result of diversification (Morgan, 1998). But we cannot yet support a claim that sport tourism is for all. Most people are not tourists, let alone sport tourists. They are subsistence agriculturalists in Africa, Latin America, China, and India (MacCannell, 1996). And the trends we have noted in chapter 9 toward market-based mixed economies and away from public investment and welfare, particularly in "trivial" areas such as sport or tourism, would indicate that sport tourism will remain the privilege of a minority of the world's population.

Maximizing Benefits, Minimizing Disbenefits

Although in part II of this book we confirm the emergence of significant mutual impacts between sport and tourism, there is no guarantee that these will only be positive, and there is no unanimity as to how their interrelationship is to be understood or managed. For example, the evidence supporting the benefits to quality of life in general, and to health in particular, from an increased level of physical activity whether at home or away from home cannot now be ignored (see chapter 8). Yet the case for a positive contribution to health from a relationship between sport and tourism must be seen in the context of potential disbenefits from inadequately planned or unwisely undertaken activity.

Early initiatives linking sport and tourism were often predicated on the grounds of positive economic value, although this was largely speculative since research on the economic impact of sports-related tourism was, and remains, relatively weak (Jackson & Glyptis, 1992) and some large-scale projects have turned out to be overambitious (see chapter 5). But of all the driving forces that have sourced the increasing significance of the sport-tourism relationship, economic interest is arguably the most powerful.

Of only slightly less importance though, the environmental and sociocultural impacts we have discussed in chapters 6 and 7 were shown to be similarly two-edged. The positive opportunities were potentially offset by negative pressures.

Nevertheless, from the evidence we have accumulated there is ample confirmation of the increasing importance of an integrated approach to sport tourism if the benefits are to be maximized.

Cooperation Between Sport and Tourism Infrastructures

We have distinguished between the touristic use of sport as a special sector of tourism and the opportunities for using touristic experiences of sport as a way of developing and furthering interest and expertise in sport. These processes may be very different given the common separation of the two sectors within the leisure industry and the lack of coordination between them. This disconnection was the central discussion of chapter 9.

Although the evidence is limited and somewhat patchy, it is sufficient to support the market-place, community, and individual benefits that can arise from the interaction between sport and tourism (see particularly chapters 5 and 8). Yet at the institutional, as well as the governmental, level there are few examples of integration. Administrative infrastructures remain largely discrete and thus policy coordination is rare although some examples of growing collaboration have been cited (see chapter 9). The idea of joint marketing is already being exploited by the commercial sector, though this may well be driven by the chase for economic gain rather than based on sound market research.

Both sport and tourism can be viewed as mixed subeconomies depending upon public, private, and voluntary sector organizations. But here differences between sport and tourism are evident. For tourism, the private, commercial sector is all-important, increasing the "alternative," often specialized, touristic experiences that appeal to the heterogeneous market. Well-managed, even small, enterprises have their place, and policy has been developed from a standpoint of "production," providing jobs and income for local residents.

With sport, however, dependence upon highly specialized facilities, many of which are costly in capital, revenue, and resource terms, has led to market failure and the argument for public sector intervention. Traditionally, sport has been viewed as an area of social consumption and public provision, and much of it has been seen as an extension of welfare policy (Richards, 1995).

In terms of economic organization then, sport tourism, as a distinct sphere of operation, demands close cooperation between sectors of the economy that have, until now, been rooted in different ideological bases (see chapter 9). However, government downsizing, an almost global response to the state of world economies, and budget deficits are leading to public disinvestment in the leisure industry. Thus sport as well as tourism is becoming increasingly privatized and fragmented, and aspects that remain in the public sector must maximize their income and minimize their expenditure. The political, organizational, and value differences at the roots of the different communities (public and private) indicate the problems that lie ahead in attempting to develop trans-institution and trans-system partnerships if the integration of sport tourism is to be more functional.

Conflicts of Interest

Conflicts of interest are now nowhere more acutely focused than in sport tourism's use of the environment (see chapter 7). But this was not always so. Witness the origins of the national park system in the United States, the model followed by many other nations. Yellowstone National Park was created in 1872 for people to visit and enjoy. According to Plog (1994),

> Tourism, as an alternative to commercial development, is a message so powerful that billions of tax dollars in the United States have been poured into acquiring lands, developing them and managing their use—all for the benefit of people who travel. (pp. 46-47)

Designating areas for tourism has been a way to protect the environment, the best alternative to heavy industrial development (Plog, 1994). But Plog goes on to note the new emphasis on profit motives (referred to in chapter 9) and the way in which "large corporate conglomerates now run many public tourism facilities worldwide" (p. 47). Thus conflicts are not limited simply to the effects of sport tourism on the physical environment; they also occur between private market mechanisms and public regulations.

There are many tensions. The need, and the desire, to achieve commercial gains, coupled with the growing popularity of outdoor sporting activities, serves to increase the concentration of sport tourists in some areas. And as the number of participants increase, conflicts arise between recreation enthusiasts and the local population, and between different sports groups (see chapters 6 and 7).

Conflicts between the public in general and private developments, between sport tourists and their hosts, and among sport tourists themselves are by no means confined to environmental concerns. Discussion in chapter 6 included the potential destruction of the sociocultural environment and the opposition of some local communities to the intrusion of sport tourists.

We have identified traditional values being sustained alongside new values, which helps to account for the conflict of interests represented by different understandings of sport tourism. We described, for example, the situation where environmental protectionists were negatively perceived by those who sought improvements in transport and access to enable more people to enjoy countryside recreations. We also noted instances where the globalization of sport tourism may be held in part responsible for the erosion of cultural differences.

Two Key Issues Needing Policy Attention

From these four main themes we derive two key issues for policy attention, namely, increasing accessibility while ensuring sustainable development and managing the process of integration.

Increasing Accessibility While Ensuring Sustainable Development

It is of fundamental importance to recognize that enjoyment of sport and tourism is more than just a matter of personal choice. Many factors influence people's behavior, such as age, gender, social and marital status, family responsibilities, education, income and wealth, geographical location, personal interests and abilities, or disability to name but a few.

Although more people in the most affluent countries have become more advantaged in terms of choice, other populations within those same countries, and even more in less developed economies, have been put at greater risk. Thus, inequality in the provision of sporting opportunities—that is, that they are provided mainly to a privileged few—remains an issue of global significance. In spite of the enormous growth and increasing diversity of sport tourism, which has been a main theme of this book, it has been equally plain that sport tourism for *all* is far from a reality. Both the increase in participation and provision have been shown to touch only a small privileged fraction of the world's population. Given the benefits to be derived from participation, both personal and public, particularly in terms of improved quality of life, equity demands access to sport tourism by less privileged classes. Yet this raises the contingent problem of sustainability.

As more and more of the earth's finite resources are used up, and as aspirations of increasing numbers of people become elevated, the moral desire for equity places a premium on sustainability. As more people trample over vulnerable areas of the earth's surface in search of their ultimate sport touristic experience how can resident, often poor, communities survive? As resources diminish how can quality of life be ensured even for the majority, let alone for all?

This is not to say that sport tourism can offer any solution to such global problems; indeed, rather the reverse is true since it has the potential to exacerbate them. But given appropriate international regulations and responsible management, the downside of the sport-tourism relation can, indeed must, be controlled, and this urgently. We have included examples in this book of operators who take careful precautions not simply to limit environmental damage but, by using local services, to enhance the economic benefits visitors bring to an area. Although the number of responsible enterprises is growing and the public is generally more environmentally conscious, with some people advocating greater regulation both on a national and international scale (Culligan, 1990), we identify increasing access while ensuring sustainable development as a key global issue that demands expert management.

Managing the Process of Integration

We have identified examples of coordination, even the beginnings of integration, in restricted pockets of sport and tourism in different parts of the world. In the main, the motivation to develop sport tourism has been rooted in economic advancement—tourism is the world's largest industry and sport tourism is a growing specialization within it. Countries large and small, new and old, seek to develop their tourism especially in terms of inbound international visitors, but also on a domestic scale.

Managing the economy is a matter for governments, increasing the inflow and the internal generation of wealth, while controlling the outflow. In a small way the balance between the inflow and outflow of tourism revenues can work to the advantage of the poorer, less privileged national economies. Since they attract more tourist revenues than they expend, this contributes positively to their balance of payments. Other countries—for example, Britain and Belgium—actually see more money leaking out of the system through international tourism than comes into it, so increasing domestic tourism is vital to their national economies. Yet while economic growth is a national aspiration, such growth needs to be long-term for it to be beneficial. Thus sustainability is again the significant issue.

The potential opposition between growth and sustainability indicates the need for state interest. However, state intervention in market economies is sensitive and politically value-laden. Safety and quality control are usually seen as less controversial state roles, yet even in these vital aspects few states in the past have intervened. Examples of administration and policy making in recent years, however, have begun to take issues such as licensing seriously. Where formerly almost any individual could establish a sport touristic business enterprise and sell it to anyone who would pay the requisite cost, standards of public safety have demanded the imposition of regulations, and the more discerning market has required more consistent and guaranteed levels of quality. Only at the state level can legislation be effected to ensure such measures.

As long as the administration of sport and tourism remains fragmented, legislation is likely to be less effective, affecting some organizations but not touching others. Managing any useful form of integration between sport and tourism depends as much upon the organization of government administration as upon the will of those involved in delivering the experiences. Indeed, ensuring effective delivery in a global marketplace calls for transnational levels of activity. We can see the beginnings of this within the European Community with the establishment of multi-interest commissions charged with policy development. Yet these are fraught with major problems of political and social significance. The multiplicity of organizational infrastructures involved at national, let alone international levels, creates a highly sensitive space within which negotiations have to take place (Botterill, 1992). Any level of coordination, partnership, or, ultimately, integration is therefore likely to meet resistance. Administrative structures must be tackled first for any positive change to occur, and it is the government that has to establish the framework within which both sport and tourism operate. We now explore the future of sport tourism.

Future Trends

To develop a vision of sport tourism in the twenty-first century, two starting points are needed. First, we need a perception of what contemporary sport tourism is. This has been summarized in the first part of this chapter. Second, we need to look at the changes we can expect in the conditions of our social world, because these form the milieus that will influence the future of sport tourism.

The Changing Social Context

In this part of the chapter we identify five aspects of society wherein the most marked changes likely to affect sport tourism are expected, namely, population, globalization, urbanization, economic influences, and technology.

Population

This has been described as one of the most far-reaching changes taking place in our modern world (Giddens, 1993). Improvements in medicine and hygiene have increased longevity in most countries, although large disparities still exist. At the beginning of this century there were 1.5 billion people in the world (Giddens, 1993). By the end of the century the World Bank expects the world population to reach 6.5 billion (Giddens, 1993). In 1998 world population will grow by 81 million to 5.93 billion. India alone will have another 20 million mouths to feed (The Economist, 1997). Considering that a century ago there were only 1.5 billion people in the world, this represents growth of staggering proportions (Giddens, 1993). The fastest growing countries in the early part of the twenty-first century are expected to be China, India and Pakistan, Iran, Nigeria, Brazil, Indonesia, Mexico, and the Philippines. Growth, which is exponential, makes a demand on world resources, many of which are finite. More than this, growth is much faster in the poorer countries of Asia, Africa, and Latin America than in most industrialized countries due to a rapid drop in mortality with the more recent introduction of modern medicine. This results in two situations. First, poor countries are destined to become relatively poorer since their level of investment and resources cannot keep up with their population increase. Second, the age distribution in poor countries is very different from the industrialized rich countries. In the latter, only about a quarter of the population is under 15 years old, whereas in Mexico, for example, 45 percent is in this age group, placing a further burden of support on an already poor country (Giddens, 1993).

It seems inevitable that the disparity between rich and poor countries can only increase. Tourism, including sport tourism, is one way for poor countries to earn much needed foreign currency; but there are attendant ethical problems to be addressed (see the next section on globalization).

Age distribution within a population is also relevant to our discussion of sport tourism. In most industrialized countries the population is described as aging; that is, the average age of the population is rising. In Britain in 1800 the average (median) age was thought to be as low as 19 years of age. By the year 2000 it is expected to be 35 (Giddens, 1993). In 1980, 9.51 percent of Canada's population was age 65 and over; by 2030 the proportion is expected to rise to 22.39 percent. Figures for other industrialized countries show similar increases: the United States in 1980—11.29 percent, by 2030—19.49 percent; Japan in 1980—9.10 percent, by 2030—19.97 percent; Germany in 1980—15.51 percent, by 2030—25.82 percent (Giddens, 1993). Several implications for sport tourism can be drawn from this change.

Sport tourism, like sport, is predominantly an experience of those under 40, although the profile may be changing (see chapter 2). Reducing the age of retirement can create increased leisure time while people are still active. Moreover, as older people become a larger proportion of the population they gain more political influence. This has been particularly noticeable in Canada, where for example "elderhostelling" has become a popular form of tourism. But retirement can also involve loss of income and loss of relationships—two further factors that will influence the future of sport tourism in the twenty-first century.

Globalization

In 1928 when the Oxford Dictionary first appeared, it described the adjective "global" as rare (Briggs, 1994). Forty years later Marshall McLuhan coined the term "global village" in his co-authored book *War and Peace in the Global Village* (McLuhan & Fiore, 1968). "Global" and "globalization" are now in common parlance generally used to indicate the increasing interdependence of world society (Giddens, 1993). In spite of many formerly colonized nations regaining their independence, the process of interdependence has accelerated, primarily due to trade and the media (Giddens,

1993). One pertinent sport example was the boxing contest staged in London in 1986 between Frank Bruno and Tim Witherspoon. In order for American viewers to see it live in the early evening it actually took place after midnight, London time, and the signal for it to begin was given in New York not in London! (Briggs, 1994). Recently, Cushman, Veal and Zuzanek (1996) observed,

> A national leisure issue is seldom merely national any more. The air we breathe is polluted from faraway sources. An increase or decline in the value of the United States dollar in relation to the currencies of other countries has immediate implications for leisure expenditure, consumption and participation worldwide. (p. 254)

But it is not simply the interdependence of nations that is our concern. We need, too, to be aware that globalization has not proceeded evenly. Inequalities have persisted resulting in enormous disparities of wealth and living standards between countries. This divergence between rich and poor countries will increase (Giddens, 1993; Sage, 1994) and is especially relevant given the sport and tourist connections between them.

Urbanization

"Urbanization in the twentieth century is a global process" (Giddens, 1993, p. 566). Urban populations are growing faster than the world's overall population. In 1975, 39 percent of the world's population lived in urban localities. According to United Nations predictions, 50 percent will do so by the turn of the century, and 63 percent 25 years later (Giddens, 1993). And this process is not restricted to the industrialized countries. By 2025 the urban populations of Africa and South America will each exceed that of Europe (Giddens, 1993). At present more than 75 percent of Americans live in communities with populations of more than 2,500 people (Giddens, 1993).

Polarized views are expressed about the influence of cities on the quality of life of those who live there. Among its cities we usually find a country's most affluent and its most poverty stricken. Cities house economic and commercial centers, the arts, and built sport facilities. However, living in close proximity induces higher levels of violence and crime and poorer physical living conditions from pollution.

Many people have preferred suburban living on the outskirts of large cities. What became known as the "flight to the suburbs" reached its peak in America in the 1950s and 1960s, and as a result, the inner cities decayed (Giddens, 1993). One consequence of the growth of the suburbs has been the financial crises of large cities and of development programs created to alleviate their problems. Although the cities of Britain and the rest of Europe have not faced such serious financial problems as those of the United States, they have followed a similar pattern. Short of the injection of major public expenditure, an unlikely occurrence in the present economic climate, cities will have to rely on private investment and partnership arrangements between the public and private sectors to generate the improvements they need. American cities like Indianapolis, sometimes called "Sports City USA" (Law, 1993), led the way in partnerships in the 1960s and 1970s. Bamberger and Parham (1984) and Wilkinson (1989) note the city's appropriation of sport as a strategy for regeneration, a plan which involved downtown infrastructure improvements through joint public/private sector partnerships.

Economic Influences

Capitalism is an economic system based on the private ownership of wealth and market transactions of labor resources and products. In this system "the price mechanism is the pivotal mode of allocating labour, resources, outputs and incomes" (Dalton, 1974, p. 57). Communism, as an economic form, is based on centralized economic management that manipulates production through central planning. It rejects private ownership in favor of state control; thus the state, not the market, determines labor, resources, output, and incomes. Socialism, like communism, "presumes the idea of economic management" (Giddens, 1993, p. 667). In its dependence on strong centralized direction of economies, "pure" socialism is considered outdated (Giddens, 1993). Hence we see the socialist parliamentary party in Britain described as "New Labour," and in America the continued reduction of government involvement even under a Democratic president. That is not to forecast the disappearance of socialism in its concern for equality, community, and care. But it is to anticipate that in this present order, "there are no future alternatives to capitalism and liberal democracy, which have triumphed globally over all rival systems" (Giddens, 1993, p. 670).

The end of the 1990s is expected to be a period of economic expansion. In 1997 the world economy is forecast to grow at 4 percent, its strongest rate since 1988 (Fishburn, 1996). "More wealth will be created than in any previous year in history" (Fishburn, 1996, p. 9). It is anticipated that America's economy will break all previous records and even after seven years of healthy growth, economists confidently expect continued expansion with the budget expected to generate a large surplus by 2002 (Hale, 1996; Tyson, 1997). Britain's economy is forecast to grow faster than any major economy apart from Canada (Fishburn, 1996). In 1996 Canada ranked first in the United Nations Development Index, which measures the general quality of life across the world (Thorsell, 1996). European nations generally seem likely to be more concerned with monetary union, which may well restrict their economic growth. In May 1998 European governments will make decisions about which European countries will fix their currency exchange rates. From January 1st 1999 the first wave of fixed (irrevocably) exchange rages will come into force with the creation of the EMU, a new currency that will be accepted across identified countries of Europe and the world. This will constitute monetary union of the countries who adopt the EMU. "Africa's economic life will improve in 1997 . . . (but) this better economic news is still not going to stop most of Africa's 700m people getting poorer" (Smith, 1996, p. 89). Commentators on Africa expect the continent's stock exchanges to expand with new investors coming in to Africa's capital markets although there is a longer term nervousness about stability since just under half of Africa's 53 states are ruled by military or ex-military officers (Smith, 1996; 1997). In South Africa economic growth will come from exports with gross domestic product growth expected to reach 3.2 percent, ahead of Greece's at 3.0 percent, and Japan's at 2.2 percent but behind Australia's at 3.8 percent, and Iceland's at 5.3 percent (The Economist, 1997).

In spite of gross domestic product growth in China of around 9.5 percent, the incomes of many Chinese will fall (Miles, 1996). The gap between the richest 10 percent and the poorest 10 percent grew almost fourfold in 1995 and about a third of state-owned farms could not pay their workers (Miles, 1996). But if China's recent growth continues, it is forecast to become the world's second-largest economy soon after the turn of the century (Nye, 1996). Elsewhere in Asia, the economies of Taiwan, Singapore, Hong Kong, South Korea, and Malaysia will grow at nearly twice the pace of any European country in 1997 (Burton, 1996). However, financial crises arising from overvalued currencies and poorly controlled banks that became evident toward the end of 1997 in South-East Asia will continue through 1998, causing a slowdown in many countries. But within a couple of years many of Asia's most successful economies ". . . will be leaping forward again" (Markillie, 1997, p. 76).

In general, then, much of the world seems to be poised for a cycle of economic expansion as the century turns. This means that tourism will expand its position as the world's largest industry and that opportunities for sport tourism will continue to grow.

Technology

There are a vast number of material instruments that count as technology. We have selected just two as having the greatest potential influence on sport tourism in the next century: first, the airline business, and, second, computing and its associated features.

America deregulated its domestic airline market in 1978. Before the end of the century similar deregulation is expected to have occurred in Europe, making it possible for airlines to run services wherever they want within continental Europe. The deregulation of international services is now under way with the "open skies" agreement signed between America and Germany in 1996 (Carson, 1996). The effect will be to increase competition and reduce fares, thus increasing the possibility for longer-distance travel. Further fare reduction will be brought about by the development of larger, more efficient aircraft like the wide-bodied Boeing 777. As people's disposable incomes rise, and travel costs decline, air travel is expected to increase by 100 percent (from 1991) by the year 2010 (Boeing, 1991).

Computers and other computer-driven telecommunications continue to revolutionize the way we do things. In 1994 the Internet connected more than 2.2 million computers serving 25 million people worldwide (Browning, 1994). Two years later more than 35 million users were connected, and by early next century that number is expected to reach 300 million (Gates, 1996). But at present 75 percent of Web users live in North America (Gates, 1996). The commercial use of computers and the Web for buying and selling topped US$100 million in 1995. Soon after the turn of the century that figure is forecast to reach US$186 billion (Gates, 1996). Businesses of all types now use the Internet. With the development of "midband connections" in the immediate future, followed by the "broadband information highway" early next century, access and quality will improve. Given its characteristic as a network of networks, its potential for the international travel industry is enormous. Individual Web users can now book their holidays direct from home using the internet. American Airlines, for example, conducts last-minute auctions to sell off some of its unbooked seats. Travel services with websites can create their own database of people who show an interest in their product and, specifically for sport tourism for example, links can be facilitated from the sites of adventure tour operators to hiking or cycling clubs or from resort accommodations to trail managers.

Summary of Changing Societal Context

In summary we can state that the changing context in which sport, tourism, and sport tourism will develop over the next couple of decades will be one characterized primarily by polarization. Rich countries, and the richer people within all countries, are set to get richer, the poor relatively poorer. The two consequences will be to increase the disparity between the rich and the poor, and to increase the opportunities for the rich.

The interdependence of globalization is likely to exacerbate this situation as wealth defines power, and as transnational companies grow. The dominance of the industrialized countries will be further assisted by the internationalization of the media and the control this gives over information. Since there are few radical differences left between the political economies of much of the world, with no significant alternatives to capitalism and liberal democracy, we may expect only relatively minor differences of policy to pervade our universe. As Giddens (1993) has it, "the world is becoming more united" (p. 561). A period of boom in the industrialized countries as we approach the turn of the century will, in the inevitable cycle of economics, be followed by a recession—and given globalization it is doubtful whether any country will remain unaffected. How deep that depression will be, and when it will occur, is difficult to forecast.

With ageism (discrimination against people on grounds of their age) and sexism (discrimination on account of sex) increasingly outmoded if not illegal, the market for all kinds of opportunities will be broadened by the addition of people with adequate disposable incomes and leisure time to explore new activities.

Both urban and rural environments will need investment and conservation if they are to be sustained.

In spite of technological developments and the creation of wealth, many observers find it difficult to be confident of the long-term future. Our ecological and economic "world" is fragile, and men and women are unlikely to solve these problems, let alone produce a peaceful and fair world order.

We shall now examine the characteristics of the changes expected in sport, tourism, and sport tourism in the twenty-first century in the context of the changes we have outlined in society.

Changes in Sport

At the beginning of the last decade of the twentieth century, and writing primarily in the context of American society, Coakley (1990) reviewed various versions of what sport might be like in the year 2000. In his own assessment, "the turn of the century is not likely to bring major changes in the basic goals and rules of sport . . . the organization of sport and the content of the sport experience will remain much the same" (p. 374). This view is supported from a European perspective by Roberts (1994).

In more detail Coakley (1990) forecast that sport spectating would remain popular and that fans would form local and national organizations to represent their interests and so gain more control. High profile events such as the Olympics and major college sports would be promoted "for the purpose of attracting spectator interest and making money" (p. 382). Professional athletes would seek to improve their socioeconomic status, and typical American professional sports such as baseball would become more international due to media influences and improved transportation, according to Coakley. Hockey (ice), American football, basketball, and soccer, like baseball, would expand into international leagues.

At lower levels of sport involvement "there will be an increasing amount of diversity and participation" (p. 375). Much of this involvement Coakley (1990) expected to occur in "highly organized settings" (p. 378) with emphasis on learning to play "correctly." Roberts' (1994) discussion of emergent trends in sport in Europe predicted that increased participation would come mainly from "persuading existing participants to play more sports, or to take part in their current sports more frequently" (p. 123), rather than by increasing the number of participants among traditionally low-participant groups associated with age, sex, and socioeconomic status. He expected neither strong expansion nor decline in participation, but is in agreement with Coakley in foreseeing a greater structural differentiation among recreational sportists themselves, and between this group and professional participants. "There are likely to be clearer divisions between casual and serious players, and among the latter according to their particular sports and factions thereof" (Roberts, 1994, p. 123). In Roberts' view, converting more athletes to serious participation will be difficult due to a shortage of leisure time among those most likely to play.

Publicly funded sport programs Coakley (1990) expected would be cut in many communities in America, while the commercial aspects of sport would remain significant, particularly in the merchandising of sporting goods, events, and sponsorship. In his view, "the interests of contemporary capitalism will become more and more a part of sport" (p. 382). Coakley acknowledges the selectiveness of this trend when he says, "Sport, for those who can afford it, will offer a context in which socioeconomic status and knowledge can be displayed through appropriate patterns of consumption" (p. 378). A similar decline of public sector involvement was anticipated in Europe by Roberts (1994) with governments more likely to service the needs of young people and serious participants. Success for commercial operators would require providers to seek market niches rather than offering undifferentiated opportunities for all. Roberts attributed the rise of sport participation in Europe to the spread of prosperity, increasing the number of people able to pay user charges, transport costs, and equipment and clothing costs, and having holiday time and the cash to "go away" and pay for active recreation themselves.

Thus, expectations of what sport will be like 10, or 20, years from now are markedly similar in America and Europe. Given the influences of globalization this should not surprise us.

Changes in Tourism

Identifying future trends in tourism in North America in 1990, Mill noted structural changes in the population and the effect these would have. The increasing number of women working would result in families with more disposable income and both the means and the reason to take a holiday. The reduction in the size of the average household would also increase holiday potential. Mill expected that with more education (that is, more people graduating from college and, in general, staying in school longer) and an increasing disposable income, more people would be curious and have the means to travel. The increase in the number of middle and older age groups, combined with earlier retirement, is already changing the structure of the tourist market. Although working hours may not have reduced significantly in recent years, people are negotiating to increase their holiday entitlement. Thus, Mill foresaw an increased propensity for international travel.

From a European perspective, Cooper and Latham (1996) expect that "while the patterns of tourism remain relatively stable, the market itself is changing rapidly" (p. 29). They describe the market as "maturing" and consumers as "knowledgeable." In 1994 there were 531.4 million international arrivals in the world, accounting for a spend of US$335,780 million. Europe has the highest proportion of world tourism with 60 percent of arrivals and 50 percent of spend (Cooper & Latham, 1996).

Plog's (1994) assessment of the tourism cycle sees leisure travel in North America declining, due largely to tourists' disaffection with their destinations. At the same time, Europeans, Asians, and Latin Americans are increasing their rates of travel year on year (Plog, 1994). This anomaly Plog explains by reference to the effects of the Second World War and the way in which its influence deprived many outside of the United States of the wealth to travel. Thus, up to the year 2000, Plog expects total travel in the world to increase at healthy rates "because of the new travel binge occurring in Europe, the Far East and Latin America" (Plog, 1994, p. 50). But he expects two consequences. First, disenchantment will eventually affect these new travelers too: "Then they will also cut back on the amount of leisure travel they pursue" (Plog, 1994, p. 45). Second, overuse of some destinations by these new travelers will increase the pressure on the places and bring about resort destruction (Plog, 1994).

In America, the average length of trip has been decreasing since 1985, according to Plog (1994). At the same time as noting the European trend toward activity holidays like hiking and cycling, Usher, too, (1996) records the trend to shorter holidays: "Spaniards still go to the coastal resorts, but it's more likely to be for a week or two rather than the traditional month" (p. 47). Italians, and Germans too—among Europe's most avid travelers—likewise now take shorter breaks and make use of long weekends—signs of Plog's forecast happening.

In the context of influences on demand for tourism, it should be noted that the majority of the populations in the countries where population growth is expected to be greatest will have a comparatively small impact on the popularity of tourism, since few of those countries are in a position to generate outgoing tourists. However, as Mill (1990) notes, even if only a small proportion of Chinese, Indians, and Russians travel, their impact will be noticed. "The Russians Have Arrived" was a headline in *Time* magazine in 1996 in which Usher referred to the better-off traveling abroad with arrivals escalating at a rate of some 50 percent a year to many resorts in Italy, Spain, France, Cyprus, and Turkey (Usher, 1996).

But greater impact will be felt from increased participation by a wider variety of different people from the present tourist-generating countries, and by some present tourists, in particular early retirees and the most affluent, increasing the number and/or duration of their trips. In other words, there will be more tourism from the same or similar people.

Walkers in the Huayhuash range enjoy the descent to Lake Cannicero, a high-altitude 14-day trek with full portage in the Andes.

In more detail, Mill (1990) has identified five trends that he expects, given the scope of demographic, economic, and social changes:

1. Increased differentiation of demand—more specialized services needed for specific groups of individuals

2. Increased desire for firsthand experiences of active pursuits, adventure trips, and tourism connected with nature

3. Increased desire to make tourism a learning experience

4. Increased emphasis on tourism with health benefits related to fitness and wellness

5. Increased attention paid by tourists to planning the structure of their trips

Holloway (1994), writing from a European perspective, has also noted trends for the twenty-first century. He anticipates market growth, noting particularly the contribution of older people who are generally fitter and more adventurous than older people in the past, due to their educational experiences and specializing in sport when they were younger. This group will, therefore, be looking for more active holidays. The emphasis on physical fitness will further influence this demand. Greater awareness of the dangers of exposing skin to the sun will force tourists to reconsider the attraction of the traditional beach holiday (Holloway, 1994). Technical advancement in transport leading to reduced travel costs will both expand the market in terms of distance traveled and interest entirely new markets. Lifestyle changes will result in a trend toward shorter, more flexible, more frequent, and more self-directed holidays. In sport Roberts (1994) characterized this as the trend to individualization. The availability of computerized shopping, according to Holloway, could make travel agents redundant unless they become able to offer a skilled and knowledgeable counseling service.

Changes in Sport Tourism

Weiler and Hall's (1992) discussion of special interest tourism (which includes sport, adventure, and health tourism) makes a broad and brief forecast. Resulting from the demographic, economic, and technological changes in society, they expect special interest travelers to become increasingly sophisticated. Special interest tourism "will be driven by the demands of these tourists and by the opportunities and limitations of the cultural and natural environments on which special interest tourism depends . . . special interest tourism has an exciting and dynamic future" (Weiler & Hall, 1992, p. 204).

We divide our vision of the future for sport tourism into three parts, namely, what we expect in terms of the

- nature of the experience,
- participation, and
- infrastructure.

In this way we remain consistent with our basic model of the sport tourism experience and attempt to provide a comprehensive perspective on the phenomenon.

The Future Nature of Sport Tourism

The nature of sport tourism as we have described it (see chapter 2) will remain much the same. It will continue to be a two-dimensional cultural experience of physical activity tied to a cultural experience of place. We expect new sport forms to emerge as long as new physical challenges can be devised in the land-, sea-, and airscapes of our planet. But these will most likely be hybrids of present sport forms, in the same way as snowboarding developed from a combination of surfing and skiing, and sky surfing from sky diving and surfing (see chapter 4). We expect place experiences to expand and include the rise of new destinations in eastern Europe, Latin America, Africa, and Asia. Our typology of the nature of sport tourism does not limit the number of different sport forms, nor the geographical and cultural settings in which they are practiced, but it does provide an unambiguous framework against which to accept or reject some new activity as a form of sport tourism (see chapter 2).

For all the different forms that sport activities can take, they have one thing in common: they involve people, and those people take different roles. Spectators are vicarious participants who influence, but do not materially alter, the nature of the sport experience. We therefore consider the future of sport tourism spectating as a form of participation, rather than as a category of the nature of sport tourism itself.

The Future Participant in Sport Tourism

Sport tourists will increase in number and there will be increasing diversity in their profile and participation. Our view is supported by Algar (1988), Burton (1995), Churchill (1990), Holloway (1994), Jackson and Glyptis (1992), and Jolley and Curphey (1994).

As the tourist market itself broadens with the addition of new travelers from countries such as China, India, Russia, Africa, and Latin America (albeit only the most wealthy), the market for sport tourism will grow. But the addition of travelers from countries barely represented in present statistics is not the only growth we can expect. As Europeans, Japanese, other Asians, South Africans, and many others pursue leisure travel in increasing numbers, sport tourists, as a special segment of general tourists, will increase in number. More than this, their profile will become more diverse as new groups of people begin to travel.

We can expect more middle-to-older-aged tourists as this age group enlarges and finds it has both the time and the financial means to travel. Earlier retirement and more active generations will increase and diversify the sport tourism market. The shrinking family market, due in particular to the smaller number of children, is not expected to make a significant impact since families are not generally sport tourists, though smaller families might become so. However, the changing household structure with the expansion of adult-only and especially single households, a group already well represented among sport tourists, will further increase the market although some will be constrained by lack of leisure time.

The fitness boom and reduced public funding for health programs have increased people's consciousness of the links between physical activity and health. Apart from enjoyment, this will be the strongest motive force, especially for aging populations, that will increase individual participation in sport tourism (Ermisch, 1990; Morris & Collins, 1992).

New and enlarging markets will display new tastes and make new demands. Individualization is not new, but it has accelerated in recent years and has led to what Roberts (1994) calls the do-it-yourself sport movement. Robinett (1993), reporting on trends in the U.S. leisure market, noted that customers wanted to be treated as individuals in a custom-made world and that economic concerns related to value and intrinsic worth were of higher

Exodus

Older people will be a growing segment of the sport tourism market in the 21st century.

priority than loyalty. Generally better educated, more discerning participants will demand more tailor-made and specialized opportunities.

The traditional two-week or one-month holiday period will change. Flexible duration sports holidays (generally longer in duration) will be enjoyed by those with most time at their disposal. These will range from budget hiking and cycling safaris to long-haul tours with sporting experiences included for the more wealthy. Short duration trips of a weekend or five days will also increase. Weekend ski trips from Britain to mainland Europe are increasingly popular, and now one-day trips are on offer to Slovenia inclusive of two-hour flights each way. The Japanese are known for their international golfing weekends.

While specialization will characterize some sport tourists, others will choose multiactivity opportunities in club locations such as Center Parcs. The latter will be favored by many for their generally more budget-conscious provision and for the chance they provide to try out a number of new activities. Individuals with larger disposable incomes, however, will gain access to increasingly wide opportunities.

"Organized" groups will continue to be popular though the level of organization will vary. Groups of friends and families will sport tour together making their own private travel arrangements. Package tours, by definition more organized, will add sport opportunities both as novelty day options, such as white-water rafting during a visit to Nepal, or as more of a sport development program such as Kuoni's bowling holidays to South Africa, New Zealand, the Far East, and America. Sports clubs will continue to travel domestically, but also further afield internationally, to test their skills and combine social and tourist opportunities with their game; professional teams will do likewise. And professional players from countries all over the world will become increasingly visible as more of them sign contracts abroad. In turn, they will encourage fan spectators to travel. There will be a growth in the range of sports played in different countries with, for example, American and Australian codes of football increasingly popular internationally. Thus, sport tourism spectating will continue to be popular, encouraged by the addition of new sports, new teams, new stars, and new places to visit to see sport.

Technological developments that have arrived with the Internet may seem to indicate that "armchair travel" is around the corner. It has become possible to spend a whole holiday simply traveling (surfing) on the Net. However, for the active sport tourist no screen will deliver the kinesthetic satisfaction (the "feel-better" response) that comes from experiencing one's body in physical activity. Nor will any "virtual" activity replace the experience of "being there." Novak (1988) pungently describes how a visit to a big football game in America is enhanced through smell: air smelling of "soaked grass and warming sun, of shiny slick programs fresh with ink, new angora sweaters, popcorn, beer, cigars, plastic raincoats, coffee, peanut shells, mustard, hot dogs, the alkaline of new concrete" (p. 4). As yet, the Net cannot reproduce these sensations. And however interesting the people one meets on the Net, they will not be as interesting as those met on the beach or the mountainside!

The Future Infrastructure of Sport Tourism

As we have seen, the overlap of the infrastructure of sport and tourism demonstrates their shared needs (see chapter 2, tables 2.1, 2.2, and 2.3). Both require space and facilities, natural and man-made. Both need servicing by providers, administrators, organizers, leaders, and others. The new leisure genre of sport tourism, and in particular its increasing popularity, has implications for the infrastructure.

Expansion in the number and type of sport tourists will result in greater product segmentation. Planners and operators will need to deliberately gear the experiences they offer to very specific and separate markets and target those niche segments appropriately.

So far as producers and operators are concerned, the recognition of the sport-tourism relation suggests that vertical integration (i.e., where a company extends its activities from one service into offering an additional service) will increase, so keeping down costs. For example, activity operators will provide accommodations and may also provide the transport required to reach the destination, and accommodation providers will offer activities. This kind of market extension we can expect to result in the growth and popularizing of more club type organizations, creating larger corporations. However, the size, diversity, and polarization of the sport tourism market suggests that there will continue to be room for the quality small business specialist providing the marketing is right.

More participants in more venues will increase the demand for space and facilities. The growing popularity and availability of long-haul travel, often to less industrialized societies, can be seen from two perspectives. On the one hand, inbound sport tourism may improve the capacity of poor countries to develop. The opportunity to provide accommodations, goods, and services may generate employment and so strengthen their economy. On the other hand, unless local populations and services are used, and cultures and environments respected, sport tourism will simply exacerbate inequalities. But even where more ethical practices are employed, can we defend the use of water for golf course maintenance in Africa and the Middle East (see chapter 7), or the use of wood to produce hot water for tourists in Nepal (see chapter 6)? The prospect of, or the actual, deterioration of inner cities in industrialized countries has led some cities to construct new sports facilities and mount new sports events in already congested areas, and in some locations enormous stadiums and other venues remain underused. This suggests that future developments for sport, tourism, and sport tourism will need national and global administrative controls. As more controls are imposed on large-scale or eco-unfriendly developments, so smaller, more locally based enterprises will survive. Controlled growth of high-quality, intrinsically valuable opportunities is to be expected. As Sage (1994) so aptly puts it, "The objective should be to promote economic development compatible with social justice and environmental sustainability" (p. 17).

The four chapters in part II of this book demonstrated the consequences of sport tourism's interaction with the economy, the environment, the sociocultural milieu, and health. Impacts on the economy, the sociocultural and natural environment, and health have both potentially positive and negative outcomes. We expect the changes that have occurred in our global political and economic order to provide a worldwide context in which the private sector will be dominant, "producing" and delivering opportunities to the sport tourist. The marketing and merchandising of clothing and equipment will be energetically pursued as new participants engage in new activities in new places. Sage (1994) appraises the ethics of the manufacture of these goods. From his detailed research of the manufacturing conditions of some of the most eminent sporting goods corporations, he criticizes their practices:

> If we continue to consume products whose conditions of
> manufacture are known to be exploitative, unsafe or pain-

ful for those involved in its production, and harmful to the environment, we hurt ourselves; we throw off our ethical equilibrium in some unquantifiable way. (Sage, 1994, p. 17)

However, international interest in sustainable development has begun to engage the interest of the general public, international organizations, and governments. Ten years ago the concept was promoted by the World Commission on Environment and Development in its publication *Our Common Future* (Bruntland, 1987). This was followed in 1992 by the United Nations Conference on the Environment and Development signed by 160 countries and in 1995 by the World Summit for Social Development held in Copenhagen (Cushman, Veal, & Zuzanek, 1996). The pressing need to coordinate policies and strategies internationally will increasingly involve national governments and international agencies.

The Internet could become the answer to both educating people about sport tourism and the marketing of it. It has the potential to replace travel agents, covering all their functions more conveniently for the consumer, but it is more likely to expand sport tourism than contribute to its decline. A journalist, preparing for a visit from England to Michigan typed the word "Michigan" into the search engine he was using: it gave 12,000 replies (Diamond, 1995). He says,

> I finished up with as many guides as I needed to Michigan golf courses, Michigan fishing, Michigan hunting, Michigan forests . . . The Michigan Golf Course Association knows that the chances of a British travel agent bothering to stock brochures on each of the state's courses are minimal, but on the Net those courses have the same chance of getting discovered by a golfing traveller as any other attraction. (p. 2)

It is perhaps through the Net as well that the latent market can be contacted and interested in sports development.

Summary

This book has described the many multifaceted connections between sport and tourism. Our analysis of their growing interdependence has attempted to reveal the significance of their relation and identify the opportunities, problems, and prospects emerging from greater integration. Sport tourism has been identified as a significant and growing segment of the tourism industry. Unless participants, spectators, communities, providers, and ultimately governments become sensitive to the impacts of sport tourism, this increasingly popular phenomenon will destroy the very resources on which it depends—in particular, landscape, culture, and people.

Essentially, a more effective integration of the infrastructures of sport and tourism is urgently required if planning, management, operation, and training are to result in reaping the benefits available to both sport and tourism from their symbiosis. Sound research and professional training are vital to the maturing of the sport-tourism relation given its potential to enrich the quality of life in our global village.

References

Algar, R. (1988). Activity holidays a growing business. *Leisure Management, 8*(1), 37-38.

Bamberger, R.J.,& Parham, D.W. (1984). Leveraging amenity infrastructure: Indianapolis' economic development strategy. *Urban Land, 43*(11), 12-18.

Boeing Commercial Airplane Group. (1991). *Annual marketing report.* Seattle: Author.

Botterill, D. (1992). Working for change in tourism: Tourism concern, the first three years. In J. Sugden & C. Knox (Eds.), *Leisure in the 1990s. Rolling back the welfare state* (pp. 205-220). Eastbourne, Great Britain: Leisure Studies Association.

Briggs, A. (1994). The media and sport in the global village. In R. Wilcox (Ed.), *Sport in the global village* (pp. 5-20). Morgantown, WV: Fitness Information Technology.

Broom, E. (1994). Foreword. In R. Wilcox (Ed.), *Sport in the global village* (pp. xxi-xxvi). Morgantown, WV: Fitness Information Technology.

Browning, J. (1994). That damn'd explosive Internet. In D. Fishburn (Ed.), *The world in 1995* (pp. 142-143). London: The Economist.

Bruntland, G. (1987). *Our common future.* Oxford, Great Britain: Oxford University Press.

Burton, J. (1996). Asian angst. In D. Fishburn (Ed.), *The world in 1997* (pp. 77-78). London: The Economist.

Burton, R. (1995). *Travel geography.* London: Pitman.

Carson, I. (1996). Open skies at last. In D. Fishburn (Ed.), *The world in 1997* (pp. 118-120). London: The Economist.

Churchill, D. (1990, September 22/23). A sense of adventure. *Financial Times Weekend,* p. vii.

Coakley, J. (1990). *Sport in society: Issues and controversies.* St. Louis: Times Mirror/ Mosby College Publishing.

Cooper, C. & Latham, J. (1996). Foreign affairs. *Leisure Management, 16*(2), 28-30.

Culligan, K. (1990). A less harried future. *Leisure Management, 10*(2), 28-30.

Cushman, G., Veal, A.J., & Zuzanek, J. (1996). *World leisure participation: Free time in the global village.* Wallingford, Great Britain: CAB International.

Dalton, G. (1974). *Economic systems and society.* Harmondsworth, Great Britain: Penguin.

Davidson, T.L. (1994). What are travel and tourism: Are they really an industry? In W. Theobald (Ed.), *Global tourism* (pp. 20-26). Oxford, Great Britain: Butterworth-Heinemann.

De Knop, P. (1990). Sport for all and active tourism. *World Leisure & Recreation, 32*(3), 30-36.

Diamond, J. (1995, May 28). Have net, will travel. *The Sunday Times—Travel Supplement*, p. 2.

Ermisch, J. (1990). *Fewer babies, longer lives.* York, Great Britain: Joseph Rowntree Foundation.

Fishburn, D. (1996). 1997. In D. Fishburn (Ed.), *The world in 1997* (p. 9). London: The Economist.

Gates, B. (1996). The Internet grows out of nappies. In D. Fishburn (Ed.), *The world in 1997* (p. 115). London: The Economist.

Giddens, A. (1993). *Sociology.* Oxford, Great Britain: Polity Press.

Glendinning, M. (1996). Kings of sport. In D. Fishburn (Ed.), *The world in 1997* (p. 126). London: The Economist.

Hale, D. (1996). America's amazing strength. In D. Fishburn (Ed.), *The world in 1997* (pp. 64-65). London: The Economist.

Hawkins, D.E. (1994). Ecotourism: Opportunities for developing countries. In W. Theobald (Ed.), *Global tourism* (pp. 261-273). Oxford, Great Britain: Butterworth-Heinemann.

Haywood, L. (1994). Community sports and physical recreation. In L. Haywood (Ed.), *Community leisure and recreation* (pp. 111-143). Oxford, Great Britain: Butterworth-Heinemann.

Holloway, J.C. (1994). *The business of tourism.* London: Pitman.

Jackson, G.A.M., & Glyptis, S.A. (1992). *Sport and tourism: A review.* Unpublished report to the Sports Council, London.

Jennings, A. (1996). *The new lords of the rings.* London: Simon & Schuster.

Jolley, R., & Curphey, M. (1994, November 10). Agents race for niche markets. *The Times*, p. 35.

Kurtzman, J., & Zauhar, J. (1993). Research: Sport as a touristic endeavour. *Journal of Tourism Sport, 1*(1), 44-76.

Law, C.M. (1993). *Urban tourism.* London: Mansell.

MacCannell, D. (1976). *The tourist: A new theory of the leisure class.* London: Macmillan Press.

MacCannell, D. (1996). *Tourist or traveller?* London: BBC Educational Developments.

Markillie, P. (1997). Tigers: The crouch before the leap. In D. Fishburn (Ed.), *The world in 1998* (p. 74). London: The Economist.

Miles, J. (1996). A difficult year for Mr Jiang, his friends and neighbours. In D. Fishburn (Ed.), *The world in 1997* (pp. 71-72). London: The Economist.

Mill, R.C. (1990). *Tourism: The international business.* Englewood Cliffs, NJ: Prentice Hall.

Morgan, D. (1998). Up the Wall: The impact of the development of climbing walls on British Rock Climbing. In M.F. Collins & I.S. Cooper (Eds.), Leisure Management Issues and Applications (pp. 255-262). Wallingford, Great Britain: CAB International.

Morris, J.N., & Collins, M.F. (1992, Jan/Feb). Health through exercise: A law of nature. *World Health,* pp. 6-7.

Nicholls, P. (1997, March). How much? *Sports,* pp. 52-54.

Nogawa, H., Hagi, Y., Suzuki, S., & Yamaguchi, Y. (1995, August). Measuring Economic Impact of Sport Tourists During the 1994 World Cup USA: A Case Study of Japanese Sport Tourists. Paper presented at the 18th Universiade 1995, Sport and Man: Creating a new vision. Fukuoka, Japan. In Proceedings FISU/CESU Conference, pp. 152-153.

Novak, M. (1988). *The joy of sports.* Lanham, MD: Hamilton Press.

Nye Jr., J.S. (1996). Uncle Sam's Asian worries. In D. Fishburn (Ed.), *The world in 1997* (pp. 82). London: The Economist.

Ogilvie, J., & Dickinson, C. (1992). The UK adventure holiday market. EIU Travel and Tourism Analyst, 3, 37-50.

Plog, S.C. (1994). Leisure travel: An extraordinary industry facing superordinary problems. In W. Theobald (Ed.), *Global tourism* (pp. 40-54). Oxford, Great Britain: Butterworth-Heinemann.

Redmond, G. (1991). Changing styles of sports tourism: Industry, consumer interactions in Canada, the USA and Europe. In M.T. Sinclair & M.J. Stabler (Eds.), *The tourism industry: An international analysis* (pp. 107-120). Wallingford, Great Britain: CAB International.

Richards, G. (1995) Politics of national tourism policy in Britain. *Leisure Studies, 14,* 153-173.

Roberts, K. (1994). The role of leisure and recreational sport in Europe. In J. Mester (Ed.), *Sport sciences in Europe 1993—Current and future perspectives* (pp. 113-125). Aachen, Germany: Meyer & Meyer.

Robinett, J. (1993). The American way. *Leisure Management, 13*(10), 52-54.

Sage, G. (1994, July). Class, gender, and race and physical activities: Beyond the stadia, arenas, and natatoria in developed and developing countries. Paper presented at the International Society for Comparative Physical Education and Sport Conference, Prague, Czech Republic.

Savignac, A.E. (1994). Foreword. In W. Theobald (Ed.), *Global tourism* (p. vii). Oxford, Great Britain: Butterworth-Heinemann.

Smith, C., & Jenner, P. (1990). Activity holidays in Europe. *Travel and Tourism Analyst, 5,* 58-78.

Smith, P. (1996). Africa turns Asian. In D. Fishburn (Ed.), *The world in 1997* (pp. 89-90). London: The Economist.

Smith, P. (1997). The big men go. In D. Fishburn (Ed.), *The world in 1998* (pp. 85-86). London: The Economist.

Standeven, J., & Tomlinson, A. (1994). *Sport and tourism in South East England.* London: South East Council for Sport and Recreation.

The Economist. (1997). *The world in 1998*. London: The Economist.

The Economist. (1996). *The world in 1997*. London: The Economist.

Theobald, W. (1994). The context, meaning and scope of tourism. In W. Theobald (Ed.), *Global tourism* (pp. 3-19). Oxford, Great Britain: Butterworth-Heinemann.

Thorsell, W. (1996). Why Canada's happier. In D. Fishburn (Ed.), *The world in 1997* (p. 69). London: The Economist.

Tyson, L. (1997). How bright is bright? In D. Fishburn (Ed.), *The world in 1998* (pp. 66-67). London: The Economist.

Usher, R. (1996, September 2). Some don't like it hot. *Time,* pp. 46-49.

Weiler, B., & Hall, C.M. (Eds.). (1992). *Special interest tourism.* London: Belhaven Press.

Wilkinson, J. (1989, November). *Sport and regenerating cities: Worldwide opportunities.* Paper presented at the Council of Europe International Conference, Lilleshall, Great Britain.

World Tourism Organization. (1997). Travel to Surge in the 21st Century. *World Tourist Organization News*, November, pp. 1-2.

World Travel and Tourism Council. (1991). Travel and tourism. The Economist, 12 October, p. 14.

World Travel and Tourism Council. (1992). The WTTC Report: Travel and Tourism in the World Economy. Brussels, Belgium: Author.

World Travel and Tourism Council. (1993). *Progress and priorities.* Brussels, Belgium: Author.

Index

A

Accommodations
  facilities for sport tourism by, 120-122,
    146
  history of, 31
  holiday camps, 31
  hotel holidays in, 103
  impacts on the natural environment,
    247-248
  motel development in, 31
Activity holidays (sport)
  economic value of, 176-179
  holiday sport activities, 12, 13, 103-111
  increase in, 6, 34-36
  participation in, 176-178
  sport activity holidays, 12-13, 88-103
Activity problems
  for obese people, 277
Administration
  coordinated approach to, 316
  defined, 295
  levels of infrastructure in, 296
Adventure sports
  holidays in, 94-95
  increase in, 94
Adventure tourism
  defined by Hall, 60
  increase in, 34, 240
AIDS
  camp for young people, 282
Air sports
  gliding, 135
  hang gliding, 135
  sky diving, 135
  sky surfing, 135
Air travel
  changes in, 30-31
Altitude
  sport tourists problems in, 276
Americas Cup
  economic impact of, 184-186

in Australia, 185, 212-213
in New Zealand, 228
socio-cultural impact of, 228
Ancient world
  sport tourism connections in the, 14-15
Argentina
  World Cup football
    economic impact of, 183-185
Artificial climbing walls, 135-136
Athletics (track and field)
  Europa Cup in, 186-187
Australia
  aboriginal culture for sport tourists
    in, 221
  activities popular in, 36
  administration of sport in, 302-303
  administration of tourism in, 302-303
  Americas Cup in, 184-185, 212-213
  employment created by sport
    tourism in, 212
  environmental guidelines for
    Sydney Games in, 263-266
  Great Barrier Reef in, 246, 277
  health tourism interest in, 273
  Olympic Games in Sydney, 154-155,
    263-266, 311-313
  sporting events generate tourism in,
    212
  sports in, 21, 26, 137, 143, 246
  violence at sporting contests in, 222
Austria
  environmental policies in, 254, 313
  rural tourism in, 211
  sports in, 211, 254, 261
  sport tourism positive impacts in, 211
Authenticity of tourist experience, 55, 215

B

Balearic Islands
  environmental protection in, 256
Ballooning
  popular in sports tourism, 36

Barbados
  administration of sport in, 305
  administration of tourism in, 305
  cricket in, 92
  sports tourism in, 305
Bare-boat chartering, 91
Baseball
  history of, 26-27
Belgium
  administration of sport in, 298-299
  administration of tourism in, 298-299
  environmental protection in, 262
  holiday sport programs in, 105
  regulations for mountain biking in,
    258-259
  Spa (the town of), 278
  sport policy in, 298-299
  sports in, 92, 251, 252, 258
Belize
  environmental policies in, 314-315
Bicycling. See Cycling
Board sailing, 135
Boat racing
  popular in sports tourism, 36
Body boarding, 91
Borneo
  sports in, 96
Bungee jumping, 95
Business
  tourism defined as, 11
              C
Camp programs
  sports in, 147
Canada
  activities popular in, 36, 242
  administration of sport in, 301-302
  administration of tourism in, 301-
    302
  day adventure centers in, 138-140
  disabled sport tourists provision in,
    282
  Olympic Games
    in Calgary, 146, 151
    in Montreal, 183
  outdoor activities popular in, 242
  sports in, 26, 36
Canary Islands
  cultural homogeneity in, 229

Capitalism
  defined, 335
Car. See Motor cars
Caribbean
  disbenefits of sport tourism in, 216
  spa and fitness tourism in, 279
  sports in, 91
Caving. See Speleology
Changes
  in economic systems, 335
  in social milieu, 332-338
  in sport, 338-339
  in sport tourism, 342-347
    the nature of, 342-343
    the participants, 343-345
  in technology, 336-337
  in tourism, 339-342
Charter air travel, 30
Chile
  sports in, 137
China
  golf in, 122
  hot springs as a tourist attraction in, 280
  importance of tourism in, 322
  martial arts in, 18
  national parks in, 257
  sports in, 280
Cities
  regeneration through sport in, 112-114,
    189-195, 335
Classification
  of adventure holidays, 60
  of special interest travel, 60-61
  of sport tourism, 62-66
Climatic conditions
  danger potential for sport tourism
    in, 276, 277
  importance for sport tourism of, 56
Climbing. See also Mountaineering
  eliminating danger of, 278
  environmental protection in, 260
  history of, 21-22
  walls, 135-136
Club formula holidays
  Center Parcs as, 102-103
  Club Med as, 100-102
Colonialism
  sport diffusion influenced by, 19

Conflicts of interest
    among sport tourists, 329
    between visitors and hosts, 329
Commercial sector. *See* Private sector
Communism
    a form of economic organization, 35, 296
Computers. *See* Internet
Congresses on sport tourism, 5
Connections between sport and
        tourism
in the Ancient World, 14-15
    in the Middle Ages, 16
    in the 19th– early 20th centuries, 18-20
    in the Premodern world, 17-18
    in the Renaissance, 16
Coronary heart disease
        physical activity prevents, 272
Cost-benefit analysis, 182
Cricket
    history of, 26-27, 214-216
    holidays, 92
    in Barbados, 92
    in India, 98, 214
    women's World Cup, 156-158
Cruise vacations
    activity holidays in, 106
Cuba
    sports in, 217
Cultural experience
    of sport, 48-49, 54
    of sport tourism, 49
    of tourism, 10, 49
Cultural homogeneity, 227-229
Cultural understanding, 214-215, 218-219
Cycling
    increase in, 89-90
    helmets prevent accidents in, 277
    history of, 24-25
    holidays in, 89, 106
    sponsored in Iceland, 284
    tours, 89
Czech Republic
    outdoor activities increasing in, 35
    Slet sport festival in, 98-99
    spas as a tourist attraction in, 280

D
Day Adventure Centers
    in Canada, 138-140

Democratization
    of sport, 28-34
    of tourism, 28-34
    of sport tourism, 308-309, 327
Denmark
    environmental concern in, 262
De-sportification of society, 33-34
Disabled sport tourists, 281-284
    barriers to participation for, 281
Diseases
    reduced by physical activity, 272, 274-
        275
Disney's approach to sport tourism, 84-
        87
Dragon boats
    development of, 123
    festival in Hong Kong, 122-124
Dress
    cultural standards of, 218
    for safety, 277-278
Dutch. *See also* Netherlands, The
    holidaymakers favorite activities,
        36

E
Economic
    forces,
        influence democratization, 28-29
    impact
        of Americas Cup, The, 185
        of Commonwealth Games,
            184
        of day visits, 178
        of Europa Cup, 186-187
        of events, 179-189
        of Olympic Games, 183, 196
        of sport, 170-171
        of sport tourism, 173-178
        of tourism, 172-173
        of Whitbread Round the
            World yacht race, 186
        of World Student Games, 190-191
Economy
    changes in, 335-336
    types of, 296
England. *See also* Great Britain and
        United Kingdom
    city regeneration from sport events,
        189, 190-191, 191-192

England *(continued)*
  cricket history in, 26
  cycling history in, 24
  economic impact
    of Europa Cup, 186-187
    of World Student Games, 190-191
  failed bid for the Olympic Games, 191
  football history in, 22
  golf history in, 24
  hiking history in, 25
  indoor ski center in, 141-143
  participation in incidental holiday
    sport, 38
  skiing history in, 21
  Snowdome, 141-143
  sport and tourism policies in, 309
  tennis development in, 158
  tennis history in, 23
  town regeneration from sport
    tourism in, 194-195
Environment(al)
  challenge in sport, 52
  conflicts of interest in, 329
  policies of control in, 313
  protection of, 237-240, 329
  protection measures
    hard instruments for, 253
    soft instruments for, 253-255
  threats identified to, 237
Ethics
  of sport tourism, 204, 217, 218, 221,
    346, 347
Europa Cup, 186-187
Europe
  Chinese martial arts in, 18
  a collection of nation states, 298
  disabled sport tourism
    exchange scheme in , 283
    provision for, 282
  ecology unit in, 258
  economic significance of sport in, 170-
    171
  golf courses in, 148
  major events support in, 181
  rural tourism in, 210-211
  Olympic Games in, 28
  Single Act, 297-298
  spa market in, 281

sport administration in, 298
  tennis history in, 23
  tourism administration in, 298
European Sports Charter, 8
Equestrian events
  popular in sport tourism, 36
Events
  stimulate sports development, 150-155
  visitors attracted to, 4, 179-189
Exercise. *See also* Fitness and Health
  appropriateness of, 277
Exodus adventure travel company, 94-95

F

Facilities
  sports development fostered by, 151-
    155, 160
  used to attract events, 114
  visitor attraction of, 179-180
Finland
  pesapallo in, 27
Fitness. *See also* Exercise and Health
  clinics, 103
  linked to physical activity, 274
Football
  history of soccer, 22
  World cup in, 112, 323
France
  activity tourism in, 35, 36
  administration of sport, 299
  administration of tourism, 299
  climbing walls in, 136
  cycling in, 4, 24, 36
  economic impact of tourism in, 176
  environmental policies in, 313
  health tourism interest in, 273
  holidays for the disadvantaged in, 226
  language laws in, 219, 228
  Olympic Games in Paris, 28
  professional qualifications in leisure
    in, 310
  spas combat disease in, 280
  sports in, 36, 136, 251
  sport tourism activities in, 36
  thalassotherapy in, 281

G

Germany
  active holidaymakers in, 35, 37-38
  activities popular in, 36

administration of sport in, 299
administration of tourism in, 299
health tourism interest in, 273
hiking history in, 25
holiday sport programs in, 106, 147
motivation for holiday travel in, 274
Olympic Games in Munich, 151
spa tourism in, 280
sport activity holidays in, 36, 176
sport cure holidays in, 103
sport holidays in, 104-105
sports in, 25, 36, 136
sport tourist maps in, 107
Gliding, 135
Globalization, 333-334
Golf
    environmental
        impact of, 248-249
        protection measures for, 258
    history of, 16, 23-24
    holidays, 92-93, 147-148
    The Masters, 113
Government involvement. *See also*
    Public sector and State
    decreasing interest in, 328
    infrastructure of, 297
    in leisure, 297
    in sport, 171, 295, 296, 297, 306
        in Australia, 302
        in Barbados, 305
        in Belgium, 298
        in Canada, 301
        in Europe, 171
        in France, 299
        in Germany, 299
        in Great Britain, 299-300
        in Portugal, 300
        in South Africa, 305
        in Spain, 301
        in Sweden, 301
        in The Netherlands, 300
        in the United States of America,
            303-305
    in sport tourism, 294
        in Barbados, 305
        in Belgium, 298
        in Canada, 301
        in France, 299

        in Great Britain, 300
        in Ireland, 310
        in Poland, 301
        in Portugal, 300
        in South Africa, 305
        in Spain, 301
        in the United States of America,
            305
    in tourism, 295, 296, 297, 306
        in Australia, 302
        in Barbados, 305
        in Belgium, 298
        in Canada, 301
        in France, 299
        in Germany, 299
        in Great Britain, 299-300
        in The Netherlands, 300
        in Poland, 301
        in Portugal, 300
        in South Africa, 305
        in Spain, 301
        in Sweden, 301
        in The Netherlands, 300
        in the United States of America,
            303-304
Grand Tour
    history of, 17
Great Britain. *See also* United Kingdom
    activity holiday makers in, 35, 37
    administration of sport, 299
    administration of tourism, 299
    climbing walls in, 136
    cycling history in, 24
    hiking history in, 25
    hooliganism in sport, 222-223
    ownership of land, 219
    sport on holiday in, 5
    sport tours from, 96
    violence among spectators, 223
Greece
    first modern Olympic Games in, 27
    sport and tourism in ancient, 14-15
    water sports in, 90-91
                    H
Halls of fame, 115
Hang gliding, 135
Hawaii
    sports in, 248

Health. *See also* Exercise and Fitness
  implications of sport tourism for,
      273-278
  linked to physical activity, 272, 273,
      278
  sport tourism's positive impacts on,
      273-275
  tourism market segments in, 273
Health farms, 278-279
Heritage
  damaged by sport tourism, 219, 220, 221
  maintained by sport tourism, 215
Hiking. *See also* Walking
  environmental protection measures
      in, 261
  history of, 25-26
Himalayas
  cultural impacts felt in the, 218, 221
  employment created by sport
      tourism in, 211
  environmental protection in, 221,
      260
  problems created by language in,
      219
  sports in, 93
Holiday resorts
  impact on the natural environment,
      246-247
Holiday sport activities
  independent, 107-111
  organized, 104-107
Hong Kong
  activities popular in, 36
  Dragon boat festival in, 122-124
Horse racing, 113
Hotels
  facilities for sport tourism in, 120-122
  health and fitness programs in, 278-279
Hot springs
  linked to sport tourism, 274, 278, 280
Humanistic perspective, 7
Hungary
  health tourism interest in, 273
  tourism commodifies local facilities
      in, 161

I

Ice climbing, 274
Iceland

cycling sponsored to combat disease
    in, 284-285
India
  cricket in, 96, 214-215
  sports in, 89, 94, 96, 137, 214-215
Indoor ski center, 141-143
Industrial revolution
  impact of, 18-20
Infrastructure
  connections between, 328-329
  economic indicator of, 178
  fragmented, 295
  improvements bring benefit to, 212
  of government, 297
  of sport, 66-68
  of sport tourism, 70, 295, 345-347
  of tourism, 68-70
International agencies, 347
International conferences, 239, 240
International Charter of Physical
    Education, 8
Internet
  use in sport tourism, 5, 32, 338, 345, 347
Ireland
  golf holidays in, 93
  sport tourism an economic policy in,
      310
Israel
  health tourism interest in, 273
  spa tourism promotion in, 279
  sports in, 137
Italy
  health tourism interest in, 273
  sports in, 96

J

Japan
  health tourism interest in, 273
  Olympic Games in, 261
  Seagaia complex in, 122
  spa tourism in, 279, 280
  sports in, 93, 137, 143, 144, 248, 261
  tourism policy in, 310
Japanese sport tourists, 35, 184, 274
Journal of Sports Tourism, 5
Jousting
  tournaments in, 16

K

Kentucky Derby, The, 113

Kite flying
    popular in sports tourism, 36

L

Lacrosse
    introduced to England, 18
La Manga
    golf in, 149-150
Land yachting, 92
Language
    cultural understanding of, 219, 220
    threatened by sport tourism, 228
Leisure swimming pools, 144-146
Le Tour, 150-151
Lodgings
    for athletes, 14
    for tourists, 31-32

M

Malta
    spa and fitness hotel in, 279
Man-made resources
    as an attraction, 84
    ski facilities in, 140-143
    sports development from visits to,
        140-146
    swimming pools in, 143-146
Market
    based economies, 296
    free, 296
    mechanisms, 294
Marketing
    sport tourism joint, 328
Maps
    of sport tourism routes, 107
Masterclass holidays, 92
Masters, The, 113
Mediterranean
    sports in, 91
Mexico
    Aztec ball players in, 16
    violence due to sport tourism in, 223
Morocco
    cycling sponsored in, 284
    sports in, 96, 137
Middle Ages
    sport tourism connections in, 16
Motivation
    for sport tourism, 273-274, 343
    for tourism, 274

for tourism in Japan, 280
    sports as, 174
Motor cars
    use of for leisure travel, 30
Motor sports
    popular in sports tourism, 36
Mountain biking
    development of, 134-135
    environmental impact of, 247, 249-250
    regulatory measures in, 258-260
Mountaineering. *See also* Climbing
    bodily conditions imposed by, 276
    environmental concerns in, 260
    history of, 21-22
Museums
    of sport, 115

N

Naghol ritual in Vanuatu, 215
National Parks
    benefit from tourism, 210-211
    in the United Kingdom, 258
    in the United States, 238, 257
    protection measures in, 257-258
Natural resources
    as an attraction, 83-84
    as a challenge, 134
    sports development from visits to,
        137-140
Nepal
    dress codes for sport tourists in, 218
    problems created by language in,
        219
    sports in, 91
    sport tourist impacts in, 219, 221
    sport tourism for the disabled in,
        283-284
Netherlands, The
    administration of sport, 300
    administration of tourism, 300
    environmental measures in, 256
    golf history in, 16, 24
    holiday and non-holiday-takers in, 224
    regeneration of cities, 144-146
    sports in, 144-146
    Tropicana, 144-146
    sport team tours in, 96
New York
    marathon in, 96-98

New Zealand
  Americas Cup, 229
  Commonwealth Games in, 185
  climbing walls in, 136
  cultural homogeneity in, 229
  economic impact of events in, 185, 186
  environmental protection measures
    in, 261
  Queenstown adventure capital of,
    108-111
  sport activity tourism in, 35
  sports in, 22, 134, 136, 137
  Whitbread Round the World Yacht
    race in, 186
Nineteenth and Early Twentieth
    Centuries
  sport tourism connections in, 18-20
Nonholiday time
  active sports in, 118-22
  passive sports in, 122-124
Norway
Olympic Games
  in Lillehammer
    economic impact of, 194
    environmental measures in, 256
  social impact of, 213, 214, 256
  skiing history in, 20-21
  supporters club, 115

O

Observers
  casual, 117-118
  connoisseur, 113-118
Olympic
  sports museum, 115-117
Olympic Games
  ancient, 14
  benefit to host nation of, 213
  bids to host the, 191, 213, 310-311, 311-313
  economic impact of, 183
  environmental concerns about, 263,
    263-265
  facilities aid sports development,
    146, 151
  history of modern, 27-28
  imitated by, 112
  modern, 27-28, 146, 151, 192-193,
    194, 212, 213, 256, 261, 263-266,
    311-313

  television rights for, 323
  a tourist attraction, 27, 182
Outdoor sports
  participation increasing in, 236, 237,
    239, 240-242

P

Pakistan
  sports in, 87
Participation
  in sport tourism increasing, 34-38
  limited to holidays, 158-159
Passive sport on holiday
  casual observers, 14, 117-118
  connoisseur observers, 13-14, 113-
    119
Physical activity
  combats disease, 274-275
  linked to heart disease, 272
  modern lifestyle antidote, 274
  risks in, 275-277
Physical education, 131-132
Place
  sense of, 58-59, 60-62, 194, 195
Placelessness
  of sport, 218, 229
Poland
  administration of sport, 301
  administration of tourism, 301
  spa tourism in, 280
Policies
  of control, 313-315
  of development, 308-311
  of ensuring sustainable develop-
    ment, 330
  of increasing access, 330-331
  revenue driven, 315
Policy
  defined, 296
  integration needs in, 316
  joint sport and tourism, 309
  leisure policy in, Europe, 298
  makers need to, 316
  making, 296
  role of government in, 296
  in sport tourism, 301
Political influences
  on travel, 32-33
Population

changes in, 332-333, 339
urban growth in, 334
Portugal
administration of sport, 300
administration of tourism, 300
holiday and non-holidaytakers in, 224
sports in, 93
Premodern world
sport tourism connections in, 17-18
Private sector
increasing interest in, 328
provider of sport tourism, 294, 328
responsible for leisure provision, 300
Professional
specific to sport tourism, 308
Professionalisms
types of, 307
Professionalization
defined, 307
of leisure services, 307
Profile of
sportists, 70-73
sport tourists, 73-75
tourists, 73
Public sector
as providers of sport tourism, 294
decreasing involvement of, 328
needed to provide sport, 328

Q

Queenstown
adventure capital of New Zealand,
108-111

R

Racquet sports
holidays in, 93
Red Sea
for scuba diving, 92
Riding holidays, 92
Risk
in activity holidays, 275-277
Roman empire
activities in, 15
influence of, 15, 32
Running
popularity of, 36
Rural areas
changing patterns of use, 211, 212
land use in, 210-212, 216-218

popular for active holidays, 211
Russia
activity holidays increasing in, 35
sports in, 137

S

Safety
clothing for, 277
equipment for, 278
Scandinavia
spa tourism in, 280
Scotland
active holidaymakers in, 37
golf history in, 16, 23-24
Scotsmen
influence in the USA, 19
Scuba diving
causes damage, 246
popularity of, 246
risks of, 276, 277
Seagaia complex, 122
Skiing
bodily conditions imposed by, 276
developed as a sport form, 134
economic impact of, 177-178
environmental
impact of, 250-251
protection measures in, 260-261
extreme type of, 274
history of, 20-21
holidays, 86, 137
steep skiing, 134
Sky diving, 135, 274
Sky surfing, 135
Snorkelling, 277
Snowdome, The, 141-143
Social context
changes in, 332-338
Socio-cultural impacts
dangers of ignoring, 204
employment benefits in, 211
negative, 205, 216-219
positive, 210-216
of tourism, 204-205
South Africa
administration of sport, 305
administration of tourism, 305
golf holidays in, 91
sports boycott of, 214-216

South Africa *(continued)*
    sports in, 143, 215-216
South America
    sports in, 96, 134
Soviet Union
    sports in, 136
Spa tourism
    ancient reason for traveling, 15, 278
    described, 278-279
    importance of, 17
    traditional spas, 278-281
    visits made to, 6
Spain
    administration of sport, 301
    administration of tourism, 301
    city regeneration by sport in, 192-
        193
    golfing holiday in, 149-150
    Olympics in Barcelona, 151, 192-193,
        212, 311
    sports in, 93
Speleology (Caving)
    environmental
        impact of, 251
        protection measures in, 261
Sport
    active involvement in, 9
    activity holidays in, 12, 37
    a cultural experience of activity, 51-
        54, 215
    analysed, 51-54
    as work, 50-51
    challenge in, 51-54
    conditions imposed on, 54
    connections with tourism
        in the Ancient World, 14-15
        in the Middle Ages, 16
        in the 19th – early 20th centuries,
            18-20
        in the Premodern world, 17-18
        in the Renaissance, 16
    definitions of
        European, 7
        in this book, 8, 12
        North American, 7, 8
    economic impact of, 170-171
    environmental challenge in, 52
    favorite on holiday, 36-38
    for all, 8, 33, 308-309
    forms/types of involvement in, 9
    for the disabled, 282
    growing segment of tourism
        industry in, 82-83
    holiday sport activities, 12, 37
    infrastructure of sport, 66-68
    interpersonal challenge in, 53
    model of sport, 51-54
    multibillion dollar business in, 323
    museums of, 215
    nature of experience in, 50-55, 325
    on holiday
        occupying a minor place, 101
    passive involvement in, 9
    a playlike activity, 50
    spectator vacations in, 4-5
    symbiotic with tourism, 5, 6
    as therapy, 6
    types/forms of involvement, 9
Sport and tourism
    joint policy statements for, 309
Sport camps, 99
Sport for all, 8, 33, 308-309
Sportification of society, 33-34
Sportists
    characteristics of, 70-73
Sport cures, 103
Sport festivals, 98
Sport participation
    influences holiday market, 81
Sports coaches
    sports development by, 158
Sports development
    assisted by programs of instruction,
        146-148
    constrained by, 159-162
    definition of, 130
    elite performers stimulate, 156-158
    evolution of sports forms, 134-136
    excellence level in, 133-134
    foundation level in, 131-132
    introduction/reintroduction level in,
        132
    major events as a catalyst for, 150-
        155
    model of, 130-131
    participation level in, 132-133

performance level in, 133
sport tourism as catalyst for, 136-
    146
summer camps assist in, 146-147
visits to man-made resources assist
    in, 140-146
visits to natural resources assist in,
    134-136, 137-140
Sports museums, 115-117
Sport tourism
    activities impact the natural
        environment, 247
    activity holidays increasing in, 34-36,
        179
    administrative frameworks for, 316
    benefits local communities, 210-216
    changes in, 342-347
    city regeneration results from, 189-195
    classification schemes of, 60-66
    combats antisocial behavior, 226
    combats disease, 274-275, 284-285
    conceptual classification of, 64
    congresses in, 5
    connections
        in the Ancient World, 14-15
        in the Middle Ages, 16
        in the 19th – early 20th centuries, 18-
            20
        in the Premodern world, 17-18
        in the Renaissance, 16
    dangers in, 275-277
    definitions of, 11-12, 60
    development policies for, 308-311
    disbenefits to local communities, 216-
        219
    economic
        benefits of, 179
        impact of, 173-176
        interest in, 327
        value of, 174, 196
    elite athletes, 118-119
    emerging as a profession, 307
    endangers the natural environment,
        236, 237
    forms/types of sport tourism, 12-14
    fragmented nature of, 161-162
    growth of, 326
    health implications of, 273-278

holiday taking volume of, 174, 176,
    177, 178, 195
increase in, 4, 5, 6, 34-38, 92
infrastructure in, 70, 297-306
integration in, 300, 328, 331-332
man-made resources as an attraction
    in, 81
market share for, 319, 321
market value of, 319
minimizing negative impacts of, 252-
    262, 277-278
model of, 5, 61-66
motives for participation in, 273-274
natural resources as an attraction for,
    81
nature of sport tourism, 58-62
negative impacts of, 230, 275-277
new genre of leisure in, 70
nonholiday taking in
    active sports, 118-122
    passive sports, 122-124
on holiday, 88-118
    active sports, 90-110
    passive sports, 113-117
participation increasing in, 34-38, 240-
    242, 282, 327, 328
physical risks of, 275, 277
place significant in, 58-60
policy for, 307, 308-315
popular activities in, 36-37
positive impacts of, 230, 273-275
professionalism in, 307-308
profile of participants in, 327
providers of, 294
sponsored by, 284-285
significance of place in, 58-60
summary of, 324-332
threat to the natural environment,
    247-252
two dimensions of, 58-59, 62-66
types/forms of, 12-14
Sport Tourists
    characteristics of, 73-75, 343-345
    responsible for violence, 222-223
Sport tours, 96
State, The
    different forms of, 296
    role of, 296

Surfing, 135
Sweden
    administration of sport, 301
    administration of tourism, 301
    sport activity holidays in, 176
Swimming
    health tourism interest in, 273
    man-made facilities important in, 140
    pools, indoors for, 143-146
    physical risks of, 277
    popularity of, 36
    Tropicana resort for, 144-146
Switzerland
    climbing history in, 21-22
    environmental protection in, 239
    holidays for the disadvantaged in, 226
    motivation for tourism in, 274
    Olympic museum in, 115-117
    skiing history in, 21
    spa tourism in, 280
    sports in, 96

T

Tanzania
    sport tourism for charity in, 285
Team tours
    popularity of, 6
Technological innovations
    influence sport and tourism, 30-32
Television
    economic value in, 191
    influence on sport of, 32
Tennis
    history of, 23
    holiday sports development in, 147
    pre-Wimbledon tournament in, 113-114
    real tennis history of, 16
    World Medical Tennis Society, 119-
        120
Thailand
    cultural impacts of dress, 218
    sports in, 87, 91, 92, 93, 248
Thalassotherapy, 281
Themes in sport tourism
    cooperation in infrastructure, 328-
        329
    conflicts of interest in, 329-330
    growth and diversification in, 326-
        327

    maximizing benefits of, 327-328
Therapeutic recreation
    for special populations, 282
Thermal air currents, 135
Tourism
    as a cultural experience of place, 55-
        57, 325
    changes in, 339-342
    connections with sport
        in the Ancient World, 14-15
        in the Middle Ages, 16
        in the 19th – early 20th centuries,
            18-20
        in the Premodern world, 17-18
        in the Renaissance, 16
    constrained by, 158
    damages the natural environment,
        242-246
    definitions of, 9, 10, 12
    economic impact of, 172-173
    forms of tourism, 11
    health tourism, 6
    host response to, 209-210
    increased by sport, 4, 214
    infrastructure of tourism, 68-70
    nature of touristic experience, 55-58
    resident impact models , 206-209,
        209-210
    resident relations in, 204, 206-208,
        209-210
    rural land use for, 210-212
    schedules include sport, 36
    sport spending generated by, 175
    sustainability of, 239, 239-241
    symbiotic with sport, 5, 6
    world's largest industry, 322
Tourist
    facilities lead to sports development,
        146
Tourists
    characteristics of, 73, 206-208
    defined as
        business, 11
        holiday, 11
        nonholiday, 11
    impact of, 206-209, 227-229
    models of impact, 206-208, 209-210
Transport

development of, 19-20, 29-31
influences sports development, 20
railways develop, 20
Travel agents, 6, 32, 275-276
Trekking
preparation recommended for, 95,
277
places to trek, 95-96
Tropicana
indoor swimming pool, 144-146
Tunisia
tourism policy in, 310
Turkey
sports in, 91, 137
Turnerverein societies
in the United States, 19
Typology
of special interest travel, 60-61
of tourists, 206

U

United Kingdom
boat industry in, 90
economic impact of sport tourism in,
173-175, 176, 177-178
economic significance of tourism in,
172-173
employment created by sport
tourism in, 211
environmental protection measures
in, 261
health tourism interest in, 273
health and fitness resort in, 279
holiday activities in, 36, 38
holidays for the disadvantaged, 226
hooliganism at sports events in, 223
national parks in, 258
negative socio-cultural impacts in,
217-218
Olympic bid failure in, 191
Outdoor activities popular in, 242
spa tourism in, 279
spas as tourist attraction in, 280
sport activity holidays in, 38, 176,
177
sports in, 136, 141-143, 217, 218, 248
sport team tours, 96
sport tourism for the disabled, 282-
283

value of activity holidays, 177
United Nations
environmental concerns of, 239, 240
United States of America
administration of sport, 303-305
administration of tourism, 303-305
baseball history in, 26-27
boat industry in, 90
Caledonian clubs in, 19
cities regeneration through sport in,
189-190
cricket history in, 26
cycling history in, 24, 89-90, 134
disabled sport tourists provision in,
282
environmental policies in, 313-314
facilities used to attract events in,
114
football history in, 22
golf history in, 23-24
golf courses in, 148
health tourism interest in, 273, 279
hiking history in, 25-26
holiday sport programs in, 147
national parks in, 238, 257, 314
New York marathon, 96-98
Olympic bids in, 213
Olympic Games
in Atlanta, 154, 183
in Los Angeles, 183
in St. Louis, 28
regeneration of cities, 114, 213
revenue driven policies in, 315
soccer development in, 155
spa tourism in, 279, 280
sports holiday makers in, 35
sports in, 134, 135, 136, 246, 248, 259
sport tourism to combat antisocial
behavior in, 226
tennis academy in, 147
tennis history in, 23
therapeutic recreation in, 282
Turnerverein societies in, 19
World Cup soccer in, 155, 184
Urban areas
negative impacts on, 218, 262-263
positive impacts on, 212-213
sport tourism to, 212-213

Urbanization, 334- 335

V

Vanuatu
Naghol ritual in, 215
Violence
associated with sport tourism, 221-223
Voluntary sector
as providers of sport tourism, 294

W

Walking
environmental
impact of, 244
protection measures in, 261
holidays in, 93-94
physical risks of, 276
popularity of, 36
socio-cultural impact of, 220-221
Waterparks
as a holiday sport activity, 109-110
Water sports
boating in decline, 90-91
board sailing, 135
environmental
impact of, 251-252
protection measures in, 262

holidays in, 90-92
surfing, 135
white-water rafting, 91
windsurfing, 135
West Indies
sports in, 217
Wheelchair sport, 284
White-water rafting, 91
Windsurfing, 36, 135
Winter sports
holidays in, 86
World Cup cricket, 156-158
World Cup football
in Argentina, 183-184
in the United States, 112, 155
World Medical Tennis, 119-120
World Student Games
in Sheffield, 152-154, 190-191
Wushu (martial arts)
in China, 18

Y

Youth hostels
worldwide numbers of 25

Z

Zimbabwe
sports in, 93

About the Authors

Joy Standeven earned her DPhil at the University of Sussex. Formerly a Principal Lecturer, she was also a Division Coordinator for Leisure and Recreation Studies at the University of Brighton between 1987 and 1994. As a recreational sport tourist, she has participated in sport activities in 60 countries on four continents. She has researched sport tourism for many years and has lectured extensively worldwide. Standeven conducts ongoing research and consulting through her private consultancy.

Paul De Knop, PhD, is a professor in the Faculty of Physical Education at Vrije Universiteit Brussel in Brussels, Belgium, and in the Leisure Studies Department at the University of Brabant in Tilburg, Netherlands. His articles on sport tourism have appeared in such prestigious publications as the *Journal of the World Leisure and Recreation Association* and the *European Journal of Sport Management*.

Related Books from Human Kinetics

Recreational Sport Management $38.00 ($56.95 Canadian)

(Third Edition)
Richard F. Mull, MS, Kathryn G. Bayless, MS, Craig M. Ross, ReD, and Lynn M. Jamieson, ReD

Outdoor Recreation in America $35.00 ($52.50 Canadian)

(Fifth Edition)
Clayne R. Jensen, EdD

The Story of Leisure $36.00 ($53.95 Canadian)

Context, Concepts, and Current Controversy
Jay S. Shivers and Lee J. deLisle

Outdoor Recreation Safety $35.00 ($52.50 Canadian)

A publication for the School and Community Safety Society of America
Neil J. Dougherty, IV, Editor

Effective Leadership in Adventure Programming $38.00 ($56.95 Canadian)

Simon Priest, PhD, and Michael A. Gass, PhD

Contemporary Sport Management $45.00 ($67.50 Canadian)

Janet B. Parks, DA, Beverly R.K. Zanger, MEd, and Jerome Quarterman, PhD, Editors

Understanding Sport Organizations $38.00 ($56.95 Canadian)

The Application of Organization Theory
Trevor Slack, PhD

Sport Marketing $44.00 ($65.95 Canadian)

Bernard J. Mullin, PhD, Stephen Hardy, PhD, and William A. Sutton, EdD

To request more information or to order, U.S. customers call 1-800-747-4457, e-mail us at humank@hkusa.com, or visit our Web site at www.humankinetics.com. Persons outside the U.S. can contact us via our Web site or use the appropriate telephone number, postal address, or e-mail address shown in the front of this book.

 HUMAN KINETICS
The Information Leader in Physical Activity
P.O. Box 5076, Champaign, IL 61825-5076
2335